THE REMNANTS OF WAR

D1316457

THE REMNANTS OF WAR

JOHN MUELLER

CORNELL UNIVERSITY PRESS
ITHACA AND LONDON

A VOLUME IN THE SERIES
CORNELL STUDIES IN SECURITY AFFAIRS
edited by Robert J. Art, Robert Jervis, and Stephen M. Walt

Copyright © 2004 by Cornell University
Preface to the Cornell Paperbacks Edition copyright © 2007 by
Cornell University

All rights reserved. Except for brief quotations in a review, this book,
or parts thereof, must not be reproduced in any form without permis-
sion in writing from the publisher. For information, address Cornell
University Press, Sage House, 512 East State Street, Ithaca, New York
14850.

First published 2004 by Cornell University Press
First printing, Cornell Paperbacks, 2007

Printed in the United States of America

Library of Congress Cataloging-in-Publication Data

Mueller, John E.
    The remnants of war / John Mueller.
        p. cm. — (Cornell studies in security affairs)
    Includes bibliographical references and index.
    ISBN-13: 978-0-8014-4239-1 (cloth: alk.paper)
    ISBN-13: 978-0-8014-7387-6 (pbk.: alk.paper)
    1. War.   2. Military history, Modern—20th century.   3. World
politics—1995–2005.   I. Title.   II. Series.

    U21.2.M8397 2004
    355.02—dc22

                                        2004006695

Cornell University Press strives to use environmentally responsible
suppliers and materials to the fullest extent possible in the publishing
of its books. Such materials include vegetable-based, low-VOC inks
and acid-free papers that are recycled, totally chlorine-free, or partly
composed of nonwood fibers. For further information, visit our website at www.cornellpress.cornell.edu.

Cloth printing   10 9 8 7 6 5 4 3 2 1
Paperback printing 10 9 8 7 6 5 4 3 2

to JAM and ESM,
to Karl, Michelle, Karen, Erik, Susan, and Kraig,
to Timothy, Samuel, Clara, Kara, Malcolm, and Atticus
and to the memory of
Curtis Maki,
Jim Hoover,
and Karen and Jon Harder

CONTENTS

PREFACE TO THE CORNELL
PAPERBACKS EDITION

Two years after *The Remnants of War* was first published, the basic patterns it traces have continued.

The number of ongoing wars has held at historically low levels. As the figure on page 87 documents, there were five wars in 2003, and, applying the same definitions, there were seven in 2004 and five again in 2005.[1]

The only international war that has thus far taken place in the twenty-first century by these definitions is the one that has attended the American and British invasion of Iraq (though some might be inclined to label the venture an imperial rather than an international war). That war, of course, persists, and it has become progressively more destructive as an insurgency against the occupiers and against the government they set up continues to rage. Moreover, an increasing measure of intercommunal violence, particularly between Sunnis and Shiites, some of it criminal in nature, has been added to the destructive mix.

The results of the war (or disaster) in Iraq are still to be played out, but the experience seems likely further to dampen the enthusiasm of developed countries for sending their soldiers into environments that could prove to be hostile—that is, into what I have called "policing wars." In the middle of the decade, the Sudan regime employed collections of criminal marauders to put down a nascent secessionist movement in the western part of the country, and this rather predictably resulted in criminal predation, ethnic cleansing, rape, substantial refugee flows, and massive suffering. The international community, after ten years of mea culpa breast-beating over its failure to intervene in Rwanda, responded with little more than huffing and puffing, pressure on the Sudan government, and the setting up of inadequate and underfunded refugee camps.[2]

For the United States something of an "Iraq Syndrome" seems likely to emerge from its fiasco in the Middle East. Among its casualties for American policy could be the Bush Doctrine, empire, unilateralism, preemption (actually, preventive war), last-remaining-superpowerdom, and indispensable-nationhood. Indeed, these once fashionable (and sometimes self-infatuated) concepts are already picking up a patina of quaintness.[3]

In part because of the attention the Iraq War has drawn, little notice has been paid to the continuing low levels of civil war. In 2005, there were only four, and all barely surpassed the 1000 battle-death threshold required for the conflict to be included in the count. Indeed, if that threshold were raised to the not-unreasonable 1500, the only war in the world in 2005 would have been the one in Iraq. (It should be stressed, however, that conflict situations that generate few battle deaths can still become humanitarian disasters for civilians through criminal predation, massacre, ethnic cleansing, and severe economic and infrastructure disruption.)

As I noted in the book, many civil wars endured for years, and the growth pattern through the early 1990s was mostly the result of a process of cumulation; it did not happen because in each year more civil wars started than concluded. In recent years, however, this process seems to have reversed itself. Many of these wars—or perhaps we should think of them as competitive criminal enterprises—have exhausted themselves, and new ones have failed to arise to take their place.

Some observers argue that peacekeeping efforts by international organizations have often proved effective at keeping the wars from reigniting.[4] International bodies and consortiums of developed countries may not be able—or, more often, willing—to stop a war when the combatants are determined to continue fighting, but they sometimes can usefully seize the opportunity to stabilize a shaky peace when the combatants have become exhausted. However, as I have argued in this book, it seems clear that a truly effective, long-term solution to the problems presented by civil warfare lies in the establishment of competent domestic military and policing forces.

War's apparent decline has excited remarkably little comment or even notice. In 2004, the United Nations issued a press release, "10 stories the world should hear more about." One of these was called "The Peacekeeping Paradox," in which it was observed that many civil wars had of late ended, providing many hopeful opportunities for international peacekeeping.[5] The story was picked up by the Lehrer News-Hour on PBS and by *Business Week*, but that was about all. Newspaper columnist Gwynne Dyer has noted the process in a few columns, and Gregg Easterbrook published a cover story, "The End of War?" in *The New Republic* in 2005 that attracted a small amount of media attention.[6] Within the political science community, Robert Jervis, in his Presidential Address to the American Political Science Association in 2001, took notice of the phenomenon (or potential phenomenon) as it pertains to international war, Raimo Väyryen has edited a set of essays on that subject, and Christopher Fettweis has assessed its potential impact on international relations theory.[7] Among scholars who have been leaders in assessing and measuring war and conflict, Monty Marshall and Ted Gurr have produced an extensive discussion of the decline of both international and civil war, and Canadian political scientist Andrew Mack has done so in a well-received report that makes prominent use of data sets produced by Norwegian and Swedish researchers.[8]

It is obviously much too early to be certain that the apparent waning of war will persist—and at least as long as the Iraq War continues, few will notice anyway. Moreover, several armed civil conflicts that have sputtered intermittently could again rise above the violence threshold in the future, though most of these seem to be currently in decline—in 2006 even the dangerous civil war situation in Nepal improved. Ethiopia and Eritrea continue to glare at each other, and plenty of problems remain in the Middle East—where in 2006 Israel took on a substate group, Hezbullah, based in another country, and where the Iraq disaster could have spillover effects. And, of course, new wars could emerge in other places: concerns about China and the Taiwan issue, for example, are certainly justified. Moreover, there has been intercommunal violence in such countries as Nigeria (and Iraq) that often seems to resemble warfare but is removed from consideration by the definitional requirement that something labeled a "war" must have a government on at least one side. Moreover, crime and criminal predation will persist, and so will terrorism, which, like crime, can be carried out by individuals or by very small groups.[9]

But war has, at least for the time being, become a remarkably rare phenomenon. A further, or continuing, decline in this ancient and venerable institution would constitute one of the most monumental developments in the history of the human race.

JOHN MUELLER

February 26, 2007

NOTES

1. For data, consult the Uppsala Conflict Database at http://www.pcr.uu.se/database/index.php.
2. Scott Straus, "Darfur and the Genocide Debate," *Foreign Affairs* 84(1) January/February 2005: 123–46.
3. See also John Mueller, "The Iraq Syndrome," *Foreign Affairs* 84(6) November/December 2005: 44–54; Mueller, "Force, Legitimacy, Success, and Iraq," *Review of International Studies* 31(S1) December 2005: 109–25.
4. Andrew Mack, *Human Security Report 2005* (New York: Oxford University Press, 2005). James D. Fearon and David D. Laitin, "Neotrusteeship and the Problem of Weak States," *International Security* 28(4) Spring 2004: 5–43. Virginia Page Fortna, *Where Have All the Victories Gone? War Outcomes in Historical Perspective* (New York: Saltzman Institute for War and Peace Studies, Columbia University, 2005).
5. www.un.org/events/tenstories.
6. Gregg Easterbrook, "The End of War?" *New Republic*, May 30, 2005: 18–21. According to Easterbrook, the article generated a few radio interviews as well as John Tierney's "Give Peace a Chance" in the *New York Times* of May 28, 2005. Dyer's columns are at gwynnedyer.com.
7. Robert Jervis, "Theories of War in an Era of Leading-Power Peace," *American Political Science Review* 96(1) March 2002: 1–14; see also his *American Foreign Policy in a New Era* (New York: Routledge, 2005). Raimo Väyryen (ed.), *The Waning of Major War: Theories and Debates* (New York: Routledge, 2006). Christopher J. Fettweis, "A Revolution in International Relations Theory," *International Studies Review* (8)4 December 2006: 677–97.
8. Monty G. Marshall and Ted Robert Gurr, *Peace and Conflict, 2005: A Global Survey of Armed Conflicts, Self-Determination Movements, and Democracy* (College Park, Md.: Center for International Development and Conflict Management, University of Maryland, 2005). Mack, *Human Security Report.* See also John Mueller, "Ideas, Thugs, and the Decline of War," in Manus I. Midlarsky (ed.), *Handbook of War Studies III* (Ann Arbor: University of Michigan Press, forthcoming).
9. However, as noted in the book, terrorism, or at least international terrorism, rarely kills more than a few hundred people a year worldwide. For an extended discussion, see John Mueller, *Overblown* (New York: Free Press, 2006).

ACKNOWLEDGMENTS

In various shapes and guises, the argument of this book has been presented at a conference organized by Raimo Väyrynen, The Waning of Major War, at Notre Dame University in 2001 and later at the Redefining Sovereignty conference at Ohio State University, the Economics of Civil War conference in Oslo, Norway, sponsored by the World Bank, and the Identifying Wars conference at Uppsala University in Sweden, as well as at conferences of the International Studies Association and of the American Political Science Association. I benefited greatly from graduate and undergraduate students in seminars at Ohio State University and the University of Rochester and from a stint as Guest Fellow at the Norwegian Nobel Institute in Oslo in 2001.

At points helpful comments, suggestions, and criticisms have been registered, sometimes quite forcefully, by Peter Andreas, Raimo Väyrynen, Robert Art, Stathis Kalyvas, Jacques Hymans, Geir Lundestad, Russell Hardin, Jacques Hymans, Michael Desch, Yakayuki Nishi, Karl Mueller, Benjamin Valentino, Stanley Engerman, Amanda Rosen, Patricia Weitsman, Richard Rosecrance, Etel Solingen, Geoffrey Parker, and Olav Njølstad. Nils Petter Gleditsch and Kristian Gleditsch have been especially helpful with comments, advice, suggestions, and data acquisition. Special thanks to Timothy Mueller-Harder for research assistance.

I also thank participants, many with sharp questions, at seminars and talks at the University of Chicago; RAND (Washington and Santa Monica); Salisbury University; Brown University; the University of California, San Diego; Ohio State University; Jagiellonian University in Kraków, Poland; Ohio University; the Norwegian Nobel Institute; the University of Belgrade; the University of Pennsylvania; the National Security Study Group, Washington, D.C.; Georgetown University; UCLA; the University of Cincinnati; MIT; Columbia University; the University of Alberta; the University of California, Irvine; Roberts Wesleyan University; the University of Rochester; and Stanford University. And thanks as well to the people at Cornell University Press: Roger Haydon, Karen Hwa, and Kathryn Gohl.

Portions of the argument have appeared in articles in *Journal of Peace Research* and *International Security*.

J. M.

Columbus, Ohio

INTRODUCTION

The Decline of War, the Persistence of Warfare

In some very important respects, the institution of war is clearly in decline. Certain standard, indeed classic, varieties of war—particularly major war, or wars among developed countries—have become so rare and unlikely that they could well be considered obsolescent, if not obsolete. Also in notable decline, it appears, are international war more generally, conventional civil war, colonial war, and ideological civil war. In this book I explore the possibility that war is in the process of, well, disappearing altogether.

With only a few exceptions, two kinds of war remain. By far the more common is unconventional civil war, most of which take place in the poorest countries of the world. Many of these wars have been labeled "new war," "ethnic conflict," or, most grandly, "clashes of civilizations." But in fact, most, though not all, are more nearly opportunistic predation waged by packs, often remarkably small ones, of criminals, bandits, and thugs. They engage in armed conflict either as mercenaries hired by desperate governments or as independent or semi-independent warlord or brigand bands. The damage perpetrated by these entrepreneurs of violence, who commonly apply ethnic, nationalist, civilizational, or religious rhetoric, can be extensive, particularly to the civilians who are their chief prey, but it is often scarcely differentiable from crime.

The other remaining type of war, much less frequent, includes what might be called "policing wars." These comprise militarized efforts, mostly successful, by developed countries to bring order to the civil conflicts or to topple the thuggish regimes that are, after the apparent demise of international war, the chief remaining sources of artificial deadly human destruction in the world.

This book explores these trends in warfare. Its scope and approach can be summarized in four related and more or less cumulative arguments.

The first seeks to explain the very remarkable decline in war among developed countries. I begin by presenting a distinction between disciplined combatants and criminal ones and suggest that sometime in the middle of the last millennium, disciplined military and police forces began to triumph over essentially criminal ones in Europe and, in the process, gradually brought civil order and the state system to that continent. As a result war, previously an almost continuous fact of life there, came under more coherent political control. Then, when people and politicians in the developed world became disillusioned with war—something that happened at the time of the First World War—they increasingly used their control over war to keep it from happening at all, at least in their relations with each other. In this view, the Second World War in Europe becomes a spectacular anachronism, fabricated almost single-handedly by history's supreme atavism, Adolf Hitler. Then, over the course of the last half century, the war aversion of the developed world seems to have become increasingly adopted elsewhere, with the result that several other kinds of warfare are becoming progressively more rare as well.

The decline of war, it seems to me, stems chiefly from the way attitudes toward the value and efficacy of war have changed, particularly during the last century. The key lies in the machinations of idea entrepreneurs, not in wider-ranging social, economic, or technological developments or in the fabrication of institutions, trade, or patterns of interdependence, which often seem to be more nearly a consequence of peace and of rising war aversion than their cause. War, in this view, is merely an idea, an institution, like dueling or slavery, that has been grafted onto human existence. It is not a trick of fate, a thunderbolt from hell, a natural calamity, or a desperate plot contrivance dreamed up by some sadistic puppeteer on high. And it seems to me that the institution is in pronounced decline, abandoned as attitudes toward it have changed, roughly following the pattern by which the ancient and formidable institution of slavery became discredited and then mostly obsolete.

The second argument assesses civil war in the wake of the Cold War. Most, though not all, civil war consists primarily of criminal and warlord predation, not clashes between ethnic or civilizational groups, and it is often carried out by small numbers of people. To a substantial and perhaps increasing degree, then, warfare has been reduced to its remnants—or dregs—and thugs are the residual combatants.

The third argument deals with the prospects that the international community, particularly developed countries, will be able to pacify criminal wars and topple thuggish regimes through a series of policing wars. Experience during the post–Cold War period suggests that this is not a terribly formidable task: because thugs tend to be opportunistic and cowardly, they can generally be defeated by an organized, disciplined, and sizeable army. Developed countries, however, despite their general consensus on how the post–Cold War world should be ordered, are unlikely systematically to carry out such actions for several reasons. These include a severe aversion to casualties, a fundamental lack of interest, an aversion to long-term policing, the lack of political gain from success, a deeply held bias against war and aggression, and the misguided but convenient assumption that civil conflicts stem from immutable and inexplicable ethnic hatreds that cannot be remedied by well-intentioned outsiders.

The fourth argument suggests that governmental effectiveness, not ethnic tension or other more cosmic concerns, is the key to the existence of much contemporary civil warfare. It follows that the fabrication of capable government, following the historic pattern of Europe, is ultimately the most promising method for the long-term control, and even potentially for the eradication, of most of the remnants of war. There is some suggestive, but by no means conclusive, evidence that governments are becoming generally more effective even in the poorest areas of the world, and thus that criminal warfare (and criminal regimes) may, like disciplined warfare, be in terminal decline.

BACKGROUND AND CONTRASTS

This book develops, reworks, and very substantially extends the argument contained in a book I published in early 1989, *Retreat from Doomsday: The Obsolescence of Major War*, which dealt with war among developed countries. At the time, military and diplomatic historian Michael Howard reviewed the book with considerable skepticism about its central thesis, helpfully suggesting that the "prudent reader will check that his air raid shelter is in good repair." But then, in 1991, he mused that it had become "quite possible that war in the sense of major, organised armed conflict between highly developed societies may not recur, and that a stable framework for international order will become firmly established." Two years later, the military historian and analyst John Keegan concluded in *A History of Warfare* that the kind of war he was principally considering could well be in terminal demise: "War, it seems to me, after a lifetime of reading about the subject, mingling with men of war, visiting the sites of war and observing its effects, may well be ceasing to commend itself to human beings as a desirable or productive, let alone rational, means of reconciling their discontents." By the end of the century, Mary Kaldor was suggesting that "the barbarity of war between states may have become a thing of the past," and at the beginning of the new one, Robert Jervis concluded that war among the leading states "will not occur in the future" or, in the words of Jeffrey Record, may have "disappeared altogether."[1] The world seems, then, to have continued, even accelerated, its retreat from doomsday—a word that has, in fact, picked up a slight aura of quaintness since 1989. And, however imprudently, many air raid shelters seem to have been allowed to lapse into disrepair.

Retreat from Doomsday came out just before the end of the Cold War and was concerned almost entirely with major war, whereas the present book deals with all warfare, not just wars among developed countries. It incorporates and extends the earlier book's emphasis on the consequential importance of changing attitudes toward war. It also proposes and explores a sort of bottom-up approach to warfare, one that focuses on methods used to recruit, retain, and motivate combatants. At base, I stress, the violence of war is committed not by grand and essentially imaginary communities such as cultures, civilizations, or peoples but rather by groups of armed men specifically mobilized for the process. Except in some primitive warfare, combatants comprise only a small portion of the society or group they are taken to represent, and in very many instances their numbers are exceedingly small by any measure: in the dozens, hundreds, low thousands.

My approach thus contrasts markedly with that of those who hold that most present (and future) warfare embodies cosmic clashes of civilizations and with those who see civil conflicts as expressions of deep-seated, immutable, and ancient if newly exploding hatreds. It also takes substantial issue with the Hobbesian image of civil warfare as a desperate conflict of all against all, neighbor against neighbor, rather than as a social disaster mostly perpetrated by small bands of predatory thugs. And it critically disagrees with the perspective of military historian Martin van Creveld, who argues, correctly in my view, that "armies will be replaced by police-like security forces on the one hand and bands of ruffians on the other" but still insists that war is "a highly attractive activity for which no other can provide an adequate substitute."[2] The central burden of this book is that war is merely an idea. Unlike breathing, eating, or sex, war is not something that is somehow required by the human condition or by the forces of history. Accordingly, war can shrivel up and disappear, and it seems to be in the process of doing so.

This book is chiefly about war, not terrorism. In a set of definitions developed in chapter 1, I designate terrorism as intermittent violence carried out for dedicated purposes by individuals or small groups. As such, it is more like crime than war in its fundamental dynamic if not in its purposes. Some of the suggestions put forward in this book to deal with the remnants of war may also help to reduce the incidence of terrorism. But whereas it is possible to imagine a world in which war has been policed to extinction, terrorism, like crime, has always existed and, it seems likely, always will.

I argue that much remaining warfare is fundamentally trivial—perpetrated by small bands of predatory thugs and criminals, very often drugged or drunken, who are chiefly motivated, like ordinary criminals, by a quest for fun and profit, not by grand ideological, cultural, ethnic, or civilizational visions. But I emphatically do not want to suggest that the *results* of the maraudings of these entrepreneurs of violence are trivial, particularly cumulatively. These predators can lay waste to entire societies and, because they often profit so nicely in the process, they have an incentive to continue their activities for years, often for decades. Through direct predation and through famine-causing and disease-spreading disruption and forced migration (or "ethnic cleansing"), their actions can lead to massive numbers of deaths—far more, for example, than in many conventional, disciplined wars. The Bosnians, as it happens, have an appropriate if understated lament for the condition: "Teško narodu kad pametni ućute, budale progovore, a fukare se obogate." That is, "It is difficult for the people when the smart keep quiet, fools speak out, and thugs get rich."[3]

THE PLAN OF THE BOOK

I begin by discussing the appeals of war and of battle, and the processes by which people are able to become organized enough to engage in such murderous and destructive activities. In chapter 1 I develop a distinction between criminal and disciplined warfare and discuss what happens in wars between and among disciplined and criminal militaries.

Chapter 2 deals particularly with developments in Europe before 1914. It traces the rise of disciplined military and policing forces and their success over criminal ones, something that led to the consolidation of the state system and, in an important sense, to the control by states of war (and peace). It also discusses the notable rise for the first time in history of an active antiwar movement in the years before World War I, and it concludes with an appraisal of the appeal war continued to inspire in Europe at the time.

A profound disillusionment with war arose in Europe at the time of World War I. Chapter 3 argues that this came about not because that war was peculiarly destructive and costly, but because the prewar antiwar movement was successful in presenting its once-novel argument that war—by which they primarily meant war among developed states—ought to be abolished.

Chapter 4 considers the determined quest for peace in Europe after the First World War, and it argues that the Second World War there was almost single-handedly created by one man, Adolf Hitler. Historical conditions in no important way required another continental war in Europe, and major nations there were not on a collision course. That is, but for Hitler, history's greatest war would most probably never have taken place. The implications of this conclusion are also assessed.

I am concerned in chapter 5 with conflict during the Cold War. I believe the Cold War was caused primarily by Communist devotion to an ideology about violent revolution and international class warfare that seemed threateningly expansionary to the democratic, capitalist West. Once this ideology was convincingly abandoned, the Cold War and ideological civil war (which

the Communists had once avidly supported) ceased to exist. Despite the severe ideological dispute between the Communist and the non-Communist
world, however, major war was never in the cards. The chapter also deals with
the decline over the period of international war and of disciplined civil warfare—both within the developed world and outside it—as well as with the remarkable demise of colonialism and therefore of colonial war.

Chapter 6 assesses civil war after the Cold War. Using the conflicts in the
former Yugoslavia as examples, it argues that the main violence in many "ethnic wars," far from being an expression of deep and long-lasting hatreds between neighbors or civilizations, is chiefly perpetrated by thugs and criminals
acting essentially as mercenaries under the sometimes vague direction of
weak or desperate governments and political leaders. Many other civil wars,
such as those in Africa, seem substantially to be violent and predatory enterprises conducted by warlord and brigand gangs. The chapter also argues that
it is often better to see these conflicts as high-intensity crime or criminal businesses rather than as low-intensity war. It contrasts the Hobbesian image of
civil war as a continual and unrelenting combat of all against all with the reality of contemporary civil wars in which small numbers of predatory combatants are able to destroy societies and make miserable the lives of helpless
and bewildered populations.

Today, after the Cold War, a remarkable consensus exists among developed states. Chapter 7 examines their mostly successful experience of trying
to regulate—that is, to order—the new world through policing wars.

Chapter 8 then evaluates the prospects for using international policing to
deal with civil warfare and with thuggish regimes. In most cases, I suggest,
the task would not be terribly difficult or costly for any sufficiently large and
well-armed disciplined military force. However, there are a number of reasons why the developed states are unlikely systematically to create and substantially to support such forces.

Chapter 9 compares trends in war with patterns in attitudes toward public
killing more generally. It also includes an examination of other explanations
for the decline of warfare: it considers, and rejects, the popular notion that
the long peace in the developed world has been a product of the development of nuclear weapons, and it explores arguments that credit the expansion of democracy, international trade, and international institutions, concluding that these are more nearly the consequence or fortuitous correlate
of changing attitudes and the decline of war than their cause.

The chapter, and the book, conclude with the argument that the best
hope for ordering the new world lies in the establishment of effective governments in countries that now have incompetent or vicious ones. In some
important respects, in fact, the central cause of much civil war is not ethnic
or economic or social or national or civilizational grievance but rather venal

or incompetent governments, which often inspire, sometimes profitably engage in, and always facilitate armed conflict and organized criminality. There are signs that an increasing number of once conflictual and ill-policed states are beginning to grasp this fact. Accordingly, criminal warfare, the chief remnant of war, may, like other forms, be in decline.

CHAPTER 1

CRIMINAL AND DISCIPLINED WARFARE

In October 1990, three months before ordering half a million troops into combat in the Gulf War of 1991, U.S. general Norman Schwarzkopf observed, "War is a profanity because, let's face it, you've got two opposing sides trying to settle their differences by killing as many of each other as they can." War, as the general so vividly suggests, is centrally about violence, and particularly about killing. Or, as Geoffrey Parker puts it laconically, "The business of the military in war is killing people and breaking things." From the perspective of the combatant, it is also about deprivation and boredom—in Napoleon's words, "The first qualification of a soldier is fortitude under fatigue and privation."[1]

The combat experience has therefore been aptly characterized as consisting of long periods of tedium punctuated by episodes of sheer terror, and the prosecution of a war requires the recruitment, retention, and motivation of men who can withstand both challenges. They must be able to live with and to commit intense violence, and they must also be able to endure long intervals—months at least, often years—of various kinds of deprivation. Among the problems: lice, maggots, leeches, and other vermin; debilitating and very often fatal battles with dysentery and other diseases; the absence of women; terrible, even inedible, food; germ-ridden water; stale cigarettes; bone-deep fatigue; syphilitic prostitutes; watered or even poisonous liquor; sleep deprivation; family separation and homesickness; absence of privacy; constant and often brutal and pointless harassment or physical abuse by superiors and by an incoherent system; exposure to extremes of weather; masturbatory fantasies that become decreasingly stimulating; and boredom that can become cosmic, overwhelming, stupefying—an emotion, though only rarely remarked upon, that is far more common in war than the rush that comes with combat.

This chapter explores the problem of creating and sustaining military forces under such conditions. It distinguishes between criminal and disciplined warfare, and it then explores the implications (and difficulties) of the distinction around which much of the argument in the rest of the book is centered.

WHY PEOPLE FIGHT

People seem to relate to violence in various ways. Some enjoy it and seek it out both for the thrill and for the profit it can bring. Others (perhaps the considerable majority of the population) can commit violence when appropriately organized—that is, they are capable of acts of violence, even very horrible ones, when the circumstances are right even though the activity gives them no notable pleasure, supplies them with no material gain, and may even cause some of them considerable psychic pain, particularly at first.

Violence for Fun and Profit

It is probably sensible to begin with the most basic motivations. Some people actively enjoy violence: for them it is something of a high. Some are drawn to it compulsively—serial killers, for example, or some sadists, who continue to perform violent acts even though they know this enhances the likelihood they will be apprehended. There are also those who are, or become, addicted to violence and will feel anxiety if they do not experience it. They exult in the thrill of violence and spend a great deal of time anticipating it and seeking it out. Many criminals find a sensual high in the criminal act, and many soccer hooligans apparently have an affinity for, even a lusting after, the thrill, exhilaration, and euphoria of violence.[2]

In addition to these people, there are some who, although they do not actively need or seek out violence, find, often to their own surprise, that they enjoy committing violence when the conditions are opportune. For example, a study conducted at Stanford University found that a considerable amount of brutal and sadistic behavior emerged in at least a few people when a group of apparently average students were put into an experimental situation in which they were randomly selected to play the role of prison guards.[3]

The opportunistic enjoyment of violence is often found in battle. As the pacifist William James once lamented, war can be "supremely thrilling excitement" and "the supreme theater of human strenuousness." For some soldiers—perhaps quite a few—battle turns out to be a high. As the young Winston Churchill observed, "Nothing in life is so exhilarating as to be shot at without result." And Glenn Gray, an American soldier in World War II, discusses what he calls "the enduring appeals of battle," stressing "its ecstatic character in the original meaning of the term, namely, a state of being outside the self." Soldiers in the American Civil War found that combat "quickened all your ideas to their highest pitch," put them into "an almost entirely dreamlike state," and that "no tongue, or pen can express the excitement."

Vietnam veteran William Broyles has come to a similar conclusion. He admonishes that "war is ugly, horrible, evil, and it is reasonable for men to hate all that," but he goes on to argue that "most men who have been to war would have to admit, if they are honest, that somewhere inside themselves they loved it too, loved it as much as anything that has happened to them before or since." It is "an experience of great intensity"; it "replaces the difficult gray areas of daily life with an eerie, serene clarity"; "if you come back whole [a notable qualification] you bring with you the knowledge that you have explored regions of your soul that in most men will always remain uncharted." He suggests that "war may be the only way in which most men touch the mythic domain of our soul. . . . War is, in short, a turn-on."[4]

Many, probably most, of the people who enjoy violence opportunistically do not in any important sense actually need it, nor do they become addicted to it. Afterward they can often descend back into what we like to think of as normality without further necessary reversion to violent behavior. For all the exhilaration he found in combat, Broyles (who has since gone on to a substantial literary career) concludes, "I never want to fight again," and "I would do everything in my power to keep my son from fighting." And Gray, who became a professor of philosophy at Colorado College, concludes his book by speculating about what would be required to extirpate war.[5]

War has also been, or seemed to be, economically profitable for those who engage in it. Some commanders have been able to pay their charges well—in money or often in liquor or drugs. In other cases, the opportunity for pillage and to seize land and booty have often been the chief form of payment. Warriors have gained as well by ransoming captives or selling them into slavery. It has been found routinely that the unemployed are more easily recruited than the employed.

Narcosis

Liquor—"liquid courage"—and other drugs have been commonly and often liberally applied before, during, and after battle.[6] They dull the mind and may sometimes help people overcome whatever inhibitions might otherwise restrain them: consider, for example, the mindless cruelty that often comes out during fraternity hazing. Because warfare requires a degree of control, however, this time-honored method for shoring up courage has notable defects.

Coercion

It is possible to force people to commit violence. Historically, men have been impressed into service, and then battle conditions have been arranged so that they must participate if they hope to survive. One common technique is to back up combatants with special rearward troops whose sole purpose is summarily to kill any who desert or fail to advance—"file closers" they are sometimes called. Thus John Keegan notes that in the First World War, "the exits of the trenches were patrolled during battle by specially detailed battle police, and there was no realistic alternative to going forward when ordered to do so." According to a British general in that war, "Not a man shirked going through the extremely heavy barrage, or facing the machine gun and rifle fire that finally wiped them out. . . . [I] have never seen, indeed could never have imagined, such a magnificent display of gallantry, discipline and determination." A British sergeant, however, described it this way: "You were between the devil and the deep blue sea. If you go forward, you'll likely be shot. If you go back, you'll be court-martialed and shot. . . . What can you do?" It is a procedure Genghis Khan worked out to a science.[7]

Once in battle, killing can become essentially a matter of self-defense, of killing to prevent being killed. Further, if surrender means death, combatants will fight simply because that alternative is the only one that promises some possibility of survival, something seen particularly in combat between the Germans and Soviets in World War II.[8]

To rely entirely on coercion in forming a combatant force is unwise, however.[9] The incentive to desert at the first opportunity is great of course, as is the incentive to shirk whenever one can get away with it.

Drill, Discipline, Leadership, and Submission to Authority

Under the appropriate circumstances, people seem to have a considerable capacity for committing violence even when they find no enjoyment or profit in it, even when utterly sober, and even when essentially uncoerced. Important in this process are various training techniques and the development of leadership skills that play upon a tendency for many to follow authority.[10]

Traditionally, brutality in training has been used to instill the requisite attitudes and fighting skills in potential warriors. However, the very substantial reduction in the use of the technique in the United States military—where drill sergeants are no longer even allowed to use profanity—does not seem to have diminished the fighting capacity of the final product. Nor has its rampant persistence in the Russian military turned out a polished and dedicated fighting man. In general, fighting capacities are likely to be heightened when combatants have an appropriately nuanced fear, love, and/or respect for their officers.[11]

Important in discussions of this phenomenon have been the experiments of Stanley Milgram, who subjected ordinary people to situations in which they were to administer what seemed to them to be electric shocks to other people when requested to do so by an experimenter. He found that a remarkably large percentage were willing to follow the experimenter's orders even when the person being shocked (a confederate of the experimenter) feigned great pain and cried to be spared.[12]

Honor, Duty, Glory, and the Fear of Shame

The ability to inflict violence can be enhanced if combatants are convinced that they have a duty to fight and that honor and glory are important and at stake in the conflict. These motivations were seen in great measure, for example, among German and Japanese troops during the Second World War and among combatants in the American Civil War. Often related to the honor phenomenon is acceptance of the notion that there is great shame and humiliation in surrender, something particularly notable among Japanese combatants in World War II, who typically died or committed suicide rather than give up.[13]

Love

Studies of combat motivation generally conclude that the most reliable quality inspiring people to risk deadly combat is one variously known as small group loyalty, unit cohesion, primary group solidarity, male bonding, or the buddy system.[14] A fifteenth-century soldier put it this way: "What a joyous thing is war. . . . A great sweet feeling of loyalty and pity fills your heart on seeing your friend so valiantly exposing his body to execute and accomplish the command of our Creator. And then you prepare to go and live or die with him, and for love not to abandon him. And out of that there arises such a delectation, that he who has not tasted it is not fit to say what a delight it is." A Confederate soldier in the American Civil War wrote about "a feeling of love—a strong attachment for those with whom one has shared common dangers, this is never felt for any one else, or under any other circumstances." Somewhat more prosaically, an American soldier in World War II commented, "It took me darn near a whole war to figure out what I was fighting for. It was the other guys. Your outfit, the guys in your company, but especially your platoon."[15]

For Broyles, the most "enduring emotion of war" is "comradeship" and "brotherly love," a "utopian experience" in which "individual possessions and advantage count for nothing, the group is everything." Or there is Gray's observation about "the delight in comradeship," and his suggestion that "there must be a similarity between this willingness of soldier-comrades for self-sacrifice and the willingness of saints to die for their religious faith." And Christopher Browning notes that a crucial motivation for many of the policemen who slaughtered Jews in Poland was the feeling that they would be letting their comrades down if they refused to do the "dirty work."[16]

In fact, it was the discovery that love—love for one's fellow combatants, for one's comrades in arms—could be used to inspire men to fight and die in combat that has made warfare so effective and so lethal. The basic idea has been noted incidentally in the past, as by the fifteenth-century soldier quoted earlier. And it has often been used ingeniously, as in the American Civil War, by arranging to have combatant units made up of men from the same community, thus multiplying the buddy effect. However, explicit, official, and conscious identification and appreciation of the process seem to have come comparatively recently—indeed, apparently only during and after the Second World War.[17] Thus, the importance of this quality has probably not been intuitively obvious. It has, however, proven to be very important in the development of disciplined combatant forces: to a significant degree, all you need to fight a war is love.

Beliefs

Most studies suggest that ideology and abstract beliefs are not among the most compelling motivations, particularly over the long term and in combat.[18] For example, consider the reflections of U.S. sergeant Keni Thomas about a battle he had been in: "I loved Casey. And I've heard his dad say, you know, 'Did my son die in vain?' He died for what I find important, which is the sense of duty, and the man next to you. . . . But if you say that anybody died over there in vain, you're invalidating everything that we fight for and everything that we believe in."[19] By this testimony, what "we fight for" and what "we believe in" are the sense of duty and the guys in your unit.

Nevertheless, some combatants do fight and die for ideas, ideals, and beliefs as they are usually defined.[20] This process works most effectively if soldiers are imbued with a degree of credulity, which is probably one reason why armies tend to prefer young men to older ones.[21]

Historically, religion—in particular the notion that an instrumental and guiding god is one's ally—has very often served that purpose. In A. A. Milne's irreverent observation, God participates in war by "fighting on both sides in that encouraging way He has." Gerald Linderman notes that in the American Civil War, "a conviction of wide currency was that God would ensure the victory of the army whose collective faith was the sturdiest."[22] Religion, prayer, and the belief in god can also aid the conduct of warfare by helping soldiers deal with the inevitable terror and stress of battle; there are, as they say, no atheists in foxholes.[23] For this reason, commanders have often used religious ritual and appeals to buck up their forces as they gird for battle. Religion is not the only mechanism for accomplishing this, of course, but there can be little doubt that the belief in the existence of a guiding and instrumental god has helped to facilitate war. Sometimes this process can be enhanced if combatants come to believe that there is a special heavenly reward for death in battle. This seems to have impelled thousands of young Iranian recruits to flock to their deaths in the country's war with Iraq in the 1980s. Similarly, the Vikings subscribed to the belief that a combatant would go to Valhalla only if he met death in battle, a truly ingenious myth because those so convinced would not only fight to the death in battle but would avoid getting into lethal conflicts outside of war.

Other impelling beliefs have been ideological, racial, nationalistic, or patriotic. At least some soldiers have probably sincerely subscribed to such slogans as "Give me liberty or give me death" or "Let us die to make men free." In general, however, beliefs, like the patriotic fervor the French call *rage militaire*, seem to be most effective at getting people to sign up, whereas other motivations become more important in helping them endure the long-term rigors of hardship. And beliefs tend to be more important to officers than to the ranks.[24]

Discussions of war, particularly ethnic war, have often held that hatred, anger, and revenge, which can be considered kinds of belief, are crucial to the process and that violence can erupt from deep-seated or newly induced hatreds between combatants or peoples. These emotions can also spring from love—the desire to avenge the death of a buddy, for example.[25] I do not wish to dismiss completely the role of these qualities and discuss the issue in more detail in later chapters: many of the chief killers and instigators of violence are indeed dedicated and highly focused haters and revenge seekers. But there are a number of difficulties with using hatred, anger, and revenge as central explanatory variables.[26]

To begin with, there is the problem of sustaining these emotions. As time wears on in violent conflicts, the actual process of warfare tends to become routine—intensely boring in fact. Maintaining a high state of hatred and anger and a desire for revenge becomes increasingly difficult. Indeed, cynicism often becomes far more common than anything else.[27] Some people, of course, are able to operate at continuing high levels of hatred and rage— some Irish Republicans and some of those hostile to the existence of Israel, for example. But such people seem to be rare, and the very passions that impel them may be self-destructive, or "consuming," as it is often put. In prosecuting a war, a commander would be unwise to rely on being able to sustain a continuing intense hatred or anger.

In addition, although expressions of hatred between groups and peoples are exceedingly (and rather drearily) common—Archie Bunkers are everywhere—violence among supposed haters is remarkably rare. Proportionately, it fact, it almost never happens.* By one calculation only five one-hundredths of one percent of potential ethnic conflicts in Africa over a

---

*If hatred without violence is common, so is violence without hatred and with only the most artificial of identities. For example, soccer or football hooligans who may all come from the same class, religion, and ethnic or national group frequently engage in violence even at local amateur matches (Buford 1991; see also Tilly 2003, 81–87). Something similar can be said for battles among urban street gangs, whose members often distinguish themselves by establishing exquisitely differentiated, if thoroughly artificial, loyalties to separate street corners.

twenty-year period actually erupted into violence. Furthermore, although there may be plenty of hate, hostility, and animosity between various peoples, warfare does not seem to correlate well with these qualities. That is, it is not notably found in the areas with the most intergroup hostility and cleavage. Indeed, people in supposedly hate-filled societies frequently manage to live peacefully side by side, sometimes for centuries, and they frequently intermarry at prodigious rates. Moreover, the casual notion that groups are unified by their antagonism toward another group appears to be deeply flawed. Serbs in Serbia have often been able to contain their affection for the desperate and often rough rural Serbs who fled to their country from war-torn Croatia and Bosnia, regarding them as "hicks" and "flotsam from the boondocks."[28]

Finally, some hatreds that appear to be elemental can vanish with amazing suddenness and apparent completeness once a conflict is over. As Lawrence Keeley notes, there is an "incredible plasticity of human conduct" in which relationships often "change from familiar friendship to bitter enmity and back again with remarkable rapidity." For example, Daniel Goldhagen argues that there had long been a "pre-existing, pent-up antisemitism" in Germany that Hitler and the Nazis merely needed to "unshackle and thereby activate," but that after the war, democracy and legal proscriptions against making anti-Semitic statements quickly transformed Germans into liberal democrats "like us." But then, as some critics have pointed out, if they could vanish so quickly and so completely, how elemental were these hatreds to begin with? Somewhat similarly, John Dower has documented the savage, almost animal, hatreds that appear to have burgeoned during World War II between Americans and Japanese, many of which had roots in various racist incidents and policies that went back decades. After the war, however, these hatreds dissipated quickly and almost completely, and postwar polls were soon to discover that the foreigners the Japanese most admired had become the Americans—the very people who in 1945 had bombed Tokyo, Hiroshima, and Nagasaki.[29]

In fact, if people were unable to control the expression of hatred in a more or less rational manner, war would be impossible or at least exceptionally difficult. For wars to be fought most effectively, combatants must be able to let their passions go only on command, and they must be able to rein them in when ordered even when severely provoked (holding their fire when being fired upon, for example). Indeed, hatred (and the desire for revenge) often seems to be more the result than the cause of violent conflict, or, like soccer rivalry, it may sometimes more nearly serve as an excuse than as a cause for violence.[30]

DEVELOPING ARMIES: CRIMINAL AND DISCIPLINED WARFARE

This checklist should not lead one to conclude that recruiting, retaining, and motivating a combatant force is easy. The devices I've outlined can be effective, but efforts to get people to commit individual or collective violence have often failed miserably, and desertion and defection have been exceedingly common in warfare, even when, as is very often the case, the penalty is death. That is, for all the psychological and historical literature about the importance of honor, about obedience to authority, and about loyalty to the group, the central problem in warfare through the ages has been to keep men from flagrantly disobeying orders by deserting at the earliest opportunity. The behavior of the Iraqi army in the Gulf War of 1991 furnishes a vivid example. But even in the comparatively well-oiled German military machine of World War II there were 15,000 executions for various infractions.[31] Moreover, the problem is not simply to create forces that will conduct themselves well during the violence of combat but ones that can also endure the long periods of boring and uncomfortable languor between engagements.

Thus, historian James McPherson makes a strong case that soldiers in the American Civil War were probably impelled much more by beliefs and ideology than were most combatants in most wars. But even he presents considerable evidence that only about half the men did the real fighting while the rest, variously known as skulkers, shirkers, sneaks, beats, stragglers, skedaddlers, coffee-coolers, or tree-dodgers, had a tendency when combat loomed to melt away, become sick, desert, or find it necessary to help a wounded comrade to the rear. He is justifiably impressed that more than half of the early Union volunteers retained enough enthusiasm to reenlist when their terms were up, but he also makes it clear that this enthusiasm was laced with manipulative appeals to unit pride, a massive financial incentive, and provisions for a lengthy furlough.[32] Indeed, if peer pressure can lead many (probably most) people to commit violence under appropriate circumstances, it can also lead them away from it. This conclusion is supported in one of the variations Milgram tested in his study. When the naive subject was put among two peers (confederates of the experimenter) who, on cue, defied the experimenter's instruction to shock the supposed victim, almost all of the naive subjects broke off the experiment and refused to administer further shocks.[33]

Broadly speaking, there seem to be two methods for developing combat forces—for successfully cajoling or coercing collections of men into engaging in the violent, profane, sacrificial, uncertain, masochistic, and essentially absurd enterprise known as war. The two methods lead to two kinds of warfare, and the distinction can be an instructive one.

Intuitively, it might seem that the easiest (and cheapest) method for recruiting combatants would be to rely on the first motivations mentioned earlier and enlist those who revel in violence and routinely seek it out or who regularly employ it to enrich themselves, or both. We have in civilian life a name for such people—criminals—but the category would also encompass those popularly known as bullies, hooligans, toughs, goons, and thugs. Violent conflicts in which people like that dominate can be called criminal warfare, a form in which combatants are induced to wreak violence primarily for the fun and material profit they derive from the experience.

Criminal armies seem to arise from a couple of processes. Sometimes criminals—robbers, brigands, freebooters, highwaymen, hooligans, thugs, bandits, pirates, gangsters, outlaws—organize or join together in gangs or bands or mafias. When such organizations become big enough, they can look and act a lot like full-blown armies.

Or criminal armies can be formed when a ruler needs combatants to prosecute a war and concludes that the employment or impressment of criminals and thugs is the most sensible or direct method for accomplishing this. In this case, criminals and thugs essentially act as mercenaries.

It happens, however, that criminals and thugs tend to be undesirable warriors, no matter how much they may be drawn to combat by their inclination to relish violence or to find profit in it. To begin with, they are often difficult to control. They can be troublemakers: unruly, disobedient, and mutinous, often committing unauthorized crimes while on (or off) duty that can be detrimental or even destructive of the military enterprise. This natural unruliness is often enhanced by the deprivation and boredom that commonly envelop the long periods between military actions—and, for relief, they may decide to return to familiar conduct except that their victims may now be fellow soldiers.

Most importantly, criminals can be disinclined to stand and fight when things become dangerous, and they often simply desert when whim and opportunity coincide. Ordinary crime, after all, preys on the weak—on little old ladies rather than on husky athletes—and criminals often make willing and able executioners of defenseless people.[34] However, if the cops show up they are given to flight. The motto for the criminal, after all, is not a variation of "Semper fi," "All for one and one for all," "Duty, honor, country," "Banzai," or "Remember Pearl Harbor," but "Take the money and run."

Indeed, for a criminal to perish in battle (or in the commission of a bank robbery) is essentially absurd: it is profoundly irrational to die for the thrill of violence and even more so for the procurement of booty, because you can't, after all, take either one with you. In general, then, although they seem more willing than ordinary people to accept risk, and although they can be induced to engage in battle by the appeal of pay or booty and by the prospect of inflicting violence, they tend to fight reliably only when the probability of being killed is low enough or when they are massively coerced.

Testimony from some of the Civil War diaries and letters examined by McPherson is suggestive. "With remarkable unanimity," he found, "fighting soldiers of middle-class origins commented in their letters home that 'it isn't the brawling, fighting man at home that stands the bullets the best.' 'Roughs that are always ready for street fighting are cowards on the open battle field.' 'I don't know of a single fighting bulley but what he makes a *cowardly* soldier.' 'As a general thing those at home that are naturally timid are the ones here that have the least fear.' " They had similar contempt for the paid substitutes and bounty men who joined the Union ranks late in the war: "The big bounty men are no men at all," one wrote. "Most of them came out just to get the bounty, & play out [shirk] as soon as they are able." Substitutes were characterized as "miserable surly rough fellows" who were "far inferior to the old patriotic vols. who came 'without money and without price.' " "*Money* soldiers are not worth as much as they *cost* for when [there is] firing ahead you may see them hid in the woods."[35] As these statements suggest, the presence of such people in the ranks can affect the fighting morale of noncriminals in the combatant forces. They routinely avoid criminals and other social undesirables in civilian life, and they may sensibly distrust their reliability in combat.

These problems with the employment of criminals as combatants have historically led to efforts to recruit ordinary men as combatants—people who, unlike criminals and thugs, commit violence at no other time in their lives (although they may watch a lot of it on television). Combat studies, in fact, generally find performance positively correlated with social class, education, intelligence, and personal stability.[36]

The result has been the development of disciplined warfare in which men primarily inflict violence not for fun and profit but because their training and indoctrination have instilled in them a need to follow orders; to observe a carefully contrived and tendentious code of honor; to seek glory and reputation in combat; to love, honor, or fear their officers; to believe in a cause; to fear the shame, humiliation, or costs of surrender; or, in particular, to be loyal to, and to deserve the loyalty of, their fellow combatants.[37] They may also, like the criminal combatant, fight to experience the thrill of battle and to enrich themselves; coercion and drugs or alcohol may also be variously relevant. Their primary motivations, however, lie elsewhere.

CRIMINAL AND DISCIPLINED WARFARE, CRIME, TERRORISM

Bands of criminal combatants seem often to be comparatively small in number, reflecting, in part, the relatively low proportion of criminals in the general population, the difficulty of controlling them, and the limits to resources that can be looted. By contrast, disciplined armies can, subject only to economic and training constraints, be very large.

Disciplined combatants generally fight to win, to conclude the war in order to return to a safer life as civilians or as professionals in a peacetime army. Criminal combatants, on the other hand, frequently are less likely to want to see the war end because they often are better off in war and face unemployment or a return to criminality in a country that has been impoverished by the very war they have just waged.[38]

In disciplined warfare, combatants principally seek to inflict violence upon each other, and in some cases they may even try to avoid harming civilians, particularly directly. In criminal warfare, combatants commonly seek to wreak violence on civilians, particularly defenseless ones, because that is where the psychic and material rewards are greatest and the risks are lowest.

Table 1.1 expands these comparisons. The routes by which criminals and thugs become organized enough to be considered to be in war or warlike situations—by becoming mercenaries or by forming warlord bands, for example—are found at the bottom of the table. The table breaks disciplined warfare into two categories: conventional (Clausewitzian or regimental) and unconventional (guerrilla or primitive).

As the table suggests, when criminal methods are applied sporadically and by individuals or small groups, we usually designate the activity "crime." When disciplined methods are applied sporadically and by individuals or small groups, the process can be designated "terrorism." When either form

TABLE 1.1
War, crime, and terrorism

	Large-group violence (war)		Individual or small-group violence
Disciplined	Conventional	Unconventional	Terrorism
	Clausewitzian Regimental	Primitive Guerrilla Partisan Insurgency People's war	
	Mao phase 3	Mao phase 2	Mao phases 1 and 2
Criminal		Brigandry Warlordism Mercenarism Freebooting	Crime banditry mafia organized crime riots

of violence is perpetrated by substantial groups and becomes continuous or sustained enough, it will look like, and be called, "war."*

The relationship between terrorism and disciplined warfare can be illustrated by the writings on guerrilla warfare by Mao Tse-tung. He distinguished three phases. The first is essentially defensive and involves setting up rear bases and gaining popular support. At the end of this phase, his combatants would begin to engage in offensive terrorism against the enemy, targeting both the military and civilians such as government officials and teachers. As this approach is developed through phase 2, full-fledged guerrilla warfare would be employed, built around a hit-and-run approach. "The ability to run away," declares Mao, "is the essence of the guerrilla." Finally, in phase 3, the weakened enemy would be engaged, and crushed, by conventional, stand-and-fight warfare.[39] The shift between phases 2 and 3 can be a tricky one. If attempted prematurely, the shift can play into the hands of a conventional enemy, as Communist guerrillas found in Greece in the late 1940s and in 1972 in Vietnam.

The goal for those engaged in counterguerrilla or counterinsurgency warfare is to stop and reverse the process by reducing guerrilla activities to more bearable terrorist levels. Similarly, those combating criminal warfare will seek to reduce the size of the groups perpetrating it and the frequency of the violence they commit. When these efforts are successful, "war" will cease to exist, and any violence and predation that remain will be called terrorism or crime.

Criminal warfare should not be confused with the sort of unconventional, yet disciplined, warfare carried out by guerrillas or by those warriors anthropologists call "primitive." The tactics applied by such unconventional combatants often resemble those employed by criminal ones—a reliance on hit-and-run raids that target civilians and a wariness about set-piece battles. Moreover, as with criminal warfare, such warfare is often waged with limited logistic backup and without much in the way of a well-developed strategy beyond attrition. But unconventional warfare actually can be quite dedicated in the sense that combatants, who have sometimes been trained from birth, often fight with ordered devotion and a willingness to die for their cause or group—or each other.[40] Combat like that would be considered disciplined by the definitions developed here.

---

*It is common to define terrorism by its target and to consider only attacks on civilians to be acts of terror. However, this means that strategic bombing of cities or the application of economic sanctions would have to be considered to be terrorism, thus distorting the meaning of the term as it is usually applied. To deal with this problem, some definitions require that terrorism must be carried out by substate actors. But this means that at least one side in almost any civil war—including the one in Vietnam—would have to be considered terrorists, particularly in the early stages. What the Vietnamese Communists were doing to the civilian population in the early and middle 1960s—assassination, ambush, harassment, sabotage, assault—has generally been considered to be war, not terrorism, because it was so sustained and was accomplished by a sizeable, well-organized group (see Pike 1966, chap. 8).

WAR BETWEEN AND AMONG DISCIPLINED AND CRIMINAL MILITARIES

With these definitions as background, it is possible to discuss the likely outcome of wars in which disciplined armies are on both sides, in which criminal armies are on both (or all) sides, and in which criminal and disciplined
armies fight each other.

Most of the literature on war deals with organized violent conflict between
disciplined conventional armies. The outcome of wars between disciplined
forces tends to depend on the adequacy of training, leadership, logistic support, weaponry, and, particularly, morale. The armies tend to continue until
one side "breaks"—something that can happen suddenly, even precipitously,
seemingly caused by an event that is later held to have been "decisive."[41]

Such wars often involve substantial and dramatic set-piece battles or engagements in which armies essentially agree to have it out and in which great
destruction is inflicted over a short period of time. Reflecting this characteristic, such wars are often designated "high-intensity" conflicts.

Sometimes wars between disciplined armies can be quite short because
one side collapses early and precipitously—as in the case of France when invaded by Germany in 1940. The exertions of battle can lead to profound las-
situde and exhaustion, and if this happens before a battle is over, it can express itself in panic and intense fear and thus in "decisive" defeat.[42] At other
times, the sides can remain stalemated for considerable periods of time.
World War I went on so long because disciplined conventional armies had
successfully been created on both sides and because neither could score a decisive breakthrough. Men fought on and on without questioning their orders
or even seeking to understand their purpose.

Though less discussed, there have also been large numbers of wars that pit
unconventional disciplined forces against conventional ones. As Keeley has
convincingly demonstrated, primitive and guerrilla combatants have very
frequently done well against conventional ones. When the latter have triumphed, it has usually been not because of superior weaponry but because
they have far greater economic and logistic capability, because they have
been crucially aided by diseases that have affected the enemy disproportionately, or because they adopt primitive or guerrilla tactics.[43]

The most common type of disciplined warfare has been that conducted
among unconventional forces, particularly by primitive combatants. Although there may be direct fighting between primitive or guerrilla armies,
concentrated battles will be far less common than feints, skirmishes, and
raids. And contact is likely to be broken off before very many casualties are
suffered in the engagement. Because of this characteristic, wars with or
among primitive or guerrilla combatants are often held to be a form of low-
intensity conflict. However, although the death and destruction resulting
from direct military confrontation between such armies or bands are likely

to be low in any single engagement because the armies would rather run than fight, the death and destruction visited upon combatants and civilians over time by the behavior of these armies can come to be quite high—devastatingly so, in fact.[44]

Wars among criminal armies are also often considered to be low intensity. But they too can be extremely costly over long periods of time, particularly to the civilian population upon whom they prey. It is often difficult to designate the beginnings of wars between criminal combatant forces, and determining their ends is even more so. The conflicts are more likely to fade away, to diminish in intensity—and therefore to become indistinguishable from ordinary crime—than they are to end with a clear-cut termination of hostilities. Furthermore, they are likely to become more like a business than a war in the sense that, because the perpetrators are profiting from the enterprise, they may have little interest in ending it—although they may at times work out de facto accommodations to divide up turf. Warfare, if that is what it is called, then becomes a continuous way of life, routine and self-perpetuating, and these kinds of low-intensity wars may be scarcely differentiable from high-intensity crime.

When a criminal army comes into direct armed confrontation with a competent disciplined one, the disciplined one, essentially by definition, will prevail. Because of the successful development of some of the devices discussed earlier, a disciplined combatant will fight even if the likelihood of being killed is high, whereas criminal armies simply do not have the ability, or more accurately the will, to stand and fight, and they will fade away. As burglars scatter when the cops show up, criminal armies disintegrate when an effective disciplined force emerges on the scene.

Often, however, the victory of the disciplined army in these conflicts will not look terribly decisive. The criminal combatants will still be around, and many of them will simply revert to more ordinary crime. Consequently, in an important sense, they do not go from combatant to noncombatant status in the manner of, say, the armies of World War II. Rather, their predations will continue, but at a different level—one that can continue to be highly destructive to the societies in which they prey. And controlling them will require patient, dreary, endless, routine, and often frustrating police work, not warfare. If the former criminal combatants take a fancy to taking pot shots at the cops, it can be dangerous work as well. "Decisive" is a military term and does not pertain to police work. Wars may end, but policing never does.

THE DISTINCTION BETWEEN CRIMINAL AND DISCIPLINED WARFARE

The discussion thus far has dealt with ideal types. But, as will be seen in later chapters, conditions can sometimes be rather fluid, even slippery.

Determining the background of combatants is not easy. Census takers may duly enumerate people by occupation, but their categories do not include one for criminals, much less ones for thugs, goons, bullies, misfits, hooligans, or drunks. As will be seen, combatants sometimes have been directly and deliberately recruited from prisons, so to designate these participants as "criminal" can be pretty reasonable. But many people in militaries that seem to be essentially criminal in nature may not be criminals in a technical sense, although people who meet up with them have often been willing to apply that term, or the more general one, "thugs," to them.

In fact, military forces have been something of a mix of the criminal and the disciplined, and the only cases in which a clear-cut distinction can be made is with some of the best modern militaries, which systematically seek to avoid enlisting criminals and the criminal-like into their forces. Moreover, sometimes criminal armies, including mercenary bands, are able to get their act together and operate like disciplined forces, or disciplined armies may disintegrate into collections of criminal and bandit bands. Sometimes disciplined militaries use criminal means to fund themselves, and some essentially criminal warlords may establish order within their area of control to the point that what they have constructed will look a great deal like a disciplined authority.

I argue in subsequent chapters, however, that the distinction—indeed, its very slipperiness—can be useful for analytic purposes in a discussion of the history of warfare over the last thousand years. As will be seen, the creation of essentially disciplined forces from bands of people who are, or act like, criminals and thugs has been at the center of much state building. And if most of the warfare that remains today is essentially or primarily criminal in character—rather than disciplined expressions of deep ethnic, political, religious, or civilizational angst and grievance—this fact holds out the possibility that disciplined forces can bring it under control. Potentially, this could even bring about the demise of the ancient and seemingly inevitable institution of war.

THE CONTROL OF WAR AND
THE RISE OF WAR AVERSION

Over the course of the last millennium, warfare in Europe has gone from the commonplace and routine to the uncommon and avoided. This chapter ranges through some nine hundred years of history to trace the success of disciplined forces in Europe, the consequent creation of the state system there, the increasing control of war by political authorities, the persistence of enthusiasm for war, and the rise, for the first time in history, of focused, dedicated, vocal bands of war opponents in the decades before World War I.

THE TRIUMPH OF DISCIPLINED FORCES IN EUROPE

At one time, Europe was probably the most warlike place in the world. In the early Middle Ages, notes Philippe Contamine, "years without military expeditions were always sufficiently exceptional for them to be mentioned in the Annals." Richard Kaeuper stresses that war was an "essential and characteristic function" of the medieval states of Europe. It commanded "a vast share of the treasure of governments, a major part of the time and energies of kings and their advisers," and it was conducted in an ethos that "glorified war as greatest test and expression of manhood." War was, notes Michael Howard, "an almost automatic activity, part of the natural order of things." Accordingly, as Charles Tilly observes, "it is hardly worth asking *when* states warred, since most states were warring most of the time."[1]

The recruitment process for these armies was singularly unselective: about all that the military normally required of recruiters was that they enlist warm bodies. Moreover, it was frequently possible for potential conscripts to buy (or bribe) their way out of service or to furnish substitutes. The process essentially guaranteed that the ranks of the soldiery would be manned disproportionately by criminals, thugs, and rogues, as well as by vagabonds, vagrants, undesirables, loiterers, misfits, social failures, beggars, derelicts, root-less people, drunks, and the unemployable, idle poor, and mentally dis-turbed. As Tilly observes, "a king's best source of armed supporters was some-times the world of outlaws" and kings often "hired sometime bandits to raid their enemies, and encouraged their regular troops to take booty." At a me-dieval battle, such as Agincourt in 1415, notes Keegan, "a high proportion of the men on the battlefield, at least among the common soldiery, would have been guilty of bloody murder before joining up and had indeed done so in order to escape civil punishment."[2]

Taverns and brothels frequently proved fertile recruiting grounds, and jails could be ideal: they housed men awaiting trial or sentencing, very often for capital offenses, for whom even the worst form of soldiering would be an improvement. For their part, the locals could at least temporarily get rid of undesirables and at the same time accomplish a net financial gain: not only was it unnecessary to pay the prisoners much of anything to sign up, but the community would be spared the cost of their upkeep. This scheme was espe-cially attractive when recruiters were trying to dragoon participants for for-eign armies because many locals saw this as a welcome opportunity to banish criminals and other undesirables from the community quite likely forever. Additionally, men fleeing the law (or irate fathers) frequently found escape and refuge in the military. Some of the armies in the Hundred Years War that took place in France between 1340 and 1453 (it was a long century) con-sisted of from 2 to 12 percent convicted criminals, many of them murderers seeking royal pardons for their services.[3]

One reason foreigners were commonly recruited for armies was that they were less likely to desert in unfamiliar territory. However, despite this, and despite the fact that the punishment was death, desertion rates were often prodigious—5 to 20 percent per month—making it impossible for generals to know the exact size of their forces at any given time. There are even in-stances in which whole armies almost entirely vanished. This was especially true during the long, enervating sieges that were the most common form of military action during the period; not uncommonly, deserters fled in large numbers to the very town they were besieging.[4]

Although there was a professional core to the combatant forces in the War of the Roses in fifteenth-century England, the vast majority of the soldiers were ill disciplined, untrained, and inexperienced. Liquor was commonly ap-plied as incentive to join, it was imbibed daily, huge quantities were con-sumed before battle, and combatants remained under its influence when they sacked towns. One contemporary chronicler protested about "the mis-rule of the king's gallants," who "went wet-shod in wine" and "robbed the town, and bare away bedding, cloth, and other stuff, and befouled many women."[5]

Accordingly, much of the warfare that plagued the Continent at the time seems in large part to have resembled criminal enterprise. As Tilly puts it, "In an era of intensely fragmented sovereignty . . . the differences among soldiers, bandits, pirates, rebels, and lords doing their duty blurred into a continuum of coercive action." Soldiers and sailors in royal service were often expected "to provide for themselves by preying on the civilian population: commandeering, raping, looting, taking prizes. When demobilized, they commonly continued the same practices, but without royal protection; demobilized ships became pirate vessels, demobilized troops bandits." To the French they were known as *écorcheurs,* scorchers of the earth. During the Thirty Years War in the first half of the seventeenth century, war often became a vast profit-making undertaking, and one of the more successful armies has been characterized pointedly as "the greatest business enterprise of the age."[6]

Knights in the fourteenth century, observes Kaeuper, "seem to have accepted arson and pillage as normal and expected accompaniments of campaigning"; as Henry V put it jauntily, "war without fire is like sausages without mustard." In the 1530s an Italian writer observed that for more than twenty years, civilians had seen "nothing but scenes of infinite slaughter, plunder and destruction of multitudes of towns and cities, attended with the licentiousness of soldiers no less destructive to friends than foes."[7]

In examining the conduct of the Hundred Years War, Nicholas Wright finds it useful to differentiate between the "official" war—campaigns led by the kings and their commanders, who "on very rare occasions" met on the battlefield—and the "unofficial" war that filled the gaps between princely campaigns, as soldiers moved out of royal field armies into various freebooting activities. Few soldiers "did not stray into the area delineated by the lawyers and theologians as criminal." Because soldiers were engaged by short-term contract and simply dismissed when their service was no longer required, they very often then "sought-out, or created, frontiers of war" in which "the difference between friends and foes, especially amongst the noncombatants, was likely to be of little immediate relevance" in their "constant search for profits and sustenance." Official and unofficial marauding armies could commonly burn and destroy a track of up to fifty kilometers in width as they progressed. It appears that boys were often kidnapped to perform sexual services, while "the capture of women for such purposes . . . is mentioned so often in the remission records that it has been reduced to a bland formula." In all, suggests Wright, the features of this form of warfare "are instantly recognizable by those with experience of wars in the so-called 'Third World' of today."[8]

That image certainly holds for the predatory and parasitical mercenary bands, or "companies of adventure," that plagued Italy around the fourteenth century. They operated under fanciful, self-infatuated names like the Company of the Star, the Company of the Hook, and the Company of the

Hat (Rambo had yet to be invented) and proudly promulgated graffiti-like slogans such as "Enemy of God, Pity, and Mercy." Their camps reminded one observer of "brothels of harlots and the taverns and bistros of gluttons." One of the most destructive and effective of these bands was led by John Hawk-wood, who inspired the observation that "an Italianized Englishman is a devil incarnate," and who is famed for solving a problem that arose during the plundering of a monastery: when two of his men argued over which would get to ravish a beautiful young nun, he plunged a dagger into her heart, thereby, observes an admiring chronicler, at once solving the dispute in his army and preserving her virginity. Since Hawkwood lived by war and would be out of business in peacetime, wrote one Italian novelist, "he managed his affairs so well, that there was little peace in Italy in his times." Not only did these marauders practice extortion on a wide scale and destroy people and property—especially in the countryside, where they regularly seized livestock and could bring agriculture to a halt—but they greatly exacerbated the effects of plagues and famines by seizing what food remained for themselves.[9]

Eventually, some of these warring units innovated and began to create disciplined militaries. For example, as early as 1445 France's Charles VII set out at considerable cost to form a permanent, standing army from among the best soldiers. They were, as Keegan notes, "officially recognized as military servants of the monarchy, whose function would be to extirpate the rest." The new regiments "rapidly acquired a character different from that of the mercenary bands of late feudalism and the Wars of Religion, which had usually disbanded when funds dried up," and they became "permanent royal—eventually national—institutions" with a culture ideally stressing "total obedience, single-minded courage, self-sacrifice, honour." Sometimes this process could involve hiring and eventually domesticating the most effective mercenary armies. Ehrenreich points out that "medieval wars had been fought not by 'armies' in any recognizable, modern sense but by loose collections of men, often under little or no central command." By contrast, the new forces were characterized by rigid systems of discipline and command in which officers often had absolute control over the destinies—and the lives—of their men. "Instead of being trained once and then trusted to use their skills on the battlefield, troops were to be trained incessantly from the moment of induction to the very eve of battle" to the point that, "for the average soldier, courage was less in order than fatalism and a kind of stolid passivity."[10]

These armies tended to be not only permanent but much larger, and almost certainly they were composed of higher portions of ordinary men than were earlier armies. The pool of talent in the dregs of society simply is unlikely to be deep enough to furnish manpower for a large army. Furthermore, the increasing emphasis on drill, discipline, and rigorous training probably decreased the attraction of military service to thugs and criminals. And because the military required skilled, or at least trainable, recruits, many criminals and other undesirables who did join were soon mustered out or given duty where they could least harm combat effectiveness. Drill masters undoubtedly found that they could mould some thugs into effective, disciplined soldiers by one method or another—mostly violent ones. But that takes time and effort, and it seems likely that tolerance for troublemakers declined over time.

This process was surely enhanced by the economics of the situation. Increasingly, soldiers were paid directly with cash rather than indirectly with opportunities to pillage. Moreover, as armies grew larger, it was no longer physically easy or even possible to house them among the (often resentful) civilian population, and so armies needed to be provided with costly billeting facilities.[11] One is likely to put up with an incompetent or venal soldier much more readily when he is essentially working on commission than when he must be paid and housed out of current revenues. Although enormous improvements in military effectiveness were made, brutal treatment remained the order of the day. Even while considering it crucial for commanders to take great care for the soldiers' welfare, Prussia's Frederick the Great in the eighteenth century insisted that it was "necessary always to make them observe the most exact discipline" so that they "fear their officers more than all the dangers to which they are exposed." He praised sternness and severity since many soldiers "can be held in check only through fear." In part, this approached stemmed from the observation that his armies, like others in Europe, were mostly "composed of the dregs of society—sluggards, rakes, debauchees, rioters, undutiful sons, and the like." The same view was held in the next century by Britain's most famous general, Wellington. Although he thought it "wonderful" that rigid discipline had made so much out of his soldiers, he considered them to be "the scum of the earth—the mere scum of the earth" who "all enlisted for drink—that is plain fact—they have all enlisted for drink."[12]

By that time, however, the institution of conscription—something that only an effective government can carry off—had begun to enhance the process of bringing in higher proportions of ordinary men to the ranks. Wellington was impressed in this regard by the troops of his principal enemy: "The French system of conscription brings together a fair sample of all classes," he observed approvingly.[13]

There may also have been an effect from the gradual development of penal servitude—the routine locking up of criminals for substantial periods of time. Earlier, reliance had been on much cheaper but probably less effective methods of punishment: banishment or exile, which, if everyone is doing it, merely churns the criminals (unless authorities could afford to ship them off to a distant place like Australia); killing or execution, which is treacherous because the pursued have every incentive to fight back murderously and none to surrender peacefully even as courts often failed to convict for comparatively minor offenses; corporal punishment, which leaves the (embittered) punished free to return to crime after recuperating; or fining, which only makes much sense for small crimes and isn't exactly useful against the indigent. Crime, like war, is mainly perpetrated by young males, and, although there is no way to stop them from being young, an increasingly popular punishment was to lock them up until they cease being so. It is a remedy that not only separated them from potential victims (except for fellow prisoners), but often also from military service.

THE POLITICAL CONTROL OF WAR IN EUROPE

These new and superior military forces were used to eliminate rivals who still relied on less-disciplined and criminal (and therefore militarily unreliable) forces. Thus princes (or warlords) who managed to create such costly military organizations were able to conquer, control, and pacify substantial chunks of territory.[14] For example, disciplined forces eventually prevailed in England, often previously the scene of nearly continuous internal armed conflict, and that country has experienced virtually no civil war now for some 350 years.

The process of developing disciplined forces led, in turn, to the creation of the state system. In the words of Saint Augustine, if brigandage "grows to such proportions that it holds lands, establishes fixed settlements, seizes upon states and subjugates peoples, it assumes the name of a kingdom." As Tilly describes the process, "From 1648, if not before, at the ends of wars all effective European states coalesced temporarily to bargain over the boundaries and rulers of the recent belligerents. From that point on, periods of major reorganization of the European state system came in spurts, at the settlement of widespread wars. From each large war, in general, emerged fewer national states than had entered it."[15]

Banditry, piracy, and organized criminality and thuggery continued, of course, but the new, larger, and more effective states were much more resilient and simply could not be viscerally threatened by small groups of armed thugs. Where bandits had once become warlords, they now remained merely criminal bands, more an inconvenience than a hazard to the stability, much less the survival, of the state.

Tilly also observes that "consolidation of the state system, segregation of the military from civilian life, and disarmament of the civilian population sharpened the distinction between war and peace." That is, war (and peace) came under a degree of control, it had clearer beginning and ending points, and states went into battle with much more deliberation. Thus, relying particularly on the work of Heinz Duchhardt, Paul Schroeder notes the emergence over the course of the eighteenth century of a "capacity of the units involved in the game of international politics to impose order on their relations and on the system as a whole and thereby to avoid or reduce war and expand the possibility of peace." He suggests that "a fair generalization about international politics in the fifteenth, sixteenth, or seventeenth centuries is that most wars that could have started, did, and that most crises led within a relatively short time to war." However, increasingly in the eighteenth and nineteenth centuries "we see emerging a more stable, comprehensive state system endowed not merely with permanent players and better and more widely acknowledged rules, practices, and institutions, but also as a result with greater ability to manage international politics short of overt war. To some extent in the eighteenth century, to an even greater extent in the nineteenth, most wars that could have happened did not happen; most crises were managed more or less successfully." As Jack Levy and his associates observe, "The wars for personal honor, vengeance, and enrichment of kings and nobles that characterized the Middle Ages . . . were increasingly replaced by the use of force as an instrument of policy for the achievement of political objectives."[16]

As it came under political control, war became less frequent. However, as Tilly notes, war also became "more intense and destructive" and "more continuous once it began."[17] This may have enhanced rulers' caution about engaging in the practice. Eventually, after a series of costly continent-wide wars, Europe managed between 1815 and 1854 to lapse into an unprecedented era of near-total freedom from international warfare, and then, from 1871 until 1914, to experience another period of near-total peace within Europe that was even longer than the first. As Evan Luard observes, although there were some civil wars, these two long stretches of European peace represent a dramatic change from earlier times, when major countries were joined in recurrent warfare against each other.[18]

In the process, an interesting change in the way war was justified took place. In early Europe, notes Luard, no justification seemed necessary—war was seen as a "glorious undertaking" and a "normal feature of human existence, a favorite pastime for princes and great lords." By 1700 or so, however, attitudes had changed enough so that rulers found they were "expected to proclaim their own love of peace and their desire to avoid the tragedies of war"—although they still managed to concoct plenty of reasons to fight, and they continued to find war a "brilliant way to win glory," as Louis XIV of France put it. The notion that war was normal, honorable, and in some respects desirable, persisted, but increasingly, observes Luard, leaders "found it necessary to proclaim that war had been 'forced' on them," and the notion gained ground that wars needed to be "just," although, as Parker acknowledges, people still continued to see "their God as the Lord of Battles and had little time for pacifism."[19]

As part of this development, war, at least in some quarters, seems to have begun to be seen more as a special (and extreme) method for accomplishing desirable political goals than as a normal way of life, a conclusion stressed in an important book, *On War,* published in 1832 by a Prussian officer, Carl von Clausewitz. At its center was the often-quoted aphorism "War is merely the continuation of politics by other means." For Clausewitz, war did not have a life or existence of its own; it was not "something autonomous" but simply— merely—"an instrument of policy."[20]

A related development is also of interest. Some once-prominent members of the war system attempted to drop out of it entirely, a process I call Hollandization. The term derives from the behavior of the Netherlands, a wealthy, central, even dominant, country that once got involved in the usual quota of conflicts. In the eighteenth century, however, it began to drop out of the system to concentrate on commercial and colonial ventures. Although it has occasionally been swept into wider conflicts by others, for more than two and a half centuries Holland has generally sought to avoid all international war in Europe. Something similar happened in Scandinavia, which had once produced some of history's most storied warrior-predators. When focused at home, the Scandinavians could spend decades engaged in civil warfare— Norway, for example, was the scene of essentially continual civil war from 1130 to 1227. The more recent war record of the Scandinavian countries is summarized in table 2.1: during most of the time from 1415 to 1816 they were engaged in some sort of war someplace (often, in fact, more than one war was being waged at a time). Yet despite this violent and bloody history, they have avidly sought for some two centuries now to remain war free, quietly giving out prizes for peace, erecting tasteful museums for the display of Viking ships lovingly rescued from burial mounds and from the sea, and writing books patiently explaining that their predatory ancestors were actually not all that bad in some cases. Similarly, although Switzerland was a first-class military power in 1500, it has ever since shown what one historian has called a "curious indifference" to "political or territorial aggrandizement."[21]

The experiences of the Hollandized countries refute two popular notions: first, that international war is endemic to human nature, and second, that war or "war fever" is cyclic.[22] If either of these propositions were true, one would expect the Swiss, Danes, Swedes, Norwegians, and Dutch to be positively roaring for a fight by now.*

---

* To be sure, most of these countries were smaller and economically less impressive than, say, Britain or France during this period. But with enough effort, some of them could have lingered for a while in the war system, at least to rival some of the lesser players such as Italy or Austria-Hungary. Actually, in 1710, when they were beginning to drop out, Holland and Sweden each had armies bigger than those of Britain or Austria, and far larger than those of Prussia (Kennedy 1987, 99). The sacrifices needed to remain in the war system probably would have been proportionally no more than those the Soviet Union bore in its costly effort to keep up militarily with the United States during the Cold War, those Israel has borne in seeking to pursue its destiny in the Middle East, those North Vietnam shouldered to expand its control into South Vietnam. But the Hollandized countries have concluded that the status sim-

TABLE 2.1
Denmark, Norway, Sweden in civil and
international war since 1416

Period	Number of years with war in the period	Number of wars in the period
1416–1515	37	9
1516–1615	75	17
1616–1715	75	17
1716–1815	42	9
1816–1915	5	2
1916–	6	1

Source: Unpublished materials compiled by Nils Petter
Gleditsch.

The control and diplomatic orderliness to which war became subjected in
Europe was probably an important ingredient in the remarkable, even
miraculous, economic development that the continent experienced, particularly during the nineteenth century (see fig. 1). When rulers are constantly
in desperate need of cash to fund treasury-depleting wars—which for centuries was their principal occupation—they will periodically use their authority capriciously to confiscate the wealth of their citizens. The citizenry naturally reacts by hiding its wealth and by keeping it exceedingly mobile. As a
result, economic development is severely hampered. When rulers manage to
lapse into long periods of peace, by contrast, economic development is generally facilitated.

Adam Smith once famously declared that "little else is requisite to carry a
state to the highest degree of opulence from the lowest barbarism, but peace,
easy taxes, and tolerable administration of justice." The latter two qualities
were being developed by the end of the eighteenth century in much of western Europe, and when those countries managed to slump into a century free
from continental war after the defeat of Napoleon in 1815, the requirements
were essentially complete, and Smith's pronouncement proved sound.[23]

THE RISE OF ANTIWAR ACTIVISM BEFORE WORLD WAR I

Individual voices, some of them very eloquent, have long been raised against
war. However, as a significant political cause, the notion that war is a bad
idea and ought to be abolished is not much more than a century old (even as
the idea that slavery is a bad thing is only some two hundred years old). The

---

ply isn't worth the pain and effort. The aloofness, or neutrality, of these countries from war has
sometimes been overseen by other, stronger countries. But that didn't cause their desire to
leave the war system; it simply helped facilitate it. Moreover, some of them have, in fact, armed
themselves to the earlobes to maintain their neutrality.

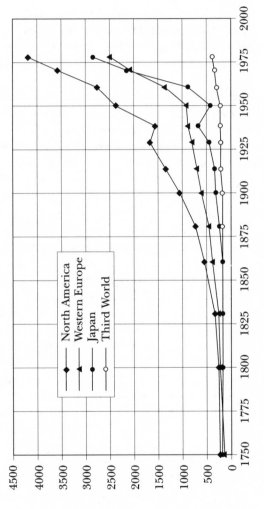

Fig. 1. Real GNP per capita (1960 U.S. dollars and prices). *Source:* Maddison 1983.

beginning of substantial antiwar agitation can be dated from 1889, when Bertha von Suttner, an Austrian noblewoman, published a vivid if stilted antiwar novel, *Die Waffen Nieder!* (*Lay Down Your Arms!*). In it she shattered standard literary precedent by describing in detail the grotesque cruelties of warfare. The novel, which was exultantly compared with *Uncle Tom's Cabin* by pacifist Leo Tolstoy, created a sensation. Published in thirty-seven editions in more than a dozen languages, it made von Suttner into perhaps the most famous woman in Europe. The antiwar movement became a political force of some potency by the end of the century. Books and pamphlets were published, international meetings were held, protests were registered, and various mechanisms and schemes to eradicate or constrain war were advocated.[24]

Constructed on arguments that had been around for centuries and sometimes related to other growing thought patterns of the era such as liberalism and the idea of progress, the antiwar movement of the late nineteenth century was a shifting, and sometimes uncomfortable, coalition. Some, like the Quakers, renounced war for moral or religious reasons. Others, like von Suttner, seem to have opposed war for reasons that were essentially aesthetic or humanistic: they found the carnage and destruction of war to be repulsive, barbaric, uncivilized, and disgusting, a perspective wryly mocked by Oscar Wilde: "As long as war is regarded as wicked, it will always have its fascination. When it is looked upon as vulgar, it will cease to be popular."[25]

Joining in the movement were a number of people who applied an economic approach. They argued that conquest, which they took to be the chief goal of war, was economically futile and counterproductive and that, as an institution of international contest, war ought now to be replaced by trade and the commercial spirit. Some of these were businessmen: Andrew Carnegie, for example, funded an Endowment for International Peace in New York, and a Swede who had become rich by discovering how to handle nitroglycerin without being blown up funded the Nobel Peace Prize to honor people who were trying to discover how the nations of the world could handle their affairs without blowing each other up. One of the most influential proponents of the economic position (and, like von Suttner, an eventual Nobel Prize winner) was an English journalist, Norman Angell, whose book *The Great Illusion* went into several editions and many printings, selling over a million copies in at least seventeen languages.[26]

Opposition to war was voiced by other activists as well. Although Socialists often shied away from the bourgeois peace societies and, indeed, often advocated revolutionary violence themselves, they tended to see international war as an evil fomented by capitalists who were using the working class as cannon fodder and to that degree added their voices to the antiwar protest. "A bayonet is a weapon with a worker at each end," as they put it.[27] Many feminists, too, accepted world peace as a desirable goal.

THE PERSISTENCE OF WAR ENTHUSIASM

By 1914, war as an institution had for the first time in history inspired a significant amount of organized disdain and opposition on moral, aesthetic, ideological, and economic grounds. However, although the peace activists sometimes caught the attention of prominent people—even the czar of Russia for a while—their protests and proposals were often frantic, muddled, and politically naive. The crusading, idealistic von Suttner was characterized by one observer as "a gentle perfume of absurdity," and the public image of her German Peace Society, as one analyst has put it, was of "a comical sewing bee composed of sentimental aunts of both sexes." Angell reports that blunt friends advised him to "avoid that stuff or you will be classed with cranks and faddists, with devotees of Higher Thought who go about in sandals and long beards, live on nuts."[28]

An important reason peace advocates were so frequently dismissed out of hand was that many people simply didn't agree that war is bad. The antiwar activists desperately needed to establish the soundness of this premise because all their proposals and gimmicks and devices to deal with war obviously sprang from it. They tried to handle their problem by proclaiming their crucial axiom loudly, repeatedly, and with shrill urgency. But most people were deaf to, even contemptuous of, their cry, and Europe remained, in Keegan's characterization, "a warrior society" or, in the words of Thomas Jefferson, an "arena of gladiators," in which "war seems to be the natural state of man."[29]

Indeed, until World War I, it was easy to find serious writers, analysts, and politicians in Europe and the United States condemning peace and hailing war. In an extensive study of the attitudes of the era, Roland Stromberg was impressed by "the mountain of tracts and manifestos in which the intellectual elite of Europe embraced the war not merely as unpleasant necessity . . . nor even as potential excitement after many dull years, but as spiritual salvation and hope of regeneration."[30]

Many of the most fervent war supporters seemed beyond logical or practical appeal because they were so intensely romantic about their subject. Others were attracted to war because they believed it to be beneficial and progressive, and many, including some who loathed war, fatalistically concluded that it was natural and inevitable.

Among the romantics was the distinguished American jurist Oliver Wendell Holmes Jr., who assured the Harvard graduating class in 1895 that a world without the "divine folly of honor" would not be endurable. At a time in which he felt he was witnessing "the collapse of creeds," the one thing Holmes found to be "true and adorable" was "the faith . . . which leads a soldier to throw away his life in obedience to a blindly accepted duty, in a cause which he little understands, in a plan of campaign of which he has no notion, under tactics of which he does not see the use." Winston Churchill, writing in

1900, observed that in civilization, "joy" is sacrificed to "luxury," whereas in the field of battle, life is "at its best and healthiest" as one "awaits the caprice of the bullet." The great French social scientist Alexis de Tocqueville concluded that "war almost always enlarges the mind of a people and raises their character," and Frederick the Great observed that "war opens the most fruitful field to all virtues, for at every moment constancy, pity, magnanimity, heroism, and mercy shine forth in it." The nineteenth-century German general Helmuth von Moltke found that war "developed the noblest virtues of man," and in England the Reverend Father H. I. D. Ryder observed in 1899 that war evokes "the best qualities of human nature, giving the spirit a predominance over the flesh." In 1866 the English essayist and art critic John Ruskin (whose military experience, speculated A. A. Milne, "must have included several drawing-room renderings of *The Charge of the Light Brigade*") declared war to be the "foundation of all the high virtues and faculties of men" and "of all great art."[31]

While war opponents were arguing that war is immoral and economically futile, war advocates were arguing that *peace* is immoral and that to preoccupy oneself with economic concerns is base and corrupt. Thus, the historian Heinrich von Treitschke in his carefully followed lectures in Germany before the turn of the century assured all listeners that "war is both justifiable and moral. . . . The ideal of perpetual peace is not only impossible but immoral as well." German general Friedrich Bernhardi was of the opinion that "all petty and personal interests force their way to the front during a long period of peace. Selfishness and intrigue run riot, and luxury obliterates idealism. Money acquires an excessive and unjustifiable power, and character does not obtain due respect." Ruskin found peace to be associated not with loving, plenty, and civilization, but rather with sensuality, selfishness, corruption, and death.[32]

For some it followed that periodic wars were necessary to cleanse the nation from the decadence of peace. Bernhardi approvingly quoted the German philosopher Hegel on this: "Wars are terrible, but necessary, for they save the State from social petrifaction and stagnation." Treitschke lamented "the corroding influence of peace" on the Dutch, who once were "a glorious people." According to Friedrich Nietzsche, "It is mere illusion and pretty sentiment to expect much (even anything at all) from mankind if it forgets how to make war," and Von Moltke declared "perpetual peace" to be "a dream and not even a beautiful one. . . . Without war, the world would wallow in materialism." Similarly, J. A. Cramb, a British professor of history, characterized universal peace as "a world sunk in bovine content." Five years before writing his treatise *Perpetual Peace*, Immanuel Kant declared war to be "sublime" and held that "a prolonged peace favors the predominance of a mere commercial spirit, and with it a debasing self-interest, cowardice, and effeminacy, and tends to degrade the character of the nation." In America, the president of the Naval War College found peace to be "more degrading" than war's "simple savagery."[33]

The notion that war could be a purifying, cleansing experience was extremely popular among European intellectuals at the turn of the century. English writer Hilaire Belloc enthusiastically declared, "How I long for the Great War! It will sweep Europe like a broom." A German lawyer, Karl von Stengel, compared war to storms that "cleanse the air and throw decayed and putrid trees to the ground." Stromberg notes that "the structure of bellicosity was the same in London (or, indeed, Dublin) to Moscow." War was seen "as restoration of community and as escape from a trashy and trivial way of life," even "as salvation." When war finally came, "the commonest images around . . . were the cleansing fire or flood."[34]

Some Social Darwinists, like the British statistician Karl Pearson, argued that "the path of progress is strewn with the wreck of nations . . . who found not the narrow way to great perfection. These dead people are, in very truth, the stepping stones on which mankind has arisen to the higher intellectual and deeper emotional life of today." In France, Ernest Renan called war "one of the conditions of progress, the cut of the whip which prevents a country from going to sleep, forcing satisfied mediocrity itself to leave its apathy," while Émile Zola found it to be "life itself. . . . We must eat and be eaten so that the world might live. It is only warlike nations which have prospered: a nation dies as soon as it disarms." In America, Henry Adams concluded that if war made men "brutal," it also made them "strong" and "called out the qualities best fitted to survive in the struggle for existence"; Admiral Stephen Luce declared that "war is one of the great agencies by which human progress is effected." Or, as Russian composer Igor Stravinsky put it simply, war is "necessary for human progress."[35]

Whether war was progressive or not, many found it to be natural. In 1895, Holmes assured his listeners that "now, at least, and perhaps as long as man dwells on the globe, his destiny is battle, and he has to take the chances of war," and Treitschke assured his that "to banish war from the world would be to mutilate human nature." Even pacifist William James agreed that bellicosity was "rooted" in "human nature," and Tolstoy, who was to become an ardent pacifist at the end of the century, concluded in 1868 that men killed each other by the millions to fulfill an "elemental zoological law."[36]

Many of these views, particularly the romantic ones, were encouraged by the widespread assumption that war in Europe would be short and cheap. Quintessential war glorifiers like Treitschke idealized war in considerable part because they believed "wars will become rarer and shorter, but at the same time far more sanguinary." In their view, long, continent-wide conflicts like the Napoleonic Wars or the Seven Years War were a thing of the past. All the midcentury wars in Europe had been brief, and war advocates deftly ignored the contemporary long wars in other parts of the world, including the

n Civil War, which one top German general dismissed as "armed
1asing each other around the country, from whom nothing can be
" They assumed that a war in Europe would be "brisk and merry," as
one German diplomat put it in 1914. Thus, although there were a few war advocates who even welcomed the prospect of a long war, much of the prewar
enthusiasm for war was based on the assumption that any future war would
be brief and bearable. As Sigmund Freud reflected in a 1915 essay, "We pictured it as a chivalrous passage of arms, which would limit itself to establishing the superiority of one side in the struggle, while as far as possible avoiding acute suffering that could contribute nothing to the decision."[37]

THE CONDITIONS IN 1914

By 1914, then, war had come under considerable control and political calculation, and some European countries had begun to seek to drop out of the
war system entirely. Nonetheless, war retained its appeal and, as Howard has
observed, "was almost universally considered an acceptable, perhaps an inevitable and for many people a desirable way of settling international differences." Or, as Schroeder puts it, "The great majority of leaders and opinion-
leaders everywhere believed . . . that war was natural and more or less
inevitable." Wrote the exasperated von Suttner in 1912, "War continues to
exist not because there is evil in the world, but because people still hold war
to be a good thing." And William James pointed out that "the plain truth is
that people *want* war."[38]

Thus war opposition was far from a majority view in 1914. And, Of course,
the essential impotence of the movement was to be demonstrated with the
cataclysmic war that began in August of that year—a war in which most peace
activists soon found themselves taking sides. (Mercifully, perhaps, von
Suttner died in June.) But peace activism was on the march in Europe by
1914, and the marchers were winning converts and felt a strong, and not entirely unjustified, sense of progress. They were about to be given an enormous boost by the very institution they so passionately opposed. World War I
may have shattered their short-term hope and clipped their sometimes giddy
optimism, but it also established their respectability, vastly multiplied their
numbers in Europe, hardened their determination, and converted almost all
of their opponents.

CHAPTER 3

WORLD WAR I AS A WATERSHED EVENT

European attitudes toward war changed profoundly at the time of World War I. There is no way to quantify this change except perhaps through a rough sort of content analysis. Before the First World War it was very easy, as documented in the previous chapter, to find serious writers, analysts, and politicians in Europe and the United States exalting war as desirable, inevitable, natural, progressive, and necessary. After the First World War, such pronouncements become extremely rare, although the excitement of the combat experience continued (and continues) to have its fascination to some.[1]

This suggests that the appeal of war, both as a desirable exercise in itself and as a sensible method for resolving international disagreements, diminished markedly on that once war-racked continent. In an area in which war had been accepted as a standard and permanent fixture, the idea suddenly gained substantial currency that war there was no longer an inevitable or necessary fact of life and that major efforts should be made to abandon it.

This change has often been noted by historians and political scientists. Arnold Toynbee points out that World War I marked the end of a "span of five thousand years during which war had been one of mankind's master institutions." In his study of wars since 1400, Evan Luard observes that "the First World War transformed traditional attitudes toward war. For the first time there was an almost universal sense that the deliberate launching of a war could now no longer be justified." Bernard Brodie points out that "a basic historical change had taken place in the attitudes of the European (and American) peoples toward war." Eric Hobsbawm concludes that "in 1914 the peoples of Europe, for however brief a moment, went lightheartedly to slaughter and to be slaughtered. After the First World War they never did so again." And K. J. Holsti observes, "When it was all over, few remained to be convinced that such a war must never happen again."[2]

Obviously, this change of attitude was not enough to prevent the cataclysm of 1939–45 or the many smaller armed conflicts that have taken place since 1918. But the existence of these wars should not be allowed to cloud an appreciation for the shift of opinion that occurred at the time of World War I. The notion that the institution of war, particularly war among developed countries (which is what was mostly meant at the time by the term *war*), was repulsive, uncivilized, immoral, and futile—a notion voiced only by minorities before 1914—was an idea whose time had come. This chapter explores and seeks to explain why and how the First World War had this impact on attitudes toward war.

THE WORLD WAR I EXPERIENCE

What was so special about World War I? There seem to be several possibilities. The first is the most obvious: the war was massively destructive. On evaluation, however, it appears that World War I was not terribly unusual in its duration, destructiveness, grimness, political pointlessness, economic consequences, or breadth. Nor was it new in that it was the first "literary" war or that it followed a remarkable period of economic progress. Further, although World War I may have been the first to raise the specter that the next such war could bring world annihilation, this belief was probably less a cause of changed attitudes toward war than a consequence of them. In the end, the war seems to have been unique in one important respect: it was the first major war in history to have been preceded by substantial, organized antiwar agitation.

Destructiveness

The Great War, as it was known for two decades, was extremely costly of course: casualties were enormous, and they were intense, suffered over what could be considered a rather short period of time. But in broader historical perspective, the destructiveness of the war does not seem to be all that unique.

To begin with, it was not the first war of that magnitude. The Taiping Rebellion, a civil war that raged through China between 1851 and 1864, probably caused a greater loss of life in absolute terms: more than 30 million were killed as compared with less than 20 million in World War I.[3] If one looks at the costs of previous wars in relative terms, the uniqueness of World War I is even less obvious. A high estimate is that of the approximately 430 million people in Europe in 1914, some 17.8 million died in the war—11.9 million military personnel and 5.9 million civilians. This estimate of the death rate suggests that about 4.1 percent of the European population perished in the war.[4] A death rate like that is calamitous, but there had been hundreds, probably thousands, of wars previously in which far higher casualty rates were suffered.

For example, the destruction of Carthage by Rome in 146 BC was essentially total. Indeed, in ancient times it was not uncommon for victors to "consecrate" city-states to the gods by killing every person and animal in them and by destroying all property.[5] History is filled with examples of such slaughter. Josephus's classic account of the Jewish War, which ended in AD 79, catalogs massacre, pestilence, human sacrifice, famine, cannibalism, and the slaughter of prisoners, resulting in the death of hundreds of thousands, perhaps millions. When Genghis Khan's hordes moved into Russia in the thirteenth century, whole towns "vanished"—they were smashed, burned down, and depopulated. In Riazan, for example, the captured men, women, and children were killed with swords or arrows, thrown into fires, or bound, cut, and disemboweled, and, of the 160,000 inhabitants of Herat in Afghanistan, they spared only 40. When Constantinople fell to the Crusaders in 1204, the victors were soon "transformed into a mob driven by hate, greed, and lust," as Donald Queller puts it; they sank into a frenzy of pillage, rape, and massacre, and reduced it to ruins. As Lawrence Keeley documents, far higher death rates have routinely been suffered in primitive warfare than those inflicted in the First World War—or in the Second, for that matter.[6]

Most appropriately, perhaps, World War I should be compared with earlier continent-wide wars fought in Europe such as the Thirty Years War of 1618–48, the Seven Years War of 1756–63, and the Napoleonic Wars that ended in 1815. In proportionate and sometimes in absolute terms, these wars were often at least as costly as World War I for individual belligerent countries. According to Frederick the Great, Prussia lost one-ninth of its population in the Seven Years War, a proportion higher than almost any suffered by any combatant in the wars of the twentieth century. Germany's population dropped by about 15 or 20 percent in the Thirty Years War, and Holsti calculates that "if measured in terms of direct and indirect casualties as a proportion of population," the Thirty Years War was Europe's most destructive armed conflict.[7] Using a high estimate for the death rate for World War I and a low one for that of the Napoleonic Wars, proportionately about three times as many people died in the later war as in the earlier one—a substantial difference, perhaps, but not clearly a revolutionary one. Using a low estimate for deaths in World War I and a high one for deaths in the Napoleonic Wars, we find that the death rates for the two wars are about equal.[8] Winners lost heavily in World War I, but some of the worst loses of the Napoleonic Wars were also suffered by a winner, Russia. And the expression "Pyrrhic victory" stems from a battle fought in 279 BC.

Not only were there many hideously destructive, even annihilative, wars before 1914, but there was a substantial belief that many of the wars had been even more horrible than they actually were. Often—in fact, *typically—*

war stories substantially exaggerated the extent of the destruction and blood-shed. For example, a legend that prevailed for centuries after the Thirty Years War held that the war had caused Germany to suffer a 75 percent de-cline in population.[9] Yet beliefs and experiences like this had never brought about a widespread desire to abandon war as an institution. Instead war con-tinued to be accepted as a normal way of doing things.

Nor was World War I special in the economic devastation it caused. Many earlier European wars had been fought to the point of total economic ex-haustion. Richard Kaeuper's analysis of the economic effects of decades of war in the late Middle Ages catalogs the destruction of property, the collapse of banks, the severing of trade and normal commerce, the depopulation of entire areas, the loss of cultivated land, the decline of production, the reduc-tion of incomes, the disruption of coinage and credit, the hoarding of gold, and the assessment (with attendant corruption) of confiscatory war taxes. The Thirty Years War set back the Germany economy by decades, and the Seven Years War brought Austria to virtual bankruptcy, whereas many primi-tive wars have essentially destroyed whole societies. By contrast, within a few years after the First World War, most of the combating nations had substan-tially recovered economically: by 1929 the German economy was fully back to prewar levels, while the French economy had surpassed prewar levels by 38 percent.[10]

World War I toppled several political regimes—in Germany, Russia, and Austria-Hungary—but it was hardly unusual in this respect. And to suggest that World War I was new in the annals of warfare in its tragic futility and political pointlessness would be absurd; by most reasonable standards, huge numbers of previous wars would rival, and often surpass, it on those dimensions.

In some respects World War I could be seen to be an *improvement* over many earlier wars. Civilian loss, in the West at least, was proportionately quite low, whereas earlier wars had often witnessed the annihilation of entire cities.[11] Moreover, logistics were vastly improved in World War I so that, un-like in olden days, soldiers did not routinely have to forage among the civil-ian population for food, sexual release, and shelter. Nor were pillage and booty seeking, a commonplace in many wars, the standard in World War I. Starvation, both of soldiers and of civilians, very often found in earlier wars, was far less of a problem in World War I. In addition, prisoners of war were generally well treated by many standards. In ancient (and in much primitive) warfare it was routine for the victors to slaughter the retreating enemy. Nor, of course, were soldiers or civilians enslaved in World War I, an accepted rou-tine in many earlier wars. And with the successful development of modern medicine and of institutions such as the Red Cross, a wounded soldier was far more likely to recover than in earlier wars, when the nonambulatory wounded were characteristically abandoned on the battlefield to die in lingering agony from exposure and blood loss. Disease was also becoming much less of a scourge than in most earlier wars.

World War I is often seen to be unusual because it was so unromantic. But if that is so, it is because people were ready to see, and to be repulsed by, the grimness of warfare. Mud, filth, leeches, and dysentery were not invented in 1914 but are standard accompaniments of warfare. As in countless wars before it, men met in swarms and attempted to annihilate one another with projectiles and by hacking and slashing with sharp or blunt instruments. Why the 1914 method should somehow be seen to be worse than earlier is not at all clear. The machine gun was an innovation, but the air of battle had been filled with showers of deadly lead since firearms had been invented. Tanks and long-range artillery (like the longbow before them) may have made some aspects of battle more "impersonal," but men generally tend to find killing each other at long range less repugnant than up close. Technological advances could have been taken to be a psychic improvement, making warfare less crude and dirty, more nearly immaculate. People found gas to be a repulsive form of warfare, but in fact gas was not a great killer—it accounted for less than one percent of the total battle deaths—and those incapacitated by it were far more likely to recover than those wounded by bullets or shrapnel.[12] Therefore it would have been entirely possible to embrace gas as a more humane form of warfare—one allowing battles to be decided with minimal loss of life.[13]

A most instructive comparison can be made with the American Civil War, which, fought in 1861–65, is often called the first modern war. There are quite a few similarities between the two wars. Both were triggered by incidents that, in historical perspective, were fairly trivial. Both initially inspired great enthusiasm. Both were expected at the outset to be brief and decisive. And both were fought substantially by ordinary men and degenerated into four years of warfare characterized by grindingly inconclusive battles, appalling bloodshed, and rising bitterness. Thus, in its own terms, the American Civil War was as brutal and horrible as World War I. Yet the experience did not bring about a rejection of war among the American people; indeed, quite soon Americans were romanticizing war just like Europeans who had not yet undergone the experience of "modern" war.[14] The notion that war should be eliminated from the course of human affairs was an idea whose time had yet to come.

World War I as a "Literary War"

The American Civil War experience also casts doubt on the popular notion that World War I was special because it was the first literary war. As Edmund Wilson points out, much the same could be said about the American Civil War. J. M. Winter suggests one difference between the two was that the writing about World War I became "vastly popular," producing such spectacular best sellers as Erich Maria Remarque's *All Quiet on the Western Front,* which was also a huge success as a film (as was King Vidor's 1925 antiwar film *The Big Parade,* which became the highest grossing silent movie ever). Such literature, Winter argues, "emphatically and repeatedly touched a chord in public taste and popular memory."[15] However, this suggests that the war was new not because it affected the writers but because it touched the postwar readers.

Economic Expansion during the Nineteenth Century

For Europeans, as figure 1 (p. 33) demonstrates, the Great War was special in that it followed a century characterized by phenomenal economic growth, something that was in part facilitated by the century of near-total peace that the Continent had just undergone. Thus Europeans were enjoying the benefits of peace even as they continued to assume war to be a normal fact of life and even as most continued to thrill at the thought of it. Accordingly, they were peculiarly set up to experience the cataclysm of World War I as a special shock.

This is a reasonable speculation, but the American experience calls it into question. As figure 1 makes clear, the United States had also undergone an enormous period of economic growth (and freedom from significant war) before its civil war. Yet the experience of that shattering conflict did not lead to widespread demand that war be abolished.

Premonitions of Apocalypse

World War I was unique in that it raised the specter that through some combination of aerial bombardment and gas or bacteriological poisoning, the next large war could lead to world annihilation—the destruction of winner and loser alike. In 1925, Winston Churchill observed that war was now "the potential destroyer of the human race.... Mankind has never been in this position before. Without having improved appreciably in virtue or enjoying wiser guidance, it has got into its own hands for the first time the tools by which it can unfailingly accomplish its own extermination." And Sigmund Freud concludes his famous 1930 book, *Civilization and Its Discontents,* by declaring, "Men have brought their powers of subduing nature to such a pitch that by using them they could now very easily exterminate one another to the last man." British prime minister Stanley Baldwin was one of many who declared, "When the next war comes ... European civilization [will be] wiped out."[16]

As these statements suggest, it was largely the impressive achievements of science that were inspiring these apocalyptic visions, and it is true, of course, that during the war, science had fabricated effective new methods for killing large numbers of people. With the development of long-range artillery and particularly the bomber, it was reasonable to anticipate that these methods of slaughter might well be visited directly upon the civilian population in the next great war. In fact, of course, they were—although not to the point of extermination.

There are at least two reasons for discounting this phenomenon as an important cause of the shift of opinion on war, however. First, as indicated earlier, wars of annihilation and wars in which civilians were slaughtered were hardly new: history is filled with examples. The fact that annihilation could now be *mutual* was new perhaps, but this distinction may be a bit delicate. In eras in which wars of annihilation were common, the fact that winner and loser were not simultaneously destroyed was more a matter of sequencing than anything else. Side A might annihilate side B, but unless A could then dominate all others, it stood a significant risk that in the next war with side C it would itself be annihilated. A war syndrome with similar stakes had not led to substantial efforts to abolish war in the past.

Second, it seems likely that this phenomenon was more a result of antiwar feeling than its cause: that is, people opposed to war *wanted* everyone to believe that the next one would be cataclysmic in the desperate hope that this belief would make it less likely to occur. This is suggested by the fact that the apocalyptic literature about the next war for the most part emerged in the 1930s, when the danger of another war was growing, not in the 1920s as a direct result of World War I. A few stories and novels depicting the next war as a worldwide cataclysm did appear shortly after World War I, but, as I. F. Clarke notes in his study of the fiction of the era, "It is noteworthy that the large-scale production of tales of the future did not begin until 1931." He concludes tellingly that "the authors all described war in order to teach peace."[17]

Existence of a Prewar Antiwar Movement

As discussed in the previous chapter, a substantial, antiwar movement had been organized for the first time in history in the decades before World War I. It was growing, but it was still very much a minority movement and largely drowned out by those who held war to be a method for resolving international disputes that was natural, inevitable, honorable, thrilling, manly, invigorating, necessary, and often progressive, glorious, and desirable. But although the antiwar people were often ridiculed, their gadfly arguments were persistent and unavoidable, and the existence of the movement probably helped Europeans and Americans to look at the institution of war in a new way when the massive conflict of 1914–18 entered their experience.

World War I served, therefore, essentially as a catalyst. It was not the first horrible war in history, but because of the efforts of the prewar antiwar movement it was the first in which people were widely capable of recognizing and being thoroughly repulsed by those horrors and in which they were substantially aware that viable alternatives existed.

THE BRITISH AND AMERICAN CONTRIBUTION

Although the idea that war ought to be abolished had received considerable notice before World War I, it appears that the ascendance of the idea was greatly aided by two key, and somewhat interlinked, phenomena relating to the victors. First, permanent peace became a central British war aim from the start of the war, and second, the promise of a war to end war became important to entice the Americans into the conflict.

Most of the belligerents—France, Russia, Germany, Austria-Hungary— were fighting for motives that were rather old-fashioned and easily understood: they were locked into mortal combat over issues of turf and continental hegemony. The British, on the other hand, were fighting to a large degree for more ephemeral reasons. Although such tangible issues as their naval arms race with Germany and strategic calculations about the military balance on the Continent were hardly irrelevant, Britain's entrance into the war was triggered when Germany brutally invaded neutral Belgium and Luxembourg. It was this circumstance, more than any other, that impelled the remarkable public outcry in Britain against Germany as the war broke out in August 1914. As David Lloyd George recalls, the war "leapt into popularity" with "the threatened invasion of Belgium," which "set the nation on fire from sea to sea."[18] Thus, Britain was fighting in part for a somewhat pacifistic principle: small countries that wish to avoid being engulfed by conflicts between larger countries, and that in fact wish to drop out of the war syndrome entirely—to be "Hollandized"—should be allowed to do so.

As early as September 25, 1914, Britain's Liberal prime minister, H. H. Asquith, was making this clear: the smaller countries "must be recognized as having exactly as good a title as their more powerful neighbors . . . to a place in the sun." He was also broadening the principle, calling for "the definite repudiation of militarism as the governing factor in the relations of states and in the future molding of the European world" and for "the substitution for force . . . of a real European partnership based on the recognition of equal rights and established and enforced by a common will." This is impressive because, although Britain had been a hotbed of antiwar agitation before 1914, Asquith had not been in those ranks. Accordingly, in his 1914 speech he appears to be somewhat startled to hear himself suddenly making noises similar to those made by the most idealistic members of the antiwar movement: "A year ago," he observed, his proposals "would have sounded like a Utopian idea." But, he argued, victory would also allow that ideal to "come within the range and before long the grasp of European statesmanship."[19]

Before the year was out, H. G. Wells, also no particular friend of the pre-war peace movement, had penned a book on the issue of war aims in which he apparently created the slogan later to be recalled with such bitterness and irony, "The War That Will End War." The immediate cause of the war, Wells observed, was the invasion of Luxembourg and Belgium, but the war had quickly become not one of "nations but of mankind," and its object should be to "exorcise a world-madness and end an age." It was, he urged, "a war for peace."[20]

Thus, for the British at least, peace early on became a war aim—not merely victorious peace but, if at all possible, perpetual, permanent, enforced peace.

The United States also played an important role in the growth of the idea of a permanent, enforced peace. In an illuminating study of this process, the Swiss political scientist William Rappard observes (with flourish) that although the "seed" of the idea may largely have been developed in Britain, it "fructified in America, where it was transplanted with assiduous care by British gardeners and whence it was later carried back to Europe in countless specimens upon the wings of President Wilson's eloquence."[21]

From the beginning the British took a considerable interest in American opinion on the war and were seeking to entice the country to enter the war on their side. Accordingly, as David Lloyd George, who became prime minister in 1916, frankly recalled later, "Peace aims were framed in such a way as to convince America, and especially the pacific and anti-Imperialist American President, that their objectives were fundamentally just."[22]

During his tenure in office, that president, Woodrow Wilson, twice ordered American troops into Mexico and rather halfheartedly even sent some to Russia during the civil war that followed the 1917 revolution there. Accordingly it would certainly not be accurate to characterize him as the purest of pacifists. Nonetheless, as the British were well aware, his inclinations were strongly in that direction: his "distaste for war," observes Russell Weigley, was "so acute that it verged on pacifism." Similarly Arno Mayer notes Wilson's "pronounced horror of war," and Alexander and Juliette George discuss his "antipathy to violence." In fact, Wilson had long been an enthusiastic supporter of such devices promoted by the antiwar movement as arbitration and free trade. He had joined the American Peace Society in 1908, had addressed the Universal Peace Union in 1912, and had appointed a man strongly hostile to war, William Jennings Bryan, as his first secretary of state. He was no tool of the antiwar movement, but much of his idealistic thinking about foreign affairs was consonant with its point of view.[23]

To play on Wilson's proclivities, the British emphasized arguments to which they were naturally inclined anyway and which, further, were sensible for maintaining the morale of their own troops. They stressed that they were "waging, not only a war for peace, but a war against war," as Asquith put it in

1917. And they exaggerated stories about atrocities committed by German soldiers against Belgian civilians, embellished the fiendishness of chemical warfare, which had been introduced into combat by the Germans in 1915 (for dramatic effect they quintupled the gas casualty figures from the first German attack), and condemned the Germans from the start for their addiction to the evil of "militarism."[24]

Gradually, Wilson and the American people came around. There were many reasons for the entry of the United States into the war, but high among them, as Arthur Link stresses, was Wilson's desire that the "United States fulfill its mission to insure a just and lasting peace of reconciliation." A desire to make his mark in world history was also not entirely absent from Wilson's motives: as one of his principal advisors, Colonel Edward M. House, wrote strokingly to him in 1918, "The sentiment is growing rapidly everywhere in favor of some organized opposition to war and I think it essential that you should guide the movement. . . . It is one of the things with which your name should be linked during the ages." Indeed, Wilson's famous desire to "make the world safe for democracy" was in large part an antiwar motivation. He and many others in Britain, France, and the United States had become convinced that, as Lloyd George put it later, "Freedom is the only warranty of Peace."[25]

The idea that war ought to be abolished in the "civilized" world, however, probably did not require Wilson to be its entrepreneur. It was already common currency by 1914 and had plenty of supporters in Britain and France— and, for that matter, in Germany and Austria. And, as noted earlier, the idea was quickly embraced and promulgated by prominent British decision makers and intellectuals as soon as the war broke out. When war erupted, the American peace groups, already a formidable presence, grew enormously in number and activity, and their ranks soon included not only prominent members of Wilson's own Democratic party but also hard-nosed leading Republicans like Theodore Roosevelt and William Howard Taft.[26] Even if someone else had been president, the idea that this ought to be the last war would in all probability have been American policy—as it was British policy.

WAS WORLD WAR I NECESSARY?

The idea that war ought to be abandoned as a way of doing business in the developed world was rapidly growing before World War I. Peace societies were proliferating, famous businessmen were joining the fray, various international peace congresses were being held, and governments were beginning to take notice and to participate. Political liberals and feminist leaders were accepting war opposition as part of their intellectual baggage, and many Socialists were making it central to their ideology and had agitated impressively and effectively against the Italo-Turkish War of 1911–12 and the

Balkan wars of 1912–13, helping to prevent escalation of those conflicts.[27] Because of such developments, peace advocates were beginning to feel a not entirely unjustified sense of optimism. As the distinguished British historian G. P. Gooch concluded in 1911, "We can now look forward with something like confidence to the time when war between civilized nations will be considered as antiquated as the duel."[28]

World War I, of course, shattered the optimism of the peace advocates even as it gave them new credibility and caused them to redouble their efforts. In retrospect, some of its members remember the prewar era with satisfaction, and one of them, Norman Angell, argues in his memoirs that if the war could have been delayed a few years, "Western Europe might have acquired a mood" that would have enabled it to "avoid the war."[29]

It is possible that the antiwar movement was in the process of gathering an unstoppable momentum similar to that of the earlier antislavery movement, and it may have been aided by the fact that in the century before 1914, Europeans gradually became, perhaps without quite noticing it, accustomed to the benefits, particularly the economic ones, of peace. The central problem, however, was that before 1914, the institution of war still retained much of the appeal and sense of inevitability it had acquired over the millennia. Despite the remarkable and unprecedented century of semipeace in Europe, war still appealed not only to wooly militarists but also to popular opinion and to romantic intellectuals as something that was sometimes desirable and ennobling, often useful and progressive, and always thrilling.

Good promoters always stand ready to use fortuitous events and circumstances to advance their product, and successful promotion is often less a matter of artful manipulation than a matter of cashing in on the tides of history or of being in the right place at the right time. One must be there when opportunity knocks, and one must be prepared to lurch into action while the sound of the knock is still reverberating. Thus, although antiwar advocates were able to show as time went by that peace is markedly superior in several important respects to the competition, this was not enough to assure success. Indeed, before 1914 the movement was still being discredited as a flaky fringe group.

For the abolition of war to become an accepted commodity, then, it was probably necessary for there to be one more vivid example of how appalling the hoary, time-honored institution really was. World War I may not have been all that much worse than many earlier wars, but it destroyed the comforting notion that wars in Europe would necessarily be long on dashing derring-do and short on bloodshed, and it reminded Europeans of how horrific wars on their continent could become. They were at last ready to begin to accept the message.

CHAPTER 4

WORLD WAR II AS A REINFORCING EVENT

Europeans brought war under a degree of control in the middle of the last millennium with the development of disciplined military and policing forces and with the consequent rise of coherent states. But they still considered it to be a natural, inevitable and, often, desirable fact of life. After the trauma of World War I, they moved to use their control of war to eliminate the institution entirely from their affairs with each other.

Since that war, countries in the developed world have participated in four wars or kinds of war: first, the cluster of wars known as World War II; second, wars relating to the Cold War; third, various wars in their colonies; and fourth, still to be defined and delimited, policing wars: assorted applications of military force after the Cold War to pacify civil conflicts and to topple regimes deemed harmful. The second and third of these are taken up in the next chapter, and the fourth is the central subject of chapters 7 and 8.

This chapter deals with the first. It surveys the aggressor states that launched World War II, and it concludes that, but for the machinations of one man—Adolf Hitler—the Second World War in Europe would likely never have come about. It also explores the implications of this conclusion, and it assesses the impact of World War II on the developed world's developing sense of war aversion.

THE QUEST FOR PEACE AFTER THE GREAT WAR

The Great War (as it was to be called for more than two decades) chiefly inspired bitterness, disillusionment, recrimination, and revulsion in Europe. For the most part, war was no longer embraced as supreme theater, redemptive turmoil, a cleansing thunderstorm, or an uplifting affirmation of manhood. It was what the first modern general, William Tecumseh Sherman, had called it a half century earlier: hell. People who often had praised war and eagerly anticipated its terrible, determining convulsions now found themselves appalled by it. Within half a decade, war opponents, once a derided minority, had become a decided majority: everyone now seemed to be a peace advocate.[1]

The peacemakers of 1918, substantially convinced now that the institution of war must be controlled or eradicated, adapted, at least in part, many of the devices peace advocates had long been promoting. A sort of world government, the League of Nations, was fabricated to speak for the world community and to apply moral and physical pressure on potential peace-breakers. Aggression—the expansion of international boundaries by military force—was ceremoniously outlawed, and in the League Covenant, signatory states solemnly undertook for the first time in history "to respect and preserve . . . the territorial integrity and existing political independence" of all League members.[2] Legal codes and bodies that might be able to deal peacefully with international disputes were also set up, and much thought went into the issue of arms control, in part because of the theory that the Great War, like lesser ones before it, had principally been caused by the greed of munitions makers.

For many, then, the real threat and the true enemy had become war itself, and the preservation of international peace became a prime national interest goal. Haunted by the 1914 experience, many concluded that the best way to prevent war was to be accommodating and unthreateningly reasonable. Grievances might be ironed out, and hostilities, many of them based on misperception or simplistic mindsets, might be lessened. There are historians who doubt this process would have been successful in 1914, because in their view Germany was looking forward to a fight and anticipating a victory that would greatly expand its area of control and firmly establish it as the dominant country in the area. But it was often touch and go in 1914, and a few wise moves could have averted war at least at that time. And perhaps, given some breathing space, the protagonists' momentum toward war might have eventually abated or been diverted. The lesson is not unreasonable, and it was one prominently derived by Western peace-preferrers from the political and military maneuvers that led to continental catastrophe in 1914.[3]

Three countries, as it happens, had leaders who were prepared, in various ways, to exploit such attitudes: Italy, Japan, and Germany.

ITALY AND JAPAN

Benito Mussolini, who came to power in Italy in 1922 and seized dictatorial, or near dictatorial, control in 1927, was one of those few souls in Europe after the Great War who still thrilled in public at the thought of war. His Fascist philosophy believed "neither in the possibility nor the utility of perpetual peace," he once wrote, and he found pacifism to be "an act of cowardice," because "war alone brings up to its highest tension all human energy and puts the stamp of nobility upon the peoples who have the courage to meet it."[4] Impelled in part by such anachronistic ravings, Mussolini cast about for a war he could wage courageously and energetically in order to win his nobility stamp, and he soon found an appealing target: Ethiopia, a weak, backward, landlocked, underpopulated, tribal/feudal country in Africa that was of little or no interest to other European colonizers.

Still, Mussolini had to struggle to win acceptance in Italy for his distant war. The army, the monarch, the conservative establishment, and even prominent members of his own Fascist party were extremely reluctant to take what they saw as "a great gamble." The venture received some support from the Roman Catholic Church, which was looking forward to converting and civilizing the Ethiopians, and it also enjoyed a certain amount of public popularity because it would avenge a humiliating defeat the Italians had suffered there in 1896 and were still smarting over.[5] It took seven months, but Italy finally managed to subdue Ethiopia. Mussolini was emboldened by this popular victory in a land whose value was apparent to no one else in Europe, and he was greatly encouraged by the unwillingness of the peace-preferring nations to do much of anything about his aggression. Accordingly, he tinkered onward, more or less following his old theories of advance. In 1938 he sent arms and troops to help the Fascist cause in the Spanish Civil War; in 1939 he annexed Albania; and on June 10, 1940, he joined Germany in war against France and Britain.

But he dragged his country kicking and screaming every step of the way. Glorious plans to attack Egypt were scuttled by the army, and the generals and admirals went along with his war declaration only after it was obvious that the Germans had defeated France (Italy quickly flew over a few planes to get in on the kill) and only after Mussolini had tricked them with assurances that there would not be any actual war to fight thereafter. "The generals," he complained disgustedly later, "didn't want to make war." And although a superior demagogue, Mussolini was unable to generate much popular enthusiasm for war. As MacGregor Knox has observed, he "struggled in vain for years to prepare the date when the Italian public would rise to its feet and demand war."[6]

Thus, even under the leadership of a charismatic and fairly crafty war enthusiast, Italy was hardly the model of a modern major aggressor. Without the coordinated machinations of their German ally and, later, master, the puffed-up adventures of Mussolini and his reluctant Italians would have been only a minor blot on the European peace that broke out in 1918.

More formidable was Japan, a distant, less-developed state that had barely participated in World War I. Many Japanese could still enthuse over war in a manner that had become largely obsolete in Europe: it was, as Alfred Vagts points out, the only country in which old-style militarism survived the Great War.[7]

By the 1920s the new Japanese army had become the center of a militant, romantic ideology that stressed nationalism and expansion. Scorning materialism—which they associated with the classes they despised as well as with the nation they found most threatening, the United States—the ideologues latched onto the mystical notion that it was Japan's historic mission to expand into East Asia, thereby securing peace in the area and preserving their hundreds of millions of fellow Asians from imperialist oppression. By 1936, people with these ideas had achieved control of the country often by assassination. War, the Japanese war ministry proclaimed, was "the father of creation and the mother of culture."[8]

However, they had no clear plan of action and achieved war mainly by bumbling into it. Their first move occurred in 1931 when portions of the Japanese army stationed in Manchuria, acting largely on their own authority, essentially took control of the area. In 1937, after several military incidents in China as well as a series of ill-considered policy lurches, Japan decided that it was "irrevocably committed to the conquest of China."[9] With the China "incident," Japan went onto a war footing, both economically and psychologically, but the costs of the vast war in China soon brought economic strain, even as the prosecution of the war itself brought deteriorating relations with the British, Americans, and Soviets (with whom Japan fought two costly border clashes in 1938 and 1939). Then, when Japan forcibly established bases in southern Indochina in the summer of 1941, the United States reacted with an economic embargo scheduled to continue until Japan backed down on its imperial ambition. Japan's oil stocks and other supplies needed for its war were rapidly dwindling, so a decision was made to seize the necessary raw materials and to establish the New Order by a coordinated attack on possessions of Holland, France, Britain, and the United States. Included was a lightning raid on December 7 on the U.S. fleet reposing so temptingly within range at Pearl Harbor.

The Japanese were willing to risk major war rather than give up on their grand schemes. When War Minister Tojo assessed the prospects, he opined that at some point in a lifetime one might find it necessary to make a dangerous jump with eyes closed—a romantic pronouncement, Robert Butow observes, that was in "the tradition of the samurai" from whom Tojo was descended, whose "willingness to take up any challenge, regardless of the odds, was legendary." In Japan, unlike in Europe, this willingness to take risks ran rather deep in the society. No one was asking the Japanese people for their opinion on these matters, but quite a few groups within the army and within the civilian population were noisily crying for immediate war, and some were threatening to assassinate any leaders who might disagree.[10]

Thus, Japan was in general a backward country in 1941—one in which major or total war was still seen to be a possible benefit or an honorable necessity, and in which imperial status was held to be crucial.[11] It took a cataclysmic war for the Japanese to learn the lessons Europeans had garnered from World War I. But the Japanese were to learn the lesson well.

HITLER AS A NECESSARY CAUSE OF WAR IN EUROPE

The war in the Pacific, then, although not inevitable, was clearly in the cards as a result of Japan's general willingness to risk all to achieve its extravagant imperial ambitions. In Europe, by contrast, it appears that hardly anyone embraced such sentiments, but one proved to be crucial. If not for Germany's leader, Adolf Hitler, the war in Europe would likely never have come about.

This conclusion is accepted, at least in passing, by quite a few prominent historians. For example, Donald Cameron Watt concludes: "What is so extraordinary in the events which led up to the outbreak of the Second World War is that Hitler's will for war was able to overcome the reluctance with which virtually everybody else approached it. Hitler willed, desired, lusted after war. . . . No one else wanted it, though Mussolini came perilously close to talking himself into it. In every country the military advisers anticipated defeat, and the economic advisers expected ruin and bankruptcy." Gerhard Weinberg: "Whether any other German leader would indeed have taken the plunge is surely doubtful, and the very warnings Hitler received from some of his generals can only have reinforced his belief in his personal role as the one man able, willing, and even eager to lead Germany and drag the world into war." F. H. Hinsley: "Historians are, rightly, nearly unanimous that . . . the causes of the Second World War were the personality and the aims of Adolf Hitler. . . . it was Hitler's aggressiveness that caused the war." Similarly, William Manchester observes that the war Hitler started was one "which he alone wanted," John Lukacs finds that the Second World War "was inconceivable and remains incomprehensible without him," and John Keegan notes that "only one European really wanted war: Adolf Hitler."[12]

These statements suggest that there was no momentum toward another world war in Europe, that historical conditions in no important way required that contest, and that the major nations of Europe were not on a collision course that was likely to lead to war. That is, had Adolf Hitler gone into art rather than into politics, had he been gassed a bit more thoroughly by the British in the trenches in 1918, had he succumbed to the deadly influenza of 1919, had he, rather than the man marching next to him, been gunned down in the Beer Hall Putsch of 1923, had he failed to survive the automobile crash he experienced in 1930, had he been denied the leadership position in Germany, or had he been removed from office at almost any time before September 1939 (and possibly even before May 1940), Europe's greatest war would most probably never have taken place.

In order to bring about another continental war, it was necessary for Germany to desire to expand into areas that would inspire military resistance from other major countries and to be willing and able to pursue war when these desires were so opposed. To be considered, therefore, are three issues: policy, tactics, and personal abilities. First, to what extent did others in Germany accept Hitler's policy of expansion into areas that would trigger a military response by other major countries? Second, to what extent did others share his willingness to use war as a tactic to carry out these visions? And third, to what extent were Hitler's personal abilities—his capacities as a leader, his organizational, political, and public relations skills, his single-minded, ruthless devotion to his goals—necessary to create the war?

The Policy of Expansion

The somewhat mystical notion that Germany needed *Lebensraum*, living space, in the non-German lands to its east is an old one. As it had developed by 1914, the concept combined an intense nationalism and an opposition to industrialization with an appeal for migrationist and annexationist colonialism in the territory to the east—a concept similar to that of America's westward expansion. *Lebensraum* imperialism survived World War I, at least among several right-wing parties. It was variously expressed in demands for the return of Germany's overseas lost colonies (an idea popular even among parties of the center and left), the return of pre-1914 German lands in Europe that had been impounded by the 1919 Versailles peace treaty, exploitation of "underused" agricultural areas within Germany itself, and, for some, expansion into areas to the east. Some on the right also connected these notions with a quasi-mystical form of geopolitics, with racism—particularly anti-Semitism and antipolanism—and with the goal of economic autarchy.[13]

Woodruff Smith argues that the contribution of the Nazi party was "to combine the major tendencies in German imperialism much more successfully than any previous political organization, mainly by fitting them into a larger ideological structure embodied in the party's program." The crucial synthesizer in all this, notes Smith, was Hitler: "Of all the major spokespersons for Nazism, the one most responsible for the strongly imperialist direction of the Nazi program as it evolved in the 1920s and 1930s was Hitler himself." Hitler apparently did not contribute substantially to the party's first programmatic statement of February 1920, which deals with the issue rather incidentally and ambiguously. But after he had obtained "dictatorial powers" within the tiny party in 1921 and by the time he finished his book, *Mein Kampf*, in 1926, Hitler had clearly embraced a *Lebensraum* position that called for expansion to the east, expressing it mostly in italics: he proclaimed "*land and soil as the goal of our foreign policy*"; he argued that "*state boundaries are made by man and changed by man*"; he noted that "*we National Socialists . . . turn our gaze toward the land in the east*"; and, in case that wasn't entirely clear, he explained that when he spoke of the "soil policy of the future . . . we can primarily have in mind only *Russia* and her vassal border states."[14]

Thus, although the general theme of eastern expansion had been around for quite a while and although it was still in the air after World War I, Hitler seems to have been important, and probably crucial, for its incorporation not only into effective German foreign policy but also into Nazi ideology. That is, it was neither obvious nor natural that it would emerge as an important theme. As Geoffrey Stoakes concludes, "In Hitler's hands—and it does seem to have been his own concoction—*Lebensraum* became the key concept in Nazi philosophy." In fact, even after Hitler took control of the party and even after he had shaped, indeed invented, Nazi ideology, there remained significant opposition to the expansionary *Lebensraum* plank of the Nazi platform even within the party itself.[15]

Even if Hitler was crucial in making *Lebensraum* a central part of Nazi ideology and policy, however, it could be argued that the notion of expansion, plain to see in *Mein Kampf,* must have generated appeal, for otherwise Hitler never would have been able to obtain office or to maintain himself there. Thus, if Hitler hadn't been around, the expansionary impulse in the German spirit would probably have found another outlet.

The problem with this argument is that Hitler's own political tactics suggest that the expansionary theme was not significantly popular: he found it tactically wise to mellow and downplay this element of his thinking as he neared and then attained office. Indeed, it appears that after *Mein Kampf,* Hitler never again in public specifically referred to Russia as a potential area of expansion. As Norman Rich points out, "especially during his first years in power," Hitler "vigorously disavowed all expansionist ambitions."[16]

In his speeches Hitler stressed issues that resonated with the public, such as resentment over the Treaty of Versailles and discontent with economic, social, and political disorder. But in virtually every foreign policy speech in the 1930s he forcefully proclaimed his abhorrence of war. As part of this, he vigorously denied any expansionist ambitions and repeatedly argued that his racism actually dictated a *non*-expansionary policy. Because he clearly wanted to "purify" the German race, he argued, expansion would pointlessly and absurdly require the assimilation of inferior races into his precious Reich. "We are," he proclaimed, "by conviction and basic tenant, not only non-imperialistic, but anti-imperialistic. . . . National Socialism regards the forcible amalgamation of one people with another alien people not only as a worthless political aim, but in the long run as a danger to the internal unity and hence the strength of a nation." In particular, he argued, an expansionary war would be utterly senseless:

> Our racial theory therefore regards every war for the subjection and domination of an alien people as a proceeding which sooner or later changes and

weakens the victor internally, and eventually brings about his defeat. . . . National Socialist Germany wants peace because of its fundamental convictions. . . . Are two million men to be killed to conquer a territory with two million inhabitants? Besides for us that would mean to sacrifice two million of the best Germans, men in the flower of their strength, the elite of the nation, in order to win a mixed population which is not to the full extent German and which does not feel itself to be German.[17]

Hitler's actions also supported this interpretation. He may have appeared to call for an invasion of Russia in *Mein Kampf,* but one of his first foreign policy moves after becoming chancellor in 1933 was to conclude a ten-year nonaggression pact with Poland, the country that lay directly on his invasion route. "The problem was not to know what Hitler had written" in *Mein Kampf,* observes P. M. H. Bell, "but what to make of it."[18] Why should one accept the ramblings of *Mein Kampf,* written a decade earlier when Hitler was in prison, over his current speeches and actions as the responsible chancellor of Germany?

Thus, in his aggressive policy of eastward expansion—the issue that was to trigger continental war in Europe—Hitler was playing on old themes. But, although these themes had support from some Germans, there was nothing remotely natural or inevitable about the process with which they came to dominate German foreign policy in the 1930s. Moreover, to get his policies adopted, Hitler had not only to mislead his own public but to override the objections of some of his most important cronies and co-workers, some of whom opposed aggressive eastward expansion and tried to divert Hitler's policy. As Hitler put it late in 1938, "Circumstances have forced me to talk almost exclusively of peace for decades."[19]

The Willingness to Use War as a Tactic

Although in Germany there may have been some enthusiasm in the abstract for Hitler's policy of expansion to the east, the notion that war should be used to carry out that policy inspired little support. In Germany, as in the West, there was a great fear of war. Some people had come to reject war entirely and in principle, whereas others opposed it because they anticipated huge costs like those suffered in World War I and/or because they believed Germany would lose.

As it happens there is quite a bit of information about German public opinion during the Nazi era. There were, of course, no public opinion polls, but countless confidential and apparently objective reports on opinion and morale were regularly filed by government, police, and justice officials, by the security service, and by Nazi party agencies. These materials can be augmented with a set of reports about German public opinion in the 1930s that were smuggled out of the country by supporters of the opposition Socialists and compiled by their leaders in exile. An analysis of this mass of material has led Ian Kershaw to conclude that the German population, like that in other areas of Europe, was "overwhelmingly frightened of the prospect of another war" and approached the prospect of "another conflagration" with "unmistakable dread." As Manchester has put it, "The German people hated war as passionately as their once and future enemies."[20]

None of this is to deny that the German public found many of Hitler's foreign policy aspirations attractive. Kershaw observes that "there were affinities between popular aspirations favoring a growth in Germany's national prestige and power, and Hitler's racial-imperialist aims. Expansion of Germany's borders, especially the incorporation of 'ethnic' German territory into the Reich, was massively popular"—but only "as long as it was attained without bloodshed."[21] It may have been much like post-1945 opinion in West Germany with regard to the portions of Germany then occupied by the Soviet Union. In a sense, the West Germans wanted to expand to the east (and eventually they did), but they were decidedly unwilling to use force to do so.

Nor was there notable enthusiasm for continental war within the military. "In 1914," observes Watt, "a belligerent military urged a reluctant civilian leadership into war, even to the extent of using deceit and misrepresentations to secure the vital orders from the Kaiser, the Austrian Emperor and the Czar. In 1938–9 the reverse was the case. It was the military leadership, whatever its nationality, which dragged its feet." The military leaders were among that near-consensus in Germany that, as Weinberg puts it, "could conceive of another world war only as a repetition of the last great conflict."[22] Hitler was not in this consensus, and his leadership was necessary to overcome this concern and to bring war to Germany.

To carry out his schemes, Hitler needed to deal both with tactical and with strategic objections from the military to his expansionary policies. At the tactical level his intervention was "decisive," Barry Posen argues, in establishing what came to be called *Blitzkrieg* as a central doctrinal innovation in the German Wehrmacht, and he was even more important in developing a strategy that would use the tactic. He agreed with most of his advisers that Germany was unlikely to be able to win a war of attrition from its current base. But unlike them, he believed that he could isolate his enemies, taking them on one by one.[23] In particular he also appears to have been utterly unique in his belief that he could intimidate his opponents into standing idly by as he carried off some dramatic conquests. Thus, Hitler invented not only a theory of expansion and conquest but also a military methodology for carrying it out.

Then, riding over internal and external opposition, he proceeded to put his theory into action. His unique daring contributed importantly to German rearmament and to his first major military success—the reoccupation, in March 1936, of the Rhineland that had been demilitarized under the terms of the Treaty of Versailles. His forces were substantially outnumbered by the French, but he had concluded that the French and British wouldn't fight over the issue. His military advisers found it "inconceivable" that "Britain and France would not resist such a violation of their foreign policy," and they "feared the worst," as Matthew Cooper has put it. Emboldened by this remarkable coup, Hitler next cast his eye covetously upon Austria and Czechoslovakia. Although the top generals liked the idea of incorporating Austria into the Reich and were not necessarily averse to destroying Czechoslovakia, they were firmly of the belief that military efforts to do so would be opposed and that this would lead to another general European war. Under Hitler's leadership and through the direct application of his will, Germany took over the portion of Czechoslovakia he had not been given by agreement with the West. Subsequently Germany invaded, in succession, Poland, Denmark, Norway, Holland, Belgium, Luxembourg, France, and finally the Soviet Union. Of these unprovoked aggressions, as Manchester notes, the attack on Norway was the only one that had not originally been Hitler's idea.[24]

The invasion of the Soviet Union proved, of course, to be Hitler's ultimate undoing, but all the others were successful, and all were accomplished at remarkably little cost. Given the experience of 1914–18, it might not be unreasonable to consider Germany's deft destruction of Dutch, Belgian, British, and French forces in 1940 to be the most spectacular military success in history. Impressed by Hitler's steadily lengthening record of unalloyed success, doubters and opponents became fewer at each step, and the objections gradually focused less on strategic judgment and more on minor matters of tactics.[25]

Hitler's Personality and Leadership Skills

Throughout, Hitler was in total and personal control. After seizing leadership of the country in 1933, he moved quickly and decisively to persuade, browbeat, dominate, outmaneuver, downgrade, and, in many instances, murder opponents or would-be opponents. By the end of the 1930s he had eliminated the naysayers, taken over the war ministry himself, and surrounded himself with sycophants. As Rich puts it, "The point cannot be stressed too strongly; Hitler was master of the Third Reich." Or, in Fest's words, "From the first party battle in the summer of 1921 to the last few days of April, 1945 . . . Hitler held a wholly unchallenged position; he would not even allow any principle, any doctrine, to hold sway, but only his own dictates." Smith points to "the dominance of Hitler over the foreign policy aspects of the Nazi program and over the making of German foreign policy under the Nazi regime." Moreover, "Hitler's long-range view of foreign policy, full of delusions and contradictions though it was, constituted the basis on which the most crucial decisions on foreign relations were made in Germany from 1933 to 1945." The decision to go to war, notes Weinberg, was made by "Hitler alone," and, concludes Geoffrey Stoakes, "despite what has been called the 'pluralism' of foreign policy conceptions inside the Nazi state, the chief author of policy remained Hitler."[26]

Although Hitler could be laughable with his cartoonish posturings and Chaplinesque moustache, to stress these would be to continue the underestimations that helped to mislead and entrap his contemporaries. As Lukacs notes, "Much that was successful in Hitler's career was due to his opponents' underestimation of his abilities." It seems clear that Hitler possessed extraordinary qualities as a leader. Rich stresses his enormous energy and stamina, an exceptional capacity to persuade, an excellent memory, strong powers of concentration, an overwhelming craving for power, a fanatical belief in his mission, a monumental self-confidence, a unique daring, a spectacular facility for lying, a mesmerizing oratorical style, and an ability to be utterly ruthless to anyone who got in his way or attempted to divert him from his intended course of action. Like Alan Bullock and Hugh Trevor-Roper, Rich considers him to be "a political genius."[27]

There was simply no one else around who had this blend of capacities. Most of the other top German leaders were toadies or sycophants, and certainly none could remotely arouse the blind adulation and worship Hitler inspired. As Hermann Göring, one of his chief henchmen, remarked, "I have no conscience. Adolf Hitler is my conscience." When another of his main associates, Rudolf Hess, flew off to Britain in an addled effort to persuade the British to give in to the Germans, the joke in Germany was that "the 1,000-year Reich has now become a hundred-year Reich. One zero is gone."[28]

As Weinberg suggests, Hitler was "the one man able, willing, and even eager to lead Germany and drag the world into war." And Hitler was well aware of this. As he told his generals in 1939, "Essentially all depends on me, on my existence, because of my political talents." He was, he boasted, "irreplaceable. Neither a military man nor a civilian could replace me."[29]

A War by the Generals?

Historian Henry Ashby Turner has suggested that it is quite possible, indeed likely, that democracy was doomed in Germany and that a military dictatorship would have emerged in the 1930s even without Hitler.[30] If we assume, in addition, that even without Hitler there to manage and manipulate, this dictatorship would have come to embrace expansionary desires, it still seems unlikely that it would have embarked on a major war. First, Germany probably would never have been ready for war as the German generals defined it. The West, rather belatedly, had begun to respond to the German arms buildup and was rapidly outfitting itself with planes and tanks that were of newer and superior design than those of the Germans. Because the military leaders were convinced in 1937 and 1938 that Germany was unable to fight a general war, they were unlikely to revise this view as time wore on and the arms race began to shift in favor the West. Second, to achieve war, a German military leader would have had to be, like Hitler, something of a political wizard. But, as Cooper points out, "None of the military leaders of those critical years from 1933 to 1938 possessed any political ability."[31]

Turner suggests a milder possibility. He sees nothing to indicate that military leaders would ever have embraced Hitlerian continental ambitions, much less go to war to carry them out. But even without Hitler, he argues, it is possible that a German military dictatorship would have been willing to initiate a limited war against Poland to restore German territory that had been given to it at the end of World War I:

> The territorial aims of a military dictatorship would . . . have been quite different from Hitler's sweeping goals for conquest. Whereas the Nazi leader scorned as hopelessly narrow the idea of restoring the Reich's boundaries of 1914, the aspirations of most German generals remained conventionally revisionist. They were resolved, above all, to recover at the earliest opportunity some of the territory that the victorious powers at Versailles had severed from the Reich and assigned to the resuscitated Polish state. . . . For the Polish Corridor and Danzig . . . a German military dictatorship would have been prepared to go to war.

He further suggests that Britain and France, in a mood to appease and in desperate fear of another continental war, would likely have acquiesced in the seizure, particularly if the territorial revisions were reasonably modest, while the Soviet Union would likely have greeted it with "benevolent neutrality, and possibly even active collaboration." The Poles would no doubt have resisted a military incursion, but, suggests Turner, the war "would probably have been a relatively brief conflict, with the larger, industrially superior country prevailing." After a few years of tension, the Continent "could conceivably have settled down," with "Germany's wounded pride assuaged and everyone else—except the Poles—reconciled."[32]

This posited war would not, of course, have been anything like either world war. It would have been only a fairly minor revisionist incursion at the expense of a secondary country. But it seems unlikely that a German military dictatorship would, or could, have led the country into even this kind of limited war.

To begin with, the two issues mentioned earlier apply as well to Turner's proposition. First, only Hitler seemed to believe that Germany was ready for war in the late 1930s; the generals all wanted to wait until the country was stronger militarily before waging any military ventures, during which time the allies would also have become stronger. And second, to pull off any kind of war, the country required some sort of effective political leadership, and none of the generals had much political ability.

Moreover, as noted earlier, the military leaders were consumed with fear of another war. Although Turner, with the benefit of hindsight, may be right that the British and French would not have fought for Poland, the German generals were not at all convinced of this. After all, the British had unexpectedly declared war when Germany invaded tiny Belgium in 1914, and the generals were fearful of a similar result at each of Hitler's expansions in eastern Europe and were vastly relieved when these did not trigger continental war.

In addition, it seems difficult to find any German military leader who genuinely wanted anything like war. It was part of their business to consider war and to plan for it, and some could perhaps see some advantage in a quick, successful war. But unlike their war-eager pre-1914 counterparts, who mainly anticipated that the next war would be brief, decisive, and even redemptive, the German generals of the late 1930s, like their counterparts in the West, almost invariably anticipated, and feared, a repetition of World War I, as noted earlier.

Finally, it is possible that a deal between Germany and the appeasers could have been worked out more or less to everyone's satisfaction. Germany did have grievances after the Great War. As Daniel Byman and Kenneth Pollack summarize them: "The German people detested the Treaty of Versailles. Most believed that Germany should rearm, regain its pre-Versailles territory in the east, and demand integration with Austria and the German populated Sudetenland." But most of these grievances could not by themselves have led to another world war because the victors—the British in particular—later came to believe that the peace terms had been unduly and unwisely harsh. Accordingly, they either assisted in removing the grievances or stood idly by as the Germans rectified the peace terms unilaterally. Thus not only was Germany allowed to default on reparations payments, to abrogate the "war guilt" treaty, to reoccupy the lands along the French border, and to rearm, but it was even permitted to take over lands that had never before been parts of the country—the republic of Austria and the German-speaking portions of Czechoslovakia. On the key remaining issue, the demand to restore German lands lost to Poland, the victors stood ready in addition to work for peaceful accommodation of those areas that contained substantial numbers of Germans. They continued to be open to this even *after* Germany had forcefully taken over the remainder of Czechoslovakia. Without that Hitler-inspired act of aggression, the appeasers would likely have been even more willing to work things out and to pressure the reluctant Poles who, though anything but gleeful about ceding any territory, were themselves open to possible deals. For example, at one point Colonel Josef Beck, Poland's foreign minister, proposed that the two countries work out a compromise on the administration of the city of Danzig, which previously had been part of Germany.[33] Given the German generals' genuine fear of war, it seems highly likely that their grievances could have been substantially appeased by peaceful deal-making.

Implications

Clearly, if, against all odds, history's greatest cataclysm came about only because one spectacularly skilled, lucky, and determined man willed it into existence, this circumstance has substantial implications. It suggests, for example, that the Second World War in Europe was not a continuation of the First World War. In many respects, World War I can be seen as a sort of "natural" war: it was in the cards and likely to emerge out of the various conflicts of the war-anticipating, even war-eager, contestants. By contrast, World War II was in no sense inevitable, and World War I had not "planted the seeds" of the later one, nor was the international "system" notably unstable or its institutions critically ill designed.[34] The war had to be willed into existence by a lucky and highly skilled entrepreneur facing gullible and uncomprehending opponents.

It also suggests that the 1920s and 1930s were not peculiarly unstable. As in any era, there were plenty of grievances and problems. But the terrible war that emerged after those decades was not a natural consequence of their character but rather the result of one man's peculiarly successful machinations. Thus, the Weimar Republic and the often-chronicled (and exaggerated) bawdiness of Germany during that period were not compellingly disgraceful and were not important causes of World War II. The democracy of Weimar was probably no less admirable and perhaps no less viable than the kind that prevailed in France after World War II. If a consolidating leader like Charles de Gaulle, rather than a fanatical aggressor like Hitler, had come along to put things back in order during Weimar, the era would have been seen merely as a colorful growing period for German democracy (rather like the Yeltsin era in Russia in the 1990s). Nor did World War II grow out of the depression of the 1930s. Economic troubles may have helped Hitler gain office in Germany, but war came only after he had apparently pulled the country out of the depression and felt economically comfortable.

Moreover, the war in Europe does not appear to have emerged out of the militarism of German society or character. That a degree of (often rather thuggish) militarism persisted in Germany after the Great War is suggested by the quasi-military movements of the 1920s, like the street fighters of the Free Corps, and also by the generally militaristic form taken in the ritual and organization of the Nazi party and its ancillary organizations like the Hitler Youth: although Hitler may have been giving speeches about peace in the 1930s, these were sometimes incongruously being delivered to regimented audiences decked out in full military uniform. However, militaristic show has a wide, nearly universal, appeal, and it does not necessarily imply warfare. After all, the putting on of uniforms and fancy braid, the parading of military gear, the waving of flags, and the staging of mass spectacles was, and is, found almost everywhere—from Boy Scout campouts to Fourth of July commemorations to Ku Klux Klan or Shriner rituals to May Day celebrations to Olympics ceremonies. The Nazi version looks ominous to us today because we know what it all came to.[35] In fact, much of what passed for militarism in Germany was pretty shallow. The vast majority of World War I veterans, as Robert Waite points out, went into quiet civilian pursuits, not into the Free Corps, and for most of its first dozen years, the Nazi party was a laughable fringe group. Although the vivid, somewhat Ramboesque novels of Ernst Jünger may have been popular, it was Erich Remarque's 1929 antiwar novel, *All Quiet on the Western Front,* that sold well over two million copies in Germany to become the top best seller in the history of German literature.[36] And, as indicated earlier, for all their oratory and ritual, for all their fulminations and parades, for all their flag-waving and solemn ceremony, Hitler and his Nazis were never able to get the German people to view war with anything other than horror and foreboding. It was the peace talk of their "General Bloodless" that the people most welcomed. Militarism was not impelling Germany toward war in the 1930s. Hitler was.

The experience further suggests that totalitarianism does not require war to function, nor does it necessarily lead to war. Many postwar thinkers, including George Orwell in his famous novel *1984,* tended to associate the two. However, but for Hitler's maniacal expansionary zeal and extreme willingness to accept risk, even a totalitarian Nazi Germany would not have gone to war—and in consequence could conceivably still be there in the center of Europe today in some form or other.

Additionally, it appears that key individuals can be vital in shaping history. The "great man" theory of history of Thomas Carlyle and others has been substantially discredited, and today, as Fest observes, we tend to "ascribe little importance to personality compared with the interests, relationships, and material conflicts within the society." However, in the case of Hitler, "an individual once again demonstrated the stupendous power of a solitary person over the historical process. . . . He made history with a highhandedness that even in his own days seemed anachronistic."[37]

It may well be, finally, that appeasement has gained an undeservedly bad reputation. The appeasers like British prime minister Neville Chamberlain almost had it right, and their strategy of accommodation might well have worked with any other German leader and averted war. The key issue, as Chamberlain put it at the time of Munich, was whether "the object of [Hitler's] policy was racial unity" or "the domination of Europe." On this he guessed wrong, even as his political opponent Winston Churchill guessed right. However, Chamberlain's efforts were not at all unreasonable, particularly given Hitler's consummate abilities as a liar, and without Hitler, Chamberlain might today be celebrated as a great visionary, and the Great War of 1914–18 might have lived up to its billing as the war to end war. That is, the deliriously optimistic and often-ridiculed sloganeers of 1914 might now be held up as seers who were right at least about the kind of war they were seeking to will into oblivion—wars among developed countries in Europe. And accordingly we might now be celebrating, or taking for granted, nearly a century of peace there.[38]

THE IMPACT OF WORLD WAR II

World War I shattered what some have called the "war-like spirit" in Europe and North America and made large majorities there into unapologetic peace mongers. World War II, it appears, reinforced that lesson there (probably unnecessarily), and it converted the less advanced Japanese in Asia. When the rubble had settled, the notion that appeal and wisdom existed in a direct war between developed countries was about as discredited as any idea can be. The lessons of the Great War had been massively enhanced by those induced by an even greater one.

Lessons about the strategy and tactics of peace were also gleaned from the experience. To opt out of a war system, a war-averse country might take one of two central paths. One is the pacifist (or Chamberlain) approach: be reasonable and unprovocative, stress accommodation and appeasement, and assume the best about one's opponent—an approach that, as suggested previously, might have worked with just about any German leader except Adolf Hitler. The other is the deterrence (or Churchill) approach: arm yourself and bargain with troublemakers from a position of military strength. The chief lesson garnered by the end of the 1930s—in particular by the experience with Hitler—was that although the pacifist approach might work with some countries, an approach stressing deterrence and even confrontation was the only way to deal with others. To that degree, war remained part of the political atmospherics even for the war averse.

CHAPTER 5

WAR AND CONFLICT DURING THE COLD WAR

"A general unwillingness for war," notes Evan Luard, can be exceedingly helpful in dampening pressures for war: crises that could be exploited to justify war are likely to be handled with "prudence, caution, and a general concern to avoid provocation."[1] The Cold War between the Western and Communist worlds that burgeoned after World War II cannot be said to have been free of crises, but when things got tense, war-averse leaders mostly worked to keep them limited—or at any rate, to prevent them from escalating into direct war between their countries.

Meanwhile, outside the Cold War, developed countries enjoyed relations that were, by historical standards, so amicable that it sounds strange, even banal, to suggest that they displayed a notable "unwillingness for war" with each other. Nonetheless it is of considerable significance that for many decades now no one in France or Germany in any walk of life has advocated a war between these two once war-eager countries. And the fact that scarcely anyone ever even bothers to comment on this phenomenon (or nonphenomenon) may be even more impressive.

There were also notable declines in other kinds of war during the Cold War period: colonial war, international war generally, disciplined conventional civil war, and ideological civil war. This chapter explores these trends and patterns.

SOVEREIGNTY AND THE ATTEMPT TO BAN AGGRESSION

The general response to World War II, none too surprisingly, was "let's not do that again." For countries to carry out this deeply compelling desire, it was necessary to determine what that conflagration had, after all, been about. A central conclusion was that it had been about territory: Hitler sought living space to the east, Mussolini domination in Africa and the Balkans, the Japanese glorious empire in East and Southeast Asia. This was not a new or unique discovery or conclusion. Wars may have been immediately motivated by ideology, religion, pique, aggressive impulse, military rivalry, nationalism, revenge, economic deprivation or exuberance, or the lust for battle, but such impelling motives and passions have generally been expressed in a quest to conquer and to possess territory for as far back as history has been recorded—and probably long before. Thus, observes John Vasquez, territory is "a general underlying cause of war," and "few interstate wars are fought without any territorial issue being involved in one way or another."[2]

Therefore, it would appear that a potential cure for most war, at least international war, would be to disallow territorial expansion by states. And after a certain amount of shuffling around, that is what the peacemakers of 1945 set out to do. Building on efforts conducted after World War I, they essentially declared international boundaries to be sacrosanct no matter how illogical or unjust some of them might seem to interested parties. And the peoples residing in the chunks of territory contained within them would be expected to establish governments that, no matter how disgusting or reprehensible, would then be dutifully admitted to a special club of "sovereign" states known as the United Nations. Efforts to change international frontiers by force or the threat of force were pejoratively labeled "aggression" and sternly declared to be unacceptable.

Amazingly, this process has, for various reasons and for the most part, worked. Although many international frontiers were in dispute, although there remained vast colonial empires in which certain countries possessed certain other countries or proto-countries, and although some of the largest states quickly became increasingly enmeshed in a profound ideological and military rivalry known as the Cold War, the prohibition against territorial aggression has been astoundingly successful. In the decades since 1945, there have been many cases in which countries split through internal armed rebellion (including anticolonial wars). However, in a reversal of the experience and patterns of all recorded history, there have been scarcely any alterations of international boundaries through force. Indeed, the only time one United Nations member tried to conquer another to incorporate it into its own territory was when Iraq "anachronistically" (to apply Michael Howard's characterization) invaded Kuwait in 1990, an act that inspired almost total condemnation by the nations of the world and one that was reversed in 1991 by military force.[3]

THE COLD WAR

With the annihilation of the aggressive, war-endorsing regimes that had started history's most destructive war, the United States and the Soviet Union rose to central international prominence. Once wary wartime allies, the two big countries—superpowers, they were quickly labeled—gradually became contesting and often hostile opponents. Their conflict generated crises and surrogate wars, but it appears that direct war between them was never close and became decreasingly likely as time passed.

Ideology and the Arsenal of Struggle

On one level, the Soviet Union was essentially content with the postwar status quo; indeed, except for the dismemberment of Germany, even a war-exhausted Hitler might have been satisfied with the empire his archenemy Josef Stalin controlled. On another level, however, it was viscerally opposed to it.

According to the ideology on which the regime had been founded in 1917, world history is a vast, continuing process of progressive revolution. In a theory propounded by Karl Marx and Friedrich Engels, updated and pragmatized by Vladimir Lenin, modified and enshrined by Stalin, and institutionalized by Nikita Khrushchev and Leonid Brezhnev, the Communist revolution in Russia was only the first step in a process of terminal world Communization. Steadily, in country after country, the oppressed working classes would violently revolt, destroying the oppressing capitalist classes and aligning their new regimes with other like-minded countries. Eventually the world would be transformed, class and national rivalries would vanish, and eternal peace and utopian bliss would inundate the earth.

This theory can seem a little hostile to those it brands oppressors, and from the start it has inspired enmity. As John Gaddis observes, "Moscow's commitment to the overthrow of capitalism throughout the world had been the chief unsettling element in its relations with the West since the Russian revolution."[4]

There has been a considerable debate about the degree to which ideology actually impelled Soviet policy.[5] Over the decades, however, prominent Soviet leaders have repeatedly made statements such as the following:

Lenin: The existence of the Soviet Republic side by side with the imperialist states for a long time is unthinkable. One or the other must triumph in the end. And before that end supervenes, a series of frightful collisions between the Soviet Republic and the bourgeois states will be inevitable.

Lenin: As soon as we are strong enough to fight the whole of capitalism, we shall at once take it by the neck.

Stalin: The goal is to consolidate the dictatorship of the proletariat in one country, using it as a base for the overthrow of imperialism in all countries.

Stalin: To eliminate the inevitability of war, it is necessary to destroy imperialism.

Khrushchev: Peaceful coexistence [means] intense economic, political, and ideological struggle between the proletariat and the aggressive forces of imperialism in the world arena.

Khrushchev: All the socialist countries and the international working-class and Communist movement recognize their duty to render the fullest moral and material assistance to the peoples fighting to free themselves from imperialist and colonial tyranny.[6]

Of course, there is some possibility that sentiments like these are simply theological boilerplate. However, after they have been uttered and recited millions of times in speeches, pronouncements, books, leaflets, brochures, tracts, training manuals, banners, pamphlets, proclamations, announcements, letterhead, billboards, handbooks, bumper stickers, and T-shirts, one might begin to suspect they could actually reflect true thought processes. At any rate, because they are explicitly and lethally threatening, responsible leaders of capitalist countries ought, at least out of simple prudence, to take them seriously.[7]

Duly alarmed by Soviet actions and the implications of its ideology, Harry Truman's United States came up with a policy to deal with the Soviet threat that might have worked against Hitler: containment. While reluctantly conceding that it would be difficult and dangerous to push the Soviets out of the territories they occupied in Eastern Europe after the war, Truman saw the policy of containment as a firm, vigilant, and patient process in which the West should do everything possible—short, preferably, of direct war—to prevent further Communist expansion. These measures variously included economic pressure and harassment, military buildup, support for movements resistant to Communist control, efforts to exploit fissures in the Communist bloc, and military confrontation where necessary in fringe areas. In the long run, it was hoped, the Soviets, frustrated in their drive for territory and expanded authority, would become less hostile and more accommodating.[8]

Of central concern to international Communists were the wisdom and efficacy of methods that might be used to confront and undermine the decadent capitalist world. The basic shape of things was clear: history was the ally, capitalists were the shifty-eyed opponents, and "struggle" was the order of the day. However, although history was moving generally in a favorable direction, it was important to struggle in a manner that did not cause one to be blown off the face of the globe while gingerly seeking to speed up the process. Various possibilities were available: major war, military probes, crisis and bluster, and subversion, seduction, and revolution.

Major War   When musing about major war—war among developed countries—Marxism-Leninism distinguished two kinds: war between the capitalist
and Communist worlds, and war among capitalist countries.

If the Soviet regime can brook comparison to Hitler's in some respects,
the Communists, however dynamic and threatening their ideology, have
never subscribed to a Hitler-style theory of direct, Armageddon-risking conquest. Lenin may have concluded that before international capitalism collapsed, a series of "frightful collisions" between the Soviet Republic and the
capitalist states was "inevitable," but the Soviets have expected that a major
war between the Communist and capitalist world would arise only from an attack on them by the enemy, citing continually the example of Western intervention in their civil war in the aftermath of World War I. By 1935 at the latest, however, official proclamations had abandoned the notion that such
wars were inevitable, concluding that the solidarity of the international working class and the burgeoning strength of the Soviet armed forces had made
them avoidable.[9]

Moreover, Lenin's methodology contains a strong sense of cautious prag-
matism: a good revolutionary moves carefully in a hostile world, striking
when the prospects for success are bright and avoiding risky undertakings. As
Nathan Leites has pointed out, three central rules for Soviet leaders were
"Avoid adventures," "Do not yield to provocation," and "Know when to
stop."[10]

Apart from his "frightful collisions" remark, Lenin had little to say about
wars between the Communist and capitalist camps. He had a great deal to
say, however, about the other kind of major war—war *among* capitalist states.
Indeed, this type of war was central to his whole theory of imperialism. He
posited that as capitalist countries greedily carved the world into colonies,
they would increasingly clash with each other over questions of turf. These
conflicts, he believed, would eventually lead to wars among them: "Imperialist wars are absolutely inevitable *as long as* private property in the means of
production exists." These wars were capitalism's ultimate "contradiction,"
and he felt they could be transformed by crafty and agile revolutionists into
massive civil wars that would ultimately lead to capitalism's final collapse. In
his last major tract, published in 1952, Stalin continued to insist that although intracapitalist rivalries were currently being held in check by the
"jackboot of American imperialism," temporarily inconvenienced capitalist
states such as Germany and Japan would eventually rise again and "try to
smash the U.S.," and thus "the inevitability of wars between capitalist countries remains in force." A few years later, however, his successor, Khrushchev,
declared that Lenin's dictum about the inevitability of war had become out of
date: although "acute contradictions and antagonisms between the imperialist countries . . . still exist," they "are compelled to heed the Soviet Union and
the entire socialist camp, and fear to start a war between themselves." There-

fore, "the likelihood is that there will not be wars" between them, "although this eventuality cannot be ruled out."[11]

Over the course of time, then, Communists took varied stances on intracapitalist wars. But all believed that such wars spring from the peculiar competitive nature of avaricious capitalism, not from their own efforts.

Military Probes: The Korean War   Although Communist states were never able to see much sense in initiating, or even risking, major war with the capitalist world, they were willing at times to use military force—that is, aggression—to advance their interests. Thus, there was some toying in the early days with the idea that Red Army troops might be sent to aid revolutions in neighboring countries.[12] And in the prelude to World War II, Stalin's Soviet Union invaded several small neighboring countries, expanding its borders. Then, after the war, it incorporated into its empire several Eastern European states it had overrun in the course of the war, and it also tried unsuccessfully to cling to the portions of northern Iran it had occupied during the war.

Most importantly, in 1950 the Soviets and the new Communist regime in China approved an invasion of South Korea by Communist North Korea, a distant war of expansion by a faithful ally that was expected to be quick, risk free, and cheap. In the view of Khrushchev, Stalin had no choice: "No real Communist would have tried to dissuade Kim Il-sung from his compelling desire to liberate South Korea from [political leader] Syngman Rhee and from reactionary American influence. To have done so would have contradicted the Communist view of the world." Stalin may have been a "real Communist" in those terms, but he also took precautionary steps to limit the war by withdrawing most Soviet military advisers and Soviet equipment from North Korea.[13]

For the most part, leaders in the West also viewed Stalin's actions as those of a "real Communist," and they saw them as confirming their worst fears of what that meant. As he sent troops to turn back the invasion, Truman declared that "the attack upon Korea makes it plain beyond all doubt that Communism has passed beyond the use of subversion to conquer independent nations and will now use armed invasion and war."[14] In 1953, after a costly war, an armistice was worked out with few changes in the territorial boundary between North and South Korea.

The Korean War, possibly the most important event since World War II, capped the Cold War. It demonstrated to the West that the danger of direct over-the-border military aggression by the Communists was very real, and thus the military component of containment was vastly expanded. The American defense budget quadrupled—something that previously had been thought to be politically and economically infeasible—and the anti-Communist North Atlantic Treaty Organization was rapidly transformed from a paper organization (big on symbolism, small on actual military capability) into a viable, well-equipped, centrally led multinational armed force. At the same time the United States expanded its commitment to anti-Communist ventures throughout the globe. Popular concern about Soviet intentions is vividly suggested by the public opinion trend illustrated in figure 2. In 1946, 58 percent of the American public said it believed the Soviets were out to become "the ruling power of the world"; by November 1950 this percentage had risen to 81.

No one intended Korea to escalate as far as it did, and East and West decided thereafter to avoid limited conventional conflicts. To that degree, the Korean War may well have been an important stabilizing event that vividly constrained the methods each side could use in pursuing its policy: there were no Koreas after Korea.

The Chinese Communists, who entered the Korean War in late 1950, also underwent the Korea experience. Despite quite a bit of verbal bluster, they too became distinctly reluctant to risk direct military action with the major capitalist states, although they used force to take over contiguous Tibet and successfully launched one bit of military action—a lightning advance and orderly retreat in contested border regions of India in 1962.

Crisis, Bluster, and the Control of War: Berlin and Cuba   Somewhat less dangerous for the Communists were efforts to manipulate the various antagonisms or "contradictions" among capitalist states that Leninist theory had long held to be natural and inevitable conditions of the capitalist state of being. Stalin had been familiar with this tactic, and Khrushchev claimed in 1960 that it was related to Soviet victory in World War II: "We smashed the aggressors, and in so doing we made use also of the contradictions between the imperialist states." Moreover, when Khrushchev met various Western leaders, he discovered that they didn't present a united front. Instead, they spoke to him in many tongues (some of them forked), and from time to time they even contradicted each other—proof that Lenin had been right all along. Khrushchev intended to exploit "intra-imperialist contradictions," as he called them, pitting the Western countries against each other.[15] To accomplish this, he blustered and sometimes built tensions to crisis levels through threats and displays of force, directing a large percentage of his strutting and fretting toward the divided city of Berlin and, more generally, toward the threatening development of West German rearmament.

Crisis achieved its zenith in 1962 when Khrushchev sought to implant short-range missiles and bombers in Communist Cuba. The United States discovered the missiles while they were still being assembled, instituted a naval blockade of the island, went on military alert, and poised itself to take out the missiles with air strikes or an invasion. Eventually, Khrushchev backed away and had the offending missiles removed in exchange for a conditional pledge from the Americans that they would not invade Cuba as well

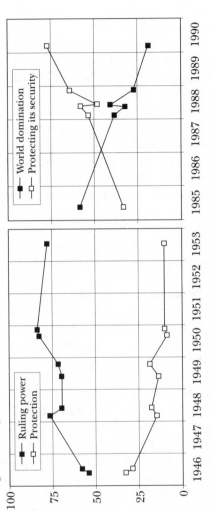

As you hear and read about Russia these days, do you believe Russia is trying to build herself up to be *the* ruling power of the world, or do you think Russia is just building up protection against being attacked in another war?

Do you believe the Soviet Union is mainly interested in world domination or mainly interested in protecting its own national security?

Fig. 2. Public opinion on the Cold War. *Source:* Roper Public Opinion Research Center.

as some informal assurances that American missiles in Italy and Turkey would be removed.[16]

At the time, war seemed uncomfortably close to participants and nonparticipants alike when they attempted to peer into the uncertain future—as it had also during the less directly confrontational crises over Berlin. From the start, however, Khrushchev saw the potential for a major war and had no intention of working his way closer to that calamity. As he responded in a speech a year later to the claim that he was afraid of war: "I should like to see the kind of bloody fool who is genuinely not afraid of war." Or in an earthy comment to some naval officers shortly after the crisis: "I'm not a czarist officer who has to kill himself if I fart at a masked ball. It's better to back down than to go to war." For their part, the Americans were also intensely concerned about escalation, though perhaps less colorfully so. President John Kennedy had been greatly impressed by Barbara Tuchman's book *The Guns of August* and concluded that in 1914 the Europeans "somehow seemed to tumble into war . . . through stupidity, individual idiosyncrasies, misunderstandings, and personal complexes of inferiority and grandeur." He had no intention of becoming a central character in a comparable book about his time, *The Missiles of October*.[17]

Although there were some dicey moments, particularly during the first day or so of the crisis, although there were hotheads on both sides, and although it was certainly possible to imagine an escalation sequence that could lead to war, the United States had many lower rungs to climb first—tightening the blockade, bombing the sites, invading Cuba, and fighting limited battles at sea—before getting there. A minimal escalatory step, an air strike against missile sites in Cuba, was scheduled, but one of the American decision makers, George Ball, says he "doubted if that schedule would be kept, in view of the President's manifest desire to avoid any irrevocable act." Moreover, the president was apparently willing to consider formally removing U.S. missiles from Turkey if that is what it would take to get the Soviet missiles out of Cuba without further escalation. Defense Secretary Robert McNamara recalled Kennedy saying, "I am not going to war over worthless missiles in Turkey. I don't want to go to war anyhow, but I am certainly not going to war over worthless missiles in Turkey." Transcripts of some of the climactic meetings at the White House tend to corroborate this view, as does the remarkable disclosure by Secretary of State Dean Rusk twenty-five years after the event that Kennedy had actually established mechanisms for arranging the missile trade should it come to that.[18] For their part, the Soviets never even went on a demonstration alert.

Some of the Americans who participated in the 1962 decisions were inclined to estimate in retrospect that the probability of an escalation to a nuclear exchange was something like one in fifty—still far too high, they would argue, and few would disagree. But even this figure may well be exaggerated.

As two analysts who have worked with the transcripts of the American meetings have observed, even if the Soviets had held out for a deal that was substantially embarrassing to the United States, the odds that the Americans would have gone to war "were next to zero."[19] It's very difficult, as Luard suggests, to have a war when no one has the slightest desire to get into one.

Most analysts have trouble seeing how a major war could come about unless an episode of crisis or at least of heightened tension and threat were to precede it. After 1962 the United States and the Soviet Union largely abandoned crisis, tension, and threat as devices for dealing directly with each other.[20] To that degree they spent decades forgetting how to get into a major war.

Subversion, Seduction, and Revolutionary War: Vietnam In complicity with the neighboring Soviet Union, the Communist Party in democratic Czechoslovakia fomented a coup in 1948, taking over the country and bringing it into the Soviet camp. In the West, there was great fear that a similar process might take place elsewhere in Europe, especially in Italy and France, where Communism seemed to have a substantial following. But its appeal gradually waned on that continent.

International Communism could cast its eye with more pleasure on the less-developed areas of the world, where dozens of new nations were emerging, most of them carved out of colonial empires that were gradually dismantled in the postwar era. Communism could be advanced in the third world, as it came to be called, through example, aid, persuasion, and perhaps, as in Czechoslovakia, a bit of judicious subversion.* Most of the new states and many of the old ones in the area had leaders and elites who, although not Communists in the classic sense, seemed susceptible because they bubbled over with ideas about economics, politics, and society that could comfortably be labeled "progressive" by Communist ideologues.[21] Thus, successful anticolonial wars brought in a Communist regime in North Vietnam in 1954, and potentially congenial regimes in Indonesia in 1949 and in Algeria in 1962. And Cuba joined up after Fidel Castro's victory there in 1959.

In the West, dealing with subversion, revolution, and revolutionary civil war in the third world was seen as an important containment challenge, and the process underwent its bloodiest development in South Vietnam. By 1965,

* The potential for this process was greatly boosted by the Soviet launch in 1957 of the first artificial satellite, *Sputnik*. Impelled in no small degree by the public relations blitz Khrushchev launched immediately afterward, many came to believe that the remarkable Soviet achievement in space said something tangible about the basic comparative worth of capitalism and Communism. Impressed, the Central Intelligence Agency in 1960 extrapolated that the Soviet Union's gross national product might be triple that of the United States by the year 2000 (Reeves 1993, 54). The impact of the space race can hardly be overstated. For the better part of a decade, the Soviets scored triumph after triumph as the United States struggled desperately to get into the game.

insurgents there, increasingly aided and supported by Communist North Vietnam, appeared to be on the verge of victory, and it seemed that the only way to rescue the situation was to send American troops. Vietnam was seen to be an important testing ground of the efficacy of such wars. As McNamara put it at the time, the conflict was "a test case of U.S. capacity to help a nation meet a Communist 'war of liberation.' " North Vietnamese leaders agreed: "South Vietnam is the model of the national liberation movement of our time. If the special warfare that the United States imperialists are testing in South Vietnam is overcome, then it can be defeated anywhere in the world."[22]

The strategy chosen to confront the Communists in Vietnam was attrition. The basic idea was to send over large numbers of American troops to "seize the initiative" and to carry the war to the enemy and in the process reach its breaking point: the enemy would become "convinced that military victory was impossible and then would not be willing to endure further punishment," in the words of the general in charge, William Westmoreland.[23]

There were at least three ways the American strategy might have been successful, all with historical precedents. Weakened, the Communists might "fade away"—"choose to reduce their efforts in the South and try to salvage their resources for another day," as McNamara put it—something like what had happened previously in Greece, the Philippines, and Malaya.[24] Another possible path to U.S. success was through a combination of military effectiveness and diplomatic maneuver: denied military victory, the Communists might have tried to cut a deal as they had done previously in Korea in 1953, in Indochina in 1954, and in Laos in 1961. A third possibility was that the Soviet Union, an important North Vietnamese ally and supplier, might become discouraged and, wary of the costs and escalatory dangers of the war, pressure its little client into a more accommodating stance, as it had in 1954.

In their calculations, American decision makers made one crucial mistake: as Rusk observed in 1971, they "underestimated the resistance and determination of the North Vietnamese." But experience suggests that this misestimation, however unfortunate, was quite reasonable. As it happened, the North Vietnamese Communists and their southern allies proved to be exceedingly bad Leninists. Instead of pursuing their venture with prudence and caution about losses, they continued to send young men by the tens of thousands to the south to be ground up by the American war machine. Indeed, their willingness to accept punishment was virtually unprecedented in the history of modern warfare. If the battle death rate as a percentage of prewar population is calculated for each of the hundreds of countries that have participated in international and colonial wars since 1816, it is apparent that Vietnam was an extreme case. Even discounting heavily for exaggerations in the "body count," the Communist side accepted battle death rates that were about twice as high as those accepted by the fanatical, often suicidal, Japanese in World War II, for example. Furthermore, the few combatant countries that did experience loss rates as high as that of the Vietnamese Communists were mainly those such as the Germans and Soviets in World War II, who were fighting to the death for their national existence, not just for expansion like the North Vietnamese. In Vietnam, it seems, the United States was up against an incredibly well-functioning organization—patient, firmly disciplined, tenaciously led, and largely free from corruption or enervating self-indulgence. Although the Communists often experienced massive military setbacks and periods of stress and exhaustion, they were always able to refit themselves, rearm, and come back for more. It may well be that, as one American general put it, "they were in fact the best enemy we have faced in our history."[25]

When the decision of 1965 to send U.S. troops to Vietnam was taken, a consensus existed in the United States about its necessity and wisdom.[26] Within a year, however, support for the war both among the elite and among the public had begun to decline. Not only were the costs of keeping South Vietnam out of Communist hands increasing, but the Cold War value of doing so was declining. A violent anti-Communist reaction was occurring in previously Communist-leaning Indonesia to the south, and in China, although still verbally belligerent, energies were turned inward as the country embarked on a bizarre ritual of self-purification known as the Great Proletarian Cultural Revolution.[27]

After a Communist offensive in 1968, which seemed to demonstrate that the end of the war was likely to be a long way off, the U.S. administration under Lyndon Johnson essentially decided to cease the American escalation and to begin to turn the war over to the South Vietnamese.[28] In 1973 the United States agreed to withdraw its already substantially reduced direct military participation in the war and to allow Communist troops to remain poised for action in the south, and the North Vietnamese agreed to give the Americans their prisoners back. After a long, costly struggle, the American will broke, and so, although it did not come out the way American strategists had planned, the war did represent a triumph for the strategy of attrition.

After the substantially abandoned and ill-led South Vietnamese forces collapsed to the Communists in 1975, the United States spent a few years in a sort of containment funk. For the most part it stood idly by while the Soviet Union, in what seems in retrospect to have been a fit of absentmindedness, opportunistically collected an overseas empire of several unimportant countries, all of which reacted by almost instantly becoming economic and political basket cases and by turning expectantly to the Soviet Union for maternal warmth and sustenance. These included Vietnam, Cambodia, and Laos in Southeast Asia, Angola, Mozambique, and Ethiopia in Africa, South Yemen in the Middle East, and Grenada and Nicaragua in Latin America. The "correlation of forces," the Soviets came happily to believe, had magically and decisively shifted in their direction.[29]

In 1978, Afghanistan moved into the Soviet embrace. A military coup brought in a Marxist government, and the Soviet regime delightedly welcomed it with aid and seven thousand advisers. A rebellion soon developed, however, and grew stronger as local Communist leaders instituted unpopular reforms and fought among themselves. Fearing a rebel victory that would set up an intensely hostile regime in this large, neighboring state, the Soviets invaded Afghanistan in December 1979, murdered the ruling Communist leader, placed a right-thinker of their own choosing in charge, and took over the war themselves. They soon found themselves bogged down in a long, enervating war like the one Americans had suffered through in Vietnam. The rebels obtained sanctuary in neighboring Pakistan, and they were supplied aid, including increasingly sophisticated weapons, by the United States and other countries.

At about the same time, the Vietnamese Communists invaded neighboring Cambodia after a number of border clashes and toppled the even more brutal Communist government there. With substantial financial aid from the Soviets, they continued their occupation, despite lingering guerrilla opposition—"Vietnam's Vietnam" some called it—and despite a punitive attack across their northern border by the Chinese Communists, who were angered at what they took to be Vietnamese imperialism.

The Demise of the Cold War

By the early 1980s, some Soviets were beginning to tally up what all this revolutionary progress was doing for—or to—number one. Ideologically, some saw it all as quite a lark: "The feat accomplished in Nicaragua," enthused a Soviet spokesman, "reflected the intensification of revolutionary processes on the Latin American continent" and "doubtless will be an inspirational stimulus in the struggle . . . against imperialism and its henchmen." Others saw a downside. Not only did the apparent Soviet advances in the late 1970s alarm the West in ways that were sometimes costly and unpleasant, but the economic bill to the Soviet Union for maintaining its growing collection of dependencies around the world was rising dramatically.[30]

In March 1985, when the reins of the Soviet Union were given over to Mikhail Gorbachev, he found plenty to be concerned about. Not only were the costs of the Soviet Empire rising, but there were major domestic problems like slackening economic growth rates, persistent agricultural inadequacies, industrial stagnation, energy shortages, severe technological deficiencies, declining life expectancy, rising infant mortality rates, and rampant alcoholism.[31] Moreover, these distressing phenomena were presided over, and in many important respects caused by, an entrenched elite of bureaucrats and party hacks who compensated for any administrative and intellectual failings with a truly virtuosic flair for bureaucratic infighting that allowed them to hang on to their privileges. In many important aspects, then, the system was, not to put too fine a point on it, rotten to the core.

Adding to all this was the overbearing burden of defense expenditures, which took up at least twice the percentage of gross national product as did the defense expenditures of the United States. The economic prognosis was also clouded by two unpleasant developments in world trade: declining prices for the Soviet Union's largest export, oil, and increased competition in the third world for its second largest, arms. The colonies in Eastern Europe were also stagnating and were becoming a considerable burden on the Soviet Union and on its long-suffering and often-resentful citizenry.[32]

Thus over the years the arsenal for furthering Communist internationalism was rendered ineffective or proved to be inadequate: major war never made any sense; Korea undercut the perceived viability, if any, of direct military probes; crisis and bluster mostly went out with Khrushchev; revolution and subversion in the capitalist world soon lost whatever potential they ever had; revolution in the third world proved costly and inconclusive; and progress by example and seduction became, by the 1980s, something of a joke.

Gorbachev responded by leading the Soviet Union toward abandoning its revolutionary commitment to worldwide revolution, that is, giving up on just about everything Lenin preached for, Stalin murdered for, Khrushchev finagled for, and Brezhnev spent for. In this Gorbachev followed the path, essentially, of such other former ideological hard-liners as Yugoslavia and China. As early as 1948, an important schism in the Soviet Empire developed when Stalin booted Yugoslavia out of the fraternity, and Yugoslavia turned from an ardent and even aggressive advocacy of international Communism to a circumspect, pragmatic nationalism. Even though the country was still a Communist dictatorship and was to remain one for decades, the West responded almost immediately by supplying aid, and it was soon declaring that Yugoslavia was "of direct importance to the defense of the North Atlantic area" and even to the security of the United States. For a while it was close to becoming an informal participant in NATO. Similarly, in the 1970s, after years of government-induced internal chaos and increasing enmity with its former ally, the USSR, China abandoned its commitment to worldwide anticapitalist revolution and revolutionary war. As with Yugoslavia before it, China was quickly embraced by the capitalist world. As early as 1980 there were official discussions about the possible transfer of American defense technology to China and about "limited strategic cooperation on matters of common concern." All this even though the Communist Party remained (and remains) fully in control in China, even though democracy has never been allowed to flower there, and (although later considerably reformed) even though the domestic economy remained strongly controlled from the center.[33]

Now Gorbachev's Soviet Union began to act like an old-fashioned, self-interested participant in the world community rather than like a revolutionary, system-shattering one as it abandoned its threateningly expansionary ideology and its devotion to impelling ideas about class struggle. In 1985 Gorbachev announced that his country required "not only a reliable peace, but also a quiet, normal international situation." By 1988, the Soviets were admitting the "inadequacy of the thesis that peaceful coexistence is a form of class struggle," and the Kremlin's chief ideologist explicitly rejected the notion that a world struggle was going on between capitalism and Communism. Then, in a major speech in December 1988, Gorbachev specifically called for "de-ideologizing relations among states" and proclaimed that "today we face a different world, from which we must seek a different road to the future." Most impressively, Gorbachev matched deeds to words particularly by withdrawing Soviet troops from Afghanistan.[34]

With that change, the whole premise upon which containment policy rested was shattered, and the Cold War came to an end. It even began to be possible that the United States and the USSR could again become allies as they had been during World War II. In 1988, in his last presidential press conference, Ronald Reagan was specifically asked about this, and, stressing the ideological nature of the contest, he responded essentially in the affirmative: "If it can be definitely established that they no longer are following the expansionary policy that was instituted in the Communist revolution, that their goal must be a one-world Communist state . . . [then] they might want to join the family of nations and join them with the idea of bringing about or establishing peace." In the spring of 1989, his successor, George Bush, was repeatedly urging that Western grand strategy should change, moving "beyond containment" to "integrate the Soviet Union into the community of nations."[35]

Thus, judging from the rhetoric and actions of important observers and key international actors like these two presidents, the Cold War ended in the spring of 1989.[36] This timing strongly suggests that the Cold War was principally an ideological conflict in which the West saw the Soviet Union as committed to a threateningly expansionary doctrine. Once this menace seemed to vanish with the policies of Gorbachev, Western leaders and observers began to indicate that the conflict was over. Thus the Cold War was not about the military, nuclear, or economic balance between the East and the West, nor was it about Communism as a form of government, the need to move the world toward democracy and/or capitalism, or, to a degree, Soviet domination of Eastern Europe.* The Cold War was not about these issues because it came to an end before any of them was really resolved.

---

* Essentially, what was expected was that the Soviet Union would retain overall control over Eastern Europe but would work, over the years, in a businesslike manner to negotiate relative

The process can be neatly summarized with some public opinion data. Figure 2 (p. 73) displays the results from a pair of questions that crudely but clearly pose the central Cold War question: Was the Soviet Union, after all, actually out to take over the world or was it mainly just interested in its own security? In the early years of the Cold War, and particularly during the Korean War, as noted earlier, the public strongly opted for the former interpretation. By the end of 1988, however, the public had reversed itself.

THE DECLINE OF WAR DURING THE COLD WAR

Direct war between the central Cold War contestants was never really in the cards, despite occasional crises and despite the depth of the ideological conflict. Overall, in fact, several kinds of war were in decline during the period.

The most notable and striking statistic in the history of warfare is zero: the number of wars conducted between developed states since the end of World War II. This is a massive shattering of historical precedent for these once-warlike countries; indeed, they have now been at peace with each other for the longest stretch of time in their history. "Given the scale and frequency of war during the preceding centuries in Europe," notes Luard, "this is a change of spectacular proportions: perhaps the single most striking discontinuity that the history of warfare has anywhere provided."[37]

This long era of freedom from major war was not a common anticipation in the aftermath of World War II, when many felt a profound sense of despair. Not only had the human race invented new and even more effective methods for devastating itself, but it also seemed utterly incapable of controlling its own destiny. As the prominent historian Arnold Toynbee concluded in 1950, "In our recent Western history war has been following war in an ascending order of intensity; and today it is already apparent that the War of 1939–45 was not the climax of this crescendo movement." Political scientist Hans J. Morgenthau was not atypical when he glumly proclaimed in 1979 that "the world is moving ineluctably towards a third world war—a strategic nuclear war. I do not believe that anything can be done to prevent it. The international system is simply too unstable to survive for long." Moreover, the Cold War often seemed intractable, and the contestants deeply committed to irreconcilable and divergent views of the world. Coping with Soviet strength, observed Secretary of State Henry Kissinger in 1976, is a condition that "will perhaps never be conclusively 'solved.' It will have to be faced by every Administration for the foreseeable future." Zbigniew Brzezinski, a major policy maker of one of those later administrations, declared in 1986 that "the Amer-

---

autonomy for individual states and to develop an accommodation on the division of Germany. Settlement in Eastern Europe was not crucial to ending the Cold War but more nearly the first really important item on the post–Cold War agenda, one that, as it happens, was resolved with astonishing and unexpected speed.

ican–Soviet conflict is not some temporary aberration but a historical rivalry that will long endure."[38]

It is the contention of this book that the long peace among developed states was caused primarily by changing attitudes toward war. Other explanations have been advanced for the phenomenon, however, particularly the seemingly overwhelming and mind-concentrating threat posed by nuclear weapons. These alternative explanations are assessed in chapter 9.

Although the Soviet Union and the United States generally kept their disagreements, however visceral, under a degree of control, and although they became, if anything, increasingly wary of direct conflict as the Cold War progressed, a large number of wars, some of them quite costly in lives and treasure, emerged out of, or were notably impelled by, their Cold War contest. These included the Korean War as well as civil and revolutionary wars waged by dedicated, internationally supported Marxist groups in Russia, Spain, Finland, and Hungary before World War II and in Greece, the Philippines, Vietnam, Nicaragua, Thailand, Peru, El Salvador, Guatemala, Angola, Mozambique, and many other places after it. There was also a set of "rollback" wars in the 1980s in which anti-Communist insurgents, often backed by the United States, opposed established Marxist regimes in Nicaragua, Afghanistan, Ethiopia, and Angola.

In Luard's view, the main dynamic of warfare in the twentieth century sprang from ideological conflict. With the demise of the Cold War and of Communism as a dynamic, disruptive force, this form of warfare has substantially slid into notable disuse. In some cases, former leftist rebels, like those in Nicaragua and El Salvador, decided to eschew violence and to seek to advance their cause through peaceful democratic means. Others, such as those in Colombia, continued their activities after the Cold War, but they substantially abandoned their impelling ideology, and their efforts became more nearly criminal enterprises, a central subject of the next chapter.[39]

Moreover, as Communism died, so did many romantic myths about revolution. Over the last two centuries, many pundits, philosophers, and political activists have waxed enthusiastic about the alleged purifying effects of violent revolution, and Communism has for decades specifically preached that successful revolutions and wars of liberation would be followed by social, political, and economic bliss. Through the 1970s at least, even many non-Communists were still working up enthusiasm for violent, undemocratic revolution.* But in each of the countries that edged or toppled into the Communist camp

---

* For example, in her multiple-award-winning 1972 book about Vietnam, American journalist Frances Fitzgerald, in consonance with many people around the globe, fairly glowed with anticipation at what successful revolutionaries could bring to Southeast Asia. "When 'individualism' and its attendant corruption gives way to the revolutionary community," she breathlessly anticipated, "the narrow flame of revolution" will "cleanse the lake of Vietnamese society from the corruption and disorder of the American war" (589–90).

between 1975 and 1979, successful revolutionaries variously led their societies into civil war, economic collapse, and conditions of severe social injustice. Indeed, the disasters that followed the successful revolutions in Vietnam and elsewhere principally cleansed the world of the notion that revolution can be cleansing: "The search for utopia brought hell," in the words of historian Paul Johnson.[40] In result, a political construct that has inspired cauldrons of ink and acres of blood over the last two centuries was unceremoniously abandoned.

Not only did developed countries, including the developed Cold War contestants, manage to stay out of war with each other during that era, but there have been remarkably few international wars of any sort since World War II, and scarcely any in the last decade and a half of the Cold War. The only truly notable exception between 1975 and the end of the Cold War in 1989 (and it is an important one) was the bloody war between Iran and Iraq that lasted from 1980 to 1988. In addition, aside from armed interventions in civil wars in neighboring countries by Israel, Syria, and the Soviet Union, there were border skirmishes and conflicts in the 1970s between China and Vietnam and between Ethiopia and Somalia; regime-changing invasions by Tanzania of Uganda in 1978–79 and by the United States of tiny Grenada in 1983; and a brief armed dispute between Britain and Argentina in 1982 over some remote and nearly barren islands in the South Atlantic. Moreover, it is probably significant that although armed contests between the Israeli government and Palestinian rebels remained plentiful throughout the period, no Arab or Muslim country was willing after 1973 to escalate the contest to international war by sending its troops to participate directly.

As international war declined during the Cold War era, so did an important form of civil war—conventional armed conflicts waged by disciplined or at least semidisciplined armies of the sort seen in the later stages of the Vietnam War, from 1972 to 1975. Depending on one's definition, some of the civil wars in Africa, Afghanistan, and perhaps Latin America may nudge into this category, but not without strain.

Finally, there is the demise of colonial war. Throughout the last two centuries there have been a large number of wars resulting from the efforts of imperial countries to gain, and then to maintain, control over distant, or sometimes attached, colonial territories. Indeed, fully 199 of the 244 wars Luard identifies as having taken place between 1789 and 1917 were wars of colonization or decolonization. Another analysis enumerates 149 colonial and imperial wars waged between 1816 and 1992.[41]

One of the great, if often undernoted, changes during the Cold War was the final demise of the whole idea of empire—previously one of the great epoch-defining constants in human history.[42] The last of the great empires, that of the Soviet Union in Eastern Europe, was abandoned at the end of the Cold War. Colonialism's demise has meant, of course, an end to its attendant wars—although there is some lingering residue in China's control of Tibet and, most problematically, in the continuing contention over Israel's decades-long occupation, if not exactly colonization in the traditional sense, of adjoining Arab territories.

THE PERSPECTIVE AT THE END OF THE COLD WAR

By some calculations, it took exactly one hundred years to extinguish slavery as a major institution in human affairs: the first notable antislavery protests erupted in 1788, and the last substantial slave system, that of Brazil, was dismantled (at considerable economic pain) in 1888. As noted in chapter 2, the antiwar movement really began, or at any rate, took off, with the publication of Bertha von Suttner's potboiler, *Die Waffen Nieder!* in 1889. One hundred years later, in 1989, war—at least the kind of war von Suttner was primarily concerned about—had slumped if not into obsolescence then at least into considerable disuse.

Shattering centuries of bloody practice, the developed countries of Europe and elsewhere had substantially abandoned war as a method for dealing with their disagreements. Moreover, the Cold War, a serious global contest between developed countries that often seemed likely to explode into major war, was no more. With its demise and with the peaceful exit of the Soviet Union from Eastern Europe in that year, the prospects for a war among developed countries seemed to begin to sink out of sight. Of course, a very costly international war between less-developed states—Iran and Iraq—had come to an uneasy end only the year before, but even that kind of war had become remarkably unusual by that time. In many respects, then, the institution of war, like slavery before it, has shown evidence of being in notable decline in many of its forms, including and especially the ones that have traditionally been the most examined, discussed, and feared.

Nonetheless, war, or at any rate warfare, continues to be waged in quite a few places around the globe. The next chapters consider these remaining post–Cold War wars and the possibility that developed countries, in a new and remarkable era of substantial consensus, could apply military force— that is, war—to police them.

CIVIL WAR AND TERRORISM
AFTER THE COLD WAR

There may have been a decline in the appeal, and therefore in the frequency, of war—or of certain kinds of war—over the course of the last century or so. But this in no way suggests that war, or any specific kind of war, has become impossible.

Nuclear weapons still exist in large numbers, and perhaps some states one bright morning will start slinging them at each other. France and Germany, countries that used to be remarkably good at figuring out how to get into wars with one another, could one day resume their time-tested custom; they certainly don't lack for resources. China could attack Taiwan, North Korea could plunge south, Pakistan east, Syria west, Tajikistan north. Hitlers, fortunately, seem to be very rare, but a new one could always erupt in an important country somewhere to ply his (or her) diabolical magic. Moreover, the excitement of warfare and of violence continues to appeal to quite a few people: it does not appear that human nature (or the general level of testosterone) has changed notably in recent years or decades.

In addition, a new romantic revolutionary movement, perhaps one based on religion or nationalism, could capture the imagination of young people out to improve the world. That is, new destructive ideas might come back, "reworked by a new set of discontented and brilliant young visionaries who are even now being hatched by sour intellectuals in our enlightened universities," as Daniel Chirot warns.[1] In the past, economic collapse or strain has often inspired revolutionaries to attempt to use violence to remake the world. Admittedly, after the death of Communism in its various forms, economic crisis—as seen in Mexico in 1994, in East Asia in 1997, in Russia in 1998, and in Argentina in 2002—seems mainly to have been met with grim resignation and with varying efforts to repair the damage within a fundamentally capitalist perspective. That is, there seems at present to be no economic alternative that has much appeal. But that circumstance could change.

Overall, however, the immediate prospects for old-fashioned, conventional international war or for full-out ideological war do not seem to be terribly bright. Nonetheless, there is still plenty of violence in the world, and war, or at any rate warfare, continues to be waged in quite a few places each year.

These remaining wars have been almost entirely of two types. The most common form, civil war, is considered in this chapter along with terrorism, particularly international terrorism, something that seems in the eyes of many to have become a major threat, even a warlike one. The other remaining type is the policing war, in which developed countries, through various applications of military force, attempt to bring order to civil violence or to topple regimes they find dangerous or otherwise reprehensible. Policing wars are discussed in chapters 7 and 8.

Some analysts see contemporary armed civil conflict as a new, or even "postmodern," kind of war. Martin van Creveld argues that war has become "transformed" as we enter a "new era, not of peaceful competition between trading blocks, but of warfare between ethnic and religious groups" waged not "by armies but by groups whom we today call terrorists, guerrillas, bandits, and robbers." Barbara Ehrenreich, too, points to a "new kind of war," one "less disciplined and more spontaneous than the old," and one "often fought by ill-clad bands more resembling gangs than armies." In a similar vein, Mary Kaldor writes about "new wars," ones centrally about "identity politics," fought in a context of globalization by "a disparate range of different types of groups such as paramilitary units, local warlords, criminal gangs, police forces, mercenary groups and also regular armies including breakaway units of regular armies." Samuel Huntington extrapolates broadly, even heroically, from the civil wars that erupted in Yugoslavia in the 1990s, proclaiming them to be harbingers of an entirely new orientation for world politics in which whole civilizations clash, particularly in "fault line" areas such as Yugoslavia, where various civilizations happen to abut each other.[2]

But as demonstrated in chapter 2, banditry and depredations by roving militias are anything but new, and as disciplined, conventional warfare has become comparatively rare, we are increasingly left with the ravages, often savage ones, of irregulars. Virtually all of the armed conflicts that remain in the world are civil or primarily civil, as figure 3 demonstrates. And most of these, as it happens, are essentially ancient forms of criminal war in which criminals and thugs—or "entrepreneurs of violence," as Virginia Gamba and Richard Cornwell have aptly labeled them—engage in warfare in much the same way they did in medieval and early modern Europe: as mercenaries recruited or dragooned by weak (or even desperate) state governments or as warlord or brigand gangs developed within failed or weak states.[3] A few contemporary civil wars, however, variously betray elements of disciplined, if mainly unconventional, conflict, and so does much terrorism. The form and content of such organized and semiorganized violence are investigated in the next sections.

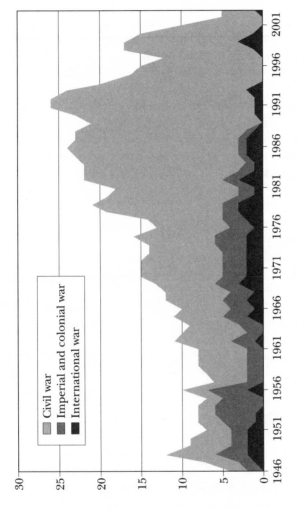

Fig. 3. Frequency of war, 1946–2003. The data are for violent armed conflicts that resulted in at least 1,000 military deaths over the duration of the dispute for international wars, an average of at least 1,000 military deaths per year for imperial and colonial wars, and at least 1,000 military and civilian (but battle-related) deaths per year for civil wars. *Source:* Gleditsch 2004.

CRIMINAL WARFARE: THE MERCENARY APPROACH

The wars in the former Yugoslavia illustrate the mercenary process best, and there are plenty of other instances elsewhere.

Croatia and Bosnia

In contrast to Huntington's view that the wars in Yugoslavia were major "fault line" wars between clashing civilizations and to Kaldor's depiction of the one in Bosnia as the "archetypal example, the paradigm of the new type of warfare," the violence that erupted there in the early 1990s derived not from a paroxysm of civilizational angst nor from a frenzy of nationalism, whether ancient or newly inspired.[4] Rather, it principally came from the actions of recently empowered and unpoliced thugs. Politicians may have started the wars, and they may have whipped up a fair amount of hatred. But the effective murderous core of the wars was composed not of hordes of ordinary citizens ripped loose from their repression or incited to violence against their neighbors. Rather, the politicians found it necessary to recruit fanatics, criminals, and hooligans for the job.[5]

It is a fact of considerable significance that the Serbian (or Yugoslav) army substantially disintegrated early in the hostilities. There may well have been hatreds, and there surely was propaganda designed to induce it, but neither was enough to inspire the kind of determined ethnic violence that was called for.[6] After years of supposedly influential media propaganda and centuries of supposedly pent-up ethnic and civilizational antagonism, ordinary Serb soldiers were finally given an opportunity to express these proclivities in government-sanctioned violence. Overwhelmingly, however, they responded to the opportunity by pointedly declining to embrace it: professing they did not know why they were fighting, they often mutinied or deserted en masse. Meanwhile, back in Serbia itself, young men mainly reacted by determined draft dodging.[7]

This phenomenon is almost too vividly illustrated by the experience of General Slavko Lisica, who tried to shame Serb conscripts in Croatia into fighting by declaring that all those who were not prepared to "defend the glory of the Serbian nation" should lay down their arms and take off their uniforms. To his astonishment, he says, "they all did, including their commanding officer." Furious, he shouted at them "to remove everything including their underpants, and with the exception of one man they all removed their military-issue underpants and marched off completely naked. I was still hoping they would change their mind, but they didn't." Later, he says, the recruits managed to commandeer a cannon and used it to shell his headquarters.[8]

Because Serbs from Serbia proper were unwilling to fight outside their own republic, Belgrade had to reshape its approach to the wars in Croatia and Bosnia in major ways. As a Serbian general put it, modification of the military plans was made necessary by "the lack of success in mobilisation and the desertion rate." Part of the solution involved arming the locals, particularly in Serb areas of Croatia and Bosnia.[9] But in general their fighting quality, especially initially, was very poor: there was a lack of discipline, ineffective command and control, and a reluctance to take casualties.

Such deficiencies, as Steven Burg and Paul Shoup observe, "led all sides to rely on irregulars and special units"—especially, as Anthony Oberschall notes, for offensive operations. In all, there were at least eighty-three of these groups operating in Croatia and Bosnia, comprising 36,000 to 66,000 members. Like many of the lords and kings of medieval Europe, the politicians recruited criminals and hooligans to man them. As part of this process, it appears that thousands of prison inmates, promised shortened sentences and enticed by the prospect that they could "take whatever booty you can," were released in Serbia for the war effort. The most dynamic (and murderous) Serbian units were notably composed, then, not of committed nationalists or ideologues, nor of locals out to get their neighbors, nor of ordinary people whipped into a frenzy by demagogues and the media, but of common criminals and thugs recruited for the task essentially as mercenaries. Similarly, the initial fighting forces of Bosnia and of Croatia were also substantially made up of small bands of criminals and violent opportunists recruited or self-recruited from street gangs. The paramilitary units generally worked independently, improvising their tactics as they went along. However, there seems to have been a fair amount of coordination in Serb areas mainly by the Serbian secret police, while the (increasingly thuggish) army enforced an overall framework of order and sometimes directly participated in the depredations as well.[10]

The appearance of the thugs in the wars was caused in part by the collapse of army morale, but their presence may also have helped to aggravate that collapse. An internal Yugoslav army memo from early in the conflict found them to be dangerous to military morale because their "primary motive was not fighting against the enemy but robbery of private property and inhuman treatment of Croatian civilians." Lisica called them "types who would kill a man of ninety for a lamb," and he reports that his men would say to him, "The paramilitaries rob, they rape, they steal. Why are we fighting and what are we fighting for?"[11]

Avenues of Entry Some of the thugs bolstered what remained of the Yugoslav army. According to Miloš Vasić, a leading Serb journalist, however, "they behaved in a wholly unsoldierly way, wearing all sorts of Serb chauvinist insignia, beards and knives, were often drunk (like many of the regular solders, too), looted, and killed or harassed civilians. Officers rarely dared discipline them."[12]

Others joined semicoherent paramilitary groups such as Vojislav Šešelj's

Chetniks (whose members seemed to be "always drunk") and Arkan's Tigers, organizations already heavily composed of criminals, adventurers, mercenary opportunists, and, in the case of the Tigers, soccer hooligans. Arkan (Željko Ražnjatović) had been the leader of Delije, the official fan club of Belgrade's Red Star soccer team, which, not unlike other soccer clubs, had become a magnet for hoodlums and unemployable young men, and the Tigers were substantially built from that membership. For their part, the Muslims were protected by paramilitary bands led by Ćelo, a convicted rapist, and by Juka, a former mob boss, racketeer, and underworld thug. And the Croats had Tuta, a former protection racketeer.[13]

Still other thugs seem to have gone off on their own, serving as warlords in the areas they came to dominate. These independent or semi-independent paramilitary and warlord units, estimates Vasić, "consisted on average of 80 per cent common criminals and 20 per cent fanatical nationalists. The latter did not usually last long (fanaticism is bad for business)." There were also many "weekend warriors," part-time predators who intermittently entered the war from Serbia and elsewhere and then mainly to rob and pillage, many becoming rich in the process. One of these was Ceko Dacevic, who is characterized by Serb officials as a "criminal, pathological thief" and "an ignorant, uneducated man who attracted stupid and violent criminals." With his band of "a few dozen unemployed people" and "riff raff" from "all across Serbia," Ceko would regularly foray into Muslim areas in Bosnia to loot.[14]

Thus, as Warren Zimmermann observes, "the dregs of society—embezzlers, thugs, even professional killers—rose from the slime to become freedom fighters and national heroes." David Rieff points out that "one of the earliest, deepest, and most pervasive effects of the fighting" was "to turn the social pyramid on its head. . . . Simple boys from the countryside and tough kids from the towns found that their guns made them the ones who could start amassing the Deutschemarks and the privileges, sexual and otherwise." There was also Rambo-like affectation: each dressed as if "he had been cast as a thug by a movie director," observes Robert Block. The degree to which these men styled themselves on characters they had seen in films such as *Rambo* and *Road Warrior* led a Sarajevan theater director ironically to call for a war crimes trial for Sylvester Stallone: "He's responsible for a lot that has gone on here!" (see table 6.1). Indeed, one Serbian paramilitary unit actually called itself the Rambos and its members went around in webbed masks and black gloves, with black ribbons fetchingly tied around their foreheads.[15]

Thus, as Susan Woodward notes, "paramilitary gangs, foreign mercenaries, and convicted criminals roamed the territory under ever less civil control." Reportage from Bosnia by Peter Maass is peppered with such phrases as "drunken hillbillies," "death and thuggery," "they don't wear normal uniforms, they don't have many teeth," "the trigger fingers belonged to drunks," "the Bosnians might be the underdogs, but most of their frontline soldiers

TABLE 6.1
The Rambo® movies: The body count

	I	II	III
Number of bad guys killed by Rambo with his shirt on	1	12	33
Number of bad guys killed by Rambo with his shirt off	0	46	45
Total number of bad guys killed by Rambo no matter how attired	1	58	78
Number of bad guys killed by accomplices of Rambo acting on their own	0	10	17
Number of good guys killed by bad guys	0	1	37
Total number of people killed	1	69	132
Number of people killed per minute	0.01	0.72	1.30
Time at which the first person is killed	29'31"	33'34"	41'9"
Number of people killed per minute from that point until the end of the film (not including the ending credits)	0.02	1.18	2.39
Sequences in which Rambo is shot at without significant result	12	24	38
Number of sequences in which good guys are tortured by bad guys	2	5	7
Number of sex scenes	0	0	0

Note: I, *First Blood* (1982; R rated; 93 minutes); II, *Rambo: First Blood, Part II* (1985; R rated; 96 minutes); III, *Rambo III* (1988; R rated; 102 minutes).

The body count includes only those who visibly fall inert after being bombed, garrotted, blasted, stabbed, or strangled; blown up by mines, artillery, grenades, or other explosives; shot by bullets, artillery, or arrows; incinerated by fires or flame throwers; blugeoned or beaten; pushed or tossed off precipices or aircraft; or had their necks snapped. In addition, there were many instances in which Rambo blows up tanks, helicopters, cars, trucks, and guard towers and other buildings that are occupied. These presumed fatalities were not included in the body count unless the people inside were clearly shown to die by, for example, bolting into the open from their erstwhile place of refuge, clutching various body parts, grimacing meaningfully, and collapsing to the ground.

Number of coders: 1. intercoder reliability: 100 percent. Rambo® is a registered trademark owned by CAROLCO.

were crooks," "a foul-smelling warlord," "only drunks and bandits ventured outside," "goons with guns," "Serb soldiers or thugs . . . the difference is hard to tell." Reporter Ed Vulliamy describes the warriors as "boozy at their best, wild and sadistic at their worst" or as "toothless goons" with "inflammable breath." Vladan Vasilejevic, an expert on organized crime, says that most of the well-documented atrocities in Bosnia were committed by men with long criminal records. And a United Nations commission notes a "strong correlation" between paramilitary activity and reports of killing of civilians, rape, torture, destruction of property, looting, detention facilities, and mass graves. In all, as one reporter put it, Yugoslavia became "a land where former football hooligans and neofascist ganglords [ran] riot with assault rifles and mortar bombs instead of boots and bottles," or, in the words of another, a place "where warlords and gangsters tried to pass themselves off as professional soldiers."[16]

The Stages of War and Ethnic Cleansing   What passed for "ethnic warfare" in Bosnia and Croatia seems then to have been something far more banal: the creation of communities of criminal violence and predation. In the end, the wars resembled the movie images of the American Wild West or of gangland Chicago, and they often had less to do with nationalism than with criminal opportunism and sadistic cruelty, very commonly enhanced with liquor. There seem to have been four stages to the process: takeover, carnival, revenge, and occupation and desertion.[17]

In the takeover phase, an often remarkably small group of well-armed thugs, recruited and encouraged by leading politicians and often operating under a general framework of order provided by the army, would emerge in an area in which the former civil order had ceased to exist or in which the police actually or effectively were in alliance with them. As the only group willing—indeed, sometimes quite eager—to use force, they would quickly take control. Members of other ethnic groups would be subject to violent intimidation at best, atrocities at worst. Because there was no coherent or unbiased police force to protect them, their best recourse was to flee, and it would not take much persuasion to get them to do so—indeed, rumors or implied threats were often sufficient.[18] Co-ethnics were intimidated into ostracizing other ethnic groups and behaving toward them with hostility, and any who might oppose the predators' behavior would be subject to even more focused violence and intimidation and would be forced out, killed, or cowed into subservience.[19]

The dynamic of the carnival phase is captured by Lord Acton's famous observation that "absolute power corrupts absolutely." The predators often exercised supreme power in their small fiefdoms and lorded it over their new subjects. Carnivals of looting and destruction would take place, as would orgies of rape, arbitrary violence and murder, and roaring drunkenness. Sadists may make up a small percentage in any population, but in these circumstances, they rose (or were drawn) to the occasion and reveled in it. In this unrestrained new world, run (in the words of a UN official) by "gunslingers, thugs, and essentially criminals," others—sometimes including local police—might opportunistically join in the violence, sometimes to settle older grudges. After all, if the property of a local Muslim is going to be looted and set afire (like the store of a local Korean during the Los Angeles riots of 1992), it may come to seem sensible—even rational—to join the thieves: no high-minded moral restraint about such behavior will do the departed owner any good. In the process, many ordinary residents might become compromised, sometimes willingly. For example, one Bosnian Serb policeman used his position, Schindler-like, to save the lives of several Muslims, but under the extraordinary conditions of the time he also probably raped two or more of them—in at least one instance after proposing marriage.[20]

The third phase was one of revenge. Some among the brutalized might wish to fight—and to seek revenge—against their persecutors. In general, they found that they were best advised not to try to improvise local resistance but rather to flee with their fellow ethnics and then to join like-minded armed bands in more hospitable parts of the country. Thus the Muslims' "elite" Seventeenth Krajina brigade was labeled "the angry army of the dispossessed," although questions have been raised about how adequately it actually fought.[21] Members of each group would then quickly find, sometimes to their helpless disgust, that their thugs at least were willing to fight to protect them from the murderous thugs on the other side. Often the choice was essentially one of being dominated by vicious drunken bigots of one's own ethnic group or by vicious drunken bigots of another ethnic group.

Finally, there was a stage of occupation and desertion. Life under such conditions could become pretty miserable because the masters argued among themselves and looked for further prey among those remaining, whatever their ethnic background. For example, the Yellow Wasps, a band of some sixty-six men who assembled in Zvornik in Bosnia to "defend the Serbian people," eventually spent most of their time looting and extorting Serbs. In war-torn Sarajevo, the criminal gangs that had helped defend the city from the Serbs in 1992 soon began plaguing the defended without regard to ethnicity. They stole automobiles; extorted money and valuables; abducted, abused, and raped civilians; looted warehouses and shops; "requisitioned" private vehicles; assaulted foreign journalists; stole from aid agencies; hijacked vehicles from the United Nations protective force; and monopolized the black market, earning fortunes in a city in which many people spent their days scavenging for water and bread.[22]

Those in the right positions quickly discovered an especially lucrative opportunity: weaponry, ammunition, fuel, and goods worth hundreds of millions of deutschmarks were traded with the enemy. The Serbs in Bosnia inherited masses of weaponry from the Yugoslav national army, and once the war settled down a bit, many went looking for buyers and found them nearby: the Croats and the Muslims were eager for weapons with which to attack the Serbs in Croatia and Bosnia (and, for a time, each other). There were opportunities in the other direction as well, and the speaker of the Bosnian Serb assembly made millions buying fuel from Croatia and then selling it to Croatia's Serb enemies in Bosnia. Croats could sometimes rent tanks from the Serbs at a going rate of DM1,000 per day. Whether they had to pay extra for insurance is not recorded. Gradually, many of the people under the thugs' arbitrary and chaotic "protection," especially the more moderate ones and young men unwilling to be impressed into military service, would manage to emigrate to a safer place. In time the size of the "protected" group would be

substantially reduced—by half or more.[23] The remnants ever more disproportionately consisted of fanatics, economic marauders, militant radicals,
common criminals, opportunistic sycophants, embittered revenge seekers,
and murderous drunks.

The Role of Ethnicity The connection of such banal behavior to nationalism, to identity politics, and to ethnic hatred, ancient or otherwise, is less
than clear, as is its bearing on the notion of clashing civilizations. The relation of the behavior to common criminality, however, is quite evident.

Ethnicity was important in all this as an ordering, organizational, sorting,
or predictive device or principle, not as a crucial motivating force. It was the
human characteristic around which the perpetrators and the politicians who
recruited and encouraged them happened to have arrayed themselves, and it
furnished them with a degree of predictability. If you were a member of the
opposite group you could be sure they would persecute you, but if you were a
member of their group, they would more or less protect you (at least initially), as long as you seemed to be reasonably loyal. That is, they may have
been thugs, but they were not *random* thugs.

However, the same sort of dynamic could hold if the thugs' organizational principle were class or ideological allegiance—or, for that matter,
handedness or loyalty to a specific soccer team. If they took control in a town
and were determined to cleanse it violently of, say, left-handers or of supporters of an opposing team, those in that group would quickly find it in
their interest to leave. Meanwhile, right-handers or fans of the thug-favored
team would, often reluctantly, come to recognize that the thugs had become
their only protection against revenge-seeking thugs of the other group. As
they hunkered down behind their "protectors" or as they sought to flee the
war zone, members of each group would probably reflect in bewilderment
from time to time that before the thugs came, they often didn't even know
the handedness or the soccer loyalties of their friends, neighbors, and
schoolmates. Under such conditions, identity, as Chaim Kaufmann notes, "is
often imposed by the opposing group, specifically by its most murderous
members."[24]

None of this is to argue, of course, that hatred played no role or that no
neighbor ever persecuted a neighbor in these conflicts. Some locals did enthusiastically join in the process, sometimes out of ethnic hatred, sometimes
to settle old scores, most often, it seems, opportunistically to pursue profit
in the chaos. In some cases, the war conditions brought out the worst in
people, and victims sometimes did know their victimizers—although this is
something that happens in most civil wars, not just ethnic ones. And, of
course, once the thugs took over, cross-ethnic relationships and friendships
were often warily broken off because the thugs were likely to punish such
sympathies.

The key dynamic of the violence, however, was not in exploding hatreds or in the rising of neighbor against neighbor, still less in the clashing of civilizations. Rather it was in the focused predation of comparatively small groups of violent thugs and criminals recruited and semicoordinated by politicians. Identity, ethnicity, nationalism, civilization, culture, and religion proved more nearly to be an excuse or pretext for the predation than an independent cause of it.

Kosovo

What happened in Kosovo at the end of the 1990s often resembles the process seen earlier in Croatia and Bosnia, except that the brutality may have been even more focused.

The ruling Serbs under the leadership of Slobodan Milošević substantially created the problem, especially after 1989, by officially discriminating against the Albanians. Then, when some Albanians resorted to anti-Serb terrorism in 1998, the Serbs foolishly moved against them with excessive violence that included massacres and the creation of masses of refugees, especially in rural areas. Although the terrorists of the Kosovo Liberation Army did not enjoy great support among the Albanians, particularly in the cities, the Serb depredations, carried out mainly by special paramilitary units under the direction of the ministry of the interior in Belgrade, greatly increased the support for the terrorists by essentially forcing Albanians to make a Bosnia-like decision: they had to choose between rule by brutish racist thugs from their own ethnic group or rule by brutish racist thugs from the other ethnic group. The KLA, which numbered no more than 150 before the massacres, quickly increased to an estimated 12,000.[25]

Kosovo is much closer to Serbia's core interests, or, at any rate, sentiments, than Bosnia or Croatia, and Serbs had been dutifully weaving fanciful myths and legends about the region for a good six hundred years. Nonetheless, following the earlier pattern found in the wars in Croatia and Bosnia, an amazingly large percentage of Serbian youth was able to contain its enthusiasm for actually fighting for dear old Kosovo. As one Serb journalist put it, "You won't find anyone prepared to send their children into the battlefield." Indeed, one Serb writer went so far as to call Kosovo "dead history," a place containing a lot of beautiful old monasteries that are, however, hardly worth spilling blood over. Others simply saw it as a "lost cause" or concluded, in the words of a Belgrade truck driver, that "now we would be fighting for Milosevic's throne. I wouldn't give one hair for Kosovo or for Milosevic." Belgrade's newspapers cited despairing letters from army conscripts on this issue, and some policemen were dismissed for refusing assignment to Kosovo. Many of the Serb policemen who did go were sent as a demotion or as punishment for misbehavior.[26]

In a doom-eager willingness to repeat the mistake of 1998, Milošević allowed himself in 1999 to believe assurances that a really substantial offensive could wipe out the KLA in five to seven days. He needed dedicated fighters for this assignment, and he found many of them in the same place as before: criminals were released from prison to join and to form paramilitary forces. As one of them put it, "Let me tell you, that for freedom we would do just about anything." Some of the victims specifically refer to their persecutors as criminals. "Those people are from prisons, are out from prison now, criminals and gypsies with big weapons, with black masks," screamed one Albanian refugee. "They were not policemen. They were criminals Milosevic let out of jail," recounted another.[27]

In the meantime, NATO was threatening to bomb if the offensive took place. Concerned about this possibility, those running the Serb offensive appear to have tried to keep it under some degree of control. Given the quality of the personnel principally carrying it out, it was likely the offensive would be brutal (and ultimately counterproductive) like the offensive of the year before, but efforts were made to keep it localized and focused mainly on KLA strongholds. Serbian "special police," presumably in an effort to deter, pointedly announced to Western journalists that they "would kill every Albanian in sight" if NATO bombed. Ethnic Albanians and others in Kosovo expressed the fear that this was not an idle threat.[28]

Dismissing such threats as "foolish Serbian bravado," NATO launched air strikes in March 1999 under the assumption, as U.S. president Bill Clinton admitted later, that after "a couple of days" of bombing the Serbs would halt their offensive. Instead, the bombing had a sort of Pearl Harbor effect on the Serbs: like Americans in 1941, they were sent into a state of outraged fury. Virtually all vocal opposition to Milošević vanished, and, in a major shift, draft and mobilization orders were now frequently obeyed.[29]

The Serbs couldn't take out their fury directly on Brussels, London, or Washington, but they had an enemy conveniently close at hand: the Albanians of Kosovo. After the bombing began, control, such as it was, collapsed, and the frenzy began: it was "a breakdown in already poor discipline," as one observer put it.[30] Serb forces in Kosovo went into an orgy of vengeful violence and destruction that lasted for several weeks and was apparently intended to carry out the goal, previously considered unrealistic, of driving the majority Albanians from Kosovo.

The violence, however, seems to have been committed largely by marauding, if sometimes uniformed, thugs rather than by conscripts in the army. As in Bosnia and Croatia, the army provided a sort of generalized support for the rampage; it participated directly in some areas, and it hardly escapes blame for the results in any case. But, as one report puts it, "in hundreds of interviews," Kosovo Albanians "have said that nearly all the killings of civilians were committed by Serbian paramilitary forces and not by the regular army." The overall pattern was similar to that in Bosnia: "The army held the ground; special police and paramilitary units, sometimes with long hair, beards and bandannas, cleared the villages, often killing those who resisted leaving; the civilians were channeled toward buses or the border; bodies were often cleared out by other police units. Then the army checked the village again."[31]

If the marauders, as in Bosnia and Croatia, were in some sense brutally (and ultimately counterproductively) carrying out nationalist goals, they, like their predecessors, also seem to have had less noble aspirations on their minds: pure sadism, mindless violence, debauched boozing, and mainly focused, if opportunistic, looting. Although killing and other brutalities were common, the true name of the game seems to have been personal enrichment. As one of them put it philosophically, "I am a Serbian patriot. I fought for the Serbian cause. And also for the sake of money. Money was the main thing." Thus, the Serb paramilitaries in many cases made special efforts to concentrate their activities on the homes of wealthy Albanians. A true ideologue would scarcely have been so picky. And, although there were plenty of murders, Albanian lives were routinely spared by the payment of cash. Serb reservists report that "everywhere in Kosovo they were surrounded by Serbs in uniform carrying stolen televisions, satellite dishes and other electronic equipment." The experience generated what a soldier called "one of the best jokes of the war": a "Rambo," asked why he had quit the war, responds, "I couldn't carry a gun and a television set at the same time."[32]

Rwanda

Much of the writing about the Rwandan genocide of 1994, in which some 500,000 to 800,000 perished in a matter of weeks—mostly by being hacked to death with machetes—gives the impression that the conflict was one of all against all, friends against friends, neighbors against neighbors, even Cain against Abel. Friends and neighbors (and even brothers perhaps) did kill each other, but it seems that by far the greatest damage, as in Croatia, Bosnia, and Kosovo, stemmed from the rampages of murderous thugs guided by a government and essentially performing as mercenaries.

The conflict was far from a spontaneous eruption in that the basic elements of the genocidal process had been planned for years by Hutu extremists who were substantially in charge of the ruling party, the government bureaucracy, the army, and the police.[33] A civil war between Hutu military forces and the Tutsi-dominated Rwanda Patriotic Front (RPF) was going badly for the Hutus, and a power-sharing agreement was worked out. Rather than let this agreement take effect, the fanatics, seizing an opportunity provided when a plane carrying the country's president was shot down, ordered the murder of all Tutsis in the country. With this, the RPF, which had ceased to engage in hostilities because of the power-sharing agreement, remobilized and launched an offensive.

Initially, killings were mainly of carefully selected Tutsis who were known to be in opposition to the Hutu extremists, as well as of unreliable Hutus. But the process quickly expanded as Hutu party and government leaders and local administrators responded to orders to carry out the genocide throughout the country. They urged—or ordered—Hutus and Hutu police everywhere to engage in the killing, and many responded enthusiastically. The Presidential Guard probably engaged in the most focused and systematic of the killings. Also contributing was the Hutu army, the Forces Armées Rwandaises (FAR). Most of its members had been hastily recruited in the previous few years from landless peasants, the urban unemployed, and foreign drifters who had joined up mainly for the guaranteed food and drink (each man was entitled to two bottles of beer a day, a luxury by Rwandan standards) and for the opportunity to loot, since pay was low and irregular. Because the RPF was in the process of advancing during the genocide, the FAR was also devoted to fighting that threat. Although its complicity in the genocide was comparatively incidental, it seems to have participated in all the largest massacres, and it was frequently called in when other génocidaires met determined resistance.[34]

Finally, there was the interahamwe, militia bands that had been created and trained by Hutu extremists. As Philip Gourevitch points out, the interahamwe had its genesis in soccer fan clubs, and it recruited jobless young men who were "wasting in idleness and its attendant resentments." Extremist youth leaders sped around on motorbikes and sported "pop hairstyles, dark glasses, and flamboyantly colored pajama suits and robes, preached ethnic solidarity and civil defense" at interahamwe rallies, "where alcohol usually flowed freely. . . . and paramilitary drills were conducted like the latest hot dance moves." The interahamwe tended to see the genocide as a "carnival romp."[35]

Moreover, their ranks were expanded by hordes of opportunists once the genocide began. Gérard Prunier stresses that a "social aspect of the killings has often been overlooked": as soon as the killing groups

went into action, they drew around them a cloud of even poorer people, a *lumpenproletariat* of street boys, rag-pickers, car-washers and homeless unemployed. For these people the genocide was the best thing that could ever happen to them. They had the blessings of a form of authority to take revenge on socially powerful people as long as these were on the wrong side of the political fence. They could steal, they could kill with minimum justification, they could rape and they could get drunk for free. This was wonderful. The political aims pursued by the masters of this dark carnival were quite beyond their scope. They just went along.

"Drunken militia bands," notes Gourevitch, "fortified with assorted drugs from ransacked pharmacies, were bused from massacre to massacre." As in Yugoslavia, criminals were released from jail to participate in the destruction, and many youth gangs, "originally no more than gangs of small-time criminals, young thugs who worked for the highest bidder," also actively participated, notes Peter Uvin. The prospect for enrichment by looting was vastly escalated during the genocide and was used as a specific incentive by the leaders, many of whom were happy to take booty as well. Rape and sadism were also common. Not surprisingly, discipline among the rampaging killing bands was poor, particularly among the new recruits, who, observes Prunier, "tended to be street boys who were drunk most of the time." During the later part of the war, "the militias crumbled into armed banditry . . . as the administrative structure which had recruited and supported them fell apart." The ideology of the genocide was specifically devoted to expanding the numbers of the murderers, and fellow Hutus were often forced, on pain of instant death, to join the killings. Others participated by manning roadblocks or by pointing out local Tutsis to the menacing and marauding génocidaires.[36]

Many Hutus, however, protected and hid Tutsi neighbors and sometimes strangers, despite the pressure and despite the fact that the punishment for such behavior could be instant, brutal death. The number who did so probably was as high as the number who, under pressure from the often-drunken and always murderous génocidaires, indicated where some Tutsis might reside or be hiding. Most of the rest, it appears, simply withdrew whether in approval or disapproval of the cataclysm surrounding them: "We closed the door and tried not to hear," said one.[37]

An extensive study by Human Rights Watch ventures no direct estimates of the numbers of Hutus who actually took part in the killings. However, it suggests at various points that the killers numbered in the "tens of thousands." There were some 600 or 700 in the Hutu elite who directed the genocide, the Presidential Guard comprised some 700 to 1,500 men, and the police, initially numbered about 1,200, had recently been expanded to between 4,000 and 6,000. The formal organization of the army has been estimated at around 5,200 personnel by Western sources and was reported at the time of the power sharing agreement to be 20,000. Some sources put its strength as high as 50,000. There were about 1,700 "professional interahamwe" who received training and uniforms, and thousands or tens of thousands joined up (sometimes under coercion) after the genocide began. The interahamwe, described by one witness as "terrifying, bloodthirsty, drunk," therefore may have totaled 20,000 to 30,000, or as many as 50,000.[38]

It seems reasonable to suggest from all this that there might have been some 50,000 hardcore killers. This would easily be enough to have accomplished the genocide: if each of these people killed one person a week for the course of the hundred-day holocaust, more than 700,000 would have perished.[39] This number would represent some 2 percent of the male Hutu population older than thirteen. It is conceivable that 200,000 participated in the massacres, but this would almost certainly be a high figure that would include people who, under pressure from the hardcore génocidaires, did nothing more than point out where local Tutsi lived or simply manned roadblocks under orders. Even this higher figure would represent about 9 percent of the Hutu male population over the age of thirteen.[40]

In some sense, these are very high—astoundingly high—figures, and they demonstrate how extraordinary the event was. In a normal year, by comparison, the proportion of males over thirteen who committed murder in Rwanda was probably something like 1 in 1,000. Nonetheless, a situation in which more than 90 percent of the over-thirteen male Hutu population did not participate in killings hardly seems to justify the notion that the situation was one of all against all or neighbor against neighbor. In this extreme case, as in Croatia, Bosnia, and Kosovo, the chief dynamic of the predations seems to have been furnished by marauding bands of violent, opportunistic, and often drunken thugs who were hired or recruited by the government for the purpose.

East Timor and Other Cases

The Indonesian army, particularly in the last years of its occupation of East Timor, found it useful to band together East Timorese "toughs" and "musclemen," as Samuel Moore calls them, into paramilitary units, and to coordinate their activities with those of the army. Each group seems to have consisted of a few hundred men at most, and they were financed through direct payment (initially using counterfeit money or through the granting of special privileges: one of their leaders, for example, was given control of a gambling racket in the capital city). These groups, notes Moore, "allowed the army to terrorize the pro-independence supporters without the army itself appearing as the perpetrator." At the end of the occupation, for example, the paramilitaries were sent on a rampage—a "killing spree by proxy," Moore calls it— calculated to intimidate voters in an upcoming independence referendum. The effort was spectacularly counterproductive and, as the army was removed in the wake of the vote in 1999, the paramilitaries went on a savage campaign of looting and destruction that was finally halted by international peacekeepers, mainly from Australia.[41]

Other instances in which governments and armies have recruited criminals and thugs essentially as mercenary forces include some of the death squads in Latin America and elsewhere. After the dissolution of the Soviet Union in 1991, the new government in one of Russia's provinces, Chechnya, quickly became substantially criminalized, and the government actively recruited criminals, many of them released from prison, for its national guard. In its 1994–96 war in the secessionist province, the Russians invaders tried, with limited success, to fabricate mercenary "Cossack" units to fight for them. The more successful effort of the Americans to hire and direct mercenary units in Afghanistan in 2001 is discussed in the next chapter. In Zimbabwe, President Robert Mugabe has supported rampaging, land-seizing "war veterans," many of whom are far too young to have participated in a war that ended in 1982. The often-hated religious police in places like Iran and Saudi Arabia are frequently bands of thugs. In Kenya, government officials essentially staged something that looked like "ethnic conflict" against people who might support the wrong party by hiring thugs to kill, maim, and rape them, to burn their dwellings, and to seize their livestock at a reward pegged at US$200 for each permanent house burned and US$20–40 for each person killed or thatched house burned.[42]

CRIMINAL WARFARE: THE BRIGAND APPROACH

When governments become weak, it is likely (almost by definition) that criminal activity will increase—not the least because prisons become insecure. And sometimes the resulting criminality will be organized enough to look like war. In some cases such organized criminal predation focuses on kidnapping, extortion, banditry, looting, armed robbery, marauding, and even, in at least one instance in Nigeria, ambushing taxiing commercial jets at international airports. It may be especially likely to occur—and most likely to look like war (or warlordism) and to become international in scope—in countries in which there is an exportable primary commodity, and particularly where that is just about the only thing around of value. Often the government itself, or even one from a neighboring country, can essentially become one of the criminal or warlord bands.[43]

Several wars in Africa illustrate the brigand process best. As Bill Berkeley puts it, "Ethnic conflict in Africa is a form of organized crime. . . . Africa's warring factions are best understood not as 'tribes' but as racketeering enterprises." A common approach is to "tease out someone else's latent prejudice and inflame it with scapegoating rhetoric, mobilize gangs of thugs and criminals and the unemployed, arm them, stoke them with drugs and drink, and loose them upon defenseless civilians with the promise of vengeance and booty." In some respects, the long war in Colombia essentially fits this pattern, as do several others. As a number of observers have suggested, a notable similarity exists between the patterns of such warlord warfare and those once found in medieval and early modern Europe.[44]

Liberia

Samuel Doe, a master sergeant who seized control of Liberia in 1980, ruled through Cold War largess supplied particularly by the United States and through the establishment of a patronage network that has been described as "rape and plunder by armed marauders whose ideology is to search for cash and whose ambition is to retain power to accumulate and protect wealth." In late 1989, after the United States, no longer so concerned about the Cold War, had cut off its funding of his regime in disgust, Doe's weakened rule was threatened by an armed group of about a hundred led by an accused embezzler ($922,382) and jail-break artist, Charles Taylor, and by a somewhat larger group that had spun off from Taylor's forces, led by a psychopathic, hymn-singing drunk named Prince Yormi Johnson. The rebels quickly gained adherents in large measure because of the excessive and arbitrary violence Doe's forces visited upon the citizenry in a counterproductive effort to put down the rebellion. In 1990, Johnson captured Doe and drunkenly had him executed, videotaping the brutal murder to prove that it was he, not rival rebel Taylor, who had accomplished the deed.[45]

In the chaos, the United States sent a two thousand–strong Marine amphibious force to evacuate American nationals, and it could have used this force to pacify the situation. It declined the honor, however, and encouraged instead the creation of a West African force, mainly from Nigeria, that came sonorously to be called ECOMOG. This force proved to be strong enough to keep Liberia's capital, Monrovia, out of rebel hands, but the rest of the country was soon dominated by some seven warlord bands, which engaged in occasional battles over turf but mostly were involved in looting, rape, torture, occasional cannibalism, and selling commodities like iron ore, timber, rubber, gold, diamonds, and drugs on the international market. Charles Taylor proved to be especially adept at this illicit export business and quickly became very rich, sometimes inventively selling concessions to foreign companies several times over. Poorly paid and badly supplied, ECOMOG also effectively became a warlord operation, distinguished from the others mainly by the fact that it was protecting a rump government that was internationally recognized. Its members routinely looted, traded in contraband, dismantled and sold off industrial equipment, connived in the drug-smuggling business, had sex with underage Liberian girls, and rented ports to, provided protection for, and sold weapons to rebel groups. So adept was it at selling off looted property that Monrovians quipped that its ugly name had come to stand for Every Car Or Moving Object Gone.[46]

According to one official, "Most of the rebel fighters were criminals before the war—petty thieves, pickpockets, trouble-makers. At least 80 per cent of them were like that." This statement is probably an exaggeration, but it is clear that the brigand bands were singularly unselective in their recruiting methods, put forward the opportunity to loot and rape as primary recruiting incentives, and doubtless attracted, as Stephen Ellis puts it, "some of the worst people in society." Berkeley describes the recruits as "orphans bent on revenge, illiterate teenage peasants and school dropouts seizing the main chance, unemployed street toughs known as 'grunah boys' (grown-up boys), and others merely driven by fear, hunger, peer pressure." For the most part the brigand bands avoided engaging each other in combat, and their "main aim," notes Ellis, "was to intimidate and loot, and this was often achieved by committing individual acts of exemplary atrocity and terror." One estimate is that there eventually were some "sixty thousand Liberians under arms, of whom no more than a handful had received any form of formal military training." Carnivals of looting and pillage took place, as well as occasional massacres. Brigand gangs even looted from each other. With amazing frankness, Taylor's final offensive against Monrovia was labeled Operation Pay Yourself.[47]

Combatants routinely styled themselves after heroes in violent American action movies like *Rambo, Terminator,* and *Jungle Killer,* and many went under such fanciful noms de guerre as Colonel Action, Captain Mission Impossible, General Murder, Young Colonel Killer, General Jungle King, Colonel Evil Killer, General Monster, General War Boss III, General Jesus, Major Trouble, General Butt Naked, and, of course, General Rambo. Particularly in the early years, rebels decked themselves out in bizarre, even lunatic, attire: women's dresses, wigs, and pantyhose; decorations composed of human bones; painted fingernails; even (perhaps in only one case) headgear made of a flowery toilet seat. Such behavior and, more generally, life as a combatant were routinely facilitated by alcohol and drugs, and it is estimated that 25 to 30 percent emerged from the war with a serious drug problem.[48]

None too surprisingly, the thrill of the enterprise often soon wore off, particularly as the promises of instant wealth overwhelmingly proved visionary, and disillusionment, desertion, and defection became common. In the rare battles, rearward checkpoints were established to keep combatants from fleeing the front. Informed estimates suggest that 10 to 15 percent of the combatants were children—boys and girls under the age of fifteen.[49] Some of these children proved to be dangerously, even recklessly, dedicated warriors, but they could quickly become disillusioned and unreliable as well.

In 1997, Taylor and ECOMOG reached an agreement to hold an election. Taylor received three-quarters of the vote because he seemed to be the strong leader that the war-exhausted and war-devastated Liberians thought they needed and because the voters feared he would re-open the civil war again if he lost. He entered the presidency after the election, exactly the outcome ECOMOG had been organized in 1990 to prevent, and continued to rule there for several years, mostly though a set of subwarlords, spending 80 percent of the government's budget on personal security while his thugs, now labeled "civil servants," continued to prey on the locals. In 2003, Taylor was ousted through a combination of internal and external pressure. Although Liberians desperately pleaded with the United States to come to their aid, and although a contingent of 2,000 U.S. Marines was stationed offshore for a while, the administration declined to deploy them on land and left matters, once again, to the ministrations of a West African policing force.[50]

Sierra Leone

In quest of further profit and to complicate life for his opponents, Charles Taylor looked across the border to the diamond areas in neighboring Sierra Leone and, when fighting broke out in 1991, threw his support behind a rebel group in that country, under the warlordship of a former corporal in the Sierra Leone army. The government, already characterized by what Michael Chege calls "venal incompetence," then predictably made a disastrous decision: it rapidly expanded its not-very-good army of 3,000 to a really terrible one of 14,000. This ragtag force, consisting mostly of "drop-outs and robbers" according to a prominent Sierra Leonean human-rights campaigner, was sent, underpaid, undertrained, and underfed, into combat under commanders who had a distinct preference for leading from the rear. Rather than taking the rebels on, the troops quickly fragmented into bandit gangs and sought to profit from the chaos itself, and their countrymen soon came up with a special name for them: "sobels" or soldier-rebels. The rebels in various guises, many of them children, routinely drank blood mixed with drugs. They raped, killed, pillaged, extorted, looted, destroyed, and mutilated. The pattern was a familiar one: as an aid worker put it, "by fighting, you get a lot of money and excitement and see the country. You're going from nothing in a village to being Rambo." Indeed, before sending their charges off to what passed for battle, rebel commanders often showed them Rambo films.[51]

When the capital of Freetown came under attack in 1995, the government in desperation hired a South African–based mercenary firm, Executive Outcomes, which sent some two hundred employees to train and direct an effective military force. In a week it cleared the capital area of rebels, and within a few months it brought important diamond-mining areas back under government control—which allowed the government to pay EO's fees. Under these auspices, an election was held in 1996. For various reasons, in early 1997 the newly elected government refused to renew the Executive Outcomes contract. Within months the situation disintegrated, and a combined force of rebels and sobels looted the capital and sent the newly elected president fleeing.[52]

Eventually things were brought under a degree of control by another mercenary company and by the Nigerians from ECOMOG, who then left in late

1999 to be replaced by an amazingly incompetent UN force, five hundred of whom wandered into the bush with outdated maps and were captured and stripped of their weapons by rebels. Finally, in 2000 the British sent in a coherent force to stabilize the situation and were generally successful in this—a development discussed in the next chapter.[53]

Somalia

During the Cold War the United States had subsidized the corrupt regime of Mohammed Siad Barre in Somalia as a counter to the Marxist regime in neighboring Ethiopia, but this financial support was cut off toward the end of the Cold War.[54] Following a familiar pattern in Africa, the government was weakened—in this case to the point where it essentially ceased to exist—and the country, a remarkably homogeneous one both ethnically and religiously, descended in 1991 into criminal predation and sometime warfare organized by a set of warlords along clan lines, particularly in the south in and around the capital city, Mogadishu.

Notable in the developing chaos were the rampages of young gangsters, high on *qat*, a local drug, who loved to watch Sylvester Stallone movies, took Rambo as a role model, and committed widespread mayhem, looting, and killing in the capital. As one observer remarked, "It was total anarchy. . . . What happened is that with the collapse of the Somali government, the armed groups overran Mogadishu . . . the gates of the prisons were opened and all the common criminals with arms were going into houses and killing everybody. It was an utter misery." Routinely, people were afraid to leave their homes and shops because unguarded ones were certain to be looted.[55]

In 1992, an international force was sent to police the situation. This venture is assessed in the next chapter.

Colombia

There are three parties to the Colombian civil war, or sets of civil wars, particularly as it developed in the 1990s: the guerrillas, the government forces, and the paramilitaries. All engaged in criminal activity, sometimes as a means to an end, sometimes incidentally, and sometimes as an end in itself.

The guerrillas mainly include two fairly well-defined groups. One, the FARC, is waging a Communist-oriented insurgency that has been going on for decades. It consists of some 15,000–20,000 combatants and seems to be a fairly well-disciplined military force that sometimes engages the Colombian military in direct warfare but mostly applies guerrilla tactics. Although its ideological underpinnings have been weakened with the end of the Cold War, the FARC, under its leader, Manuel Marulanda, who began fighting at the age of fifteen and is now pushing eighty, apparently continues to yearn to take over the country and to push the national political and economic agenda sharply to the left. In the meantime, FARC acts much like a brigand force, controlling remote territory and funding its efforts through servicing the illegal demand for drugs in the United States and other rich countries and through bounties received from kidnapping and other forms of extortion. Somewhat allied with the FARC is a more hard-line (although often ideologically splintered) Communist group, ELN, of some 3,000–5,000 members. Following the distinctions developed in table 1.1, we should probably consider the ELN a terrorist group more than a guerrilla force because it seems to engage almost entirely in sporadic acts of destruction and extortion designed to undermine the country's petroleum industry and economy.[56]

In opposition, primarily against the FARC, are nearly 150,000 government troops, most of them arrayed in static defense of oil fields and infrastructure. For the most part, they are an underpaid, undertrained, poorly equipped, undermotivated, undereducated (Colombian men with a high school education are exempt from combat duty), and substantially corruptible conscript army. Despite Colombia's endless mayhem, the government spends only 3.5 percent of its gross domestic product on defense.[57]

In part because of the incompetence of the army engaged in its hopelessly monumental task of trying to protect a large country against guerrilla and terrorist attacks that can come from anywhere, a wide array of private militias have opportunistically sprung up. The paramilitaries, or self-defense forces, as they prefer to be called, are some 8,000 individuals strong. Some of them work as mercenaries for landowners or businesspeople desperate to protect their enterprises and family from guerrilla predation; others go off on their own, applying guerrilla tactics against the guerrillas, claiming turf, and setting up private fiefdoms. Many of these forces, like the guerrillas to whom they are devotedly opposed, engage in criminal activities such as trafficking in drugs, kidnapping for ransom, and setting up protection rackets. Some of their enterprises can be quite ingenious. When the guerrillas threaten an area, land prices abruptly fall as increasing numbers of rural people flee to the relative safety of the cities—some 2 million people have been displaced by the conflicts and some 800,000 have fled the country. The paramilitaries buy up (or seize) this cheap land, secure it from guerrilla attack, and resell it at much higher prices. Also, because such privately protected land is no longer guerrilla turf, it is unlikely to bring on depredation from the Colombian military in its clumsy and often vicious efforts to confront the guerrilla forces. To some degree, paramilitary forces have been enhanced by defectors from the guerrilla groups. They can provide havens from retaliation by the guerrillas, do not require guerrilla discipline, and offer a straight-forward opportunity for profit without all the obsolete and distracting ideological clutter.[58]

The bulk of the violence—or human rights violations—that has devastated very substantial sections of the country has been delivered by the military and other state agents and by the paramilitaries, not by the guerrillas.[59] In total, the war in its various incarnations claims something like two thousand lives per year, far lower than the number of Colombians killed in homicides committed by ordinary people and ordinary hoodlums.[60]

Popular opinion, none too surprisingly, is disgusted with the endless and economically debilitating violence and extortion: half of all the kidnappings in the world take place in Colombia. Approximately 5 percent of the population seem to support the FARC, fewer than those who support the paramilitaries, who may commit more violence but do not pose a strategic threat to the country. This attitude has not led to a great deal of support for the government, however, or to support for its unsuccessful and often corrupt and vicious military efforts to put down the resilient and well-heeled guerrillas. Conceivably the paramilitaries could be part of a solution to the overall problem, but they are poorly coordinated, and the government refuses to recognize them as a politically relevant force, holding them simply to be criminal enterprises.[61]

The United States has been interested in the wars in Colombia mainly as part of its campaign to interdict the supply of drugs that so many Americans are anxious to pay hefty prices for. This motivation is viewed with considerable disgust by many Colombians, who suggest that the war on drugs ought really to be focused on reducing demand back home and who point out that American efforts have thus far been almost wholly unsuccessful in reducing supply in the United States. American support to help Colombia develop a competent military force could potentially benefit the civil war effort, however limited its impact might be on the international drug trade.[62] This issue is considered more fully in later chapters.

Elsewhere

Similar criminal or criminalizing processes have taken place in a number of countries around the world, often leading to what looks very much like warfare. These countries include Sudan, Angola, Congo, Burma, Nigeria, Algeria, Macedonia, Georgia, Aceh in Indonesia, and various ones in the Caucasus and central Asia.[63]

DISCIPLINED CIVIL WARFARE

Although few of the armed civil conflicts in the post–Cold War era seem clearly and unambiguously to be disciplined wars, differentiating criminal from disciplined warfare, as suggested in chapter 1, is not always easy. Almost all wars—particularly civil wars—contain elements of both. Moreover, at various times disciplined combatants can degenerate into opportunistic criminal predators, while criminal armies can sometimes get their act together and perform like disciplined ones—standing, fighting, and risking their lives for a cause or agenda.

A good case in point is Afghanistan. Reacting to the Soviet invasion of 1979, Afghan warriors, mujahideen, fought a guerrilla war with tenacity and substantially with discipline against the well-armed but often ill-led and incompetent invaders, causing them to withdraw in 1989. In the aftermath of that victory, however, the former disciplined Afghani combatants disintegrated into dozens of squabbling and corrupt warlord and bandit gangs, plundering the population they had once defended. According to Ahmed Rashid, they "abused the population at will, kidnapping young girls and boys for their sexual pleasure, robbing merchants in the bazaars and fighting and brawling in the streets." They "seized homes and farms, threw out their occupants and handed them over to their supporters," and they "sold off everything to Pakistani traders to make money, stripping down telephone wires and poles, cutting trees, selling off factories, machinery and even road rollers to scrap merchants." The case is further complicated by the fact that many criminals, on the run from the law in Iran and Pakistan, took the opportunity to flee to the potentially profitable protection provided by the anarchic situation in post-Soviet Afghanistan, where they joined warlord bands or plied their trade on their own. In addition, large portions of the regular Afghan army defected to fight with the rebels during the Soviet occupation, and many of these may have gone back to civilian pursuits after the Soviets left, abandoning the field to the more criminal element.[64]

A similar pattern seems to have held in the 1994–96 war in Chechnya. Confronted with a heavy-handed Russian invasion, the resistance was often dedicated and tenacious in a fight for national independence—a "well-prepared, reasonably well-equipped guerilla force defending its own territory," as Olga Oliker puts it.* Once victory had been achieved, however, the combatants quickly reverted to self-destructive banditry and hooliganism, much of it inflicted on the very people they had previously fought so valiantly to protect from the Russian forces.[65]

The process can also be seen in the long civil war in Lebanon, which finally came to an end in the mid-1990s. By the definitions used here, much of the combat would be considered disciplined: forces stood and fought, for cause or sect or for revenge, occasionally risking or committing suicide in

---

* Although "clashing civilizations" would seem to have been involved in the wars between Slavic-Orthodox Russia and Muslim Chechnya, it is interesting that the Chechens received almost no support (except occasionally verbally) from their Muslim neighbors (Lieven 1998, 97; cf. Huntington 1996, 277–78).

the process. As that exceedingly complicated war progressed, however, more forces degenerated into what looks suspiciously like self-perpetuating criminal or thuggish predation, as competing fiefdoms, private armies, militias, or bandit gangs engaged in racketeering, looting, kidnapping for ransom, rape, extortion, and a bewildering array of shifting turf wars built around efforts to rob a certain bank or to control the lucrative drug trade—the country's only growth industry during the turmoil. Many of the combatants seem to have been on drugs themselves much of the time. Other combatants included "gun-toting adolescents" and crazy people: as one psychiatrist put it, "The mental hospitals are not functioning because the patients are on the streets carrying guns."[66]

In the post–Cold War era, substantial elements of disciplined civil warfare can be seen in the lengthy, persistent conflict in Sri Lanka in which a tenacious guerrilla group, the Tamil Tigers, has battled for secession. Although it partly uses criminal techniques to fund itself, including smuggling, money laundering, extortion, drug dealing, and trafficking in human beings, it has become a well-disciplined military force, forcibly conscripting young boys and girls, assassinating or intimidating moderate Tamils from negotiating with the government or joining its army, perpetrating efficient massacres, launching suicide attacks, and fighting pitched battles against military forces from the central authority.[67] In the second war in Chechnya, begun in 1999, some of the defending combatants seem once again to have reverted from banditry to disciplined, dedicated warfare against the massively destructive Russian army—which, however, entered this war, unlike the earlier one, with considerable popular support due to outrage against Chechen terrorism and attacks during the interwar period. In various ways, much of the civil warfare in Algeria and Turkey probably also qualifies as disciplined, as does, perhaps, the insurgency that emerged in Iraq after the U.S. 2003 invasion.

TERRORISM

By the definitions developed in chapter 1, terrorism is not the same as disciplined war, but this is not because it fails to be disciplined. Rather, it fails to be war because it is perpetrated by individuals or by small bands and because it is generally sporadic—insufficiently sustained. It is distinguished from crime not only because it is carried out with discipline, but also because it has a broader political or social goal than simply fun and personal profit. Precisely because it can be carried out by individuals or very small groups, terrorism, like crime, has been around forever and will presumably continue to exist.

Terrorists seek to commit enough violence that their opponents will accede to their wishes, or they hope gradually to gain enough adherents so that their efforts can graduate to a full-blown insurgent war, or both. Terrorist campaigns that lingered into the 1990s in Northern Ireland and in the Basque country in Spain succeeded in neither goal, although they continued to be a notable irritant to British and Spanish authorities. Destructive activities by the Japanese terrorist group Aum Shinrikyo created substantial fear and havoc but utterly failed to inspire the transformational apocalypse that leaders of the group apparently hoped for. Terrorist activity designed to push India from its positions in Kashmir has also failed to show much success. And efforts by the well-funded international terrorist group, or movement, al Qaeda to shift U.S. policy in the Middle East have thus far proven to be substantially counterproductive.

In general, terrorist violence causes more disruption through the panic and overreaction it often provokes than through its direct effects. In part, this conclusion is definitional because if considerable damage is accomplished—as the Communists were able to do through selective assassination and other violence in the early years of the Vietnam conflict—we tend to call the activity war rather than terrorism. Keeping that in mind, usually only a few hundred people die worldwide each year from international terrorism, and over the course of the entire twentieth century, fewer than twenty terrorist attacks managed to kill as many as 100 people, and none caused more than 400 deaths. The September 11, 2001, terrorist attacks in the United States in which some 3,000 perished were accordingly quite literally off the charts. Until then, far fewer Americans were killed in any grouping of years by all forms of international terrorism than were killed by lightning. However, even including that disaster in the count, the number of people who die as a result of international terrorism is tiny compared with the number who die in most civil wars—or for that matter from automobile accidents.

Obviously, this condition could change if international terrorists are able to assemble sufficient weaponry or devise new tactics to kill masses of people and if they come to do so routinely—and this, of course, is the central fear. But extreme events often remain exactly that—aberrations rather than harbingers.[68]

A problem with getting coherent thinking on the issue of terrorism is that reporters and politicians mostly find that extreme and alarmist possibilities arrest their audience's attention more than do discussions of broader context, much less of statistical reality: when someone interviewed on CBS's popular *60 Minutes* had the temerity to suggest that "the chances of any of us dying in a terrorist incident is very, very, very small," his interviewer summarily admonished him, "But no one sees the world like that." Both assertions, as it happens, are true. Although it is sensible to be alert and to take precautions, many of the extreme forms alarmism has taken are not reasonable—in fact, they often verge on hysteria. After the September 11 attacks, some prominent commentators came to argue that the United States had become "vulnerable," even "fragile," or that the threats posed to the United States by terrorists and by pathetic, impoverished tyrannies like those in Iraq and North Korea were "existential."[69] All societies are vulnerable to tiny bands of suicidal fanatics in the sense that it is impossible to prevent every terrorist act. But the United States is hardly vulnerable in the sense that it can be toppled by dramatic acts of terrorist destruction, even extreme ones. In fact, the country can, however grimly, readily absorb that kind of damage— as it "absorbs" some 40,000 deaths each year from automobile accidents. In fact, the major economic effect of terrorist attacks is usually not in their immediate impact but in the costly and often hasty, even hysterical, efforts to prevent a repetition.

Terrorist successes, or apparent successes, in the post–Cold War era have mostly been associated with Israel and its occupation of Arab territories in the Palestinian area and in southern Lebanon. (In both cases, however, it is certainly possible to hold that the violent activities have been committed by large-enough groups, and have been sustained enough, to be considered warfare rather than terrorism; if so, these instances, would be considered, like the conflict in Sri Lanka, to be instances of disciplined civil warfare.) Persistent attacks, many of them suicidal, by terrorists (or disciplined combatants) against Israeli occupiers in southern Lebanon eventually proved successful: they sufficiently increased the cost of the eighteen-year occupation (which was controversial in Israel from the start), and in 2000 the Israelis withdrew their forces. In the wake of that success, some terrorists have sought to adopt the tactic to force Israel to withdraw from occupied Palestine and, in their most extravagant dreams, from the Middle East entirely. Although the latter outcome is highly unlikely, the mellowing in 2003 of Israel's formerly hard-line prime minister, Ariel Sharon, on matters of Palestinian statehood likely is partly a consequence of terrorist attacks that had plagued his country for the previous three years.

Some terrorists have apparently had the goal of sabotaging talks that could lead to a settlement between Israeli and Arab Palestinian authorities. A Jewish terrorist with that in mind certainly hampered progress by assassinating the prominent Israeli peacemaker Yitzhak Rabin in 1995, and Arab terrorists did so by bombings that led Israelis to react by electing prime ministers hostile to the peace process in 1996 and 2001.

Regimes have frequently allowed their participation in peace talks to be affected in important ways by terrorists. By stating that they will not negotiate as long as terrorist attacks continue, both the Israeli government and the British government (over Northern Ireland) effectively permitted individual terrorists to set their agendas—although, of course, if those governments didn't want to negotiate anyway, the terrorist acts simply supplied a convenient excuse.

CIVIL WAR AND THE HOBBESIAN IMAGE

Michael Ignatieff has compared the conditions that prevailed in the former Yugoslavia to a Hobbesian state of nature, and Chris Hedges refers to places like the Congo as "Hobbesian playgrounds."[70] Although that image is commonly evoked for many of the post–Cold War civil conflicts discussed in this chapter, experience suggests that Hobbes—or at least the common Hobbesian image—is wrong, and perhaps profoundly so, in some important respects about the state of nature.

Hobbes was obsessed by the chaos and calamity of the English Civil War of 1642–49, which took place during his lifetime, and his important book, *Leviathan*, was, he notes, "occasioned by the disorders of the present time." In particular, he viewed the conflict as essentially one of competing ideas— in that case religious ideas, rather than nationalist, ideological, or ethnic ones. And, like Ignatieff on Yugoslavia, he envisioned the conditions as a descent into a base state of nature, a "kingdom of darkness" and a "confederacy of deceivers" in which "force and fraud" become "the two cardinal virtues," and where, without "a common power to keep them all in awe," people live in a perpetual state of war "where every man is enemy of every man," where "there is no place for industry because the fruit thereof is uncertain," where there is "continual fear and danger of violent death," and where life, as he famously put it, becomes "solitary, poor, nasty, brutish, and short." Hobbes acknowledges that humans group themselves (so the state of nature may not be quite as "solitary" as his description seems to suggest), and thus that the perpetual wars of the state of nature are waged between bands rather than between individuals.[71] However, the implication of the image, at least as commonly understood, is one of perpetual and total violence in which all, or virtually all, partake.[72]

The experience of the civil wars discussed in this chapter calls this image into question. Although there was plenty of deception, force, and fraud in those conflicts, people there did not descend into the war of all against all that Hobbes so vividly depicted and so ardently and influentially abhorred. Although the conditions of deep insecurity certainly resemble a Hobbesian state of nature, they come about not because people generally fall into, are manipulated into, or give in to murderous enmity, but because they come under the arbitrary sway of bands, often remarkably small ones, of armed and murderous thugs or fanatics.

Repeatedly it has been found that society can be devastated by the violent maraudings and intimidations of a handful of people. In the conflict to which Ignatieff applies the Hobbesian image, Arkan's much-feared forces consisted of a core of some 200 men, and perhaps totaled 500–1,000 overall. Višegrad, a Bosnian town of 50,000, was substantially controlled for years by a returned hometown boy, Milan Lukić, and some fifteen well-armed companions, including his brother and a local waiter who often went barefoot. Using violent and often sadistic intimidation (Peter Maass refers to Lukić as a "psychopathic killer"), this tiny band forced the town's 14,500 Muslims to leave and suppressed any expressions of dissent from local Serbs (many of whom, however, took advantage of the situation to profit from the Muslim exodus). The town of Teslic was controlled, it is estimated, by "five or six men, well placed and willing to use violence." One paramilitary "group" identified by UN analysts consisted of a single man, appropriately known as Adolf, who reportedly lined up 150 unarmed Muslim and Croat civilians in Brčko and then killed them individually with an automatic pistol fitted with a silencer. The 1992 violence that tore apart Srebrenica, a town of 37,000 people, was perpetrated by no more than thirty Serb and Muslim extremists. Naser Orić, the Muslim warlord who controlled that town for several years (and who was mysteriously absent with his gang when Serb forces overran the place in 1995), led an armed band with a nucleus of only fifteen men. They controlled the few jobs, lived in the larger homes, had more food than others, exaggerated the population size to get excess humanitarian aid while hoarding it to drive up prices before selling it on the black market at a killing. When three opponents to this feudal arrangement arose, they were ambushed and at least one of them was killed. Because the refugees were essentially being used as human shields to protect the property and income of Orić and his men, Muslims were not allowed to leave, yet little effort was made to improve the lives of the people, especially the refugees, unless it brought personal profit to the ruling gang.[73]

The condition seems quite general, perhaps even universal. For example, during the Dutch Revolt in the middle of the sixteenth century, notes Geoffrey Parker, small numbers of Calvinists were able to topple Catholic authority in many areas, smashing churches and wayside shrines often "in full view of great crowds who watched and lifted not a finger." In the south of the country, the destruction was carried out by a band of between 50 and 100 people—including returned exiles, unemployed manual workers, drunkards, whores, and boys in their early teens—who were hired by the day at the wage of an unskilled laborer. More recently, the forces that ended up shattering Liberia numbered 150 or less at the beginning, and those in Guatemala began with less than 500. The rebel combatants actually in the field in Colombia may number only some 5,000–6,000, whereas those in the 1994–96 war in Chechnya were never more than 3,000 at any time. The guerrillas in East Timor who gave such trouble to the vast Indonesian army forces were well under 2,000. According to a priest who lives there, a slum in Kingston, Jamaica, populated by 8,000 people is totally dominated by thirty mobsters. In Somalia, warlord Mohammed Aidid ran his fiefdom with a few dozen hired guns paid in part with drugs. The Rwandan genocide of 1994 is doubtless the event that most evokes the Hobbesian neighbor-against-neighbor image in the post–Cold War era. Yet, as demonstrated earlier in the chapter, the portion of the Hutu population that perpetrated the mayhem was much lower than it might seem, and it certainly was not a war of all against all. When a referendum was conducted in 1998 on the key traditional Irish Republican Army demand that unification should be decided through a vote of the people in the entire island, not just those in the Protestant-majority north, fully 95 percent of the voters in the Irish Republic voted against the idea—a percentage rarely, if ever, achieved in a fully democratic process. Many voters were presumably against the use of violence to advance the goal of unification, not necessarily against the goal itself. But it was the use of violence, not the goal, that was the defining and distinguishing characteristic of the IRA terrorists. Whom, one might fairly ask, did they represent?[74]

Brian Hall, in assessing the violence in Yugoslavia, reflects on the "one-to-five percent of any population, any nation," that becomes violent, "not because they were afraid, or confused, or idealistic, but because they wanted to hurt people. . . . War was their dream come true." Similarly, commenting on the situation in Sri Lanka, Stanley Tambiah makes an observation that has wide applicability to what has come to be called ethnic violence. He stresses "the awful existential fact" that a "minority of activists, populists, and terrorists on both sides" can hold "the entire society as its hostage," while the many people in between "are inexorably seduced and forced into taking sides as the spilling of blood on both sides heightens the emotions and sentiments cohering around such primordial themes as kinship, people, religion, language, and 'race.' "[75]

On December 7, 1941, as it is commonly put, "the Japanese" attacked Pearl Harbor. No one, of course, takes this expression literally to suggest that the entire population of Japan, or even a major portion of it, directly participated in the venture. Rather it is understood to mean that some of Japan's military forces, ordered into action by Japan's government and perhaps supported to varying degrees by the Japanese population, launched the attack. By contrast, in discussions of ethnic war and civil war more broadly, such distinctions are often missing. When we say "the Serbs" and "the Croats" are engaged in war, the implication frequently seems to be that those two groups have descended into a sort of war of all against all and neighbor against neighbor. In the end, in fact, the mistaken—even racist—image that an entire group is devotedly out to destroy another group is an important cause of the violence itself, and it can shatter any ability to perceive nuance and variety.

THUGS AS RESIDUAL COMBATANTS

Most, though certainly not all, contemporary civil wars have been primarily or substantially perpetrated by semiorganized and mostly opportunistic criminal predators who are drawn to, or recruited for, violence for its own sake and for the personal and material fulfillment it can often supply. Like bandit and pirate bands, their numbers are often small, although quite sufficient to intimidate the unarmed and unorganized civilians who are their chief prey and source of satisfaction.

Thus, most of what passes for warfare today is centrally characterized by the opportunistic and improvisatory clash of thugs, not by the programmed and/or primordial clash of civilizations—although many of the perpetrators do cagily apply ethnic, national, ideological, or civilizational rhetoric to justify their activities because to stress the thrill and profit of predation would be politically incorrect. So, for example, the butcher of Sierra Leone, Foday Sabana Sankoh, says he took up arms after having "a vision" and that his goal is "to defend democracy." This presumably caused him to launch his drugged, youthful charges on a rampage in which they set out to lop off the arms of people to keep them from voting in an election that had been boycotted by Sankoh's group.[76]

In a review of several studies of "ethnic" war, James Fearon and David Laitin observe that "what is described as ethnic violence looks very much like gang violence with no necessary ethnic dimension" in which what is required is simply the "availability of mobilizable thugs." They then muse: "One might ask if there has been a great upsurge in ethnic war since the end of the Cold War, or whether more insurgencies are not labeled 'ethnic' due to opportunistic redescriptions and salesmanship by rebel leaders seeking support from great power patrons newly disposed to see ethnic rather than Left–Right conflict."[77] Indeed, one might very well ask that.

Moreover, combatants in many of these conflicts don't really want the "war" to end because they are profiting so nicely from it. And there is something of a reverse causality as well: as David Keen puts it, "The longer a civil war, the more likely it becomes that people will find ways to profit from it."[78] The lengthy civil wars in Lebanon and Burma form cases in point. And so does the one in Colombia: although the government there presumably has an incentive to end the war, that is not so clear for most of the guerrillas and paramilitaries. The guerrillas, or at least their leaders, do seem to want to take over and reform the country, but failing that, they are likely to find endless war more satisfying and financially rewarding than peace, and they seem to be exceedingly patient.[79] Meanwhile, many of the paramilitary warlord and mercenary forces are doing quite well in their individual criminal fiefdoms, and some are even seeking respectability.

Although the number of wars going on at any one time has increased over much of the last forty years, for the most part there was no notable rise in the number of wars starting in any given year. What happened is that wars became longer, which is consistent with the notion that they are often criminal in nature.[80]

may be set to wondering whether many of these enterprises
Wars are fought to achieve victory (and, often, its attendant
ically profitable enterprises that one hopes will go on forever
esses, and if they are illicit, they are called crime. Assessing
...ord predation in several countries in Africa, David Keen describes a
process in which "one avoids battles, picks on unarmed civilians, and makes
money."[81] He calls this "war," but his characterization seems much more
nearly to be a description of crime.

The "true essence of warfare," argues van Creveld, "consists not just of one
group killing another but of its members' readiness to be killed in return if
necessary." Similarly, Robert O'Connell, in a wide-ranging consideration of
the history and prehistory of warfare, searches for a definition to differentiate war from blood feuds and other forms of armed mayhem and violence.
He determines that for an armed conflict to be considered a war, it should
be premeditated and directed by some form of governmental structure; it
should focus "on societal issues with the interest of resolving them by force,
using the resources of the group"; combatants should have palpable economic and/or social goals, and they should be willing "to risk injury and
death in pursuit of these objectives and in accordance with the dictates of the
command authority"; and the warring parties should understand that the results of the war "will be more lasting than momentary."[82] If these are the definitions and "true essences" of war, the rampages of bands of thugs simply
don't qualify.

But even if we consider criminal civil conflicts to be warfare, we are dealing increasingly not with a new kind of war but with the residue of warfare. It
is not, as van Creveld would have it, that such warfare has risen to dominance. Rather it is that, increasingly, warfare of that sort is just about the only
kind still going on: criminal warfare is the residual, not the emerging, form.
Nor is it, as van Creveld would also have it, that "now as ever war itself is alive
and well" and "about to enter a new epoch."[83] Instead, it seems to me, war
has increasingly been reduced to its pathetic, if often highly destructive,
remnants.

ORDERING THE NEW WORLD

In his farewell address upon leaving the presidency in January 1953, Harry Truman looked forward to the post–Cold War period, or, as he put it, "the world we hope to have when the Communist threat is overcome." It would be a "new era," he suggested, "a wonderful golden age—an age when we can use the peaceful tools that science has forged for us to do away with poverty and human misery everywhere on the earth."[1]

After 1989, the world entered that new era or, as some were given to calling it, a new world order. Over the course of a couple of years, virtually all the major problems that had plagued big-country (sometimes known as Great Power) international relations for nearly half a century were resolved with scarcely a shot being fired, a person being executed, or a rock being thrown. Among them were the unpopular and often brutal Soviet occupation of Eastern Europe; the artificial and deeply troubling division of Germany; the expensive, virulent, crisis-prone, and apparently dangerous military contest between East and West; the often-resented hegemonic hold of Russia over various non-Russian neighbors; and the ideological struggle between authoritarian, expansionist, violence-encouraging Communism and reactive, sometimes panicky, capitalist democracy.[2]

For many, however, the post–Cold War era does not really feel much like "a wonderful golden age." The developed countries may be in substantial agreement about most major issues, and there may be little or no fear of armed conflict among them. But notable problems remain. High among these, certainly, is managing the entry of Russia and China, the main losers of the Cold War, into the world community—a process that generally seems to be going well. Indeed, by the dawn of the new century, the post-Communist era seemed substantially to be over, and a considerable stability had enveloped most of the area after a very turbulent decade. Problems remain, of course—especially concerning China's deep desire to bring Taiwan back into

for the most part, the losers of the Cold War came to see the
:h the same way as the winners.

entral problem, more ambiguous and tentative, is the establish-
:hanisms for dealing with residual disorder in the new world
order. Since 1918, developed countries, as noted earlier, have engaged in
four kinds of warfare. For differing reasons, three of these are now firmly in
the past. One, discussed in chapter 4, was the cluster of wars known as World
War II, and the other two were colonial war and warfare emerging from the
Cold War contest, both considered in chapter 5. The fourth application, or
potential application, of warfare is being developed in the aftermath of the
Cold War. In their new era of essential consensus, the developed countries
have been free to explore various devices for managing the world. Some of
these devices are diplomatic, social, or economic, but the judicious application or threat of military force—in ventures that might be called "policing
wars"—is also potentially available.

It may be time to go back to first principles. The problem with war, of
course, is not in its essential point—it often does resolve contentious issues—
but rather in the decidedly unnatural death and destruction that are part of
its essential workings. Although the once-perennial problem of international
war seems to have been substantially brought under control, two notable
sources of artificial death and destruction continue to exist—and to persist.

One of these is civil war, the chief remaining form of war and the central
subject of chapter 6. The other is government. In fact, over the course of the
bloody twentieth century, far more people were killed by their own governments than were killed by all wars put together.[3] For example, during the
1990s, the government of Rwanda, as discussed in the previous chapter, systematically tried to kill off a minority group, resulting in perhaps half a million deaths or more in about a hundred days. In North Korea at around the
same time, as discussed in this chapter, the regime so mismanaged and exacerbated famine conditions that hundreds of thousands of people died, with
some careful estimates putting the number at more than two million.

In principle, the international community is ill prepared to deal with civil
conflict and with vicious or criminal or cosmically incompetent domestic
governments because it is chiefly set up to confront problems that transcend
international borders, not ones that lurk within them. However, having substantially abandoned armed conflict among themselves, the developed countries can, if they so desire, expand their efforts and collaborate on international police work to deal with civil war and with destructive domestic
regimes. During the Cold War, the leading countries often found themselves
supporting opposite sides in domestic conflicts and often ended up exacerbating the problem. That is unlikely to be the case in the era of post–Cold
War consensus.

The opportunities are considerable. Most civil warfare, although certainly not all, can readily be policed because it is chiefly perpetrated by poorly co-ordinated, if often savage, thugs. Moreover, many of the most vicious governments are substantially of the criminal variety, and many could be toppled by coordinated forces sent from outside. This is because, as observed in chapter 1, a criminal or near-criminal force tends to be cowardly and incompetent when confronted by an effective disciplined one.

Some of the policy implications of the new post–Cold War consensus are assessed in this chapter and the next. This one discusses the use of force by developed countries in the aftermath of the Cold War, and chapter 8 examines the prospects that, with this experience behind it, the international community, led by the developed countries, can systematically use policing wars to order the new world.

POLICING WARS AFTER THE COLD WAR

Since the end of the Cold War, there have been a number of instances in which developed countries have applied, or threatened to apply, military force in an effort to correct conditions they considered sufficiently unsuitable (see table 7.1). Most of these military ventures, or policing wars, either have been led by the United States or have been conducted as solo enterprises by that country in its self-proclaimed (and perhaps self-infatuated) post–Cold War role as "the world's only remaining superpower" or as "the indispensable nation."[4]

The developed countries were able to engage in these ventures at remarkably little cost to themselves, particularly in casualties, though they often seem to have had rather little concern about the casualties they might themselves have been inflicting in the process. The experience suggests that a sufficiently large, impressively armed, and well-disciplined policing force can often be effective in pacifying thug-dominated conflicts and in removing thuggish regimes. A review of this experience follows.

Panama, 1989

Manuel Noriega was a certifiable thug who had abrogated an election in Panama in order to continue running the place himself. He also played around in the drug trade, made some hostile references to the United States in speeches, and remained unapologetic when his goons shot and killed an American soldier in a checkpoint altercation, beat up another American serviceman, and sexually threatened his wife. There were also concerns about the security of the famous Panama Canal, even though Noriega was wary of threatening that piece of real estate, which was due to be turned over to Panama in a decade anyway. U.S. president George H. W. Bush had made

TABLE 7.1

Applications and notable threatened applications of military force by developed countries since the Cold War[a]

| | | Battle deaths by developed countries | | | |
| | | Actual | | | |
	Anticipated	United States	Other developed countries	Other deaths	Reason for intervention
Panama 1989	10s	26	NA	Hundreds	Regime change
Gulf War 1991	500–1,000	146	63	Thousands	Reverse an act of aggression
Gulf area 1991–2003	Near 0	Near 0	0	Hundreds[b]	Contain Iraq; regime change
Somalia 1992–94	Near 0	26	0	Hundreds	Police civil war; provide humanitarian assistance
North Korea 1994	Tens of thousands	0	0	0	Reverse nuclear weapons development
Haiti 1994–96	Near 0	0	NA	Few	Regime change; police the aftermath
Bosnia 1995–	Near 0	Near 0	Near 0	Low hundreds	Support one side in civil war; police the aftermath
Kosovo 1999	Dozens	0	0	Thousands	Support one side in civil war; police the aftermath
East Timor 1999	Near 0	NA	0	Few	Police peace settlement
Sierra Leone 2000–2002	Near 0	NA	Near 0	Dozens	Police civil war
Afghanistan 2001–2	Hundreds, thousands	19	Near 0	Thousands	Pursue international terrorist organization; regime change
Iraq 2003–	Scores, low hundreds	Hundreds	Dozens	Thousands	Regime change; police the aftermath

Note: NA, not applicable.

[a]Does not include cases in which troops were sent to rescue or extricate nationals.

[b]In addition, sanctions imposed as part of the policy were a necessary cause of tens, probably hundreds, of thousands of deaths.

many tough anti-Noriega statements during his election campaign of 1988, and he seems to have seen the dictator as "an unpleasant symbol of American impotence in the face of illegal drugs," which Bush had made a high-priority issue. Bush was also concerned, it appears, by lingering suggestions that he was an indecisive, hesitant wimp. Outraged at the Panamanian dictator's insolent statements and behavior, Bush ordered 24,000 American troops into action at the end of 1989. They were up against 16,000 troops in the substantially criminalized Panamanian Defense Forces, of whom 3,500 were reckoned to be capable of combat; few fought with much vigor.[5]

Like the Cold War–related invasion of the tiny island of Grenada in 1983 by Bush's predecessor, Ronald Reagan, Panama was raided and occupied at little cost to the Americans. Noriega gave himself up and was sent to Florida, where he was tried by an American court, convicted by an American jury, and locked up in an American prison. In Panama, a new government, not ideal, but a distinct improvement by most standards, was set up. The venture seems to have had no significant impact one way or the other on the drug trade.

Gulf War, 1991

During 1990, Saddam Hussein, a former hit man who was now the president and resident dictator of Iraq, had become particularly aggrieved by the behavior of his neighbor country, Kuwait. Iraq was in desperate economic straits, and he argued that Kuwait should forgive a debt Iraq had incurred by fighting the mutual enemy, Iran, in an eight-year war that had ended in 1988. He also claimed that Kuwait was stealing Iraqi oil by slant-drilling at the border and that Kuwait was violating agreements by overproducing oil and thus lowering the world price for a product vital to Iraq's well-being. To signal his anger, he moved troops to the border. In various meetings over the issue, Kuwait, urged on by British prime minister Margaret Thatcher, refused to budge, and Kuwait's Crown Prince and prime minister reportedly shouted in a meeting on August 1 that if the Iraqis needed funds, they should "send their wives out onto the street to earn money for them."[6]

Iraq's invasion of oil-rich Kuwait the next day caught almost everyone by surprise, including Arab rulers in Kuwait and other countries in the Middle East, who had brushed off the troop buildup as a bluff.[7] This act of war in an area of importance alarmed most world leaders, particularly Thatcher and Bush, who saw it as a form of "naked aggression" comparable in its way to that of Adolf Hitler in the 1930s, but not comparable, of course, to Bush's venture into Panama a few months earlier.

And in an important sense, it wasn't. The policing war against Panama restored that country's elected government, after which the aggressors quite willingly left. Saddam's aggression against Kuwait was carried out as a matter of conquest. It did not stay that way long.

Encouraged by Thatcher ("Remember, George, this is no time to go wobbly"), Bush led a determined international effort to impose a punishing economic blockade on Iraq, and the Americans and others sent warships to the area. Cooperating were not only the Western countries but most Arab ones. Moreover, in the wake of the Cold War, Iraq's former friend and ally the Soviet Union joined the boycott—something that took Saddam by surprise.[8] In short order Iraq's economy was fractured, making these sanctions far more punishing than any others ever imposed.[9]

By October, however, Bush had decided that the economic sanctions were not working fast enough. He apparently felt that public support for the venture would decline and that the coalition aligned against Iraq might eventually become unstuck, making the use of the military force to remove Iraq from Kuwait problematic. Moreover, if sanctions dragged on, observed a sympathetic columnist, "Bush would lose face, popularity, and reelectability."[10]

Accordingly, shortly after the 1990 U.S. congressional elections, Bush announced that troop levels in the Middle East would be substantially increased in order to attain an "offensive military option." The hope was that this threat, combined with the sanctions, would cause Iraq to withdraw as demanded. At the end of the month, Bush was able to sharpen the threat by getting the United Nations Security Council to authorize the use of force unless Iraq left Kuwait by January 15, 1991. Bush's earlier policy in the Gulf had been strongly supported by the political leadership of both parties, but his unilateral November escalation, with its apparent rush to war before sanctions were given a full chance to take effect, alarmed many. Eventually, Bush formally asked Congress to authorize him to use force after the deadline, and after extensive debate, a majority—a rather slim one in the Senate—did so in a vote that largely followed party lines.

Over time, Bush became emotionally absorbed, even obsessed, by the crisis and felt he was being "tested by real fire." To some, he seemed to yearn to have a war. He insisted that there could be no deals: in his view, Saddam must withdraw unconditionally and ignominiously, suffering maximum humiliation for his aggression. There were also growing concerns that Iraq might be able to produce a crude atomic bomb, complicating the eventual use of force. Moreover, persistent reports about atrocities committed by Iraqi troops within Kuwait deeply outraged Bush. Military planners, meanwhile, were concluding that a war against Iraq's forces could easily be won, or as Bush put it, "We're going to kick his ass out." An influential supporter of war, House Armed Services Committee chairman Les Aspin, a Democrat, publicly concluded that "prospects are high for a rapid victory" and suggested that American casualties might be between 3,000 and 5,000, with 500 to 1,000 dead.[11]

Saddam Hussein apparently became convinced that war was inevitable and that a humiliating backdown would be "suicidal" for him. Accordingly, he called Bush's bluff and refused to move his occupying troops. There was a growing sense, too, of helpless fatalism in Washington—a feeling that the United States simply couldn't back down from the expensive and heightened troop commitment that had been unilaterally instituted by the president two months earlier. Unleashed by Congress, Bush proclaimed that there would be a "great promise of a new world order" in victory and began the war on the moonless night of January 16, 1991, a few days before huge antiwar demonstrations were scheduled to take place in Washington.[12]

A great deal of postwar discussion and lesson-drawing concluded that the war showed, as one analyst put it, "the revolutionary potential of emerging technologies" or the "power of coherence and simultaneity." However, it seems that the war mainly demonstrated how easy it is to run over an enemy that has little in the way of effective defenses, strategy, tactics, planning, morale, or leadership. As it transpired, there is little evidence that the Iraqi leadership, such as it was, gave a great deal of coherent thought to how it might devise an effective strategy. Nor, it seems, did they trouble themselves to think very deeply about what their opponents might do, leaving their right flank open for hundreds of miles.[13]

Saddam Hussein had promised the mother of all battles, but his troops and commanders delivered instead the mother of all bugouts. Many officers, it seems, abandoned their troops early, leaving their pathetic charges to fend for themselves. However, because the Iraqi leadership seems to have had no feasible idea about how to deal with its opponent, this was probably best for all involved; thus the most popular "tactic" was to dig in at a respectable distance from potential bombing targets and to wait to surrender. The few battles organized by tank forces of the Republican Guard were brief (none lasted more than seventy-five minutes) and showed little coherent thought in that they were too far to the south, allowing the brunt of the U.S. offensive to flank them to the north. As Major General Barry R. McCaffrey of the 24th Infantry Division put it, the war resembled "an eighth grade team playing a pro football team." Or as one U.S. Marine suggested, "on a combat scale of 1 to 10, it was a 1."[14]

Indeed, the real achievement for U.S. combat forces in the Gulf War may well be in the way they routed their pathetic and terrified, but rather well-armed, enemies without killing many of them. In all, it seems likely that only a few thousand Iraqis were killed in the air and ground war in Kuwait and southern Iraq. The chief military lesson of the prosecution of the Gulf War may be, in John Heidenrich's words, that "military effectiveness is not synonymous with human slaughter."[15]

Containing and Harassing Iraq after the Gulf War, 1991–2003

As it turned out, the aftermath of victory in the Gulf War was messy. Egged on by Bush and by U.S. propaganda, groups opposing Saddam Hussein within Iraq—Kurds in the north, Shiite Muslims in the south—seized the opportunity and rebelled, expecting help from the victorious Americans. Then, even while triumphantly proclaiming the "Vietnam syndrome" to be a thing of the past, Bush proceeded to apply it: after blasting the pathetic Iraqi defenders out of their bunkers, he refused to intervene to get Saddam or to help the rebels because he did not want American troops to become involved in a Vietnam-style quagmire.[16] As the United States watched from the sidelines, the remnants of Saddam's army brutally put down the rebellions, causing a massive and well-publicized exodus of pathetic, fleeing Kurds toward and into Turkey, an important NATO ally. Meanwhile, Saddam Hussein remained defiantly in control in Iraq—very much contrary to the confident assumptions, made by most analysts, of his early demise.*

Eventually the administration was goaded into action. To help the refugee-besieged Turks, it established a safe zone in the north for the Kurds and, much later, it enforced a no-fly zone in the south to help the Shiites.[17] For twelve years and at considerable cost, the United States and, occasionally, its allies kept up a military campaign of focused bombing to harass and intimidate the Iraqi regime and to maintain the no-fly zones.

Economic sanctions were also applied. Before the war, the goal of the sanctions had been to pressure Iraq to leave Kuwait. During and after the war, however, the United States and the UN substantially escalated the requirements for sanctions to be lifted, demanding reparations and insisting that Iraq must allow various inspection teams to probe its military arsenal, particularly to make sure it had no nuclear, biological, or chemical weapons.

Iraq was peculiarly vulnerable to sanctions because so much of its economy was dependent on the export of oil, because it had not recovered from its lengthy war against Iran, and because the effects of sanctions were enhanced by the destruction of much of its rather advanced infrastructure during the Gulf War and by the truculent, even defiant, policies of the regime. The impact appears to have been devastating: analysts David Cortright and George Lopez call it "an appalling humanitarian tragedy," and a 1999 UN report concluded that "the gravity of the humanitarian situation of the Iraqi people is indisputable and cannot be overstated": the country has experienced "a shift from relative affluence to massive poverty."[18] Estimates are that the sanctions contributed to the deaths of hundreds of thousands of people in Iraq because of inadequate food and medical supplies as well as breakdowns in sewage and sanitation systems and in the electrical power systems needed to run them—systems destroyed by bombing in the Gulf War that

* In its first Sunday edition after the war, the *New York Times* published in adjacent columns two confident and entirely sensible predictions. In one, James E. Atkins, a career foreign service officer and Middle East specialist, asserted that "there is little reason to concern ourselves with Saddam. He has been defeated and humiliated and will soon be dead at the hands of his own people unless some unlikely country gives him refuge." In the other, *Times* columnist Anna Quindlen predicted with "reasonable" sureness that "George Bush will be re-elected President in 1992."

often went unrepaired as a result of sanctions-enhanced shortages of money, equipment, and spare parts.[19] It was not until 1998—nearly eight years after sanctions began—that Iraq was allowed to buy material for rebuilding its agricultural sector, water supply facilities, oil fields, and once-impressive medical system. Imports of some desperately needed materials were delayed or denied because of concerns that they might contribute to Iraq's programs for nuclear, chemical, or biological weapons. Chlorine, an important water disinfectant, was not allowed into the country because it might be diverted into making chlorine gas, the first chemical weapon used in World War I but later abandoned when more effective ones were developed. The sanctioners were wary throughout about allowing the importation of fertilizers and insecticides, fearing their use in production of weapons of mass destruction, and as a result, disease-carrying pests that might have been controlled proliferated. Although humanitarian exceptions to some of the restrictions were available all along, Iraq was sometimes slow to take advantage of them, and there often was administrative chaos and delays.[20]

Early on, Bush announced that the economic sanctions would be continued until "Saddam Hussein is out of there," and his deputy national security adviser declared that "Iraqis will pay the price while he remains in power." In 1997, President Bill Clinton's secretary of state, Madeleine Albright, announced that sanctions would not be lifted even "if Iraq complies with its obligations concerning weapons of mass destruction." The British made similar statements.[21] Unlike many dictators, Saddam Hussein had no other place to go; he was reasonably safe only in office and in control in Iraq. Therefore, the rather mild-sounding notion that he should be removed from office—that he should "step aside" in Bush's words—was effectively a death sentence to him. Not surprisingly, he remained uncooperative about allowing the sanctions to have this effect, regardless of the cost to the Iraqi people, whose suffering could be used to portray Iraq as the aggrieved party. He also apparently sought to rebuild his military capabilities.

In 1996, he relented somewhat and, in order to obtain some relaxation of the sanctions, allowed international arms inspectors into the country. But he remained wary of them, fearing that their activities could be used to fix his whereabouts—and indeed, later disclosures indicated that the arms inspections were being used to harbor spies.[22] When the inspectors demanded to investigate his central party headquarters in late 1998, he refused. The inspectors were then withdrawn (thus removing people who might become hostages), and the intermittent bombing of the country that had been going on since the Gulf War was briefly intensified.

In the meantime, support for the sanctions was waning, with only the United States and Britain remaining as dedicated advocates. As more and more counties came to question the effectiveness of the sanctions, and as the sanctions, partly in consequence, were more and more evaded by Iraq, they were further relaxed. This served to alleviate at least some of the suffering, but it was often late, and it remained inadequate to the scope of the problem.[23]

Although tens, probably hundreds, of thousands of Iraqis died in the extended aftermath of the Gulf War, none of these was the man who started the whole thing. The sanctioners hoped that their policy would encourage or help facilitate a coup, an assassination, an army revolt, a popular uprising, or a rebellion or invasion by armed dissidents. However, although such an undertaking was certainly possible, the prospects never seemed very bright. The memory of Saddam's brutal suppression of the 1991 uprising against him provided a strong disincentive for a repetition, and the opposition, both within the country and outside it, was splintered and infiltrated by agents.[24] The sanctions did not loosen his control, and he seemed exceedingly unlikely to become enticed to relinquish leadership, and life, over concern for the sufferings inflicted on the Iraqi people by economic sanctions and by his policies.

Thus, in an effort to accomplish ends they considered valid, the sanctioning countries consciously adopted military and economic policies that necessarily resulted in the deaths of large numbers of civilians, and many, like former UN secretary general Boutros Boutros-Ghali, were set to wondering "whether suffering inflicted on vulnerable groups in a target country is a legitimate means of exerting pressure on political leaders whose behavior is unlikely to be affected by the plight of their subjects."[25]

Somalia, 1992–94

Because of the criminal and clan-based warfare and predation that burgeoned in Somalia with the fall of Mohammed Siad Barre in 1991, famine developed, killing hundreds of thousands and sending even more fleeing. In March 1992, a ceasefire between warring clans allowed for the importation of food relief, but armed gangs, usually high on *qat*, a local amphetamine, looted these supplies and imposed taxes and protection levies; as a result, the food aid was effectively supporting the war effort and often failing to reach its intended recipients.[26]

With over a million lives at risk, the United Nations put together a military task force late in 1992 to protect food relief shipments. It declared the situation to be a threat to international peace—the first time a problem that was clearly internal and humanitarian had been so designated—and it did so without an explicit invitation from a coherent state. That is, as Ioan Lewis and James Mayall put it, "For the first time, statelessness was acknowledged to be a threat to an international society composed of sovereign states." The United States became the largest and most important contributor to this effort—of the eventual 33,656 troop deployment, 28,100 were American. There was a humanitarian motive for U.S. intervention, but it was impelled as well by a desire by many in the outgoing Bush administration to deflect the incoming Clinton administration from sending troops into the much more dangerous and uncertain Bosnian situation.[27]

The troops almost immediately brought order to the chaotic situation, food distribution proceeded with little problem and few casualties, and most of the American troops were withdrawn. Never before, perhaps, has so much been done for so many at such little cost. According to U.S. secretary of state Warren Christopher, the lowest estimate of the number of lives saved was 110,000, although some estimates do put the number at 10,000–25,000, with an approximate cost to the United States of $2.3 billion.[28]

Efforts to disarm the clans and their semi-associated hoodlums—an essentially hopeless enterprise, given the number of weapons in the country and neighborhood—ran into resistance, however. Then in June 1993, twenty-four Pakistani peacekeepers were killed, and their bodies mutilated, by a mob associated with one of the warlords, Mohammed Aidid. Aidid was summarily declared an outlaw, and the peacekeepers, particularly the Americans, set about trying to capture him and his henchmen. A series of heavily armed raids were unsuccessful at catching anybody, but they did cause a considerable number of Somali deaths through collateral damage as well as a concomitant escalation of Somali rage against the Americans.[29]

A raid on October 3 in the capital, Mogadishu, managed to capture several of Aidid's associates, but in the process a couple of U.S. helicopters were shot down. The body of a fallen U.S. Ranger was trapped in one of the crashed helicopters, and his comrades, already pinned down by Somali fire, were unwilling, according to their code, to leave it behind, so they staged a firefight until equipment could be brought in to free the remains and to rescue them. In the process, eighteen Americans were killed, one was captured, the body of another was dragged through the streets and photographed, and hundreds of Somalis were killed.[30]

In strict military terms, the October venture could have been considered a success. Although plans went awry and emergency measures had to be hastily improvised to compensate—something that is, of course, hardly uncommon in warfare—the mission was accomplished with resultant low casualties to the United States and high ones to the enemy. However, the stakes in the Somali venture were humanitarian, not military. There was considerable support for the effort when Bush had put it into effect in late 1992. But the 1993 Clinton policy of seeking to create a viable government there, known as "nation building," was much criticized by Republicans as unwise "mission creep," and congressional and public support for the venture was dampening even before the Americans were killed in the October firefight.[31] After that, support for the venture, already substantially reduced, it seems, to its hardcore supporters, dropped even further, and criticism became rampant. Clinton judiciously retreated. To save a bit of face, however, he let the troops stay on for six months, but only after making sure that no more were killed in combat situations. With that, other contingents from the UN force were withdrawn as well. While the troops remained, the situation remained reasonably orderly. Once they left, it descended again into chaos, although apparently at a somewhat attenuated level, whereas northern sections of the country, left to their own devices by the turmoil around the capital, managed to establish a degree of local order and economic viability, if one unrecognized by the international community.[32]

Despite the enormous number of lives the international mission appears to have saved, U.S. policy there has been labeled a failure in large part because a few Americans were killed in the process.[33] In essence, when Americans asked themselves how many American lives peace in Somalia was worth, the answer came out rather close to zero.[34]

The U.S. administration remained shy of repeating the performance. When genocide erupted in Rwanda in 1994, the United States worked to keep itself, and the international community, out of it.[35]

North Korea, 1994

The United States never actually sent troops into action in its confrontation with North Korea in 1994, but it certainly edged threateningly in that direction and, in the process, indicated what its primary values, concerns, and interests were.

Already the most closed and secretive society in the world, North Korea became even more isolated after the Cold War, when its former patrons, Russia and China, notably decreased their support. Its economy deteriorated into a shambles, and it was having trouble even feeding its population, conditions that were exacerbated by the fact that it continued to be led by an anachronistic Communist Party dictatorship whose leaders celebrated theory and persistent self-deception over reality. With their incessant fear of attack from the outside, they continued to spend 25 percent of their wealth to maintain a huge, if fuel-short, military force of more than a million underfed troops.[36]

According to some U.S. analysts, North Korea was also trying to develop nuclear weapons. By 1994, a U.S. national intelligence estimate concluded that there was "a better than even" chance that North Korea had the makings of a small nuclear bomb. This conclusion was hotly contested by other U.S. analysts and was later "reassessed" by intelligence agencies and found possibly to have been overstated. In addition, even if North Korea had the makings in 1994, skeptics pointed out, it still had several key hurdles to overcome in order to develop a deliverable weapon.[37]

Nonetheless, the Clinton administration was apparently prepared to go to war with the miserable North Korean regime to prevent or to halt its nuclear development, fearing the North Koreans might produce an arsenal of atomic bombs that could be sold abroad or used suicidally to threaten a country that possessed tens of thousands of its own. Accordingly, the United States moved to impose deep economic sanctions to make the isolated country even poorer (insofar as that was possible), a measure that garnered no support even from neighboring Russia, China, and Japan. It also moved to engage in a major military buildup in the area. So apocalyptic (or simply paranoid) was the North Korean regime about these two developments that some important figures think it might have gone to war on a preemptive basis if the measures had been carried out. A full-scale war on the peninsula, estimated the Pentagon, not perhaps without its own sense of apocalypse, could kill a million people, including 80,000–100,000 Americans, cost more than $100 billion, and commit economic destruction on the order of a trillion dollars.[38] A considerable price, one might think, to prevent a pathetic regime from developing weapons with the potential for killing a few tens of thousands, if they were actually exploded—an act that would surely be suicidal for the regime.

In effect and perhaps by design, however, the North Korean leaders seem mainly to have been practicing extortion. No one ever paid much attention to their regime except when it seemed to be developing nuclear weapons, and they appear to have been exceedingly pleased when the 1994 crisis inspired a pilgrimage to the country by former president Jimmy Carter, the most prominent American ever to set foot there. Carter quickly worked out a deal whereby North Korea would accept international inspections to guarantee that it wasn't building nuclear weapons. In exchange it graciously accepted a bribe from the West: aid, including some high-tech reactors that were capable of producing plenty of energy but no weapons-grade plutonium, as well as various promises about normalizing relations—promises that went substantially unfulfilled in the hope and expectation that the North Korean regime would soon collapse.[39]

In the next years, that hope sometimes seemed justified as floods and bad weather exacerbated the economic disaster that had been inflicted on North Korea by its rulers. Famines ensued, and the number of people who perished reached the hundreds of thousands or more, with some careful estimates putting the number at over two million. Food aid was eventually sent from the West, although in the early days of the famine there seem to have been systematic efforts in the United States to deny its existence in fear that a politics-free response to a humanitarian disaster would undercut its efforts to use food aid to wring diplomatic concessions from North Korea.[40]

A large-scale war had been seriously contemplated in 1994 as a way of keeping North Korea from potentially creating a few substantially unusable atomic bombs. However, no one in high places seems to have suggested that the human calamity there could best be arrested by using a policing war to take out the principal cause of the enormous sufferings of the North Korean people: their contemptible regime.

Haiti, 1994–96

When a military coup in Haiti threw out an elected government in 1991, President George Bush reacted harshly and declared that the situation in the tiny, impoverished country somehow posed "an unusual and extraordinary threat to the national security, foreign policy and economy of the United States." (Around the same time, the discredited dictatorship in a far more important country, Algeria, abrogated an election, but the United States reacted with studied calm, perhaps because the elections there were likely to be won by Muslim extremists.) To show his outrage, Bush slapped economic sanctions on the country. As usual, the sanctions scarcely weakened the thugs in charge, but they further impoverished just about everyone else, and this led to an exodus of hordes of pathetic refugees, many of whom made it to the United States with attendant political complications.[41]

In the election campaign of 1992, candidate Bill Clinton criticized Bush's handling of the situation and expressed ambiguous support for the refugees. After winning the election, he was saddled with the lingering problem and tried to work out a deal by which the dictatorship would voluntarily remove itself in favor of the elected president. When this process failed for various reasons, the administration moved in 1994 toward an invasion to set things right. In explaining the situation to the public, Clinton chose to echo Bush's earlier amazing hyperbole about the antidemocratic coup. Because of a flow of desperate refugees to the United States, the Haiti issue was probably of more national concern than were the problems in Somalia. However, the American public never seemed to grasp the urgency of the Haiti problem, and the policy never seems to have generated much support—although Clinton came under intense pressure on the issue from the black caucus in Congress, whose votes he needed on other issues.[42]

As the invasion was nearing, citizens Jimmy Carter and Colin Powell were able to convince the reigning military leaders that honor required them to leave peacefully. U.S. forces then reinstalled the elected government, gave it aid, and brought in the United Nations to help it get on its feet. Nothing worked very well—mostly because of endless political wrangles and stalemate—and in March 1996 U.S. troops were withdrawn in disgust, an event that rated eleven inches in a lower corner of page 14 of the *New York Times*.[43]

Bosnia, 1995

Dealing with the wars that broke out in Croatia in 1991 and in Bosnia in 1992—the first civil warfare in Europe in a generation—proved difficult for the leading developed states. They did much huffing and puffing, passed self-important resolutions, held peace conferences, and authorized the

United Nations variously to provide humanitarian aid and to establish a set of ambiguous "safe areas"—lightly defended enclaves in which refugees from ethnic cleansing could be housed and fed. Also, in 1992, they sent small numbers of troops to Macedonia, a former Yugoslav republic in which civil war seemed to threaten but never materialized.

Serb forces in Croatia and Bosnia remained dominated by criminals and became increasingly so.[44] Their opponents, however, began to develop real armies. Unprepared and badly outgunned at the beginning, independent Croatia, despite an international arms embargo, gradually built up and trained a conventional military force employing Western advisers and, essentially, receiving Western, particularly American, encouragement. To build *its* army, the Bosnian government embarked on a risky but successful military operation in October 1993 to destroy two of the most important criminal gangs in Sarajevo. These gangs had helped defend the capital in 1992 but had then taken control of various areas of the city, terrorizing non-Muslims and Muslims alike. An indication of their fighting tenacity is suggested by a report that many arrested in the raid quickly "repudiated their commanders and asked for clemency."[45]

As early as January 1993, only a year after Serbs had effectively partitioned their country, the new Croatian army launched an attack on several important targets in Serb-held territory and encountered little resistance.[46] In May 1995, it achieved another success in Croatia in a central area known as Sector West, taking control in thirty-two hours. Then, over three or four days in August, using plans partly devised by retired American generals, the army pushed the remaining Serb opposition from most of the rest of Croatia. For the most part these Serbs followed the example of its erstwhile "protectors" and simply ran. As Marcus Tanner puts it, "As soon as the bombardment started the Serb troops fled the frontlines, provoking a panicked flight into Bosnia by thousands of civilians, who left their houses with washing on the lines and meals half eaten on kitchen tables." Similar results were soon achieved in neighboring Bosnia by organized Croat and Bosnian forces. Even outnumbered, the Serb defenders could have delayed the advance and engaged in guerrilla harassment if they had had a capacity for disciplined combat. Instead, they ran, and many simply blended back into the population, where they reverted to ordinary crime and continue to prey on civilians.[47]

There had been much talk from time to time among the leading states, particularly those in NATO, about bombing Serb positions. The tactic had been tried a few times, but in each case it came to an embarrassed end when Serbs calmly took West European peacekeepers into custody and essentially held them for ransom. By the time of the Croat and Muslim offensives, however, there were no longer peacekeepers to kidnap: the Serbs had brutally extinguished the "safe areas," sending their foreign overseers packing, and peacekeepers had been quietly removed from other vulnerable areas.[48] Consequently, when an excuse presented itself, extensive bombing of Serb positions began and continued for several weeks.

Although the bombing campaign probably helped to concentrate the Serb mind, it may not have been necessary to obtain the resulting agreement that ended the war. Before the bombing even began, the Serb military position was falling apart as a result of Croatian ground attacks—whose importance, as United States negotiator Richard Holbrooke notes, was not appreciated by policy planners at the time. Moreover, the Bosnian Serbs had already agreed to let Serbian president Slobodan Milošević negotiate for them, giving him virtually total control over their fate. Since he had been repeatedly urging them for more than two years to accept various peace plans offered by the West, this appointment was close to an admission of defeat. Also relevant is the fact that the final agreement involved substantial concessions on the part of the Bosnian government.[49]

Kosovo, 1999

The consortium of developed countries known as NATO had been concerned for years by what was seen as the systematic persecution in the Yugoslav province of Kosovo of ethnic Albanians—a minority in the country but a huge majority in the province. As discussed in chapter 6, when a small group of terrorists started using violence to protest Serb dominance, the Yugoslav government made things much worse for itself by responding in 1998 with extensive and often indiscriminate violence, a campaign that vastly increased the ranks of the terrorists and their supporters.

Threats by NATO to bomb in 1998 seem to have been effective in causing Yugoslav president Slobodan Milošević to rein in the troops at least for a while. In the following year, however, Milošević decided, despite continued bombing threats, to launch another campaign to destroy the terrorists, expecting it to be quickly successful. A humanitarian disaster developed as masses of refugees were created, and with its bluff called, NATO commenced bombing in March 1999, at which point Serb violence dramatically escalated.

Unlike the situation in Somalia at the beginning of the decade, this venture did not occur in a place in which government had essentially ceased to exist. And unlike the situation in Bosnia in 1995, this was not a civil war situation that was taking place within an international context. NATO has consistently held Kosovo to be a part of Yugoslavia, which has a recognized government, and therefore the organization was openly intervening militarily in a domestic conflict within a coherently governed, sovereign country.

Like the United States over Haiti, NATO had become substantially self-entrapped on the Kosovo issue. Its bluff had been embarrassingly called, and its leaders had come to believe that its credibility and relevance were crucially at stake, even to the point of maintaining that the organization (at the time celebrating its fiftieth anniversary) would disintegrate if it did not stand up to the challenge. But there was also a compelling, if geographically limited, humanitarian component to its action. Non-Communist Europe had been substantially free of the violent persecution of minorities after World War II until the Yugoslav conflicts of the 1990s, and many strongly wanted that record to be reestablished. Europe had largely failed during the course of the wars in Croatia and Bosnia, but it intended to succeed now. As British prime minister Tony Blair put it, "We either stand aside and let this man conduct a policy effectively of racial genocide in a part of Europe or we say 'I'm afraid we're not going to allow that.' "[50]

For all that, NATO was careful to make sure that it suffered few, if any casualties itself, whatever might be happening to the Albanians they were seeking to protect. To preclude the possibility that they could be taken hostage, international monitors who had been placed in Kosovo under an earlier agreement were withdrawn in anticipation of the bombing campaign. Moreover, to keep the bombers outside the range of potential antiaircraft defenses, the bombing was conducted from high altitudes, considerably reducing its accuracy and effectiveness. And no ground action was anticipated or planned for. Hopes for success through bombing seem to have been based on the Milošević back-down in 1998 and on an overestimate of the effectiveness of the bombing of Bosnian Serbs in 1995—which, however, took far longer than the two days it was hoped would be needed in Kosovo. The Central Intelligence Agency estimated that there was a 50/50 chance Yugoslavia would relent if bombed, and a 50/50 chance that it wouldn't. One frustrated State Department official, yearning for certainty rather than a reasoned assessment of probabilities, denounced this estimate by "those bastards" for "having it both ways." No planning or provision was made for the possibility that the CIA's alternate outcome would transpire and that masses of refugees would be forced out of Kosovo.[51]

After nearly three months of bombing, Milošević finally gave in. The bombing was halted, and a deal was worked out that gave Kosovo effective, if not internationally recognized, independence, together with much international guidance and largess. No one knows precisely why Milošević finally decided to capitulate. He probably came to conclude that, despite early indications of dissension within the ranks, NATO would not split over the bombing policy and thus could keep it up forever, and that Russia, though critical of the bombing, would not come to his aid. He may also have feared an eventual invasion that would directly topple him, possibly from neighboring Hungary, which had recently been admitted to NATO. In addition, the deal he accepted had better terms than the one he had previously been offered by NATO.[52]

With Milošević's capitulation, the situation became even less safe for the Serbs in Kosovo, and ethnic cleansing of them by the now-vengeful Albanians occurred, or resumed, at a heightened pace. In 2000, the opposition in Serbia managed at long last to bury its disagreements and to coordinate its efforts. Aided by considerable sums of money from Western governments, it launched a massive election campaign and then staged demonstrations that finally ousted Milošević after he tried to steal the election.

Australia in East Timor, 1999

Before and after the August 30, 1999, government-approved referendum in which the East Timorese voted overwhelmingly for independence from Indonesia, thuggish militia groups under the control, or at least the influence, of the Indonesian army went on rampages, looting, pillaging, raping, and torching. They killed a thousand or more and displaced three-quarters of the new country's population.[53]

Australia led and mostly manned a force of several thousand policing troops sent by several countries—a "coalition of the willing"—under UN auspices. The militias had publicly sworn to defend the Indonesian flag "until the last drop of blood," but when the disciplined Australian troops arrived, this proved to be empty bravado and, except for a few scuffles, the militia groups simply disappeared.[54]

The British in Sierra Leone, 2000–2002

Chaos in Sierra Leone caused, as the *Economist* noted, by "a rabble of drugged-up teenagers with Kalashnikovs" continued until 2000, when several hundred disciplined British troops joined United Nations forces in the former British colony. This venture converted what was, in Michael Maren's words, "a ragtag collection of third world armies thrown at a problem" into something capable and competent. The difference was pungently put by a nineteen-year-old student: "We love the British soldiers—they are showing some military guarantee. They are well equipped. They are not like the U.N., like the Kenyans and Zambians who just gave up their arms and were taken hostage. They are not here to take any rubbish." By 2002, notes Michael Chege, Sierra Leone had come "back from the dead." The war was declared over with the surrender of tens of thousands of rebels and renegades, Britain was training a new army for the country, and elections were held.[55]

Afghanistan and the Campaign against Terrorism, 2001–2

After it was established that the terrorists who crashed airliners into New York's World Trade Center, Washington's Pentagon, and a field in Pennsylvania in September 2001 were linked to and apparently trained by al Qaeda, a group of foreign terrorists based in Afghanistan, the United States demanded of the fundamentalist Taliban government there that those Afghan residents the United States considered responsible for the attack be turned over to it. When the Taliban waffled on this request, the administration of George W. Bush, bolstered by favorable resolutions passed by NATO and the U.S. Congress, crucially aided by cooperation from Pakistan, which had previously supported the Taliban, and supported by an outraged domestic public, actively threw its considerable military support to the efforts of anti-Taliban forces in the civil war that had been going on for years in the country.

Those forces had often seemed remarkably disunited and thuggish in their behavior over the preceding decade. Mostly they were a shifting collection of warlord bands, and just about anyone with about ten thousand dollars could set one up. As an informed Afghan patiently explained, for that sum "you hire a hundred gunmen for a month, get a few Toyota pickups, and you're in business." The bands would then be sustained through extortion of wealthy merchants and traders and through agile involvement in the lucrative opium and heroin trade.[56]

It was a game the United Stated proved fully capable of playing. Operating warily (the cautionary wisdom was, "You can't buy an Afghan but you can rent one"), Special Forces teams and agents from the Central Intelligence Agency entered the country armed with large metal suitcases each packed with $3 million in U.S. currency in nonsequential $100 bills. With such sums, platoons of combatants were hired, each liberally paid between $100 and $1,000 a month and each furnished with a shiny new weapon embossed with a serial number. (In sensible concern that the combatants might sell the weapons while claiming they had lost them, they were only paid if they could produce their assigned weapon on pay day.) In addition, the Americans supplied two other crucial elements. One was leadership and tactical direction. The Afghans had a tendency to fight only until their ammunition ran out and to retire before finally securing their objective even when they had gained the upper hand. The Americans made sure their hired charges never ran out of ammunition, and they forcefully urged them on to complete each military task. The other element was the deft coordination of precision, and sometimes massive, bombardment from the air.[57]

After eight years of chaotic and often brutal rule, the Taliban had become deeply unpopular in the war-exhausted country, and its poorly trained forces, which a few years earlier had united the country by conquering or bribing the warlord bands that had been tearing the country apart, now mostly disintegrated under the air and ground onslaught. Many al Qaeda members did stand and fight, but few Afghans seemed to be willing to battle alongside these foreigners except under duress.[58]

The enterprise proved to be a remarkable success. Anticipations were that it might take years to finally dislodge the Taliban and al Qaeda, and plans were being made to send 50,000 or 55,000 American troops into the fray if necessary. But the ground and air onslaught quickly engendered the perception that victory was inevitable, and this attitude, combined with suitable remuneration, converted an increasing cascade of Taliban fighters ("behaving like chickens," according to their religious leader) and enticed warlords to switch sides without a fight. The country was secured in two months at a cost to the CIA of some $70 million. Along with those providing the massive airpower and some Marines who helped with the final occupation, the total American personnel involved in the conflict consisted of about 110 CIA officers and 316 from Special Forces. Two Americans were killed by the enemy in the operation, three died from friendly fire, and ten from accidents. The U.S. Navy and Air Force delivered some 6,500 strike missions from the air, and 57 percent of the ordnance was precision guided.[59]

Later, an operation was undertaken to dislodge residual al Qaeda elements from bases in remote mountainous terrain using a combination of U.S. and allied forces and Afghan proxies. The venture was only a qualified success because many of the most important al Qaeda and Taliban leaders were able to escape—a result sometimes attributed to an overreliance on the somewhat undermotivated and unreliable Afghans. Eleven Americans were killed in the operation as well as three friendly Afghans.[60]

In the wake of the war, a new, broad-based government was set up, many Afghans returned to their tortured country, and foreign aid and other forms of assistance were contributed by a large number of countries. A fair amount of security was set up, particularly in the capital, Kabul, but much of the country continued to be run by, or plagued by, entrepreneurial warlords following traditional modes of conduct. The central government has set about the daunting task of trying either to defeat the warlords or to co-opt them: "Now we call them 'regional leaders,'" noted one of Afghanistan's new government officials.[61] Complicating the process were various sporadic guerrilla and terrorist attacks, apparently launched by resurgent Taliban and al Qaeda elements, some of which inflicted additional American and allied casualties.

Iraq War, 2003–

There was wide consensus, particularly among developed countries, that Saddam Hussein's criminal regime in Iraq was a contemptible one. Moreover, it was reasonable to expect that a conventional military invasion by a disciplined army could eliminate the regime, and it seemed entirely possible that Iraq's ill-led and demoralized army, which had hardly fought at all when challenged in the Gulf War, would put up little armed resistance to such an attack.[62] Moreover, a policing war by an international force held out a reasonable prospect that a bloodbath—seemingly nearly inevitable in any Iraqi civil conflict—could be avoided. Nonetheless, there was not much stomach for such a war in the 1990s.

In the wake of the September 11, 2001, terrorist attacks in the United States, however, President George W. Bush began to think seriously about launching a war to remove Iraq's leader—rather in the way his father had deposed Noriega in Panama. In 2002, after the successful Afghan venture, the Bush administration began to set its sights on such a venture. Efforts to tie Iraq to international terrorism mostly proved futile, but fears that the dictatorial and unstable Saddam possessed or could develop weapons of mass destruction remained high, and these fears were now embellished by the argument that he might palm them off to dedicated terrorists for use in the United States. This argument enjoyed quite a bit of support with the American public and Congress, still reeling from the September 11 attacks.

The notion of an Iraqi war generated much less backing abroad, however, especially publicly, and the Americans were never able to get a resolution of support from any international body, although they tried hard both in NATO and at the UN. The leaders of most countries, including those bordering Iraq, never seemed to see that country as nearly as much of a threat as did the distant United States and its only notable ally on the issue, Tony Blair's United Kingdom. Most leaders found the evidence that Iraq possessed or was developing weapons of mass destruction—which had been banned in Iraq by various United Nations resolutions—unconvincing or incomplete, and along with many American analysts, they believed that the militarily pathetic Saddam could readily be deterred and contained.[63] Some also felt that the real motive behind the American drive to war was to secure Iraq's oil or to placate neoconservatives, particularly in the Defense Department, who were mainly out to make the Middle East safe for Israel.[64] Bush did voice the humanitarian argument that Saddam Hussein was a monster whose removal from the planet would make it a far better place for the tyrannized and victimized citizens of Iraq. But this justification was not stressed nearly as much as were Iraq's apparent violation of UN disarmament resolutions as well as the threat Iraq was held to present to the United States and to American interests in the Middle East, especially through links to terrorism. The administration apparently didn't think the purely humanitarian argument would generate sufficient domestic or international support.

In any case, determined to see it out, Bush shrugged off international disapproval and fabricated a small and personalized "coalition of the willing," which included, mainly, the British and some Australians, and sent the U.S. military into action. Notably, despite widespread disapproval of the venture, the invaders did not have to worry that other states, particularly from the developed world, would come to the assistance of the beleaguered Iraqi regime—a considerable change from the days of the Cold War.

As expected, the Iraqi military performed in about the same manner as it had in 1991: basically, it disintegrated under the American onslaught and seems to have lacked any semblance of a coherent strategy of resistance. A reporter's observation from the later war could hold as well for the earlier one: "The battlefields I walked over revealed signs of panicky flight: Iraqi gas masks and uniforms abandoned; armored vehicles left in revetments where they could not see advancing U.S. armor, much less shoot at it; blanket rolls left out in the open. I searched for bodies and bloodstains but saw neither on battlefields where Iraqi vehicles hit by Marines were still smoking. Defenders must have run before Marine fire reached them. Iraqi officers deserted their men . . . and this abandonment almost certainly triggered full flight by all ranks." Putative fighting units lacked training, adequate equipment and ammunition, and the capacity to communicate with each other. Directives from Saddam's headquarters, when they came at all, were erratic and often contradictory—the "orders of an imbecile . . . like a teenager playing a video war game," one Iraqi general recalled bitterly, and, in the end, "no one was willing to die for Saddam."[65] Total battle deaths for the American and British forces during the war were well under 150, even lower than had been borne in the Gulf War of 1991.

In a matter of weeks, then, Iraq was relieved of two vicious regimes: the twenty-five-year-old one of Saddam Hussein and the thirteen-year-old one of international sanctions. In concert, these regimes had inflicted far more death in an incremental fashion than had been caused by the wars of the Bushes in combination.

The fat lady sang in Bush's father's war: once Iraq was expelled in 1991, the Kuwaiti regime came back from exile and took over, and American troops traveled home to parade victoriously in American cities. No such pleasant fate greeted their successors in 2003; they had to remain to build a viable national government out of the rubble that remained after Saddam, the sanctions, and the war had taken their toll. It had been hoped that the Iraqis would greet the conquerors by dancing happily in the streets and somehow coordinate themselves into a coherent, and appreciative, government. But although many were glad to see Saddam's tyranny ended, the invaders often found the population resentful and humiliated rather than gleeful or grateful. Moreover, bringing order to the situation was vastly complicated by the fact that the government-toppling invasion had effectively created a failed state that permitted criminality and looting of the sort found, for example, in Somalia. In addition, some people—including some foreign terrorists drawn opportunistically to the area—were dedicated to sabotaging the victors' peace and to killing the policing forces. Having been shunned by the Bush administration, the international community was not eager to join in the monumental reconstruction effort. The inability of the conquerors to find any evidence of those banned and greatly feared weapons of mass destruction (the administration's "conservative estimate" had been that Iraq possessed a stockpile of 100 to 500 tons of chemical weapons alone), much less links to international terrorism, only enhanced this reluctance.

THE POST–COLD WAR EXPERIENCE

Martin van Creveld has argued that armies are being "replaced by police-like security forces on the one hand and bands of ruffians on the other."[66] The record of developed countries since the Cold War 1990s suggests that, applying reasonable military standards, such policing is not likely to be terribly difficult or costly. In these cases, disciplined forces were in various ways mainly up against criminal ones or against ones representing criminal or substantially criminalized regimes. In all of them, the disciplined forces triumphed easily and at remarkably low cost in casualties, although in the case of Somalia the peacekeepers found that cost to be insufficiently low given the value of the stakes and in Iraq the casualty costs of the post-war occupation continued to mount disconcertingly.

There are other suggestive instances during the period as well. When the Tutsis eventually were able to get their comparatively capable army into Rwanda in 1994, they had to battle for the capital city against a small yet rather determined force but took over the rest of the country with a minimum of fighting. For the most part, Hutu authorities, like their counterparts in the former Yugoslavia, simply ordered their forces and other genocidal marauders to flee when confronted with military force.[67] Then, in pursuit of the fleeing Hutu génocidaires in neighboring Zaire, they came up against the thuggish, criminalized Zaire army, filled, in Michela Wrong's description, with "angry young men in their pimp sunglasses, Kalashnikov cartridge belts Scotch-taped together, trousers held up with bootlace." This organization, so adept at preying on civilians, simply collapsed when confronted with a reasonably coherent military force put together by the Tutsis, who defeated it in what Wrong calls "one of the swiftest campaigns in modern African history." Meanwhile in Liberia, even the minimally competent, substantially corrupt, underpaid, and undermotivated troops of ECOMOG could continue to hold the capital and other areas against the rebels. In breakaway Abkhasia, National Guardsmen supported by Russian military units easily defeated political party militias (popularly and derisively differentiated by their drug preferences as "hashishists" or morphinists") that were sent against them from central Georgia. After the Soviets had been driven out of Afghanistan in 1989, many of the mujahideen bands disintegrated into banditry and warlordism, as noted in the previous chapter, and when these formerly effective but now decadent warrior bands were confronted in 1994 and 1995 by the disciplined, even fanatical, forces of the newly created Taliban, many of them simply collapsed in disarray, sometimes without a shot being fired as noted earlier in this one. Frequently, the Taliban bribed commanders to switch over to their side.[68] And the ability of disciplined, if newly formed Croatian and Bosnian forces to rout the criminalized Serbs was discussed earlier.

Thus, it seems, "bands of ruffians" can readily be policed. The intimidating, opportunistic thugs have been successful mainly because they are the biggest bullies on the block. However, like most bullies (and sadists and torturers), they tend not to be particularly interested in engaging a formidable opponent. Moreover, they substantially lack organization, discipline, coherent tactics or strategy, deep motivation, broad popular support, ideological commitment, and, essentially, courage—and, as van Creveld aptly puts it, "but for its fighting spirit, no armed force is worth a fig."[69] Therefore, a sufficiently large, impressively armed, and well-disciplined policing force can be effective in pacifying thug-dominated conflicts and removing thuggish regimes. The thugs would still exist, of course, and many might remain in the area, but insofar as they remained unpacified, they would be reduced to sporadic and improvised crime and violence, not town or area mastery.

The record suggests, then, that it is possible to use policing wars to order the new world—or at least to eliminate many of the criminal regimes and to pacify many of the criminalized civil wars that are the main source of unnatural death and deprivation in the world. The prospect that this ordering will take place in a systematic manner is evaluated in the next chapter.

CHAPTER 8

THE PROSPECTS FOR POLICING WARS

The post–Cold War experiences with policing wars outlined in the previous chapter were generally successful—at least in their own terms. Civil wars were halted and vicious regimes were ousted or significantly constrained. It would seem, then, that the prospects for international police work after the Cold War are considerable. This chapter explores the possibility that the developed states will be able to respond to this opportunity by creating mechanisms for systematically carrying out such policing wars.

In general, the prospects seem limited. In the wake of the mostly American intervention in Iraq in 2003, extensive enthusiasm for, or fears of, a wide set of mainly U.S.-led policing wars erupted, often centered around the slippery concept of "hegemony" and around the feasibility or desirability of establishing a new "American Empire." However, it does not appear likely that the international community—or the Americans alone—will be able to rise to the challenge or maintain the required momentum to institutionalize the process. Nor are they likely consistently to support the establishment of adequate peacekeeping forces staffed by international civil servants or by hired private military companies. A systematic solution to the problems of civil warfare and of vicious regimes lies elsewhere.

IMPEDIMENTS TO INTERNATIONAL POLICING

There seem to be several reasons why developed countries are unable systematically to fabricate effective international policing forces.[1]

Lack of Interest

The dynamic of the Cold War contest caused the two sides to believe that their interests were importantly engaged almost everywhere. A central tenet of Communist ideology was that violent revolutionary conflict was pretty much inevitable and that the Communist states were duty bound to help out wherever it cropped up. Meanwhile, the Western policy of containment was based on the notion that any gain for Communism would lead to further Western losses elsewhere and therefore that just about all Communist thrusts must be actively opposed. Although few wars were directly initiated by the major belligerents during the Cold War, quite a few local wars were exacerbated by interfering Cold War contestants. At times they restrained—or tried to restrain—their smaller clients, but more often they eagerly helped.[2] Once this elemental contest evaporated, however, most areas of the world became substantially less important to developed countries. In the early 1960s, a civil war in the Congo inspired dedicated meddling by both sides; in the late 1990s, no one much wanted to become involved in the complicated and hugely destructive civil war, or sets of civil wars, that ravaged that country.

Thus, in the wake of the Cold War, two contradictory, even paradoxical, developments took place. On the one hand, East–West and major country cooperation became far easier to arrange than before. On the other hand, these countries found few trouble spots worthy of their efforts. That is, although developed countries have an interest in peace and stability, they probably will be stirred to significant action—sending their troops into harm's way—only in those few remaining areas where they feel their interests to be importantly engaged.

Determining exactly what a country will decide is in its interests, however, is a slippery process. For example, it is not always easy to see what the interest of the interveners was in the array of policing wars and interventions discussed in the previous chapter if one applies classic, hardnosed concepts of vital national interest. These concepts, suggests Robert DiPrizio, might be taken to include a state's survival; protection of its land, people, and economic vitality; and maybe protection of close allies and of a country's prestige or honor.[3]

Thus the applications of military force against Panama and against Iraq in Kuwait seem to have been impelled to a considerable degree by the personal animus of the president of the United States against those countries' resident dictators. Noriega never threatened the Panama Canal, which might seem to be the only really substantial U.S. interest in the area. And although the principle that aggression cannot be tolerated does sensibly need to be defended, sanctions had already rendered Saddam's gains in Kuwait utterly vaporous and had massively punished him. Moreover, as critics pointed out at the time, sanctions might eventually have driven him from his conquest without war, at least if accompanied by some limited face-saving gimmicks.[4]

The ventures in Haiti, Bosnia, and Kosovo seem to have emerged as much out of self-entrapping rhetoric—or sanctimonious huffing and puffing—as anything else. The idea that Haiti has much of anything to do with U.S. security can seem absurd, as can the notion that events in a fragmented, distant Yugoslavia—more nearly the armpit of Europe than its heart in the view of many on that continent—are vital to the fate of the prosperous and productive peoples to its north and west. The ventures in Somalia and Sierra Leone were almost purely humanitarian, and it is difficult to see how anyone who has looked at a map could conclude that East Timor is important to Australia because it perches on that country's doorstep. And why the United States, after a half century of living with and deterring a dedicated enemy with thousands of nuclear weapons, should be so concerned that pathetic, impoverished, distant North Korea might obtain a few is not all that clear.

The traumatic terrorist attacks of September 11, 2001, may have impelled the U.S. venture in Afghanistan, but the invasion often seems to have been as much a matter of rage and revenge as one of sober calculation of national interest.[5] International policing measures—greatly accelerated at the same time—were probably more important for dealing with terrorism. Concerns about terrorism were also in the mix in the justifications for the U.S. war against Iraq, although there was little or no evidence of a connection, and the idea that an armed Iraq was a present or future threat to the region was unclear to almost all of its neighbors. Saddam was so wary of his own army that he would not allow it to bring heavy weapons anywhere near Baghdad out of fear that the troops might turn and use them against his government. Moreover, given the country's pathetic showing in the Gulf War and given the wary hostility of its neighbors, Saddam might have been adequately deterred and contained by policies far less costly to the Iraqi people and, for that matter, to the sanctioning countries.[6]

There is nothing new, however, about this condition. As Warner Schilling observes crisply, "At the summit of foreign policy one always finds simplicity and spook." For example, he suggests that American opposition to Japan's expansion in East Asia in the 1930s "rested on the dubious proposition that the loss of Southeast Asia could prove disastrous for Britain's war effort and for the commitment to maintain the territorial integrity of China—a commitment as mysterious in its logic as anything the Japanese ever conceived." Melvin Small concurs: "The defense of China was an unquestioned axiom of American policy taken in along with mother's milk and the Monroe Doctrine. . . . One looks in vain through the official papers of the 1930s for some prominent leader to say, 'Wait a second, just why is China so essential to our security?'" And Bruce Russett notes that U.S. leaders were affected by the "sentimental American attitude toward China as a 'ward'" and may have managed to come to see China as a significant economic partner, even though by placing an embargo on Japan they were "giving up an export trade at least four times that with China."[7]

Nor did the Cold War policy of containment—with its overarching theory about confronting Communist expansionism—inspire a great deal of consis-

;y in U.S. foreign policy.[8] Even as the policy was being formulated in the 1940s, the administration was allowing China to fall into the Communist camp. In the 1950s, it proved unwilling to use military measures to prevent a Communist victory in Indochina but held fast on the tiny islands of Quemoy and Matsu off the China coast. And in the 1960s, it sought to shore up the anti-Communist position in South Vietnam even as it agreed to give the Communists effective control of large portions of neighboring Laos.

Following in this tradition, then, the post–Cold War involvement by developed countries has been quite capricious. Bosnia fired the imagination (although not much action for years), while the much worse civil war in Sudan was substantially ignored. Haiti arrested attention, but not the catastrophes in Liberia or Algeria. Efforts were made to deal with the civil war–induced famine in Somalia but not the much greater one in Congo a few years later. Disasters perpetrated on their own people by Indonesia in East Timor, the Taliban in Afghanistan, and Saddam Hussein in Iraq were tolerated for years, and the policing wars that eventually removed the problems were triggered mostly by fortuitous, and sometimes unrelated, events.

When active, militarized interest is stirred, then, it is generally because developed countries have concluded that their own concerns have (somehow) become involved, because they have been self-entrapped by their own rhetoric, because their domestic politics demand it, or because their leaders are personally piqued. Iraq and North Korea may sport regimes that are contemptible in the extreme and disasters to their own people, but the interest of the developed states is almost entirely bound up with the fear that those countries might develop weapons that could threaten the outside world. The United States was impelled into the Haitian morass substantially because of domestic pressures and because of the politically embarrassing flow of refugees that had been created largely by the economic sanctions the United States had imposed on that country. Conflict in the Balkans sent an inconvenient flow of refugees northward, and the violence there raised fears it might somehow spread elsewhere in Europe. The Australians sent policing forces to East Timor in large part because it wants to live in a stable neighborhood, whatever that means. Interventions, as Philipp Genschel and Klaus Schlichte observe, "are driven more strongly by political imperatives in the intervening states than by the circumstances of the civil war they are designed to pacify."[9]

Fears of international terrorism took on a much heightened urgency after the devastating attacks on the World Trade Center in New York and Washington on September 11, 2001, and, conceivably, this urgency could lend a degree of continuity and coherence to future interventionist policy. However, as noted, the threat of Communism did not accomplish this during the Cold War. Moreover, it is doubtful that the campaign against terrorism will lead to very many episodes like the one in Afghanistan because in the future, regimes that harbor terrorists are unlikely to be so open about it whereas, insofar as they need bases at all, international terrorists are likely to concentrate even less than they do now.

The Ancient Hatreds Image

Leaders and publics in developed states have often concluded that many civil wars are essentially inexplicable, all-against-all conflicts rooted in old hatreds that could hardly be ameliorated by well-meaning, but innocent and naive, outsiders. It follows, therefore, that intervention would at best be simply a short-term palliative and thus a pointless exertion.

This convenient excuse for inaction was developed in the early 1990s when civil war shockingly broke out in Yugoslavia, on a continent that had been free from civil war for more than forty years. The need for an explanation, preferably a simple one, was handily supplied by pundits such as the fashionable travel writer and congenital pessimist Robert Kaplan. In a book and, probably much more importantly, in a 1993 front-page article in the Sunday *New York Times Book Review,* he portentously proclaimed the Balkans to be "a region of pure memory" in which "each individual sensation and memory affects the grand movement of clashing peoples." These processes of history and memory had been "kept on hold" by Communism for forty-five years, "thereby creating a kind of multiplier effect for violence." With the demise of that suppressing force, he argued, ancient, seething national and ethnic hatreds were allowed spontaneously to explode into nationalist violence.[10] This perspective was elaborated into a cosmic worldview by Harvard's Samuel Huntington under the snappy label "clash of civilizations." Huntington acknowledged that there had been little or no ethnic violence in Yugoslavia before World War II, but he still prominently designated the Bosnian war as one of those crucial clashes of civilization or fault-line wars that "rarely ends permanently" because "when one side sees the opportunity for gain, the war is renewed." He argued that if the United States withdrew from Bosnia, the war there very likely would erupt again.[11]

This perspective informed some of the reluctance of the Bush administration to become involved in Bosnia and also, initially, in Somalia, and it was soon also embraced by the Clinton administration. Thus, waxing eloquent about the Bosnian conflict on national television in 1995, Vice President Al Gore allowed as how the tragedy had been unfolding, "some would say, for five hundred years." President Bill Clinton, not to be outdone, opined on the same show that "their enmities go back five hundred years, some would say almost a thousand years." The exact identity of the hyperbolic "some" was not specified, but one source, perhaps, was Henry Kissinger, who has noted authoritatively that "ethnic conflict has been endemic in the Balkans for centuries" (as opposed to gentle, trouble-free western Europe presumably), and, onizingly and absurdly, that "none of the populations has any experience with—and essentially no belief in—Western concepts of toleration." As the discussion in chapter 6 suggests, this explanation, so convenient to those favoring passivity, was substantially flawed. But, as Brian Hall observes, "literary clichés do not die easily, especially when informed by superficialities."[12]

In some respects this perspective derives from the Hobbesian image of civil war. Because Hobbes assumes that *every* person is, at base, "radically insecure, mistrustful of other men and afraid for his life," he concludes that the only way out of the mess is for everyone permanently to surrender to an authoritarian ruler, one who primarily values glory and stability rather than doctrinal orthodoxy or ideological (or ethnic) purity, and one who will maintain the force necessary to keep people from once again giving in to their natural proclivities for isolation, hostility, and insensitivity to the rights of others.[13]

The experience with civil war as discussed in this book, however, suggests that this monumental—perhaps even impossible—task is hardly required. Most people most of the time do not have a great deal of difficulty getting along and in fabricating useful rules and patterns of conduct that allow them to coexist peacefully.[14] Police may indeed be needed, even necessary, to maintain order, but they need not normally be numerous nor must their control be Leviathan-like. This is because they mainly need simply to protect the many from the few, rather than everyone from everyone else as Hobbes—or at least the Hobbesian image—would have it. That is, the policing forces do not have to deal with a broad population, but only with a small, violent segment.

At one extreme, the all-against-all image can lead authorities or members of a threatened group to reach the essentially racist conclusion that the only effective method for eliminating a threat that emanates from a definable group is to annihilate the group itself. This simple if horrendous conclusion has been, as Benjamin Valentino has demonstrated, a major reason for huge population transfers and for mass killing.[15] At the other extreme, the image can discourage policing by suggesting that the costs would be enormous because the entire group must be directly and completely controlled, rather than just a small, opportunistic, and often quite cowardly subgroup.

Low Tolerance for Casualties

The international community has had an extremely low tolerance for casualties in military missions that are essentially humanitarian—that is, in ventures in which important national interests are not, do not appear to be, or cannot be made to seem to be at stake.

The U.S. experience in Somalia demonstrated this axiom, as discussed in chapter 7. It can also be seen in the general reluctance to become involved in the fighting in Bosnia in the early 1990s, despite years of the supposedly action-impelling "CNN effect," despite dedicated efforts by Western journalists to impel intervention, and despite the fact that Europe is generally held to be closer to American interests than are impoverished areas of Africa.[16]

Before U.S. troops were committed to Bosnia in late 1995, some 67 percent of the American public said it would favor sending the troops if none were killed, but this figure plunged to 31 percent if it was suggested that twenty-five U.S. combatants might die. This phenomenon seems to be general. By 1997, Spanish troops had suffered seventeen deaths during their postwar policing of the deeply troubled city of Mostar, and the Spanish government, indicating that this was enough for them, withdrew from further confrontation, which greatly encouraged the Croat gangs in the city. Similarly, Belgium abruptly withdrew from Rwanda—and, to save face, urged others to do so as well—when ten of its policing troops were massacred and mutilated early in the genocide.[17] Such intolerance for casualties led to the pulling out of peacekeepers, inspectors, and other potential hostages from Bosnia in 1995, from Iraq in 1998 and 2003, and from Kosovo in 1999 before bombing was commenced. To avoid additional casualties in Kosovo, the United States carried out the bombing from some 15,000 feet, where it was far less likely to be effective.

It is sometimes argued that effective presidential cheerleading can induce a reluctant public to accept dangerous peacekeeping missions, and President Bill Clinton tried that tact at the end of 1995 as he was about to send policing troops to Bosnia. Poll data, however, demonstrate that even though it was expected that there would be few casualties, Clinton was never able to increase the numbers of Americans who saw wisdom or value in sending troops. Similarly, the Presidents Bush were unable to shift public opinion decisively in their favor in the run-ups to their wars against Iraq in 1991 and 2003.[18]

This reluctance should not be seen as some sort of new isolationist impulse. Americans were willing, at least at the outset, to send troops to die in Korea and Vietnam, but that was because they subscribed to the containment notion, holding Communism to be a genuine threat to the United States that needed to be stopped wherever it was advancing. Polls from the time make it clear they had little interest in losing American lives simply to help out the South Koreans or South Vietnamese. Thus, an unwillingness to send Americans to die for purposes that are essentially humanitarian is hardly new. Nor is it unusual for humanitarian ventures: if Red Cross or other workers are killed while carrying out humanitarian missions, their organizations frequently withdraw, no matter how much good they may be doing, essentially saying that the saving of lives is not worth the deaths of even a few of their service personnel.* Where deep national interests are, or seem to be, at

---

* On the other hand, there seems to be little political problem in keeping occupying forces in place, even in ventures deemed of little importance, as long as they are not being killed. After the Somalia fiasco, the Americans stayed on for several months and, since none were

e, however, tolerance of casualties can be high. The only policing war discussed in chapter 7 for which this is true is the U.S. intervention in Afghanistan in pursuit of the terrorist organizations that had attacked the United
States itself.[19]

I have argued that policing thug-dominated conflicts and toppling thug-
dominated regimes probably would be neither terribly difficult nor terribly
costly. In Bosnia, for example, it might have taken a fair number of troops,
perhaps more than 100,000, but there would likely have been little real fighting, and most of the troops would probably not have had to stay long. In estimates that seem to be regarded as militarily sound, the local UN commander
and other experts have suggested that 5,000 well-equipped and determined
soldiers with a free hand to fight could probably have brought the genocide
perpetrated by murderous, rampaging thugs in Rwanda rapidly to a halt.
And if the 2,000 U.S. Marines dispatched to Liberia in 1990 to extricate
Americans there had stayed on, they could in all probability have headed off
the set of civil wars that would devastate that country off and on over the next
decade and a half.[20]

It would be impossible, however, to guarantee that such operations could
be carried off with extremely few—or no—casualties. Thugs may be cowardly, but a few might fight, especially if cornered, and some might lob shells
or snipe at the policing forces. Even the most criminalized forces may contain among their membership a few dedicated, even fanatical, combatants
who are willing to die for the cause, as the United States discovered in Iraq.
The damage such people can inflict is likely to be minor by ordinary military
standards, but in many cases, the potential for damage can make such a venture a nonstarter politically.

Aversion to Long-Term Policing

As noted in chapter 6, it may be more sensible to envision civil violence in
many instances as criminal activity rather than as warfare because policing
methods are more to the point than are military ones. That is, the guiding
image should be one of dreary, restrained, methodical, patient police (or social) work rather than one of glistening technology and the "decisive" battle.
The criminals and thugs will still exist after peace is achieved, and although

---

killed, little attention was paid or concern voiced. Similarly, although there was little public
support for sending U.S. troops to Haiti, there was also almost no public concern about keeping them there as long as none were killed. At the end of 1995, Clinton told a skeptical American public that the policing troops being sent to Bosnia would only be there for a year. Although many Americans afterward came to see Clinton as a liar, this is not the instance of
deception upon which they based that conclusion. In fact, there was not much protest, or even
notice, that the troops were still there when the nation entered the new millennium. If they
are not being killed, it scarcely matters whether the troops are in Macedonia or in Kansas.

their predation will now look more like simple crime, it will still be irksome and will require continuous, routine, drab policing, just as it does in other societies that are at what we take to be peace. There may also be intense ethnic fears and hatreds—more likely the consequence of the conflict than the cause of it—to deal with.

Developed countries often have an aversion to such long-term policing, and a realistic concern about the long, unpleasant aftermath often inspires a reluctance to intervene in the first place. The experience in Somalia brought this home, and the one in Haiti enhanced it. A contrast of the edgy tedium of Cyprus and Northern Ireland with the dramatic catastrophe of Bosnia suggests that the patient police work carried out in Nicosia and Belfast probably saved thousands of lives over the years. But it tends to be a profoundly thankless job because the people whose lives have been saved don't know who they are, and they are often critical or even contemptuous of their unappreciated saviors. Such probable ingratitude further deflates the policing enthusiasm of the international community.

In the wake of the 2003 policing war in Iraq, a prominent hawkish columnist frankly observed that "two quick wars have made U.S. soldiers the main guarantors of national integrity in Iraq and Afghanistan for years to come." The difficult and costly aftermaths of those wars—in which important interests were, or seemed to be, at stake—are likely to embellish the already considerable wariness in the developed world about engaging in such activity. The problems developed countries have maintaining a momentum of commitment and concern after successful policing wars is illustrated by the Afghanistan case, where interest dropped significantly after the country no longer served as a base for international terrorists. Aid from the United States and from other developed countries was sent to assist the new, vastly improved government installed to replace the Taliban, but at levels far lower than had been promised at the height of the fighting. In fact, the U.S. administration initially forgot to include Afghan aid in its budget request a year after the war.[21]

Lack of Political Gain from Success

George Bush obviously achieved little lasting electoral advantage from his dramatic victory in the 1991 Gulf War, and lesser accomplishments have been at least as unrewarding politically. Clinton found that the more purely humanitarian (but casualty-free) intervention in Bosnia of 1995 scarcely helped in his reelection efforts a year later; by the time the election came around, people could scarcely remember the venture. Similarly, at the time of the Kosovo bombings of 1999, press accounts argued that the presidential ambitions and political future of Clinton's vice president, Al Gore, hung in the balance.[22] From the standpoint of public opinion, the Kosovo venture ns to have been a success, but when he launched his campaign for the presidency a few months later, Gore scarcely thought it important or memorable enough to bring up.

In general, it appears that the natural tendency of most publics is to pay international issues little heed and instead to focus principally on domestic matters. Attention can be diverted by major threats or by explicit, specific, and dramatic dangers, but once these concerns fade, people generally return to domestic issues with considerable alacrity—rather like "the snapping back of a strained elastic," as Gabriel Almond once put it. For example, despite all the publicity, Americans for the most part reported paying close attention to events in Bosnia only when a U.S. pilot was temporarily lost behind enemy lines and when Clinton moved to send policing troops to the country. In the last seventy years, in fact, only a few events have notably caused the American public to divert its attention from domestic matters, and at no time between the Tet offensive in the Vietnam War in early 1968 and the terrorist bombings of September 11, 2001, did foreign policy issues outweigh domestic ones when the public was asked to designate the country's most important problem.[23]

To those preoccupied by foreign affairs, this proclivity may resemble an attention deficit disorder. Yet it also means that if things go wrong in low-valued ventures, troops can be readily removed with little concern about saving face or about longer-term political consequences, although the episode will hardly be something to brag about, of course. For example, the combat deaths of U.S. soldiers in Somalia in 1993 enhanced demands for withdrawal (after the lone American prisoner of war was recovered), not calls to revenge the humiliation, and by the time the 1996 election rolled around, the public had substantially forgotten about the event. This may hold even for ventures that are highly valued initially. As noted in chapter 5, the perceived foreign policy value of maintaining the American position in Vietnam declined for years, and then, most importantly, the United States had gotten its prisoners of war back in 1973. For this and other reasons, Americans accepted the 1975 defeat there with remarkable equanimity.* Of greater electoral concern would be a situation in which peacekeepers are taken hostage, something that can suddenly and disproportionately magnify the perceived stakes because of the very high value people tend to place on the lives of their own countrymen.[24] However, the fact that politicians do not necessarily seem to suffer political damage for international policy failure hardly

---

* Amazingly, the 1975 debacle was actually used by the man who presided over it, Gerald Ford, as a point in his *favor* in his 1976 reelection campaign. When he came into office, he observed, "we were still deeply involved in the problems of Vietnam," but now "we are at peace. Not a single young American is fighting or dying on any foreign soil" (Kraus 1979, 538–39). His challenger, Jimmy Carter, seems to have concluded that it was politically disadvantageous to point out the essential absurdity of Ford's ingenious argument.

compensates for the fact that they receive little or no political gain from its success.

The Bias against War and Aggression

For effective international policing to become the norm, it would be necessary for the international community explicitly, clearly, and systematically to abandon or reinterpret the concept of sovereignty. The United Nations Security Council appears in recent years to have developed the legal ability to intervene in civil wars or to declare a state government too incompetent or too contemptible to be allowed to continue to exist, and it can accordingly authorize military intervention. That is, it can decertify a state and topple its leadership by sending in a military force of its own or by calling on others to use their forces to do so. And a number of people, including most prominently UN secretary general Kofi Annan, have suggested that it may be time for "individual sovereignty"—the fundamental freedom of each individual—to take precedence over state sovereignty in some instances.[25]

In several of the experiences after the Cold War, developed countries, or at least some of them, inched in the direction of moving beyond sovereignty. The U.S. policing war (or aggression) against sovereign, if thug-run, Panama opened the 1990s, and NATO's policing war (or aggression) against Milošević's sovereign Serbia closed it. And shortly after he took the presidency of the United States at the start of the new century, George W. Bush concluded that a policing war (or aggression) against Iraq to remove its troublesome regime made a lot of sense.

The decertification process could be a way for the Security Council to tidy up the legal issue, but it seems unlikely that the biases against aggression and war and in favor of sovereignty so carefully and deeply cultivated in the developed world and elsewhere over the last century, as discussed in chapters 2–5, can be adequately overcome except in special cases. Moreover, some members with vetoes in the Security Council are wary of the precedent. Thus, Russia, with its civil war in Chechnya, and China, with several secessionist movements in its west, were notably unenthusiastic about sanctifying the NATO venture in Kosovo in 1999. And, of course, tyrannies that have reason to believe they may find themselves on the international community's hit list have every incentive to arm themselves—in the cases of North Korea and Iran, perhaps with nuclear weapons—to deter the policing action, something that is undesirable from a different perspective.

OVERCOMING THE IMPEDIMENTS

There exist methods, at least in principle, for eliminating or significantly reducing the problems developed countries experience in policing criminal warfare. One of these is to establish a competent standing United Nations military force. Another is to hire private military companies. And a third is to rely on "coalitions of the willing," with troops contributed by interested countries on an ad hoc basis. On closer examination, however, none of these approaches seems especially promising.

The prospects for United Nations peacekeeping rose considerably after the Cold War. Indeed, of the forty peacekeeping missions the UN undertook between 1945 and 1998, more than twenty-five were begun after 1988, in the wake of the Cold War. After the Somalia fiasco of 1993, however, there was a pronounced decline of enthusiasm, and the number of personnel in UN peacekeeping operations declined. UN peacekeeping spending reached a high of $4 billion in 1993 and declined to under $900 million in 1998.[26]

There are problems with the way peacekeeping forces of the United Nations (as well as those of other such bodies) are presently formulated. Composed of essentially independent military and policing units, they are contributed by individual countries and maintain their separate identities. Thus, the U.S. force in Somalia was operating as part of a UN peacekeeping force, but it was made up entirely of U.S. units culled from the country's regular forces. Consequently, when Americans were killed in the 1993 firefight, they were taken to be direct American loses.

In some cases, military units have been contributed to peacekeeping operations simply because their impoverished home countries are being well paid to hire them out. Many of these units have been underpaid and poorly equipped and trained, and they have often simply compounded the problem, becoming as corrupt and as ill disciplined as the marauders they were sent to police. When a participating country does have fairly competent forces, these are often kept at home to protect political leaders or for domestic defense. Moreover, as Alan Ryan notes, the "UN has a poor record for the refund of the costs incurred in such operations," and UN peacekeeping missions generally follow a "bureaucratic and collegiate model of command, where national representation often has priority over operational effectiveness." And, he stresses, "there is a baseline of professional competence and capability below which a force cannot fall. To ignore this requirement is to court disaster."[27]

An alternative would be for the UN to fabricate a well-paid, well-equipped, well-trained, and risk-acceptant standing military force for peacekeeping, something that was envisioned in the UN charter but that never materialized because of profound political differences among the permanent members of the Security Council, who ultimately would be in charge of the body.[28] Individual Americans and other nationals might volunteer on their own to be part of such a force, but if they died in the line of duty in conflagrations of little national interest to their home country, they would be doing so as comparatively faceless international civil servants, not as members of identifiable national units sent into danger by domestic political authorities. Presumably, therefore, the internal political impact of such casualties would be limited.

The establishment of such a force has often been proposed in the wake of the Cold War.[29] However sensible the idea may seem to be in principle, it has run into a number of stated or unstated objections. Some countries fear that such a force could be used against their national interests, or even against themselves. Because the force would be under direct control of the Security Council in which the United States has a veto, one would think this objection would not have surfaced in that country, but it has. There have also been objections to the probable costs. It is likely that a standing force would be fairly expensive, and increasingly so as it was deployed to more and more trouble spots and as its peacekeeping duties stretched on for years—or even decades, as seems entirely possible in some cases.

These concerns have been sometimes heightened by the fact that the United Nations has often proven to be a remarkably incompetent organization with a much bloated payroll, where, as it is often charged, 20 percent of the employees do 80 percent of the work. A charitable organization so wasteful would soon run out of contributors. It is not at all clear that the organization, so encumbered by bureaucracy and ticket-balancing, can be trusted to create and manage a policing force that is both competent and cost-effective. There are all sorts of practical problems in putting together such a force as well. Ryan points out that even in the relatively smooth and trouble-free intervention in East Timor, language was a great challenge to cohesion even for English speakers, many of whom found the Australian accent difficult to decipher.[30]

In addition, experience, most notably in Bosnia, suggests that the Security Council can be racked with, or even paralyzed by, political uncertainty and disagreement even in the post–Cold War era, particularly when specifics are required and when financial costs begin to mount. The result can be directives and initiatives (or the lack thereof) that are confusing, debilitating, contradictory, or even impossible. If an important member has a specific domestic concern—as Russia and China had in the Kosovo case—no Security Council action is likely to take place at all.

Finally, although a well-crafted international police force presumably would be far more tolerant of casualties than would national forces, it is likely that there are casualty levels—and probably fairly low ones—that could still force it from the field, no matter how much good it may be doing.

Another possibility would be for international bodies to employ private security firms to do the policing work. Private security firms have burgeoned in recent years—in 1995, Americans spent more than twice as much on private security as they did on domestic police forces—and the translation of the process to the international arena seems natural. In fact, quite a few of these enterprises, often run by and employing former military personnel from developed counties, have gone into business after the Cold War. Thus, in the 1990s, private security companies have operated policing and training missions, mostly successfully, in Papua New Guinea, Angola, Sierra Leone, Croatia, Bosnia, and elsewhere.[31] And, as noted in chapter 7, the United States effectively hired locals in its policing war in Afghanistan in 2001–2.

Although they have been disparaged as "mercenary," private military companies differ from the kinds of mercenaries, often criminal or semicriminal, who have formerly gone under, and often besmirched, that label. To begin with, as David Shearer notes, private military companies advertise their services and are legally registered; their personnel are "employed with a defined structure, with established terms and conditions, and work with a degree of organization and accountability to the company"; and the company "is answerable to its client, often under a legally binding contract." Moreover, they seem to be cost-effective. The firm Executive Outcomes, now disbanded, which successfully pacified Sierra Leone for twenty-one months before the government foolishly declined to renew its contract, charged $35 million for its services. By contrast, the cost of the UN force that eventually replaced it came to $47 million for a mere eight months. Month-for-month, the UN force cost more than three times as much to perform much the same job. And judging from the problems the UN force experienced until the British sent in a disciplined contingent of troops, Executive Outcomes was far more effective.[32]

The experience thus far is that private security firms take their contracts very seriously and find it good business from a long-term perspective to make sure they do not work for monsters or undercut the foreign policy goals of the developed countries from which they hail. Fears they would run amok, especially if unpaid in the manner of mercenaries of old, have not so far materialized. Thus, when Executive Outcomes' contract was ended in Sierra Leone, the firm simply packed up and left—and in an orderly fashion, which is certainly far more than can be said for the warring criminals, sobels, and warlords it left behind. Moreover, in many cases it would be difficult to imagine how rampaging mercenaries could do any more damage than the locals have done to each other. Presumably, private security companies are not entirely immune to casualties. Thus far, they have stayed the course even after taking losses far greater proportionately than the United States sustained in Somalia (which, of course, is not saying much). However, one firm, the Gurkha Security Group, hired to train Sierra Leone military forces, withdrew after suffering what is described as "heavy casualties" in an ambush in 1995.[33]

There are, of course, legitimate concerns about private security companies, including ones about accountability. Because of that, and because the label "mercenary" sticks in the craw of many, the use of private military companies seems likely to remain a minor or ancillary (training, supply, logistics) contribution to any solution to the problem of criminal warfare.

One could also fabricate "coalitions of the willing" on an ad hoc basis. Indeed, most of the instances of policing wars discussed in the previous chapter were carried out by developed countries or coalitions of developed countries acting substantially on their own, although in most instances the perpetrators were able to fabricate legalistic justifications for their acts.[34] It is certainly possible that such ventures will continue in the future, especially after the successful, unauthorized, mainly U.S. venture against Iraq in 2003. But such efforts do not seem to be a promising general solution to the problems of civil war and of vicious regimes. They are likely to continue to be spotty and capricious and constrained by the impediments listed earlier.

POLICING DISCIPLINED WARFARE

The discussion about policing has thus far been devoted primarily to thug-dominated conflicts like the ones in Yugoslavia and in many parts of Africa. These seem to represent the most common kind of contemporary warfare. However, if such essentially criminal forces *can* be molded into disciplined and dedicated ones willing to stand and fight and to take substantial casualties, they can become highly formidable and therefore capable of inflicting substantial casualties on policing forces. Under such circumstances, it would probably be close to impossible to fabricate effective international policing forces of any sort unless the interests of major countries are, or appear to be, very much and very directly at stake. Thus it is likely to be exceptionally difficult to muster support for intervention to deal with the disciplined Tamil Tigers or with dedicated Palestinian or Kurdish guerrillas. And North Korea's seemingly formidable, and presumably disciplined, army will probably deter a policing war designed to topple its destructive regime.

Complications arise because it can be difficult to predict whether a given combatant force will behave like a disciplined or a criminal one. A force that may have once been disciplined and highly effective may descend into militarily debilitated criminality and accordingly become easy to police. This happened in Afghanistan in the early 1990s as noted in chapter 7. Or a criminal force can become disciplined, particularly if it is strengthened by combatants energized by actions of governments or interveners that have overreacted with indiscriminate brutality in trying to put down the initial criminal forces, a process considered more fully in the next chapter.

POLICING INTERNATIONAL TERRORISM

The international community is likely to be better at dealing with international terrorism than it is at policing most residual warfare. In general, as the definitions developed in chapter 1 suggest, terrorism in its essential dynamics is much more like crime than it is like warfare. Military measures may sometimes be useful in the campaign against terrorism, but for the most part, opposition to terrorism is more likely to resemble a campaign against crime than a war, however much the war imagery may get the juices flowing. What is mostly required is police work: intelligence gathering, staking out suspects, gathering evidence, tracing funding sources, checking and rechecking, guarding potential targets, and so forth. And like all good police work, it should be carried out selectively and discriminately, because overreaction can be counterproductive, doing more to create terrorists and terrorism than to snuff them out.[35]

Because terrorism, like crime, is carried out by individuals and small groups, it cannot be deterred by threatening a central authority with unacceptable retaliation. Some individual terrorists would be deterred if they knew there would be substantial punishment for their actions if they were caught, but this, obviously, would scarcely work with those who are suicidal. And although wars can be brought to an end, it seems likely that terrorism, like crime, cannot—though its incidence and effects, also like crime, can be reduced.

The shock of the September 11 attacks has probably had a salutary effect on the policing of international terrorism in that almost all countries everywhere have reason to feel they could be in similar danger. Accordingly, they have an incentive to cooperate to deal with the problem.

CRIMINALITY AND OTHER PROBLEMS CAUSED OR FACILITATED BY INTERNATIONAL POLICY

Although developed countries have often failed because of the impediments assessed earlier to police criminal regimes and civil wars, they also have adopted a number of policies that, by their very nature, have often actually rewarded, inspired, or facilitated criminality and, ultimately, some criminal warfare.

Sanctions have certainly done so, and those seeking to identify a new form of war might better focus on economic warfare. Of course, the technique itself is hardly new: it has a long history—from sieges of castles to the blockade of Germany during and after World War I—and has often caused more deaths than bombing or bombardment. What is new, however, is that the ending of the Cold War has allowed the technique to become far more effective. In their new era of comparative harmony, the major countries have at their disposal a credible and potentially potent weapon for use against small- and medium-sized foes, one that can inflict enormous pain at remarkably little cost to themselves or to the global economy. Sanctions were applied many times during the 1990s—most notably, and most conspicuously, against Iraq in 1990, against Haiti in 1991, and against Serbia in 1992.[36]

Economic sanctions, however, not only cause great human harm, as noted in chapter 7, but also almost inevitably favor criminality in the sanctioned societies. By artificially restricting the supply of various commodities, sanctions automatically benefit those who can service that demand. This process inevitably rewards those with criminal skills, and it has lead to, or notably enhanced, the criminalization of entire regimes.

In Serbia, observes Tim Judah, "the unprecedented breakdown of law and order and the fantastic business opportunities provided by sanctions-busting meant that many Yugoslav gangsters who had hitherto operated in the richer pastures of Germany and Switzerland returned to reap the profits of war. Some became involved with Serbian paramilitaries, which under cover of patriotism became rapacious looting machines. After they had stolen all the cars and other goods from the frontline towns, they turned their attention to the home front." And the condition continued after the war. In post-war Belgrade, observes Chris Hedges, a very prominent criminal class, "many of whom made their fortunes by plundering the possessions of ethnic Croats and Muslim who were expelled from their homes or killed in Bosnia during the war there," returned home to deal "in stolen clothes from Italy, stolen cars, drugs, protection rackets, prostitution, and duty-free cigarettes." The prominent Belgrade gangster Arkan made millions of dollars selling loot and smuggling oil, and operated a protection racket and a private prison used in kidnapping for ransom. All this was accompanied by a disastrous brain drain. Meanwhile, in the Serb section of Bosnia, the leaders, guarded by bodyguards with shaved heads and sunglasses, expropriated the largest houses and drove luxury sedans, while gangs of armed car thieves roamed the streets. Armed gangsters continued to reign in many places in the rest of Bosnia as well, such as the Croatian section of Mostar.[37]

It is probably not very sensible to suggest that sanctions created a criminal regime in Iraq, because Saddam Hussein, a former street tough, substantially ran the country as a criminal enterprise from the outset. The sanctions, however, tended to facilitate his control. They created artificial shortages and drove up prices for scarce commodities, demands that could be serviced only by smugglers and sanctions-busters. Insofar as the regime could control this highly lucrative market, it was able to channel the considerable benefits of such enterprises to its supporters. Moreover, the system of food rationing, made necessary by the sanctions, was used by the government to strengthen its control. As one Iraqi put it, "I have to pledge loyalty to the party. Any sign of disobedience and my monthly card would be taken away." And key supporters were rewarded with extra rations.[38] Moreover, the years of sanctions tended to sap the energies of the population as the quest for survival became paramount.

For sanctions to be effective, it is axiomatic, as Jonathan Kirshner points out, that they weaken, rather than strengthen, the ties of the leader's core support group. In most cases, they probably are counterproductive in this regard.[39]

Criminality and criminal warfare have also been enhanced by the various drug "wars" waged by developed countries—strenuous efforts to reduce the supply of an international commodity, drugs, for which there is monied demand within their own countries. Indeed, some specific ventures, such as arming incompetent, rampaging government armies or applying herbicides that kill a wide variety of crops, have sometimes enhanced the support for warlord rebels.[40] Much criminal activity, some of which often looks a lot like warfare, particularly in Latin America and in Asia, would be greatly reduced if drugs were legalized or if the developed countries—as they do now for alcohol and cigarettes—spent all their efforts on reducing demand in their own countries rather than trying to stamp out the sources of the supply.

In addition, misapplied aid has often enabled criminality and criminal regimes. During the Cold War there was often a political test for receiving aid, and tyrannical or mind-bogglingly incompetent and/or corrupt leaders were commonly rewarded for being on the right side. As Jeffrey Herbst points out, the six countries in Africa that received the most U.S. aid—Ethiopia, Kenya, Liberia, Somalia, Sudan, and Zaire—all had exceptionally poor economic and political performance, and except for Kenya, all are now considered to be "failed states."[41] The Soviet record was probably even worse. A danger in the post–September 11 era is that similarly disastrous governments will be supported because they deftly place themselves on the right side in the "wars" on terrorism or drugs.

However politically incorrect, it might also be worth considering whether the decolonization process of the post–World War II era was too hasty. In some cases, the process was effective, but in many others, decolonization led to conditions that were vastly worse in human terms as thugs, monsters, and ideologues rose to authority and viciously destroyed or looted the new countries.

When the Belgians left the Congo under pressure in 1960, they protested that it would take thirty years to prepare the colony for independence—something suggested, among other things, by the fact that only seventeen Congolese at the time had received a university education. Under the leadership of Mobutu and despite considerable Cold War aid from the outside, the country became "progressively pauperized," in the words of Michela Wrong. By the mid-1980s, telephone communication had become impossible; by 1994, copper production had sunk to less than 15 percent of its peak, the country's economy was still at 1958 levels even though the population had tripled, and 80 percent of the population was employed in subsistence activities. Less than thirty years after the Belgians left, the average wage was some 10 percent of what it had been when they were there. Ten years after the Portuguese abandoned neighboring Angola under pressure, coffee production in the country was down to 5 percent of colonial levels.[42]

The effects of premature decolonization on the rise of states with incompetent, venal, and criminal governments and the consequent increase in civil war are explored in the next chapter.

Finally, the restrictive trade and immigration policies of developed countries make the illegal smuggling of goods and people a lucrative, if risky, business even as criminality and criminal civil wars have been greatly facilitated by the arms so readily available from developed countries on the international market. Both sides in the Cold War sent a great many weapons to the people they supported: in the case of Somalia, in fact, they took turns supplying arms. Much of this hardware has been fully in use in many of the civil conflicts that continued to plague the developing world after the Cold War, and developed countries continue to be by far the largest suppliers of arms in the world.

PROSPECTS FOR INTERNATIONAL POLICING

International bodies and consortiums of developed countries can often be useful to broker cease fires and peace settlements, and they can sometimes assist with humanitarian aid and economic and political development once peace has been achieved. Although, as suggested earlier, international policy has often proved misguided and even counterproductive, a number of ventures seem to have been effective, albeit often in rather messy or clumsy ways. "People have been fed," as Mary Kaldor notes, "and fragile ceasefires have been agreed."[43] Thus, for example, further violent conflict in Cyprus has probably been averted by the international community's very long-term intervention there, Cambodia is better off thanks in part to missions from the outside, and Bosnia and Kosovo seem to be settling down under international tutelage, albeit accompanied by considerable criminality.

Developed states, however, are likely to intervene with any sort of reliability, either by themselves or through international bodies, only if they conclude that their interests are importantly engaged or if they become self-entrapped. Even then, they are likely to do so with enormous apprehension about suffering too many casualties of their own. Concerns that may arrest their attention from time to time include international terrorism, the dispersion of weapons of mass destruction to what are sometimes called rogue states, the flow of illegal drugs to their own populations, localized dangers to the flow to the international market of valued commodities like oil, and refugee incursions that cause them trouble and cost them money. For the most part, however, they are more likely to see civil conflicts and the domestic disasters perpetrated by vicious regimes as essentially irrelevant to their interests and thus to remain aloof. They are not very good at risky, onerous, and thankless missions that seem to them to be purely humanitarian. Their hearts simply aren't in it.

Thus, it seems clear that a truly effective, systematic solution to the problem of civil warfare and of brutal regimes is not in policing wars instituted by developed countries. And there may be one.

CHAPTER 9

THE DECLINE OF WAR

Explanations and Extrapolations

This book has traced what appears to be a decline in war. That venerable institution has for almost all of history been accepted as a natural, inevitable, and, often, desirable element in human affairs. However, over the course of the last century, the institution seems to have been losing that casual acceptance and is moving toward obsolescence, rather in the manner of slavery and dueling before it. In particular, although still entirely possible in a physical sense, the most often-discussed kind of war, major war—war among developed countries—is becoming increasingly unlikely as developed countries seize control of their destinies and decide that war with each other should not be part of them. By now, war between many former enemies in the developed world, such as France and Germany, has become subrationally unthinkable—it doesn't even come up as a coherent option, and if it ever did, would be rejected not so much because it is unwise but because it is absurd.[1]

Moreover, many other forms of war, including international war more generally, seem to be following the same rough trajectory. What we are mostly left with are civil wars, many of which seem to be all but indistinguishable from organized or high-intensity crime, and with policing wars—sporadic, low-casualty efforts by developed countries to pacify civil wars that happen to arrest their attention and to remove a few of the regimes they come to consider reprehensible. In seeking to explain this remarkable historical development, I have stressed changing attitudes toward war as a central independent or explanatory variable, and I have focused on the role of idea entrepreneurs in developing and selling the once-novel notion that war should be abolished.

This chapter takes up three concerns. First, I put the decline of war into broader perspective. Second, I assess alternative explanations for that decline, ones that do not focus on changing attitudes toward the institution. And third, I extrapolate the process, exploring the possibility that warfare, now substantially reduced to its criminal dregs, will fade away entirely.

THE DECLINE OF WAR IN BROADER PERSPECTIVE

The apparent decline in war, or at any rate in the most discussed types of war, may be part of a broader trend, at least within the developed world, away from the acceptance of a number of forms of deliberate, intentional killing. Infanticide, for example, has declined over the centuries, as has human sacrifice—something that, Barbara Ehrenreich reminds us, was once a "widespread practice among diverse cultures, from small scale tribes to mighty urban civilizations."[2]

A more recent development is summed up by David Garland: "At present there is a measure of agreement—though not unanimity—among historians that the period between 1700 and the present has seen a change in sentiments with respect to violence, a growing antipathy toward cruelty of all kinds, and the emergence of a new structure of feeling which has changed the nature of human relationships and behaviour."[3]

To begin with, there has clearly been a decline in unofficial justice as carried out by vigilantes, lynch mobs, or posses, and forms of private justice that previously had been tolerated—vendetta and blood feuds—seem generally to have been eliminated in many cultures. Donald Horowitz also notes the remarkable, and presumably related, decline of deadly rioting in the West. These developments seem to be closely associated with the rise of competent, coherent governments in the developed world. Formal dueling, too, once a very common practice among certain social sets, has become obsolete, although it may live on in different form in other social sectors, as in street gangs. Official murder, generally known as capital punishment, has also been eradicated in most of the developed world and is carried out only very infrequently in places, like the United States, where it is still legal practice. Corporal punishment, too, once standard practice and very common, has ceased to be either. Finally, a number of studies have suggested that homicide—and, indeed, civil violence more generally—was far more common centuries ago, particularly in rural areas. Connected to this trend, perhaps, is the decades-long decline of adult homicide in the United States—in part the result, it seems, of concerted efforts to make it clear that family and spousal violence is no longer acceptable.[4]

At the same time there has been a rise in the acceptance of some forms of what might be called lethal nonviolence. Depending on the definition of human life, society's increasing acceptance of abortion could be seen—and is seen by many—as a strong counter to the trend away from deliberate killing in developed societies. The medical eradication of human fetuses was generally condemned as a process of population management as late as the 1960s by such organizations as Planned Parenthood. The rather sudden and remarkably widespread acceptance of this once-abhorred practice has presumably been facilitated by the fact that abortion is accomplished quietly, privately, and out of sight.

Somewhat related may be the indifference in most of the world to another form of lethal nonviolence: the effects of economic sanctions during the 1990s, which caused more human suffering in an incremental manner than most wars inflict in a direct one. Indeed, if the estimates are even roughly correct, economic sanctions in Iraq were a necessary cause of more deaths than those inflicted by all the nuclear weapons used in World War II and all the chemical weapons used in World War I combined.[5]

Several explanations for this lack of concern or notice are conceivable. The devastation can be blamed at least in part on Iraqi president Saddam Hussein because he variously refused to comply with many of the sanctioners' demands, although the morality of killing one person because another refuses to do one's bidding is, to say the least, a bit shaky.[6] In addition, he sometimes seemed more interested in enhancing the nation's suffering for propaganda purposes (especially with an eye toward getting the sanctions removed) than in relieving it—that is, the people of Iraq essentially became his hostages, and the sanctioners effectively decided to let the hostages die rather than to give in to him. There was also hope that the sanctions might hamper Iraq's ability to develop threatening weaponry and that they might encourage the Iraqis to overthrow the tyrannical regime.

Much of the inattention, however, may have derived from the fact that, in contrast to the destruction of life caused by terrorist bombs, economic warfare generally kills quietly and indirectly. Deaths are dispersed rather than concentrated, statistical rather than dramatic. In addition, they are of distant, faceless foreigners and occur substantially out of sight.[7] Whatever the trends in warfare, tolerance for this sort of deliberate killing remains, it seems, remarkably high.

ALTERNATIVE EXPLANATIONS FOR THE DECLINE OF WAR

In focusing on changing attitudes toward war as a principal mechanism for explaining the institution's decline, I find myself in agreement with Robert Dahl's observation that "because of their concern with rigor and their dissatisfaction with the 'softness' of historical description, generalization, and explanation, most social scientists have turned away from the historical movement of ideas. As a result, their own theories, however 'rigorous' they may be, leave out an important explanatory variable and often lead to naive reductionism." Because beliefs and ideas are often, as Dahl notes, "a major independent variable," to ignore changes in ideas, ideologies, and attitude is to leave something important out of consideration.[8] That is, ideas are important in their own right, and if idea entrepreneurs are successful in changing them, this can have substantial, even profound, consequences.

However, a number of other explanations have been advanced to account for the rise of war aversion or the decline of war. Some of these stress the impact of technology, particularly nuclear weapons, while others point to economic development, the increasing costs of war, the rise of democracy, increased international trade, or the role of norms and international institutions.

Nuclear Weapons

In seeking to explain history's greatest nonevent—the utterly unprecedented absence of major war for more than a half century—many observers credit the fortuitous invention in 1945 of nuclear weapons and emphasize the peculiar terror they induce.[9] These analyses accept what can be called the Churchill counterfactual, a proposition that notes the emergence after World War II of a "curious paradox" and a "sublime irony" whereby nuclear weapons vastly spread "the area of mortal danger," with the potential result that "safety will become the sturdy child of terror, and survival the twin brother of annihilation."[10] Rendered in more pointed, if less eloquent, phraseology, the Churchill counterfactual holds that if, counter to fact, nuclear weapons had not been invented, disaster was pretty much inevitable. That is, the people running world affairs after 1945 were at base so incautious, so casual about the loss of human life, so conflagration-prone, so masochistic, so doom-eager, so incompetent, and/or simply so stupid that in all probability they could not have helped plunging or being swept into a major war if the worst they could have anticipated from the exercise was merely the kind of catastrophic destruction they had so recently experienced in World War II. Accordingly, those who abhor war should presumably take the advice of Kenneth Waltz and "thank our nuclear blessings" or, as Elspeth Rostow proposes, bestow upon it the Nobel Peace Prize.[11]

To me, the opposite counterfactual seems more plausible. It suggests that if, counter to fact, nuclear weapons had not been invented, the history of world affairs would have turned out much the same as it did.[12] Specifically, nuclear weapons and the image of destruction they inspire were not necessary to induce the people who have been running world affairs since 1945 to be extremely wary of repeating the experience of World War II (or for that matter, of World War I). After all, most of these figures were either the same people or the direct intellectual heirs of the people who tried desperately, frantically, pathetically, and ultimately unsuccessfully to prevent World War II. They did so in part because they feared—correctly, it gave them no comfort to discover—that another major war would be even worse than World War I.[13] I find it difficult to understand how people with those sorts of perceptions and with that vivid and horrifying experience behind them would

discernable long-term trend towards greater costliness."[19] Many people concluded from the experiences of the World Wars that they never wanted to do that again, but at least for some of the winners that conclusion could not have been inspired by the fact that these wars were unprecedentedly unprofitable politically and economically. Moreover, as with Howard's argument, the problem is that the great expansion of economic growth in Europe after the industrial revolution was accompanied not only by a rising peace movement (eventually) but also with a renewed romantic yearning for the cleansing process of war. An all-out nuclear war, to be sure, would likely be terrible for winner (if any) and loser alike. The questionable necessity of that technological development for deterring major war was discussed earlier. (And, of course, many subnuclear wars have been fought since Hiroshima.) Kaysen's argument, however, is principally about prenuclear developments.

The Expansion of Democracy

In the last decade or so there has been a burgeoning and intriguing discussion concerning the possibility that democracy causes or leads to war aversion.[20] Much of this has been inspired by the empirical observation that democracies have never, or almost never, gotten into wars with each other.

This relationship seems substantially spurious to me. Like most important ideas over the last few centuries, the notion that war is undesirable and inefficacious and the idea that democracy is a good form of government have largely followed the same trajectory: they were accepted first in northern Europe and North America and then gradually, with a number of traumatic setbacks, became more accepted elsewhere. In this view, the rise of democracy is associated not only with the rise of war aversion but also with the decline of slavery, religion, capital punishment, and cigarette smoking, and with the growing acceptance of capitalism, scientific methodology, women's rights, environmentalism, abortion, and rock music.[21] Moreover, although democracy and war aversion have taken much the same trajectory, they have been substantially out of synchronization with each other: the movement toward democracy began around 1800, but the movement against war really began about a century later. Critics of the democracy–peace connection often cite examples of wars or near-wars between democracies. Most of these took place before the experience of World War I, that is, before war aversion had caught on.[22]

Since World War I, the democracies in the developed world have been in the lead in rejecting war as a methodology. Some proponents of the democracy–peace connection suggest that this is because the democratic norm of nonviolent conflict resolution has been externalized to the international arena. However, as discussed earlier, developed democracies have not necessarily adopted a pacifist approach, particularly after a version of that approach failed so spectacularly to prevent World War II from being forced upon them. In addition, as noted in chapter 5, they were willing actively to subvert or to threaten and sometimes apply military force when threats appeared to loom during the Cold War contest. At times this approach was used even against regimes that had some democratic credentials such as in Iran in 1953, Guatemala in 1954, Chile in 1973, and perhaps Nicaragua in the 1980s.[23] And, as considered in chapter 7, they have also sometimes used military force in their intermittent efforts to police the post–Cold War world.

It is true they have not warred against each other—and, since there were few democracies outside the developed world until the last quarter of the twentieth century, it is this statistical regularity that most prominently informs the supposed connection between democracy and peace. However, the developed democracies hardly needed democracy to decide that war among them was a bad idea. (Nor is it likely they needed "American preponderance" to do so, as some have suggested.)[24] In addition, they also adopted a live-and-let-live approach toward a huge number of dictatorships and other nondemocracies that did not seem threatening during the Cold War—in fact, they often aided and embraced such regimes if they seemed to be on the right side in the conflict with Communism.

Moreover, to deal with a central concern of this book, and one little considered by theorists dealing with the democracy–peace connection, the supposed penchant for peaceful compromise of democracies has not always served them well when confronted with civil war situations, particularly ones involving secessionist demands. Sometimes democracies have handled these challenges without violence by convincing would-be secessionists to remain within the fold (as in Canada or Belgium) or by letting them depart (as in Czechoslovakia). But the process broke down into civil warfare in democratic Switzerland in 1847 and savagely so in the United States in 1861. Democracies have also fought a considerable number of wars to retain colonial possessions—six by France alone since World War II—and these, as James Fearon and David Laitin suggest, can in many respects be considered essentially to be civil wars.[25] To be sure, democracies have often managed to deal with colonial problems peacefully, mostly by letting the colonies go. But it is not at all clear that authoritarian governments have been less able: the Soviet Union, for example, withdrew from its empire in Eastern Europe and then dissolved itself, all almost entirely without violence.

It is often asserted that democracies are peaceful because the structure of democracy requires decision makers to compromise and to obtain domestic approval. But authoritarian regimes must also necessarily develop skills at compromise in order to survive, and they all have domestic constituencies that must be serviced, such as the church, the landed gentry, potential urban rioters, the nomenklatura, the aristocracy, party members, the military, eventually become at best incautious about, or at worst eager for, a repeat performance. But that, essentially, is what the Churchill counterfactual asks us to believe.

There were several additional important war-discouraging factors. The world after 1945 was ruled by the victors of World War II, and they were generally content with the territorial status quo. Furthermore, as discussed in chapter 5, although Communist ideology—the chief upsetting element during the Cold War—did embrace violence, it emphasized subversion and internal revolution, not over-the-border aggression, and it came accompanied by a cautious emphasis on tactics inherited from Lenin.[14]

None of this, of course, is to deny that nuclear war is appalling to contemplate and mind-concentratingly dramatic, particularly in the speed with which it could bring about massive destruction. Nor is it to deny that decision makers, both at times of crisis and at times of noncrisis, have been well aware of how cataclysmic a nuclear war could be. It is simply to stress that the horror of repeating World War II is not all that much *less* impressive or dramatic and that leaders essentially content with the status quo would strive to avoid anything they believe could lead to *either* calamity. A jump from a fiftieth-floor window is probably quite a bit more horrible to think about than a jump from a fifth-floor one, but anyone who finds life even minimally satisfying is extremely unlikely to do either.[15]

However, although visions of mushroom clouds haven't been necessary to keep the leaders who have actually run world affairs since 1945 cautious about major war, there are imaginable circumstances under which it might be useful to have the weapons around—such as the rise of another lucky, clever, risk-acceptant, aggressive fanatic like Hitler. Moreover, there are circumstances in which nuclear weapons could have made a difference. For example, Iraq might not have attacked Iran in 1980 or Kuwait in 1990 if those countries had had nuclear weapons with which to retaliate. The argument is not that nuclear weapons *cannot* make a difference but rather that their existence has not been necessary to create the long peace that the developed world has now enjoyed for such a long time.

Economic Development and the Industrial Revolution

In attempting to assess the rise of war aversion in the developed world, Michael Howard proposes economic development as a causative factor. At one time, he notes, the developed world was organized into "warrior societies" in which warfare was seen to be "the noblest destiny of mankind." Industrialization, he suggests, changed this situation in that it "ultimately produces very unwarlike societies dedicated to material welfare rather than heroic achievement."[16]

The main problem for this generalization, as Howard is quite aware, is that industrialization spoke with a forked tongue. Between 1750 and 1900 the developed world experienced the industrial revolution, enormous economic growth (see fig. 1 on p. 33), the rise of a middle class, a vast improvement in transportation and communication, surging literacy rates, and massive increases in international trade. But if this phenomenon encouraged some people to abandon the war spirit, it apparently propelled others to fall, if anything, more fully in love with the institution, as documented at the end of chapter 2. Howard himself traces the persistence, even the rise, of a militaristic spirit that became wedded to a fierce and expansionist nationalist impetus, as industrialization came to Europe in the nineteenth century. Thus industrialization can inspire bellicism as much as pacifism. Howard never really provides much of an explanation for how or why industrialization must inevitably lead to an antimilitary spirit, and he vaguely attributes the horrors and holocausts that accompanied industrialization to "the growing pains of industrial societies."[17]

The Rising Costs of War

Carl Kaysen has concluded that major war is becoming obsolete, and he has advanced an argument similar to Howard's, but with far more detail about the process, particularly its economic aspects. He argues that "for most of human history, societies were so organized that war could be profitable for the victors, in both economic and political terms." However, "profound changes . . . following the Industrial Revolution, have changed the terms of the calculation," causing the potential gains of war to diminish and the potential costs to rise.[18]

Kaysen tends to minimize the economic costs of war before the modern era, but, as discussed in chapter 3, they could be extremely high for winners and losers alike. Indeed, as noted there, the expression "Pyrrhic victory" refers to a battle fought in 279 BC. Moreover, civil wars have often been cosmic exercises in masochism, destroying both sides, and many primitive wars have essentially eradicated whole societies. In fact, notes Lawrence Keeley, because the costs of warfare are relatively higher for primitive societies, war should be less common among them than it is among states and empires, but the opposite seems to be the case. By contrast, Germany recovered economically from the destruction of World War II in five years, whereas Japan, poorer to begin with, and even more devastated in World War II, recovered in less than ten (see fig. 1). For the United States, one of the winners, World War II was politically and probably economically profitable, and the casualties it suffered were, as a percentage of its population, tiny compared with those borne by countries in many earlier wars. The "most meaningful question," observes Alan Milward, "is whether the cost of war has absorbed an increasing proportion of the increasing Gross National Product of the combatants. As an economic choice war, measured this way, has not shown any

though trade interconnections obviously did not prevent Europe from cascading into such a war in 1914.[30] It is peace that causes, or facilitates, the trade and other interconnections, not the other way around.

Problems also occur when one seeks to apply the interdependence argument to wars other than international ones. Civil wars, which are far more common than wars between countries—and often far more destructive to the participants—are usually fought between groups whose interdependence, economic and otherwise, is close to total. In his study of primitive warfare, Keeley concludes that "economic exchanges and intermarriages have been especially rich sources of violent conflict. . . . Exchange between societies is a context favorable to conflict and is closely associated with it."[31]

The Development of International Institutions and Norms

International institutions and norms often stress peace, but to the degree that is true, they, like expanded trade flows, are not so much the cause of peace and war aversion as their result. Many of the institutions that have been fabricated in Europe—particularly ones like the coal and steel community that were so carefully forged between France and Germany in the years after World War II—have been specifically designed to reduce the danger of war between erstwhile enemies. However, because it appears that no German or Frenchman in any walk of life at any time since 1945 has ever advocated a war between the two countries, it is difficult to see why the institutions should get the credit for the peace that has flourished in the area for the last half century and more.[32] They are among the consequences of the peace that has enveloped Western Europe since 1945, not its cause. As Richard Betts puts it for institutions of collective security, "Peace is the premise of the system, not the product."[33]

A similar argument holds for the impact of international norms. Take, for example, the norm of territorial integrity. As noted in earlier chapters, since World War II, there have been few instances in which an international border has changed as a result of warfare. But, as also indicated, this norm was specifically fabricated and developed because war-averse countries, noting that disputes over territory had been a major cause of international war in the past, were seeking to enforce and enshrine the norm. Its existence did not cause them to be war averse but rather the reverse.

ORDERING THE NEW WORLD: THE DOMESTIC DETERMINANT

A central theme in this book is tidily and conveniently summarized in a comment by John Keegan: "War is escaping from state control, into the hands of bandits and anarchists." Therefore, "the great work of disarming tribes, sects, warlords and criminals—a principal achievement of monarchs in the 17th century and empires in the 19th—threatens to need doing all over again."[34] War, of course, is not escaping anyone's control in the developed world—quite the opposite. But there are clearly substantial areas in the developing world where it has.

The developed countries have brought the civil warfare that once plagued them under control, have generally abandoned warfare among themselves, and have arrived, after the Cold War, at a substantial consensus about the desirable shape the world should take. Although they are now accordingly free to carry out the "great work" that Keegan calls for, it seems unlikely that, for the various reasons brought forward in chapter 8, they will actually expend the effort except in special circumstances and, often, for the wrong reasons.

The best solution to the problems presented by civil warfare and by criminally brutal or capable regimes lies in the development of effective domestic governments—that is, not in international policing but rather in the establishment of competent domestic military and policing forces tracing a process Europe went through in the middle of the last millennium. After all, it was not efforts by the international community that brought warfare, particularly civil warfare, under control in Europe, but rather the development of what Charles Tilly calls "high capacity" governments.[35]

Government as a Cause of Civil Warfare

To a very substantial degree, the amount of warfare that persists in the world today—virtually all of it civil war—is a function of the extent to which inadequate governments exist.

Yahya Sadowski finds that cultural and ethnic strife occurs about as much in developed countries as in poorer ones, but that such strife is less likely to turn violent in prosperous societies. Or, as Keegan puts it, "War is increasingly becoming an activity undertaken by poor rather than rich states." By one calculation, in fact, a poor country is eighty-five times more likely to experience violent conflict than is a rich one. From such data Sadowski concludes that economic advancement tends to reduce cultural violence.[36]

It seems to me, however, that prosperous societies do better than poorer ones in this regard not because they are prosperous but because they are more effective at policing—and that, in fact, is probably one of the reasons for their comparative prosperity. More generally, as several studies suggest, civil wars are least likely to occur in stable democracies and in stable autocracies, that is, in countries with effective governments and policing forces.[37] Stable democracies, almost by definition, have competent policing forces, and they deal with grievance by bringing the aggrieved into the process (as long as it is expressed peacefully) and listening to the grievance. Stable autocracies also police effectively—in fact, they are often called police states. They rule through the selective, but persistent, application of terror: through prominent business interests, the police or secret police, lenders of money to the exchequer, potential rivals for the throne, and the sullen peasantry.[26]

Democracy, as H. L. Mencken put it, is "the theory that the common people know what they want, and deserve to get it good and hard." At base, democracy is not a mystique but merely a gimmick—a good one in my view—for aggregating preferences. Democratic publics, sometimes heavily influenced by agile leaders, have at various times wanted all sorts of things, only to change their minds about it later (see table 9.1). Thus, if the people happen to come to think they want war, they will tend to get it.[27] Especially before 1914, democracies were often poised for war, even with other democracies: France and England certainly neared war in the Fashoda crisis, and both the War of 1812 and World War I could be considered to have had democrats on both sides. Moreover, if Cuba had been as brutally run by democratic Belgium in 1898 as it was by at best semi-democratic Spain, the resentment triggered in the United States about the colonial reign on that island is unlikely to have been much less. In more recent times, it is not at all clear that telling the elected hawks in the Jordanian parliament that Israel is a democracy will dampen their hostility in the slightest. And various warlike sentiments could be found in the elected parliaments in the former Yugoslavia in the early 1990s or in India and then-democratic Pakistan when they engaged in armed conflict in 1999. If Argentina had been a democracy in 1982 when it seized the Falkland Islands (a very popular undertaking), it is unlikely that British opposition to the venture would have been much less severe. "The important consideration," observes Miriam Fendius Elman after surveying the literature on the subject, does not seem to be "whether a country is democratic or not, but whether its ruling coalition is committed to peaceful methods of conflict resolution." As she further points out, the countries of Latin America and most of Africa have engaged in very few international wars even without the benefit of being democratic (for a century before its 1982 adventure, Argentina, for example, fought none at all).[28]

Thus, although democracy and war aversion have often been promoted by the same advocates, the relationship does not seem to be a causal one. And, of course, the long peace enjoyed by developed countries since World War II includes not only the one that has prevailed between democracies, but also the even more important one between the authoritarian east and the democratic west. Even if there is some connection, whether causal or atmospheric, between democracy and peace, it cannot explain this latter phenomenon.

Increased Trade and Interdependence

Peace may be associated with increased trade and other international interconnections. But to the degree this is true, peace, it seems to me, is more

TABLE 9.1
Democracy's record

Democracies variously have:		
Gone to war with enthusiasm and self-righteousness	*and*	sought to outlaw the institution.
Banned liquor	*and*	allowed it to flow freely.
Welcomed or committed naked aggression	*and*	fought to reverse it.
Raised taxes to confiscatory levels	*and*	lowered them to next to nothing.
Refused women the right to vote	*and*	granted it to them.
Despoiled the environment	*and*	sought to protect it.
Subsidized certain economic groups	*and*	withdrawn subsidies.
Stifled labor unions	*and*	facilitated their creation.
Banned abortion	*and*	permitted and subsidized the operation.
Tolerated drug use	*and*	launched massive "wars" on the practice.
Devolved into vicious civil war	*and*	avoided it by artful compromise.
Embraced slavery	*and*	determinedly sought to eradicate it.
Tolerated and sometimes caused humanitarian disaster in other parts of the world	*and*	sought to alleviate it.
Persecuted homosexuals	*and*	repealed the laws that did so.
Seized private property	*and*	turned over state assets to the private sector.
Discriminated against racial groups	*and*	given them preferential treatment.
Embraced colonialism	*and*	rejected the practice entirely.
Banned pornography	*and*	allowed it to be distributed freely.
Adopted protectionist economic policies	*and*	been free traders.
Tolerated the organization of peaceful political opposition	*and*	voted themselves out of existence by withdrawing the right to do.

nearly the essential cause of the connection rather than the reverse. Although expanding trade and interactions may enhance or reinforce the process, attitude toward war is likely to be the key explanatory variable in the relationship.

It has frequently been observed that wars and militarized disputes between countries reduce trade between them. By contrast, if a couple of countries that have previously enjoyed a conflictual relationship lapse into a comfortable peace and become extremely unlikely to get into war with each other, businesses in both places are likely to explore the possibilities for mutually beneficial exchange. For example, the Cold War, as Edward Yardeni has pointed out, was among other things a huge trade barrier; once it ended, trade and other connections grew greatly.[29] One reason for the remarkably enhanced international trade that occurred in Europe during the nineteenth century was surely the unprecedented absence of continental war, al-even worse for most of the 1990s by a double economic embargo, one imposed by Greece, the other by the international community against trade with Serbia. In 1991, Robert Kaplan ominously declared that "Macedonia is once again poised to erupt. Never in half a century has there been so much anger in Macedonia, as its people wake up from a Communist-imposed sleep." Serbia, he found, was in a much better position to cope: "Unable to stand on its own, like its more populous and historically grounded neighbor Serbia, Macedonia could implode under the pressures of Albanian nationalism from the west and Bulgarian nationalism from the east. And this is to say nothing of the pressures of Greek nationalism from the south. . . . The various popular convulsions in the Balkans are inexorably converging on Macedonia. . . . Rarely has the very process of history been so transparent and cyclical." Even later, when war had sprung up not in Macedonia but in Slovenia, Croatia, and Bosnia (with various interventions by the populous, historically grounded Serbs), Kaplan continued to see Macedonia as "ground zero for the coming century of culture clash." Over the course of a tense decade, despite those "transparent and cyclical" threats to their country, Macedonian "elites on both sides wanted to avoid violence," as Stuart Kaufman notes. Accordingly, they sought calm accommodation and substantially achieved it. Things became more difficult later with the rise of an armed insurgency based outside the country—in Kosovo—after the war there in 1999. There were some very rough moments—particularly when the government seemed on the verge of enlisting the services of Slav gangs, such as the Macedonian Action Organization, which was "closely associated" with fans of one of the local soccer clubs. However, in part because of active work and encouragement by representatives of the European Community, the Macedonian leadership again was able to keep things under control.[46] Its experience strongly suggests that the disasters in the more prosperous areas of the former Yugoslavia, far from being inevitable, could have been avoided if politicians and police had behaved more sensibly.

As David Keen has observed, "The aggression of counter-insurgency forces has repeatedly alienated their potential civilian supporters, and this has often continued even when evidently counter-productive from a military point of view." This "has frequently reflected a military ethos that prefers using massive force to winning hearts and minds," and clever rebels, as in Kosovo, have often sought to provoke such abusive repression in hopes that it "will have precisely these counter-productive effects." Europe eventually solved this problem, in part by taking seriously a simple but apparently not obvious observation from the sixth century by Saint Augustine: paying for soldiers ensures "that they do not turn themselves into brigands to recover their expenses."[47] Of course, as noted in chapter 2, the attainment of civil order did not keep European governments from engaging in international wars. However, the present aversion to international war and aggression should continue to limit such wars, even in a world filled with competent states, as it has in once-warlike Europe.

Thus, the establishment of competent government—or, more specifically, of coherent political systems and disciplined military and policing forces—is the key to engendering and maintaining civil peace—to policing the thugs, brigands, bandits, highwaymen, goons, bullies, criminals, pirates, drunks, mercenaries, robbers, adventurers, hooligans, fanatics, and children who seem to be the chief remaining perpetrators of a type of violence that can be said to resemble war.

Effective Government and Trends in Residual Warfare

It is undoubtedly much too early to be confident about the future of the remnants of war, whether criminal or disciplined, but a number of studies suggest, or at least are consistent with the suggestion, that civil war may be in, or going into, decline. People who carefully track the incidence of various forms of violent conflict, including types large enough to be labeled war, generally agree on the overall pattern of warfare and armed conflict since World War II (see fig. 3 on p. 87).[48] There was something of a tapering off after World War II, a rise (mainly in civil warfare) beginning in the 1960s that peaked in the early 1990s, and a decline since then.*

Obviously, these broad patterns mask all kinds of subtlety and variety, but their overall shape conforms fairly well to the discussion above. The key to the amount of residual (mainly criminal) warfare in the world, it has been argued, is not the degree to which there is hatred, grievance, or ethnic or civilizational cleavage but rather the degree to which governments function adequately. Where governments are inadequate, crime and turmoil will grow (not least because prisons are abandoned or become porous), and some of it will look a great deal like war, particularly if it is exacerbated by counterproductive efforts by inept governments to police it.

It appears that trends in warfare track well with the existence of weak governments. With the decolonization that occurred during the late 1950s and 1960s, a group of poorly governed societies came into being, and in part because of the processes outlined above, many found themselves involved with civil warfare. Moreover, as noted in chapter 6, as these civil wars became criminal enterprises, they tended to go on longer and to accumulate in number. This pattern may have been embellished by another phenomenon, democratization, which often is accompanied by a period in which governments become weak. Most of the data sets document a notable rise—or

---

* The rise in civil wars is not simply an artifact of the increasing number of independent countries that followed decolonization; the overall pattern holds even when the number of states is controlled for (Fearon and Laitin 2003, 77; Gleditsch et al. 2002, 621–23).

vigilant domestic spying and through focused, if often brutal, suppression. North Korea and Cuba provide contemporary examples.

In fact, in an important sense many civil wars have effectively been *caused* by inept governments. "War upon rebellion," T. E. Lawrence once observed, "is messy and slow, like eating soup with a knife."[38] Policing forces that do not understand this elemental fact are likely, through impatient overreaction, to adopt policies that are ineffective or counterproductive. If policing forces are sufficiently brutal and systematic, the methods can sometimes be successful, particularly in the short run.[39] But inept forces applying the same methods court disaster. Through closed political systems and through policing methods in which excessive, indiscriminate, and often inconsistent force is employed to try to deal with relatively small bands of troublemakers, inept governments can turn friendly or indifferent people into hostile ones and vastly increase the size of the problems they are trying to deal with.

The spectacularly counterproductive effort of the Serbs to police small bands of Albanian terrorists in their Kosovo province, noted in chapter 6, supplies a pertinent case in point: the overreaction caused the terrorists' numbers vastly to increase. More violent, and even more counterproductive, was the Indonesian military invasion and occupation of East Timor in 1975. Coming on the heels of a brief civil conflict between leftist and rightist forces in which the leftists had won, the Indonesians could probably have obtained a degree of support from the rightists as well as acquiescence from the majority of the population: as one observer puts it, "Based on my own assessment on the ground at the time, the majority of the Timorese, while preferring independence, would have remained in the towns with their families rather than flee to the interior of the island, had the invading forces shown respect for the lives, property and rights of the civilian population." But the invaders instead engaged in an orgy of indiscriminate brutality, torture, murder, rape, massacre, looting, and pillage. These measures did engender a degree of order for a while, but they also forced much of the population into rebel territory, hardened resistance, and led to an on-and-off guerrilla conflict that lasted twenty-four years, cost perhaps 10,000 Indonesian lives (and more than 100,000 East Timorese lives), and ended in an internationally supervised loss of the conquest. It is notable that when the Portuguese controlled East Timor, they did so with a military force of no more than 1,500, whereas the Indonesians needed troops in the tens of thousands.[40] Similar processes variously took place in Algeria, Sierra Leone, Liberia, Chechnya, Guatemala, and elsewhere.[41]

Something comparable can happen when the police and government, either through incompetence or lack of will, are unable to protect minorities from rioters who purport to represent the majority. In Sri Lanka, for example, Tamils variously have identified themselves by their place of emigration or by the region of the country in which they lived. But gangs of Sinhalese, reacting to incidents of Tamil terrorism, rioted against Tamils in Colombo and elsewhere in 1983, looting, killing, and setting fires in what Stanley Tambiah characterizes as an "orgy of violence," while the police mostly stood by in effective, and sometimes actual, complicity. In the process, the rioters defined for Tamils what being a Tamil meant, thus playing into the hands of Tamil extremists and terrorists who were committing violence exactly to heighten that identity. The resulting ethnic cleansing, in which Tamils of all varieties fled to safer areas, tended to concentrate them in one potentially secessionist corner of the country, one that relatively easily and substantially came to be controlled by Tamil secessionists acting as warlords.[42]

A similar pattern took place in Azerbaijan in 1988, when mobs rioted and looted over the issue of the secession of Karabagh, a local area heavily populated by Armenians. Even though many Armenians were saved from the marauders by their Azerbaijani neighbors, the conflict, and the polarization, was dramatically accelerated. Aiding in the process was the complicity—or at best the studied incompetence—of the police, the bumbling and ultimately counterproductive efforts of Soviet authorities to deal with the situation, and the facilitating machinations of some local officials.[43]

Prosperity may therefore be beneficial if it helps to develop, or comes associated with, competent governments and police forces, but wealth itself is not the key operative factor. Thus it is entirely possible to imagine Bosnian-like chaos in prosperous Quebec or Northern Ireland if the Canadian or British authorities had attempted to deal with conflicts there through murderous rampage rather than through patient, focused policing and political accommodation. This not to suggest that developed countries have an impeccable record, of course. Lack of restraint on the part of British forces during and after the Easter rising in Dublin in 1916 and on Bloody Sunday in Northern Ireland in 1972 proved to be extremely counterproductive. Similarly, a misguided and murderous American bombing raid in Somalia in July 1993 turned many moderate Somalis toward intense opposition. In none of these cases, however, did the policing forces exacerbate their mistake by going on a spree of uncontrolled and indiscriminate violence.[44]

Government as a Solution to Civil Warfare

When poor countries adopt sound and accommodating political policies, they can often do quite well. Thus, ethnic violence has been avoided in Bulgaria and Romania, even though those countries are hardly more developed than Serbia or Bosnia and even though they have variously experienced considerably greater ethnic tension.[45]

Surely the most impressive case in point in the post–Cold War era is that of Macedonia, the former Yugoslavia's poorest province—a condition made

POGG: The Canadian Redundancy

The experience in the developed world over the last millennium suggests that the essential and long-term solution to the problems of civil warfare lies not in ministrations by the international community—so often halfhearted, half vast, and half coherent—but rather in the establishment of competent domestic governments in the many places that do not now have them.

The Canadians, as it happens, have the slogan for our era. Many countries and institutions have mottos designed to get the blood flowing, ones that cry for, and are often delivered through, a thicket of exclamation points. There is, for example, "Liberty! Equality! Fraternity!" Or, "Duty! Honor! Country!" Or, "One Reich! One People! One Führer!" Canada's national slogan, by contrast, is one of studied modesty: "Peace, Order and Good Government."

Not only does POGG (as embarrassed Canadians sometimes flippantly call it) fail to get the blood flowing, and not only does the slogan eschew exclamation points, but it is cumulatively redundant: after all, order already implies peace, and good government implies both. But whatever the slogan's failings, POGG, it seems to me, is what people throughout the world in one way or another need and are yearning for.

There is plenty of "ethnic conflict" in Canada—between Francophones and Anglophones—but over the course of a third of a century that conflict resulted in exactly one death in the country.[56] And there is a reason for that: good government. The point is further illustrated by a comparison, arrestingly suggested by Keeley, concerning the westward expansion of Canada and the United States during the nineteenth century. In both countries, the Indian tribes in the way of expansion were equally warlike, but in the United States it took a series of costly, frequent, and debilitating wars to displace them whereas in Canada the job was accomplished with far less violence and with an almost complete absence of anything that could be called warfare. The central reason for this difference, suggests Keeley, is government, or perhaps better, good government. The Canadian government established treaties with the Indians before the settlers got there, not after as in the United States, and the Canadians actually lived up to those agreements, behaved as policemen, not soldiers, and administered justice evenhandedly against both whites and Indians, punishing individuals, not whole groups, for any transgressions. The Canadian success, concludes Keeley, "was predominantly the product of the mediation and police powers of the central state and the use made of them," and he suggests that "the restraint exercised by the Indians of western Canada as they were subjugated and dispossessed is evidence of how much injustice people will tolerate for the sake of peace if they are assured of receiving the means to survive, certain punishment for breaking the peace, and impartial protection of their persons and property if they keep it."[57]

As it happens, the world is not a teeming mass of frustrated, angry, hate-filled fanatics seeking to express their ethnic, religious, cultural, or civilizational angst in cataclysmic violence against each other in a Hobbesian state of nature. There are small numbers of people, it is true, who are drawn to violence and yearn to experience its exhilarations and its potential profits. Some of these are, indeed, fanatics and true believers, but most are criminals and thugs, and small, unpoliced, or badly policed bands of these people can cause vastly more devastation than their numbers would seem to imply.

As attitudes toward war have changed, disciplined international war, and for that matter, disciplined civil war, has become less and less common, and it is violence and predation by bands of thugs that most disrupts the civil peace. What is needed to keep them in check—to establish peace and order—is good government, following the path the developed world fell upon in the middle of the last millennium.

For the most part, however, the establishment of peace and order through good government—which is perhaps the way the Canadian motto should be read—needs to be accomplished by people within the countries themselves. In many areas over the last few decades—particularly in Latin America and much of Asia—progress has been made on this vital task. Sometimes international authorities, working out of or under the direction of, the developed countries, have been able to aid or speed the process. And they can certainly be of assistance when a country sincerely desires to develop the kind of competent military and police forces that have helped bring peace and prosperity to the developed world. Moreover, the example of the developed societies—civil, prosperous, flexible, productive, and free from organized violent conflict—can be very attractive, as indicated by the masses of people from the developing world who are trying to immigrate there, abandoning in fear and disgust the turmoil and violence of their home countries.

The U.S. invasion of Iraq in 2003 inspired quite a bit of discussion or pundity (some of it self-infatuated) about a new American colonialism or empire in which the "only remaining superpower" would take the lead (or imperiously foray into unilaterally) to oust contemptible regimes and to police dangerous civil conflicts. However, the spotty experience with policing wars in the post–Cold War era suggests this is unlikely to become the wave of the future. Indeed, at the same time as the Iraq venture, the United States declined (as it had in 1990) to send even a small contingent of policing troops to deal with civil conflict in Liberia even though many people there pleaded desperately for such intervention. And the lessons are likely to be embellished by the experience of the aftermath of the Iraq policing war in which the United States found itself met with scattered, but disciplined, dedicated, and often deadly, resistance—very much unlike the experience in almost all of the policing ventures discussed in chapter 7. Accordingly, it is likely that exercises in nation building that are productive of peace and order—and that ul-

acceleration in the upward trend—in civil war after 1975, a pattern that co-incides fairly closely with the rise in democracy that began at that time.[49]

Then, in the aftermath of the Cold War in the early 1990s, a further in-crease occurred in the number of incompetent governments as weak, con-fused, ill-directed, and sometimes criminal governments emerged in many of the post-Communist countries to replace comparatively competent police states. In addition, with the end of the Cold War, the developed countries, in-cluding former colonialist France, no longer had nearly as much interest in financially propping up some third world governments and in helping them police themselves, an effect particularly noticeable in Africa.[50]

By the mid-1990s, however, a large number of countries had managed to get through the rough period and had achieved a considerable degree of democratic stability—especially in Latin America, post-Communist Europe, and East and Southeast Asia—and relatively effective governments had emerged in most of them. Moreover, lingering ideological civil wars inspired or exacerbated by the Cold War contest died out (or became transmogrified into criminal ones) with its demise. Civil warfare has persisted primarily in Africa, where governments are the weakest and where democratization has only begun—though there has been a decline in war even there.

From Mobutu to Mandela?

Over the course of the last few decades there has been something of a de-cline in the number of regimes that are vicious and/or criminal and an in-crease in the number of countries that are led by effective people who, in-stead of looting their country's resources like Zaire's Mobutu, seem to be dedicated to adopting policies that will further their country's orderly devel-opment—something Robert Rotberg labels "positive leadership."[51] This has happened in almost all of Latin America as well as in many places in Asia, such as South Korea, the Philippines, Malaysia, and Thailand—areas that, not coincidentally, have also experienced a considerable decline in warfare.

Whether Africa—the area that not coincidentally has continued most to be plagued by civil warfare—will follow that pattern is yet to be determined, but there are some hopeful signs. Quite remarkable has been the transition that has occurred in South Africa. This extremely important country has managed to move to coherent, responsive democracy from a condition that was part democracy and part police state.[52] Huge problems remain, particu-larly with ordinary crime and with AIDS, but the country made the transi-tion. And key to that accomplishment were the judicious ministrations of the country's first elected post-Apartheid president, Nelson Mandela.

There are at least some indications that the Mandela approach may be gradually replacing the Mobutu one in Africa and elsewhere. At one time, the model, as found in Nigeria for example, was one in which military lead-

ers waited in line to take over the country in order to loot it even more effectively than they had been doing as senior officers. But such venal and klepto-
cratic leaders may now be in the process of being replaced by ones whose
style is not egomania and whose primary goal is not self-enrichment. Rather,
they seek to make their mark in history by guiding their countries to coherence and prosperity.

That such a change is possible and can happen quickly is suggested by the
experience in Latin America, where most countries were once run by military leaders who not only enriched themselves but also subscribed to the almost "messianic self-image" that the military was "*the* institution ultimately in-
terpreting and ensuing the highest interests of the nation," as O'Donnell and
Schmitter have put it. For various reasons, military leaders throughout Latin
America became increasingly convinced that military dictatorship was a
thing of the past, and country after country became democratic. When a
clumsy coup attempt was launched in Argentina in 1990, the country's president reacted not so much with alarm as with contemptuous dismissal. He labeled the effort "ridiculous antics," and as one observer noted, he "just said
no and it was over in a matter of hours."[53]

There does seem to be a rise in competent government in previously
failed states in a number of states, including ones in Africa. An indicator that
at least some progress has been made is William Reno's calculation that
whereas 71 percent of African rulers in the 1970s and 1980s were violently
forced from office, that figure dropped to 41 percent in the 1990s. Among
the potential candidates variously suggested as "new leaders" are Musaveni in
Uganda, the younger Kabila in Congo, Kagame in Rwanda, Obasanjo in Nigeria, Deby in Chad, Konare and perhaps Touré in Mali, Wade in Senegal,
Saakashvili in Georgia, and Karzai in Afghanistan. Whether such people will
proliferate in other countries, whether these people will truly follow the Mandela route rather than the Mobutu one, and whether they will really be able
to improve the situation in their countries remain to be seen. But because
competent government seems to be the key to civil warfare, this development could be of profound significance. As Rotberg stresses, state failure "is
largely man made, not accidental." It stems not from "structural flaws" or "in-
stitutional fragilities," but from the purposeful behavior of leaders who have
"engineered the slide from strength to weakness and willfully presided over
profound and destabilizing resource shifts."[54] It follows that human beings
can also reverse this process.

Also of importance is that strategies for achieving sustained economic development are much better understood than they were in earlier decades,
when statist economics and the severely misguided "dependency theory"
were all the rage. If the economists now have gotten the basics right, competent governments that generally follow their advice (and can avoid civil war)
are likely to prosper.[55]

NOTES

INTRODUCTION

1. Howard 1989; 1991, 176; Keegan 1993, 59; Kaldor 1999, 5; Jervis 2002, 1; Record 2002, 6. See also Mandelbaum 1998–99, 2002; Johnson 1995; Mack 2002, 523.
2. Van Creveld 1991, 225, 218.
3. Cohen 1998, 297.

1. CRIMINAL AND DISCIPLINED WARFARE

1. Schwarzkopf: Woodward 1991, 313. Parker 1994, 44. Napoleon: Chandler 1987, 74.
2. Combat studies suggest that perhaps 2 percent of combat soldiers enjoy killing; that is, they are "aggressive psychopaths" or, put a bit more mildly, "if given a legitimate reason, will kill without regret or remorse" (Grossman 1995, 180; see also Baumeister and Campbell 1999; Valentino 2004). Criminals: Katz 1988, especially chap. 2. Soccer: Buford 1991.
3. Haney, Banks, and Zimbardo 1973; Zimbardo et al. 1973. Opportunistic violence can occur, indeed it can become or seem to become rationally sensible when two conditions prevail: the violence is going to happen anyway, and the perpetrator will not suffer negative consequences from the act. Suppose, for example, that a building is going to be torn down. The contractors in charge have determined that a large glass window on the ground floor must be shattered before the demolition takes place and need to enlist someone to throw a brick through the window. Although there are a large number of glass windows in the world and an even larger number of bricks, people only rarely (rather amazingly so, it might seem) are inspired to put them violently together in this way. However, many people, probably most—perhaps even you, gentle reader—would find themselves capable of accepting, indeed seizing, this special opportunity to commit an unaccustomed act of violence and destruction. To extrapolate unpleasantly, suppose there is a riot going on, the police have withdrawn, and a liquor store is in the process of being looted. One might have some moral reservations about helping oneself to a couple of bottles of Wild Turkey, but this will be of absolutely no service to the owner-victim because someone else will snap the bottles up anyway. Or suppose order has broken down and some thugs are in the process of burning down a house. Because nothing can be done to save it, why not help with the burning—how often does one get such an opportunity? After all, arsonists get a kick out of watching things burn, and others routinely follow fire trucks and flock to view the results of the arsonists' handiwork, sharing at least that part of the experience. Suppose someone is being intimidated and humiliated in a way that seems entertaining. How often does one get to join in such behavior? Suppose a man is going to be killed, or a woman raped, and nothing can be done to stop that from happening? Somewhere along

the line, I hope, most people's sense of morality and outrage will have clicked in, and they will refuse to participate even when the prick of conscience is the only negative consequence to the perpetrator and even though the violent act will take place anyway. The examples suggest, however, that violent and predatory behavior can often spring from the peculiarities of the opportunity or from the savage appeals of the act itself. See also Valentino 2004, chap. 2; Tilly 2003, chap. 6.

4. James 1911, 282, 288. Churchill: Manchester 1988, 28. Gray 1959, chap. 2; he also stresses "the delight in destruction" or "the satisfaction that men experience when they are possessed by the lust to destroy and kill their kind"; on this, see also Bourke 1999, chap. 1. Civil war: McPherson 1997, 39–42. Broyles 1984.

5. Broyles 1984, 57; Gray 1959, 226. See also Bourke 1999, chap. 11; Hedges 2002, chap. 1. Grossman notes that even most of what he calls "aggressive psychopaths" seem entirely capable of blending back into the population after the war without finding a need to do further killing (1995, 181).

6. Keegan 1987, 196–97; Boardman 1998, 110–11, 158; Fussell 1989, 96–105; Lieven 1998, chap. 1; McPherson 1997, 52; Ellis 1999, 120–22.

7. File closers: Keeley 1996, 46; McPherson 1997, 48–51. Keegan 1987, 196. General and sergeant: Valentino 2004, 59.

8. McPherson 1997, 73; Shils and Janowitz 1948, 300–301, 309–10. Much primitive warfare has involved a no-prisoner approach: Keeley 1996, 83–86.

9. Shils and Janowitz 1948, 285.

10. McPherson 1997, 53.

11. Shils and Janowitz 1948, 297–99. On brutality in the Russian army, see Atkinson and Lee 1990; Williams 1999; Lieven 1998, 198, 290–93.

12. Milgram and others have seen resonances of these experiments in such horrors as the massacre that took place at My Lai during the Vietnam War and in German extermination camps during World War II (Milgram 1975, chap. 15; Kelman and Hamilton 1989; Staub 1989; Katz 1993). In the latter case, Christopher Browning has presented a striking study of how a substantial majority of ordinary German policemen engaged in direct executions of Jewish civilians even though they were explicitly given the freedom to refuse the duty and even though many of them apparently found it disgusting and horrifying. Among the explanations by Browning for this behavior are obedience to authority and pressures to conform in a context of warfare and ideological racism (1998, chap. 18). On replications and extrapolations of the Milgram findings, see Blass 2000; A. G. Miller 1986.

13. Second World War: Shils and Janowitz 1948, 292–97; see also Kellett 1982, 327–28. American Civil War: McPherson 1997, 22–29. Shame and humiliation: Edgerton 1992, 186–87; see also Shils and Janowitz 1948.

14. Keegan 1987, 197; Dyer 1985, chap. 5; McPherson 1997, chap. 6; Guilmartin 1997, 37–40; Hauser 1980, 188–95; Shils and Janowitz 1948, 283–88; Holmes 1985, 270–359; Grinker and Spiegel 1945, 25; Hedges 2002, 38, 40. See also Smith 1949; Bourke 1999, chap. 5; Kellett 1982, chap. 18; Valentino 2004. On the process more generally, see Sherif et al. 1961; Tajfel 1982.

15. Fifteenth century: Vale 1981, 30; see also Parker 1997, 174. Confederate: McPherson 1997, 87. American: Fussell 1989, 140.

16. Broyles 1984, 58; Gray 1959, 47; Browning 1998, 184–85.

17. McPherson 1997, 86; Keegan 1987, 197; Kellett 1982, 41, 320.

18. Shils and Janowitz 1948, 284, 300, 302–3, 309; Fussell 1989, chap. 10; Desch 1993–94; Browning 1998, 177–84; Kellett 1982, chap. 12.

19. "Ambush in Mogadishu," *Frontline*, PBS, August 29, 1998, also November 1, 2001.

20. McPherson 1997, chap. 2.

21. As Paul Fussell puts it, "Men will attack only if young, athletic, credulous, and sustained by some equivalent of the buddy system" (1989, 4). Or, in the words of Shils and Janowitz, when men "are placed in the entirely male society of a military unit, freed from the control of adult civilian society and missing its gratifications, they tend to regress to the adolescent condition. The show of 'toughness' and hardness which is regarded as a virtue

timately will produce results most likely to be lasting—will have to be primarily accomplished by domestic forces.

There are signs, particularly in the last decade, that this process is under way—that in an increasing number of places fanatics, criminals, and thugs, the chief (but not the only) instigators of what remains of war in the world, are being brought under control or sometimes aptly co-opted by effective governments. Criminality and criminal predation will still exist (there is some of that even in Canada), and there certainly will be plenty of other problems to worry about—famine, disease, malnutrition, pollution, corruption, poverty, politics, and economic travail. Moreover, terrorism, which, like crime, can be carried out by individuals or by very small groups, is unlikely, again like crime, ever to be completely expunged. Although it has caused far less damage than even quite minor warfare (at least so far), terrorism often arrests attention and inspires reaction far out of proportion to the harm it inflicts, and there is no reason to conclude that this condition will change.

However, a further (or continuing) decline in residual warfare and in the number of countries with criminal regimes, while far from certain, seems to be an entirely reasonable prospect. If the process continues, war, already substantially reduced to its thuggish remnants, will recede from the human experience.

18. Luard 1986, 58–59. See also Levy, Walker, and Edwards 2001, 17–19.
19. Luard 1986, 330–31, 354, 349, 361. Parker 1994, 42.
20. Clausewitz 1976, 87–88, 605–10. On Clausewitz's thought, see Brodie 1959, 37–38; 1976.
21. Lynn Montross, quoted in Levy 1983, 45.
22. See also Blainey 1973, 5–9. Ehrenreich vividly discusses what she calls war's "iron grip on human cultures" and its "remarkable resilience in the face of changing circumstances. . . . war appears to be far more robust than any particular religion, perhaps more robust than religion in general" (1997, 231–24, emphasis in the original). Over the last few centuries, however, a number of once-warlike cultures appear to have wriggled free from war's "iron grip" and to have been quite happy and content to alter their whole international lifestyle by seeking to avoid war entirely (see also Keeley 1996, 32). Robustness and resilience, it would seem, should be made of sterner stuff. However, this is not to suggest that religion has necessarily proven to be more robust than war: the Scandinavians have substantially managed to shuck that off as well.
23. Smith: Jones 1987, 235. Latter two qualities: Rosenberg and Birdzell 1986, 116–17. On oppressive war taxes, see Dessert 1995.
24. These people were similar to the "transnational moral entrepreneurs" identified by Ethan Nadelmann, that is, the sort of person who in the 1800s might have campaigned successfully against piracy, privateering, and slavery, and who in these times now rails against the international drug trade, pollution, and the killing of whales and elephants (1990). They were also similar to those idea entrepreneurs Neta Crawford (2002) identifies (indeed, they were often the same people) who successfully worked in the last century to promote decolonization as an international norm for the first time in human history. For a history of the movement, see Beales 1931; Hinsley 1963; Chickering 1975, chap. 1; Howard 1978, chap. 2; Mueller 1989, chap. 1; Cooper 1991.
25. Wilde 1946, 133–34.
26. Angell 1951, 145–49; J. D. B. Miller 1986, 4–8.
27. Joll 1984, 176–82. On antiwar activities of the French socialists, see Chickering 1975, chap. 8.
28. Von Suttner: Chickering 1975, 92–93, 327–28. Angell 1951, 146–47. See also O'Connell 1998, 248–49.
29. Keegan 1993, 21; Jefferson 1939, 262–63.
30. Stromberg 1982, 1–2. See also Mueller 1989, chap. 2.
31. Holmes: Lerner 1943, 20. Churchill: Weidhorn 1974, 20. Tocqueville: Stromberg 1982, 186. Frederick: Bernhardi 1914a, 27. Moltke: Brodie 1973, 264. Ryder 1899, 727. Ruskin 1866, 84, 85, 89; Milne 1935, 56.
32. Treitschke 1916, 2:599; Bernhardi 1914a, 26; Ruskin 1866, 88–89.
33. Bernhardi 1914a, 26; Treitschke 1916, 1:50. Nietzsche: Barclay 1911, 16. Moltke: Chickering 1975, 392–93. Cramb 1915, 128, 146; Kant 1952, 113 (section 28). Kant was in good philosophic company: according to Aristotle, "A time of war automatically enforces temperance and justice: a time of the enjoyment of prosperity, and license accompanied by peace, is more apt to make men overbearing" (1958, 231–22). Naval War College: Linderman 1987, 292.
34. Belloc: Stromberg 1982, 180. Stengel: Chickering 1975, 394. Stromberg 1982, 11, 189.
35. Pearson, Renan: Langer 1951, 88–89. Zola: Joll 1984, 186. Adams, Luce: Linderman 1987, 292. Stravinsky: Stromberg 1982, 51. Even some war opponents bought the notion that war could be progressive; they tried to argue, however, that although war may once have been productive and necessary, it was no longer so. In a lecture published in 1849, the American essayist Ralph Waldo Emerson concluded that "war educates the senses, calls into action the will, perfects the physical constitution, brings men into swift and close collision in critical moments that man measures man." But, he felt, "it is the ignorant and childish part of mankind that is the fighting part"; he argued that because civilization was now maturing and entering "higher stages," war was in "decline"—indeed, "on its last legs" (1904, 151, 152, 155, 156, 159). Herbert Spencer, a prominent Social Darwinist, came to a similar conclusion. Writing in 1908, he argued that although "indispensable" as a "process by which nations have been consolidated, organized, and disciplined," war had

done its work. Because "the peopling of the Earth by the more powerful and intelligent races is in great measure achieved," all that remains is to allow the workings of "the quiet pressure of a spreading industrial civilization on a barbarism which slowly dwindles" (1909, 664–65; see also Langer 1951, 89).

36. Holmes: Lerner 1943, 19–20. Treitschke 1916, 2:396. James 1911, 300–311; Tolstoy 1966, 1372.

37. Treitschke 1916, 2:443. Armed mobs: Esposito 1979, 217. Brisk: Lebow 1981, 251. On the short war illusion, see Farrar 1973; Snyder 1984; Van Evera 1984, 58–107. Bernhardi, however, thought that another seven years war "will unify and elevate the people and destroy the diseases which threaten the national health" (1914b, 233), and some other Germans agreed: see Chickering 1975, 390–91. Freud 1957, 14:278.

38. Howard 1984, 9; Schroeder 2001; see also Joll 1984. Von Suttner: Chickering 1975, 91. James 1911, 304 (emphasis in the original). As Robert O'Connell reflects of the time: "For many, the notion that an institution as apparently fundamental as warfare could have possibly outlived its usefulness was not simply implausible, it was utterly at odds with what they perceived to be happening around them. . . . [They saw] war as a palliative, an equipoise to the tedium and uncertainty of daily existence . . . [that] held out the possibility for adventure in an overcivilized world. . . . There is every reason to believe that such notions were widely held . . . by broad segments of the population in every corner of the industrialized world" (1998, 248).

3. WORLD WAR I AS A WATERSHED EVENT

1. Thus the exchange between two characters in Bernard Shaw's play *Major Barbara* is a non sequitur: "Well, the more destructive war becomes, the sooner it will be abolished, eh?" "Not at all, the more destructive war becomes the more fascinating we find it." Terrible things are often fascinating, but it doesn't follow that they will also be considered desirable.

2. Toynbee 1969, 214; Luard 1986, 365; Brodie 1973, 30; Hobsbawm 1987, 326; Holsti 1991, 175.

3. Taiping: Ho 1959, 275. World War I: Sivard 1987, 29–31 (all Sivard estimates are based on data gathered by William Eckhardt). Sivard's estimate of the Taiping Rebellion's total deaths is almost inconceivably low: see Ho 1959, 236–47.

4. This estimate takes the war death figures as detailed in Sivard (1987, 29–31) for the European combatants—that is, it excludes the deaths suffered in the war by Australia (60,000), Canada (55,000), India (50,000), New Zealand (16,000), Turkey (1,450,000), and the United States (126,000). If these non-European peoples were included in the calculations, the proportion killed in the war would be lower because their populations would dramatically inflate the percentage base. McEvedy and Jones (1978, 34) estimate that a total of 8 million military deaths were suffered in the war, substantially lower than Sivard's 12.6 million. A careful and widely accepted 1923 estimate of total military deaths is also lower: between 10 and 11 million (Dumas and Vedel-Petersen 1923, 144). Others estimate total battle deaths at 9 million (Winter 1989, 206; Small and Singer 1982, 89) or 7.7 million (Levy 1983, 91). Population estimate: McEvedy and Jones 1978, 19.

5. Botterweck and Ringgren 1986, 189–98. If the Bible is to be taken as literal truth, the Israelites launched a series of such wars. God was reportedly concerned that the current occupants of the promised land might subvert the Israelites by teaching them the "abominations which they have done unto their gods," thus causing the Israelites to sin. Accordingly it was required that they kill the heretics before such damage could come about (Deut. 20:16–18), and the book of Joshua relates the consequent utter annihilation of the peoples of Jericho, Ai, Libnah, Lachisk, Eglon, Hebron, Debir, Hazor, and the areas in between (the people of Gibeon, however, cut a deal and were merely enslaved).

6. Josephus 1982, 450–51. Riazan: Brent 1976, 117, 120. Herat: Rashid 2000, 37. Queller 1977, 149–53. Keeley 1996, 89–94.

7. Frederick: Luard 1986, 51. Twentieth-century wars: Small and Singer 1982, 82–99. Thirty Years War: Parker 1997, 188. Holsti 1991, 313.

8. Sivard estimates 2.4 million military and civilian deaths in the Napoleonic Wars (1987,

among soldiers is a response to these reactivated adolescent anxieties about weakness" (1948, 293–94).

22. Milne 1935, 222–23; Linderman 1987, 10; see also McPherson 1997, chap. 5.

23. See Smith 1949, 172–188; Keegan 1987, 197; Kellett 1982, 193–95.

24. McPherson 1997, 16; Desch 1993–94; Shils and Janowitz 1948.

25. McPherson 1997, 153; Peterson 2002; see also Judah 2000.

26. See also Valentino 2004.

27. Thus, in assessing the U.S. combat experience in World War II, Paul Fussell documents the considerable hatred combatants felt toward the Japanese and their desire for revenge for the attack on Pearl Harbor, but he also demonstrates that they mostly developed a strong sense of cynicism about the war, spent almost no time discussing ideological issues, and mainly fought out of loyalty to their buddies and to get the whole thing over so they could go home (1989, chap. 10). See also Bourke 1999, chap. 5.

28. Africa: Fearon and Laitin 1996, 717; see also Keeley 1996, 178. Poor correlation: Collier 2000; Collier and Hoeffler 2001; Fearon and Laitin 2003, 83–84; Sadowski 1998; Keen 1998, chap. 2; Valentino 2004. On the high intermarriage rates in war-torn former Yugoslavia, see Gagnon 1994–95, 134; Bennett 1995, 192. Hicks: Cohen 1998, 296; similarly for Croats on their country cousins: "I hate them. I hate the refugees. They don't want to work, and they smell" (Merrill 1999, 126). See also Spolar 1995; Woodward 1995, 364; Kinzer 1995b; Bowen 1996; Sadowski 1998, 78–80.

29. Keeley 1996, 158. Unshackle: Goldhagen 1998, 443. Like us: Smith 1996; see also Goldhagen 1998, 593–94. Critics: Bartov 1998, 34; Browning 1998, 193. Dower argues that the images initially went from being racist and vicious to racist and patronizing—the Japanese, once pictured as menacing, blood-soaked gorillas, now became appealing little monkeys, for example (1986, 302). But even this is a profound transformation, and it happened almost immediately after the war.

30. See also Kaufmann 1996, 141–46; Keen 2000, 22.

31. Desch 1993–94, 361.

32. McPherson 1997, 6–8, 59, 173. Further, as McPherson readily admits, the diaries and letters he dissects very disproportionately came from the committed—from officers, from slaveholders, from those in the professional and middle classes, and from early volunteers—and far less from draftees, substitutes, and those who enlisted for bounties. Moreover, he suspects that some who gallantly wrote of "duty, honor, country, and liberty were merely 'masking' other motives" (1997, ix, 28, 101–2). For a different perspective on Civil War combatants and on the reenlistment issue, see Linderman 1987, especially pp. 261–65; for McPherson's appraisal of this work, see McPherson 1997, 186.

33. Milgram 1975, 116–21. See also Valentino 2004, 268n78.

34. On the organized use of jailed criminals in the Turkish massacres of Armenians in 1915, see Staub 1989, 182; Valentino 2004, chap. 5. On the use of mostly criminal paramilitaries to carry out the massacre at Srebrenica in Bosnia in 1995, see Kaldor 1999, 55.

35. McPherson 1997, 8–9, 116.

36. Stouffer et al. 1949, 36–38; Watson 1978, 49; Grinker and Spiegel 1945, 11–12; McPherson 1997, 9.

37. Peer pressure may motivate at least some criminal warfare as well; showing off one's viciousness, prowess, and daring to one's buddies helps motivate some to commit ordinary crime. Criminal combatants, however, are probably far less likely to carry this to the point of being willing to die for each other.

38. Once the war is over and they are decommissioned and released among the civilian population, criminals are likely to return to their predatory ways—particularly, of course, if they are unpaid or underpaid. Even noncriminals in a criminal army may turn to crime when they return to civilian life: when most soldiers are, or seem to be, criminals, employers are likely to discriminate against all ex-soldiers as a shortcut method for avoiding the hiring of criminals and other undesirables, a process often exacerbated by the fact that war frequently weakens economies.

39. Essence of the guerrilla: Kaldor 1999, 97. Mao's phases: Griffith 1961, 20–22.

40. Keeley 1996, 42–48. See also Lieven 1998, 5, 130, 324–54; Valentino 2004, chap. 6.

41. On the mostly futile quest for "decisive" battle, see Weigley 1991. However, the results of wars so waged can be decisive in that they can cause the losing entity to cease to exist, as Keeley suggests (1996, 223).
42. McPherson 1997, 42.
43. Keeley 1996, chap. 5 and p. 175.
44. Keeley 1996, chaps. 2–4, 6, 7, and pp. 174–75. Such conflicts are often designated "low intensity" in much the same sense that the human destruction caused by the automobile in the United States can be considered low. On average, each day only about a hundred people die in automobile accidents, and this loss is spread over a huge area. Cumulatively, however, automobiles are the cause of more death than most wars: tens of thousands each year, well over a quarter million each decade.

2. THE CONTROL OF WAR AND THE RISE OF WAR AVERSION

1. Contamine 1984, 23; Kaeuper 1988, 11; Howard 2000, 13; Tilly 1990, 184 (emphasis in the original); see also Parker 1996, 1. In every year but one between 1550 and 1650, note Geoffrey and Angela Parker, there was a war going on somewhere between European states, "and even in that year great armies were on the move and a major war was just averted" (1977, 46).
2. Tilly 1985, 173; Keegan 1987, 194; see also Ehrenreich 1997, 160, 174. The recruitment process receives sardonic treatment in Shakespeare's *Henry IV, Part I*, act 4, scene 2, and *Henry IV, Part II*, act 3, scene 2.
3. Recruitment: Parker 1995, 32–39. Escape and refuge: Keegan 1998, 48–49. Hundred Years War: Wright 2000, 69.
4. Desertion: Parker 1996, 55–58; 1997, 180–82. Sieges: Parker 1995, 38.
5. Boardman 1998, 92, 110–11, see also 158.
6. Tilly 1990, 184; 1985, 173. Scorchers: Keegan 1993, 13. Business enterprise: Berdal and Malone 2000, 1. See also Parker 1996, 58–59; 1997, 179. It was the motto even of the well-organized Gustavus Adolphus that "War must support war" (Millett and Moreland 1976, 15; see also Contamine 1984, 57). Wanton destruction was central, not peripheral, to Genghis Khan's approach to war. He found the "greatest pleasure in life is to defeat your enemies, to chase them before you, to rob them of their wealth, to see those dear to them bathed in tears, to ride their horses, and to clasp to your breast their wives and daughters" (Kellett 1982, 292–93).
7. Kaeuper 1988, 84; Hale 1985, 179.
8. Wright 2000, 7–8, 4–5, 69, 72–73, 3. See also Lynn 2003, 85–93.
9. Caferro 1998, xiv (names and slogans), 2 (camps and novelist), 1 (nun), 25–30 and 36–80 (destruction). See also Singer 2003, 216.
10. Keegan 1993, 13–16. Mercenary armies: Caferro 1998. Ehrenreich 1997, 179–81. See also Parker 1997, 183–86; Levy, Walker, and Edwards 2001, 28.
11. Parker 1995, 41.
12. Frederick: Luvaas 1999, 72-28. Wellington: Brett-James 1961, 269. According to one contemporary observer, an English recruiter would "go to the very places in which he is least of all likely to meet with steady and respectable men. He goes to the public house, to the fair, the races, or the wake, the haunts of the idle and the dissolute, and in many cases, having stupefied some lazy vagabond with intoxicating drink, he slips a shilling into his hand. . . . Of those who voluntarily enlist, some few are driven by poverty, . . . some had disgraced themselves in their situation or employment, many have committed misdemeanours which expose them to the penalties of the law of the land, and most are confirmed drunkards" (Davies 1954, 68).
13. Brett-James 1961, 269.
14. Tilly 1985, 178. On the later, and somewhat related, state control over privateering, piracy, mercenarism, and armed mercantile companies, see Thomson 1994.
15. Augustine: Kalyvas 2001, 105. Tilly 1985, 184.
16. Tilly 1990, 185; Schroeder 2001; Levy, Walker, and Edwards 2001, 27.
17. Tilly 1990, 185. See also Levy, Walker, and Edwards 2001, 18–19.

14. Smith 1986, 231, 238–39; Hitler 1943, 649, 653–54 (emphasis in the original).
15. Stoakes 1986, 216. Opposition: Smith 1986, 239; Stoakes 1986, 237; Hildebrand 1973, chap. 1.
16. Rich 1973, xi. Something similar happened with Hitler's anti-Semitism. Although he never reversed his often-proclaimed anti-Semitism, he toned it down as he came closer to office; then, after becoming chancellor, he scarcely mentioned the "Jewish question" at all in public for several years, and because of their unpopularity, he was extremely careful to avoid being associated with violent anti-Semitic outrages perpetrated by his followers. See Kershaw 1987, 233–41; also Steinert 1977, 136.
17. Hitler 1942, 1216, 1218, 1220, 1260; see also 1099. For a compilation of Hitler's public statements against war, see http://psweb.sbs.ohio-state.edu/faculty/jmueller/hitpeace.
18. Bell 1986, 77. See also Kagan 1995, 340.
19. Fest 1974, 536. Hermann Göring, working with members of Hitler's Foreign Office, apparently sought to develop a peaceful foreign policy built around a strong position for Germany within Europe—one of indirect domination—while pursuing the acquisition of overseas colonies (Hildebrand 1973, 57, 71, 143, 173n21; Stoakes 1986, 237). And Hitler's foreign minister, Joachim von Ribbentrop, far from supporting an invasion to the east as the natural destiny of Germany, advocated instead the formation of an anti-British alliance with the Soviet Union and, like Göring, the acquisition of overseas colonies. This view was also supported by members of the German Foreign Office and the navy, as well as by industrial leaders (Hildebrand 1973, 48–49, 58; Stoakes 1986, 238).
20. Kershaw 1987, 2, 143; Manchester 1988, 307. Another analyst of German public opinion characterizes it as "dead set" against major war: Steinert 1977, 50. In the midst of the Munich crises of 1938, a motorized division was sent off to the Czech frontier at dusk as hundreds of thousands of Berliners were leaving work. Remembering how Berliners on these same streets had sent their troops off to war in 1914 by showering them with cheers and flowers, American journalist William Shirer was amazed to see that the citizens of 1938 "ducked into the subways, refused to look on, and the handful that did stood at the curb in utter silence unable to find a word of cheer for the flower of their youth going away to the glorious war." Hitler emerged to review the troops from his balcony, but even this failed to draw a crowd: "Hitler looked grim, then angry, and soon went inside, leaving his troops to parade by unreviewed." Shirer called it "the most striking demonstration against war I've ever seen" and concluded that the German people were "dead set against war" (Shirer 1941, 142–43). Hitler reportedly remarked disgustedly, but as it turned out inaccurately, "with these people I cannot make war" (Taylor 1979, 877).
21. Kershaw 1987, 229. The Nazis found that "enthusiasm for war itself and for an apocalyptic struggle for 'living space' was difficult to raise outside circles of nazified youth, the SS, and Party fanatics." Thus "although the overwhelming majority of the population clearly wanted 'national success'—the restoration of Germany's power and glory in Europe—it was just as clearly unwilling to entertain the idea of national sacrifices to attain them, least of all—certainly for the older generation who remembered the suffering of 1914–18—another war" (Kershaw 1987, 122).
22. Watt 1975, 11; Weinberg 1980, 18–19. See also Gat 2001, 83.
23. Posen 1984, 211–13, 218. Isolate: Weinberg 1980, 19–20, 1994, 22.
24. Cooper 1978, 53; one of the generals described the atmosphere as "like that of a roulette table when a player stakes his future on a single number" (54); see also Weinberg 1970, 262. Manchester 1988, 622.
25. Knox 1984, 42–43, 49–57; Steinert 1977, 25–102; Rich 1973, 211. The 1940 victory: see also Mearsheimer 1983, 99. Hitler often complained about the "Angst and cowardice in the army," whose officers "as yet did not understand the meaning of the new age" (Knox 1984, 50).
26. Rich 1973, 11; Fest 1974, 8; Smith 1986, 238; Weinberg 1995, 47; Stoakes 1986, 238–39. Kershaw: "There seems little agreement among historians that Hitler did personally take the 'big' decisions on foreign policy after 1933" (1985, 114); by 1936, "Hitler's power was absolute" (2000, xxxvi). John Stoessinger: "If one looks at the outbreak of World War II . . . it was the personality of Hitler that was decisive" (1982, 208). Hans J. Morgenthau: "The victories which German diplomacy won from 1933 to 1940 were the victories of one

man's mind, and the deterioration of that mind was a direct cause of the disasters which marked the last years of the Nazi regime" (1948, 107). For the rare argument that Hitler, though central to the situation, was mainly swept or buffeted into the war by the force of events, see Taylor 1961; for a deft rebuttal, see Hinsley 1963, chap. 15.

27. Lukacs 1997, 134; Rich 1973, xxxii, xxxvi–xxxix; Bullock 1952, 735; Trevor-Roper 1953, vii.

28. Göring: Overy 1989, 39. Joke: Vassiltchikov 1987, 52.

29. Weinberg 1980, 664. Depends on me: Alexandroff and Rosecrance 1977, 416–17. Irreplaceable: *Documents on German Foreign Policy* 1954, 443. See also Knox 1984, 54; Mearsheimer 1983, 112.

30. Turner 1996, 111.

31. Cooper 1978, 26; Cooper suggests Walther von Reischenau as a "possible exception." Moreover, many military leaders believed they needed broad popular support to perpetrate a war: as the army's chief of staff, General Ludwig Beck, put it, "Today an anxious disquietude affects the masses; they fear war; . . . they see no justifiable grounds for war" (Craig 1956, 488). The evidence strongly suggests that that condition was extremely unlikely to change.

32. Turner 1996, 112–14. See also Kagan 1995, 317, 327–28.

33. Byman and Pollack 2001, 115. On Poland: Read and Fisher 1988, 43; also Byman and Pollack 2001, 117–18. See also Kagan 1995, 413–15; Manchester 1988, 512–13.

34. World War I: Howard 2001. Institutions: Ikenberry, for example, seems to suggest that disaster was inevitable because the United States failed to join the League of Nations (2001, chap. 5); the name Hitler does not appear in the index of his book.

35. A few observers at the time did find it disconcerting, but many concluded that this was simply the way the Germans were reestablishing a sense of community, honor, self-respect, and national pride after the devastations of a great war and a severely troubled aftermath—and to a considerable extent that was exactly what the militaristic ritual was all about. On the relation of the uniform to a sense of honor in Germany, see Vagts 1959, 444.

36. Waite 1952, 29. Novels: Owen 1984, 81–97; a survey among 2,600 male youths as late as 1932 found it still to be the most widely read book (98).

37. Fest 1974, 5–8. See also Haffner 1979, 100; Byman and Pollack 2001. On the other hand, Hitler was also lucky. The chaos, grievance, and discontent worked for him, although he created much of it too. And he surely needed assistance—colleagues who were worshipfully subservient; a superb army that could be manipulated and whipped into action; a population capable of being mesmerized and led to slaughter; foreign opponents who were confused, disorganized, gullible, myopic, and fainthearted; neighbors who would rather be prey than fight—although he created much of this as well. Hitler took the conditions of the world as he found them and then shaped them to his own ends.

38. The many people who have tried to discredit Shakespeare (the Stratford man, as they often call him) have been impelled by information of his poor education and inadequate upbringing. Hitler rose almost literally from the gutters of Vienna to a position in which he virtually single-handedly instigated and shaped some of history's greatest and most horrible events. But if we knew as little about his background, about his innate skills, and about his ability to develop as we know about Shakespeare's, many people would today be discounting his importance and concluding that he must have been a convenient mouthpiece for backroom manipulators. Indeed, it seems a reasonable, if depressing, prediction that hundreds of years from now, when the twentieth century for most people will have been reduced to a few catch words, the name that will represent it in the popular imagination will not be Winston Churchill, Pablo Picasso, George Balanchine, Franklin Roosevelt, Albert Einstein, or even Fred Astaire. Its best-remembered figure will be Adolf Hitler.

5. WAR AND CONFLICT DURING THE COLD WAR

1. Luard 1986, 231–33.

2. Vasquez 1993, 151, 293.

3. Howard 2000, 92. For a discussion of the process and a detailed enumeration of territorial

29), when Europe had a population of 180 million (McEvedy and Jones 1978, 18); this estimate generates a death rate of 1.3 percent as against 4.1 percent for World War I. However, authoritative estimates of deaths in the Napoleonic Wars by nineteenth-century historians (which are more relevant for present purposes because these would inform the perspectives of their contemporaries) were often much higher. For example, Sivard estimates total military deaths to have been 1.4 million, but most historians held that the French alone suffered between 1.7 million and 3 million; even those who discounted that estimate argued that total military deaths in the wars were less than 2 million (Dumas and Vedel-Petersen 1923, 28). Levy's (1983, 90) estimate of battle deaths in the war, 1.9 million, is substantially higher than Sivard's. For World War I estimates, see n. 4.

9. The legend is reported in Wedgwood 1938, 516.
10. Kaeuper 1988, 77–117. Primitive wars: Keeley 1996. 1929: Overy 1982, 16. Thirty Years War: Almost two-thirds of the expenditures of the city of Nordlingen were devoted to direct military demands, and the average wealth declined precipitously. Although the city gradually recovered during the next twenty years, another cycle of wars left it "helpless to solve its own financial problems." It took fifty more years to recover (and then only with outside intervention), at which point it was plunged once again into deep debt by the wars of the French Revolution (Friedrichs 1979, 154, 169). During the fourteenth century, the Italian city of Siena was raided by mercenary armies every two years, a process that exhausted its economy and destroyed its viability as an independent entity (Caferro 1998). Nicholas Wright observes of the Hundred Years War, "If the soldiers are 'friendly' in the sense that they are of the same nominal allegiance as their victims, their very existence interrupts the work of the ramshackle fiscal structures and prevents a fair distribution of the tax-yield. If they are 'enemy' soldiers they must live off the country and their very propose is to wreck, or intercept, its taxable resources" (2000, 122).
11. Because of this phenomenon, World War I was more notably destructive compared with earlier continent-wide wars if one deals only with battle deaths. Levy calculates battle deaths as a percentage of the entire population of the Continent and concludes that World War I was 3.6 times more destructive than the Napoleonic Wars by this measure and some 2.4 times more destructive than the Thirty Years War (1983, 89–91). However, if a war generates horror, this should logically spring from its total destructiveness, not simply from the deaths it inflicts on young men in uniform. Indeed, the "unnecessary" deaths of "innocent civilians" has usually been seen to be war's chief outrage. For an able discussion, see Holmes 1989.
12. Among Americans, for example, only 2 percent of those wounded by gas died as compared with 24 percent of those wounded by bullets or shrapnel; for the British the comparison was 3 versus 37 percent; for the Germans it was 3 versus 43 percent (Gilchrist 1928, 48; see also McNaugher 1990). In the conclusion to the official British history of the war, chemical weapons are relegated to a footnote, which asserts that gas "made war uncomfortable . . . to no purpose" (Edmonds and Maxwell-Hyslop 1947, 606).
13. Some people, in fact, did draw this lesson. H. L. Gilchrist, the U.S. Army's leading expert on the medical effects of chemical warfare, concluded that gas "is the most humane method of warfare ever applied on the battle field" (1928, 47). In 1925, the British defense analyst Basil Liddell Hart speculated that "gas may well prove the salvation of civilization from otherwise inevitable collapse in case of another world war" (Mearsheimer 1988, 90). See also Stockton 1932, 536–39.
14. Linderman 1987, 266–97; Mueller 1989, 30–32, 38–39.
15. World War I as the first literary war: Fussell 1975, 157. Wilson 1962, ix; Winter 1989, 826.
16. Specter of annihilation: Brown 1968, 65, 164, 180–81. Churchill 1932, 246, 248; Freud 1930, 144. Baldwin: Kagan 1987, 26. It was also widely believed in the West that, assuming anything was left standing, a major war would lead to a worldwide depression: Milward 1977, 16. See also Bialer 1980, 46–47, 158.
17. Clarke 1966, 169–70. Similarly, official discussions in Britain about the future danger of aerial bombardment seem to have become general only in the 1930s, when another war began to loom as a distinct possibility (and when, of course, the airplane had been developed much more fully). It was, as one military analyst put it at the time, "a brain child

born in the early years of the century and turned into a Frankenstein in the early 1930s" (Bialer 1980, 12, also 1–2). It is also noteworthy that those few in Europe who still wanted war—Adolf Hitler in particular—correctly assumed that the doomsday theorists were wrong (Bialer 1980, 133–34). For nonapocalyptic visions in the 1930s of a future war, see Stockton 1932, 501–49; and Dupuy and Eliot 1937.

18. Lloyd George 1933, 65–66. For the impact of the invasion of Belgium on turning pacifist and neutralist factions in Britain into war supporters, see Robbins 1976, 30–32.

19. Rappard 1940, 20; for a similar statement by the Labour Party on October 14, see Mayer 1959, 143. On Asquith: Robbins 1976, 11.

20. Wells 1914, 9, 12, 14.

21. Rappard 1940, 21.

22. Lloyd George 1938, 22. See also Rappard 1940, 46–47; Herman 1969, 195.

23. Weigley 1976, 62; Mayer 1959, 347; George and George 1956, 173. Wilson and the antiwar movement: Patterson 1976, 205–9. See also Herman 1969, chap. 7; Mandelbaum 2002.

24. Asquith: Rappard 1940, 46. Gas casualties: Brown 1968, 14. For a discussion of the destruction of Prussian militarism as an important British war aim, see Gooch 1981, chap. 7. On the effectiveness of British propaganda, see Squires 1935.

25. Link 1957, 88–89. House: Rappard 1940, 33; see also George and George 1956, chaps. 9–11. Lloyd George: Rappard 1940, 42–44.

26. On the German and Austrian prewar peace movement, see Wank 1988; Chickering 1975, 1988. American peace groups: Chatfield 1971, 15–87.

27. The National Arbitration and Peace Conference, which packed Carnegie Hall in New York in 1907, was supported by 8 cabinet officers, 2 former presidential candidates, 10 senators, 4 Supreme Court justices, 9 governors, 10 mayors, 27 millionaires, 18 college presidents, 30 labor leaders, 40 bishops, 60 newspaper editors, and representatives of 166 businesses (Patterson 1976, 129). Socialists: Wank 1988, 48–52.

28. Gooch 1911, 248–49. For similar expressions from the era, see Mueller 1995a, 187–90.

29. Angell 1951, 178.

4. WORLD WAR II AS A REINFORCING EVENT

1. A. A. Milne crisply characterized the change this way: "In 1913, with a few exceptions we all thought war was a natural and fine thing to happen, so long as we were well prepared for it and had no doubt about coming out the victor. Now, with a few exceptions, we have lost our illusions, we are agreed that war is neither natural nor fine, and that the victor suffers from it equally with the vanquished" (1935, 9–10). To a degree, the process traced in this book, derived mainly from a bottom-up approach, parallels one set out by Alexander Wendt applying a top-down one (1999, chap. 6). He labels the medieval and early modern condition in which other states are seen as "enemies" as "Hobbesian," the later one in which they are seen as "rivals" as "Lockean," and the last one in which they are seen as "friends" as "Kantian."

2. Zacher 2001, 219–20.

3. Kagan 1995, 329–30. On German anticipations, see Fischer 1967, 1975; see also Kagan 1987, 22–24; Glynn 1987; Howard 2001.

4. Mussolini 1935, 7.

5. Knox 1984, 44–45.

6. Knox 1982, 48, 122, 290.

7. Vagts 1959, 451.

8. Luard 1986, 368.

9. Butow 1961, 99–101, 108–9, 154; Rich 1973, 224–25.

10. Butow 1961, 267. Support of Japanese people: Butow 1961, 167, 251–52, 332–33.

11. See also Brodie 1973, 272.

12. Watt 1989, 610; this passage is quoted approvingly by another distinguished historian, Gordon A. Craig, in a review of the Watt book (1989, 11). Weinberg 1980, 664, and 1994, 29–30; Hinsley 1987, 71–72; Manchester 1988, 197; Lukacs 1997, xi; Keegan 1989. See also Kershaw 2000, 841; Byman and Pollack 2001; Bullock 1993, 973.

13. Smith 1986, 209–23, chap. 5.

tant Soviet official observed in 1987 that "previously we reasoned: the worse for the adversary, the better for us. . . . But today this is no longer true. . . . The better things are going in the European world economy, the higher the stability and the better the prospects for our development" (Snyder 1987–88, 115). On the origins and development of this important ideological change, see in addition Mueller 1989, 205–13; Hyland 1990, chap. 14; Oberdorfer 1992, 141–42, 158–64; Garthoff 1994, 255–65, 358–68, 753–57, 769–78; Zelikow and Rice 1995, chap. 1; Checkel 1997; Vasquez 1998, chap. 13; Kramer 1999; Lundestad 2000; English 2001, 2002; Suri 2002; Brooks and Wohlforth 2000–2001, 2002. For analysis concluding that the decline in fervor in the Soviet Union for its ideological commitment to the international Communist revolutionary movement "could eventually result in the end of the cold war" and thus that "we may be coming to the end of the world as we know it," see Mueller 1986. See also Mueller forthcoming.

35. Reagan: quoted in the *New York Times,* December 9, 1988, A18. Bush 1990, 541, 546, 553, 602, 606, 617. Notably, Reagan tied this development to an end of the Soviet expansionary threat, not to reform of its domestic system. That is, cooperation, even alliance, was not contingent on the progress of Soviet domestic reform. Reagan was also reflecting a comment by the quintessential Cold Warrior, John Foster Dulles: "The basic change we need to look forward to isn't necessarily a change from Communism to another form of government. The question is whether you can have Communism in one country or whether it has to be for the world. If the Soviets had national Communism we could do business with their government" (quoted in Gaddis 1982, 143).

36. The *New York Times* proclaimed on April 2, 1989, that the Cold War was over. For other such declarations at the time and for a fuller development of the argument about ideology and the ending of the Cold War, see Mueller forthcoming.

37. Luard 1986, 77; see also Johnson 1995. There are a few potential exceptions. The most likely prospect is the Soviet suppression of a rebellion in its satellite, Hungary, in 1956, although in many respects this seems more like a colonial war. There are some aspects of the Croatian offensive in neighboring Bosnia in 1993–94 during the chaotic civil war that are sometimes seen to be essentially international in scope. And NATO's rather bizarre "war" over Kosovo in 1999, discussed more fully in later chapters, might also be considered an exception.

38. Toynbee 1950, 4. Morgenthau: Boyle 1985, 37. Kissinger 1977, 304; Brzezinski 1986, xiii. See also Johnson 1995.

39. Luard 1986, 64. As one reporter put it, "The Latin American left's 30-year obsession with armed struggle as a means to revolution has come to an end" (Rohter 1996; see also Brooke 1990).

40. Johnson 1995.

41. Luard 1986, 52, 60; Ravlo, Gleditsch, and Dorussen 2001.

42. See Crawford 2002; Jackson 1993; Ray 1989, 431–32; Keeley 1996, 166–67.

6. CIVIL WAR AND TERRORISM AFTER THE COLD WAR

1. Chirot 2000, 675. See also Howard 2000, 112–13.

2. Van Creveld 1991, ix, 197; Ehrenreich 1997, 227; Kaldor 1999, 6, 8; Huntington 1993b, 1993c, 1996. See also Hamburg 1993; Moynihan 1993; Brzezinski 1993; Ignatieff 1997, 3, 5–6, 132. For an able critique of this literature, see Kalyvas 2001; see also Henderson and Singer 2002. As Sandra Halperin (1998) has documented, ethnic conflict occurred frequently in Europe during the nineteenth century—far more often than in the twentieth.

3. Gamba and Cornwell 2000, 169–70.

4. Kaldor 1999, 31.

5. For an extended development of this argument, see Mueller 2000a, 2000b.

6. In all Communist countries, certainly including Yugoslavia, people were determinedly subjected to decades of Communist propaganda in the media, yet many—probably most—failed in the end to be convinced by it. If media promotion could guarantee lasting impact, all Yugoslavs would today be worshiping Tito and all Americans would be driving Edsels. For a discussion, see Mueller 1994, 129–36. See also Zimmerman 1996, xi, 209–10.

7. Cigar 1993, 315–19; Woodward 1995, 238; Bennett 1995, 167; Vasić 1996, 128; Burg and Shoup 1999, 51; Tanner 1997, 269–70; Judah 1997, 185, 189; Oberschall 2001, 142; Udovicki and Cerovic 1995; Sikavica 1995, 138; Silber and Little 1997, 177; Gagnon 1994–95, 162; Doder and Branson 1999, 98; Vulliamy 1994, 19.

8. Doder and Branson 1999, 97–98.

9. Burg and Shoup 1999, 84, 130; Judah 1997, 170–72, 192–95. Lack of success: Tanner 1997, 269.

10. Burg and Shoup 1999, 137; Oberschall 2001, 141. Eighty-three groups: United Nations Commission of Experts 1994, para. 14. Booty: Borger 1997b. See also Ron 2000a, 297; Cohen 1998, 192, 410–11; United Nations Commission of Experts 1994, paras. 3, 18, 24, 30; Firestone 1993; Thomas 1999, 98; Woodward 1995, 238, 249, 265; Vasić 1996, 128, 134; Kaldor 1999, 93; Udovicki and Cerovic 1995; Ignatieff 1997, 132; Tanner 1997, 245; Judah 1997, chap. 9; Doder and Branson 1999, 101–3, 117–18; Hedges 2002, 9; Andreas 2004.

11. Primary motive: United Nations Commission of Experts 1994, para. 100. Kill a man for a lamb: Doder and Branson 1999, 97.

12. Vasić 1996, 128. See also Thomas 1999, 99.

13. United Nations Commission of Experts 1994, paras. 125–29; Judah 1997, 186; Sudetic 1998, 97–98; Thomas 1999, 94. Arkan began as a juvenile delinquent and later developed into a skilled bank robber, plying his trade mostly in northern Europe (a dashing fellow, he often left the tellers bouquets of roses). Returning to Belgrade after breaking out of jail, the fugitive became a member of the criminal underground and enjoyed a special relationship with the police and with Serbia's internal affairs ministry (see also Doder and Branson 1999, 100–101; Kaldor 1999, 47; Ron 2000a, 295). He was assassinated gangland style in Belgrade in January 2000. The fanatical, pot-bellied Šešelj is more of an intellectual, spent a year teaching political science at the University of Michigan in his younger years, and later seems to have become mentally unbalanced as the result of the torture and beatings he endured while in prison in Yugoslavia for counterrevolutionary activities. One academic colleague described him as "disturbed, totally lost and out of his mind" (United Nations Commission of Experts 1994, paras. 107, 108; see also Judah 1997, 187). "Always drunk": Kaldor 1999, 48. Ćelo: Cohen 1998, 280; Kaldor 1999, 48; Block 1993, 9. Juka: United Nations Commission of Experts 1994, para. 74; Maass 1996, 31; Block 1993, 9. Tuta: Block 1993, 9. On these issues, see also Husarska 1995; Tanner 1997, 245; Rieff 1995, 131–32; Vulliamy 1994, 314–16; Ignatieff 1997, 131; Burg and Shoup 1999, 137–39; Sadowski 1998, 163. The percentage of soccer hooligans who have a criminal record seems to be very high (Buford 1991, 28). Also associated are racist attitudes; a proclivity for extreme right-wing politics; a capacity to imbibe huge amounts of liquor; a strident and vicious boorishness; a deep need for being accepted by the "lads"; and an affinity for, even a lusting after, the thrill, exhilaration, and euphoria of violence. On the war-anticipating pitched battle between supporters of the Zagreb and Belgrade soccer clubs in 1990, see Tanner 1997, 228; Merrill 1999, 169.

14. Vasić 1996, 134. Weekend warriors: Sikavica 1995, 137. Dacevic: Ron 2000b, 627–28.

15. Zimmerman 1996, 152; Rieff 1995, 130; Block 1993. Stallone: Rieff 1995, 130; see also Husarska 1995. Black ribbons: United Nations Commission of Experts 1994, para. 291; Cohen 1998, 126. Maass also applies the "Rambo" image: 1996, 111, 155. Naser Orić, the muscular former bodyguard who became the Muslim warlord of Srebrenica, often liked to wear leather jackets, designer sunglasses, and thick gold chains. Juka's troops, called the Wolves, variously sported crew cuts, black jumpsuits, sunglasses, basketball shoes, and masks (United Nations Commission of Experts 1994, para. 76). The Muslim paramilitary group, the Black Swans, whose members sometimes served as bodyguards for Bosnia's president when he ventured outside Sarajevo (Burg and Shoup 1999, 137), wore a round patch depicting a black swan having intercourse with a supine woman (United Nations Commission of Experts 1994, para. 142).

16. Woodward 1995, 254, also 356, 485; Maass 1996, 6, 7, 16, 30, 48, 61, 79, 80, 85; Vulliamy 1994, 19, 46, also 307–16. Vasilejevic: Firestone 1993. UN commission: United Nations Commission of Experts 1994, para. 21; see also Kaldor 1999, 53. Hooligans and gang

changes since 1945, see Zacher 2001. See also van Creveld 1999a, 28–29; Gray 2002, 2; Kaldor 1999, 5.

4. Gaddis 1974, 388.

5. For an able analysis and discussion, see Gould-Davies 1999. See also Roberts 1999; Lundestad 1999, chap. 2; and especially Macdonald 1995/96.

6. Lenin: Burin 1963, 337; Leffler 1994, 17. Stalin: Historicus 1949, 198; Taubman 1982, 224. As Taubman points out and as is discussed later in this chapter, Stalin was referring to wars *between* capitalist states, something often neglected when the West examined this statement; nevertheless, even taking this into account, the declaration clearly remains profoundly threatening to capitalist states; on this issue more generally, see Burin 1963, 334–54. Khrushchev: Hudson, Lowenthal, and MacFarquhar 1961, 214, 196.

7. The Soviet Union also developed a social and political system that was singularly repugnant to liberal Westerners. Under Lenin and Stalin, a massive tyranny was established in which a vicious totalitarian government systematically visited brutalities and spectacular economic mismanagement upon its own citizenry. During Stalin's tenure, millions were shot, sent to death camps, or deliberately starved to death. In terms of domestic human destruction, mounting evidence suggests that corpse for corpse, Stalin may have outpaced Hitler as a monster (Conquest 1986, 306; see also Applebaum 2003, 578–85).

8. For the seminal and quintessential statement of this perspective, one that stresses the ideological threat from the outset, see Kennan 1947. See also Macdonald 1995/96. In many respects, containment policy was a resurrection and a relabeling of the policy applied by the British and French against the Germans during the "phoney war" period of 1939–40. Mueller 1995a, 105; Gat 2001, 83.

9. For an excellent analysis, see Burin 1963. Even many of those most hostile to the Soviet regime during the Cold War concluded that the Soviet Union never saw major war as a productive, viable, useful, or remotely sensible procedure for advancing revolution. Thus, Michael Voslensky asserted that Soviet leaders desire "external expansions" but that their "aim is to win the struggle between the two systems without fighting" (1984, 320–30). And Richard Pipes argued that "Soviet interests . . . are to avoid general war with the 'imperialist camp' while inciting and exacerbating every possible conflict within it" (1984, 190–91).

10. Leites 1953, 46–53. Pipes also stresses the Soviet tactical emphasis on "utmost caution," patience, and prudence (1984, 52–53).

11. Lenin: Burin 1963, 336 (emphasis by Lenin). Stalin 1973, 471–72. Khrushchev: Hudson, Lowenthal, and MacFarquhar 1961, 43–44, 210–11; see also Burin 1963, 353.

12. Hosmer and Wolfe 1983, 185; Taracouzio 1940, 88–89.

13. Khrushchev 1970, 370; Simmons 1975, 163. "Real Communist": Khrushchev 1970, 368.

14. Shulman 1963, 150. See also Rees 1964, 21–24; Gaddis 1974, 396; Taubman 1982, 193.

15. We smashed: Hudson, Lowenthal, and MacFarquhar 1961, 211. Intra-imperialist: Shevchenko 1985, 103. See also Snyder 1987–88, 108.

16. Kennedy 1971, 58, 86–87. The American pledge not to invade required international verification measures; because Cuba's leader, Fidel Castro, never agreed to this, the pledge technically does not hold (Garthoff 1987, 80–83; Kissinger 1979, 633).

17. Khrushchev: Werth 1964, xii; Lebow and Stein 1994, 110. A report from a "reliable, well-placed" Soviet source says that the leadership issued a formalized secret directive that it had decided not to go to war even if the United States invaded Cuba: Garthoff 1987, 51. Kennedy: Kennedy 1971, 40, 105; see also Sorensen 1965, 513.

18. Ball: Ball 1982, 307. McNamara: Trachtenberg 1985, 146. Transcripts: Welch and Blight 1987–88, 27–28. Rusk: Lukas 1987, 58; Blight, Nye, and Welch 1987, 178–79; Lebow and Stein 1994, 127–28.

19. Welch and Blight 1987–88, 27. See also Blight, Nye, and Welch 1987, 184; Schlesinger 1978, 528–29; Lebow and Stein 1994, chap. 6; Jervis 1989; Brodie 1973, 426; Bundy 1988, 453–57, 461–62.

20. For an extended discussion of the most likely candidate for an exception to this generalization, the confrontation between the United States and the USSR at the time of the 1973 war in the Middle East, see Lebow and Stein 1994, chaps. 7–11. As they point out, the United States went on alert to try to prevent the Soviets from doing something the Soviets

had no intention of doing in the first place (p. 268). On crisis and war: Harvard Nuclear Study Group 1983, chap. 3.

21. Bialer 1986, 188–89.

22. McNamara: *Pentagon Papers* 1971, 3:500; see also 3:50–51. North Vietnam: Vo Nguyen Giap quoted by Maxwell Taylor, in Fulbright 1966, 169.

23. *Pentagon Papers* 1971, 3:482–83. Or, in 1967: "We'll just go on bleeding them until Hanoi wakes up to the fact that they have bled their country to the point of national disaster for generations" (Lewy 1978, 73). Some military leaders apparently believed the North Vietnamese supply of fighting-age men could be severely depleted, a conclusion Defense Department analysts found to be physically invalid: Lewy 1978, 82–84; Enthoven and Smith 1971, 295–300; Jenkins 1970; Thayer 1977, 85–92; McMahon 1999, 131.

24. McNamara: *Pentagon Papers* 1971, 4:624.

25. For a full treatment of this analysis, see Mueller 1980. Rusk: interview on NBC-TV, July 2, 1971. Best enemy: Kinnard 1977, 67. As U.S. general Maxwell Taylor recalls, "The North Vietnamese proved to be incredibly tough at accepting losses which, by Western calculation, greatly exceeded the value of the stake involved" (1972, 400). Or as Westmoreland put it tersely, "Any American commander who took the same vast losses . . . would have been sacked overnight" (1976, 251–52). On this issue, see also Pike 1966; Leites 1969; Karnow 1991, 19–23; and especially Kellen 1972. The extraordinary Communist tenacity could not have been confidently anticipated. Evidence from the war they had earlier conducted against the French certainly was of little help. In their major battles in the war against the Americans and South Vietnamese, the Communists suffered tens of thousands of battle deaths, whereas in the major massed battle against the French they had lost about 7,900 men—and apparently had been pushed to the limits of collapse as a result: Mueller 1980, 505, 509; Khrushchev 1970, 482.

26. In 1965, future war critic David Halberstam called Vietnam a "strategic country in a key area, it is perhaps one of only five or six nations in the world that is truly vital to U.S. interests." He opposed withdrawal because "the United States' prestige will be lowered throughout the world" and because "the pressure of Communism on the rest of Southeast Asia will intensify," and "throughout the world the enemies of the West will be encouraged to try insurgencies like the one in Vietnam" (Halberstam 1965, 315, 319). Or as reporter Neil Sheehan, another future critic of U.S. policy in Vietnam, put it in 1964, "The fall of Southeast Asia to China or its denial to the West over the next decade because of the repercussions from an American defeat in Vietnam would amount to a strategic disaster of the first magnitude." Only the United States, he argued, could meet "the Chinese Communist challenge for hegemony in Asia."

27. For more detail on this process, see Mueller 1989, 177–78. On the important impact of Indonesia, see also McMahon 1999, 119–24.

28. On these decisions, see Schandler 1977.

29. Breslauer 1987, 436–37. See also Hosmer and Wolfe 1983, chap. 12.

30. Nicaragua: Hosmer and Wolfe 1983, 59. Economic costs: Wolf et al. 1983. On the debate, see Hosmer and Wolfe 1983, 78; Hough 1986, chaps. 8, 9; Checkel 1997; English 2001.

31. Kennedy 1987, 488–98, 502; Bialer 1986; Pipes 1984, chaps. 3–4.

32. The oil price drop also meant that the Arab states, by far the largest buyers of Soviet arms, were reducing their orders for more; see Kramer 1987, 66; Kempe 1986. Defense burden: Kennedy 1987, 498–504. Eastern Europe: Bunce 1985.

33. On this process, see Mueller 1989, 184–86. Yugoslavia: Campbell 1967, 24–27. China: Pollack 1984, 159; on the potential for alliance, see also Talbott 1981, 81–113. In 1985, Reagan adviser Richard Pipes observed, "China has turned inward and ceased being aggressive, and so we are friendly toward China, just as we are toward Yugoslavia. We may deplore their Communist regimes, but these countries are not trying to export their systems and therefore do not represent a threat to our national security" (*Policy Review*, Winter 1985, 33).

34. Reliable peace: Colton 1986, 191. Inadequacy: Binder 1988. Ideologist: Keller 1988. 1988 speech: quoted in the *New York Times*, December 8, 1988, A16; December 9, 1988, A18. Perhaps recalling the 1961 party program that ringingly declared "our epoch" to be one "of struggle between the two opposing social systems" (Voslensky 1984, 319), an impor-

lords: Ron 2000a, 288. Pass as professional: Hedges 2002, 13. See also Glenny 1993, 185; Sudetic 1992; Benard 1993.

17. A partial exception to this pattern concerns the slaughter of thousands of Muslim men by Serbs after they successfully invaded the "safe area" of Srebrenica in 1995, a seemingly calculated and orderly massacre that was carried out by what appears to have been the regular army (on this issue, see Sadowski 1998, 133). Since the army had become increasingly thuggish by this time, a formal distinction with less organized bands of thugs may be somewhat strained. Moreover, many of the paramilitary groups had by that time been absorbed into the army as "Special Units," and it appears that these were sent in on the third day to carry out the main violence (Kaldor 1999, 55). Although in no way excusing the massacre, it may be relevant to point out that the Serbs were deeply bitter about the situation because they had accepted the city as a UN safe area in 1993 with the understanding that it would not be used for attacks against Serbs (Silber and Little 1997, 345; Sudetic 1998, 207). Nonetheless, the forces of Srebrenica defender Orić, regarded by some Muslims as "dangerous primitives" (Rohde 1997, 109), had repeatedly forayed from the city to attack and kill Serb civilians (Rohde 1997, 215-16, 409; see also Kinzer 1995a).

18. United Nations Commission of Experts 1994, para. 104. The phenomenon can be widely found. For example, in the first Arab–Israeli war in 1948, Israeli paramilitary and terrorist forces captured the strategically located village of Deir Yassin, slew more than two hundred Arab men, women, and children, mutilated the bodies, and then threw them into a well. Although this atrocity was immediately repudiated by the Israeli leadership, descriptions of it, sometimes exaggerated, were avidly spread by Arab leaders, with the strategically important result that many Arab communities—hundreds of thousands of people— were sent into panicky flight even before Jewish forces arrived. Sacher 1976, 333-34.

19. Husarska 1995, 16. See also Bennett 1995, 191; O'Connor 1996; Rieff 1995, 110; Judah 1997, 195; Maass 1992. The most common emotion among ordinary people caught up in this cyclone of violence and pillage seems to have been bewilderment rather than rage. Working with Muslim refugees early in the Bosnia war, Cheryl Benard found them "to be totally at a loss to explain how the hostility of the Serbs was possible. All of them, without exception, say they lived and worked with and were close friends with Serbs . . . Many found excuses for their Serb neighbors." Far from seeing the violence as evidence of the strength of ethnic ties, Benard suggests that "one could argue that Bosnia shows how weak and how fluid political identity really is" (1993, 24). Halina Grzymala-Moszczcynska, a sociologist working with Muslim refugees in Poland, reports that the refugees she interviewed never referred to their persecutors as Serbs, but always as criminals (personal conversation).

20. Acton 1948, 364. Sadism: Judah 1997, 233; Maass 1996, 52, 111; Borger 1997c. Gunslingers: Sudetic 1992. Serb policeman: Borger 1997a. On opportunism more generally, see Tilly 2003, chap. 6. On the settling of local grudges in civil wars, see Kalyvas 2003.

21. Burg and Shoup 1999, 137.

22. Zvornik: Ron 2000a, 297; see also Judah 1997, 242. Sarajevo: United Nations Commission of Experts 1994, paras. 84, 86; Burns 1993a; Kaldor 1999, 51; Merrill 1999, 285; and especially Andreas 2004. As Rieff observes, "The involvement of gangsters on all sides meant not only that the fighting took on a more and more lawless, brutal character, but also that the political aims of the war became hopelessly intertwined on a day-to-day level with profiteering and black market activities" (1995, 132). Judah notes that "local industrial and agricultural assets that would have helped sustain Serb-held areas both during and after the war were simply stripped and sold off" (1997, 254). Some of this behavior surfaced early—in the fighting in Croatia in 1991. As one Serb from the area recalled, "I don't deny that I myself did some shooting, but the worst crimes were committed by the irregulars who came in from Serbia. First they looted the homes of Croats. When they came back a second time they started looting Serb houses, because the Croat houses had already been robbed clean" (Štitkovac 1995, 160).

23. Trading with the enemy: Judah 1997, 242-52; Vulliamy 1996b; see also Burg and Shoup 1999, 138; Sudetic 1998, 90; Andreas 2004. Reduced by half: Vasić 1996, 133; Woodward 1995, 246; Boyd 1995, 29; Malcolm 1995, 9; Judah 1997, 223, 237, 296; Kaldor 1999, 49, 56; Merrill 1999, 282; Hedges 1995, 1996a; Tanner 1997, 283.

24. Kaufmann 1996, 144. See also Fearon and Laitin 2003, 88.
25. KLA origins: Hedges 1998c; O'Connor 1998a; Finn 1999; Judah 1999. Size of KLA: Steele 1998; Hedges 1999, 34–36; Judah 2000, 309. As in Bosnia and Croatia, the Serbs committed atrocities, and as in those instances, the stories of the atrocities were often even worse than the reality: see O'Connor 1998b. Before the 1999 war, the province was being ethnically cleansed of Serbs by the actions of Albanians. In reaction to Serb oppression, the majority Albanians often adopted a position of considerable hostility to local Serbs and this, enhanced by the still minor violence committed by the Kosovo Liberation Army, was easily enough to drive many Serbs from the area, even though they enjoyed the protection of the Serb-dominated police force of 20,000 (Steele 1998). Comparatively few of them actually suffered great hardship, but most were made to feel unsafe, and for many this was fully enough (Hedges 1998b; 1998c; 1999, 38; O'Connor 1998c; Erlanger 1999a). As the experience in Bosnia and Croatia had previously indicated, it does not take much to get people to flee. The Albanian rebels in Kosovo do not appear ever to have achieved genuine popularity: they did very poorly in elections held after the area achieved virtual independence in 1999.
26. Journalist: Nougayrède 1999. Writer, truck driver: Perlez 1998. Letters: O'Connor 1998c. Demotion: Hedges 1999, 32.
27. Assurances: Perlez 1999; Dinmore 1999. Release of criminals: M. Gordon 1999; Ingrao 1999; Dorsey 1999; Judah 2000, 245–47. Do anything for freedom: Judah 2000, 247. Black masks: *NewsHour* with Jim Lehrer, PBS, April 1, 1999. Not policemen: Kifner 1999a.
28. Special police: Ingrao 1999. Albanian fear: Gall 1999a, 1999b; Erlanger 1999c, 1999e; see also the warnings in Kuperman 1998.
29. Clinton: Whitney and Schmitt 1999; Broder 1999; Judah 2000, 229–30. Orders obeyed: Erlanger 1999b; Harden 1999a; Hosmer 2001, 50–52.
30. Stanley 1999. See also Daalder and O'Hanlon 1999, 107; Layne 2000.
31. Interviews: Harden 1999b; see also Kifner 1999b; Dorsey 1999. Overall pattern: Erlanger 1999f; see also Judah 2000, 245–46.
32. Money main thing: Judah 2000, 246. Wealthy Albanians: Rohde 1999. Payment of cash: Kifner 1999a; Erlanger 1999d. Rambo joke: Harden 1999b.
33. Prunier 1995, 169; African Rights 1995, 51–52; Jones 2001, 39.
34. Selected Tutsis: Des Forges 1999, 9. Police and Presidential Guard: Prunier 1995, 242–43; African Rights 1995, 49, 65. FAR: Prunier 1995, 113, 246, 254; African Rights 1995, 48, 1050; see also Feil 1998, 37.
35. Gourevitch 1998, 93.
36. Social aspect: Prunier 1995, 231–32; see also Des Forges 1999, 11, 261. Gourevitch 1998, 115. Criminals: Gourevitch 1998, 242. Uvin 1998, 219. Enrichment: African Rights 1995, 1003–6. Discipline: Prunier 1995, 243–44; see also Des Forges 1999, 13. Forced to join: Prunier 1995, 247; African Rights 1995, chap. 14; Gourevitch 1998, 307, 309. Roadblocks: Prunier 1995, 253–54; Gourevitch 1998, 136.
37. African Rights 1995, 1017–22; Prunier 1995, 253; Des Forges 1999, 11, 260–62.
38. Tens of thousands: Des Forges 1999, 2, 16, 260, 262. Elite Presidential Guard: Prunier 1995, 242–43; African Rights 1995, 49. Police: Feil 1998, 37–38. Army: Feil 1998, 37–38; Prunier 1995, 113. Interahamwe: African Rights 1995, 55, 61–62, 114; Feil 1998, 38; Prunier 1995, 243. Terrifying: Gourevitch 1998, 134.
39. For an analysis that independently comes up with similar estimates, see Jones 2001, 39–41. See also Lemarchand 1998, 42; Valentino 2004, 178–87. A year after defeating the genocidal regime, Tutsi forces had 33,000 people incarcerated under suspicion of participating in the genocide, a figure that later rose to at least 125,000 (Gourevitch 1998, 242).
40. Population data for Rwanda are given in Prunier 1995, 79n, 264; Feil 1998, 32–34. Although by all accounts they were very much outnumbered by men and boys, women and girls did join in the genocide. In addition, boys younger than thirteen often participated (Keller 1994). If these groups are added to the base, the percentages would, of course, be much lower.
41. Moore 2001, 28–29 (toughs), 32n (group size), 40 (financing), 29 (racket), 30 (perpetrator), 3 (proxy).

42. Death squads: Campbell and Brenner 2000. Chechnya: Lieven 1998, 61–62, 75, 81. Cossack units: Lieven 1998, chap. 6. Kenya: Brown 2002; Rotberg 2003, 17. See also Tilly 2003, 238.

43. Keen 1998, chap. 2; Reno 1998; Gamba and Cornwell 2000; Collier 2000; Rotberg 2003, 6, 10. Jet in Nigeria: Reno 2000, 54.

44. Berkeley 2001, 15, 140. Medieval comparison: Berdal and Malone 2000, 1; Keen 2000, 28; Ayoob 1998, 42; Wright 2000, 3.

45. Rape and plunder: Ellis 1999, 62. Cut off by U.S.: Reno 1998, 87–88. Taylor and Johnson: Ellis 1999, 2–4, 10, 15, 67–68, 74–75, 319; Reno 1998, 92. Counterproductive effort: Ellis 1999, 76–79, 113; Howe 1996–97, 149. Doe execution: Ellis 1999, 9–11; Reno 1998, 93.

46. Marines: Ellis 1999, 307. Creation of ECOMOG: Ellis 1999, 174–75; Reno 1998, 93. Warlord bands: Ellis 1999, 141; Howe 1996–97, 156, 163. Taylor's wealth: Ellis 1999, 90–91; Reno 1998, 94–102; Howe 1996–97, 173. ECOMOG as warlord operation: Ellis 1999, 98, 104, 170–75; Howe 1996–97, 156–57. Ugly name: Ellis 1999, 173; see also Howe 1996–97, 162, 169.

47. Criminals before the war: Ellis 1999, 134. Ellis 1999, 134. Berkeley 2001, 49. Ellis 1999, 312, also 122–23, 145. Sixty thousand: Berkeley 2001, 53. Loot from each other: Ellis 1999, 126. Taylor's offensive: Ellis 1999, 108.

48. Ellis 1999, 115, 121 (Rambo); 17–18 (bizarre attire); 118, 120–21, 127, 132, 134 (drugs; see also Kaldor 1999, 164n25). Nom de guerre: Goldberg 1995; Ellis 1999, 121; Reno 2000, 54.

49. Disillusionment: Ellis 1999, 125–27, 141. Checkpoints: Ellis 1999, 116. Children: Ellis 1999, 132; Howe 1996–97, 170n.

50. 1997: Ellis 1999, 109, 185; Reno 2003, 93. Budget: Reno 2003, 75. 2003: Malinowski 2003.

51. Corporal: Reno 1998, 123; Chege 2002, 149. Chege 2002, 151. Army: Keen 1998, 26–28; Reno 1998, 125, Singer 2003, 111–12. Sobels: Reno 1998, 125. Aid worker: Keen 1998, 48. Drugs and Rambo films: Ourdan 1999; Singer 2003, 111.

52. Reno 1998, 130–32; Chege 2002, 154–55; Singer 2003, 112–14.

53. Singer 2003, 114–15. UN: Maren 2000. British: Onishi 2000; Chege 2002.

54. Hirsch and Oakley 1995, 8.

55. Movies: Maren 1997, 17. Rambo as role model: Lewis and Mayall 1996, 106–7. Utter misery: interview with Mrs. Abshir, "Ambush in Mogadishu," *Frontline*, PBS, 1998, on the program's website at www.pbs.org. Homes and shops: Bowden 1999, 56, 82, 144.

56. FARC: Rabasa and Chalk 2001, xiv, 24, 39–45, 47–51, 56, 75–76; Keen 1998, 35. ELN: Rabasa and Chalk 2001, 30–31, 45. In 1992, a set of prominent Colombian intellectuals, many of them very left wing, published a polite five-paragraph open letter pointing out to the guerrillas that "your war, understandable in the beginning, now goes against the tide of history," deploring the endless violence, and urging them to "search for new and novel forms of political creativity appropriate to the realities of the world today." Ten days later, the guerrillas' umbrella organization published a polite sixteen-paragraph reply that said, in essence, "up yours" (Bergquist, Peñarand, and Sánchez 2001, 214–20).

57. Army: Rabasa and Chalk 2001, 103–4; Jenkins 2000–2001, 52. GDP on defense: Rabasa and Chalk 2001, 95.

58. Paramilitaries: Rabasa and Chalk 2001, xvi, 53–55, 58–59; Sánchez 2001, 20–25. People displaced: Jenkins 2000–2001, 48. Paramilitaries and land: Cubides 2001, 133–34, 136. Defectors from the guerrillas: Cubides 2001, 138; Rabasa and Chalk 2001, 56.

59. Sánchez 2001, 22; Rabasa and Chalk 2001, 55–56.

60. Sánchez 2001, 13.;Rabasa and Chalk 2001, 56; Jenkins 2000–2001, 47–48.

61. Kidnapping record: Sánchez 2001, 17. Popular support: Rabasa and Chalk 2001, 29, 56, 60. Paramilitaries as solution: Sánchez 2001, 25; Rabasa and Chalk 2001, xvii, 59–60; Miller 2002a, 2002b; see also Forero 2000; Miller 2001.

62. Drug issue: Jenkins 2000–2001, 51–55; Rabasa and Chalk 2001, xv, 21; Bergquist, Peñarand, and Sánchez 2001, 269–73. Develop competent forces: Rabasa and Chalk 2001, 95, 99.

63. Sudan: Berkeley 2001. Angola: Gamba and Cornwell 2000. Congo: Reno 1998; Berkeley 2001. Burma: Brown 1999. Nigeria: Reno 1998. Algeria: Kalyvas 1999. Macedonia: Hislope

2002. Georgia: King 2001. Aceh: Malley 2003, 200–1. Caucasus: Lieven 1998, chap. 1. See also Bayart, Ellis, and Hibou 1999.

64. Rashid 2000, chaps. 1–2. Criminals: conversations with Alam Payind, Ohio State University. Army: Valentino 2004, 220.

65. Oliker 2001, 72–73. Reversion to banditry: Lieven 1998, 146, 302, 348–49.

66. Mackey 1989, 162, 207, 214, 228–30, 233 (criminal predation); 214, 229–30 (drugs); 226 (patients).

67. Jenne 2003, 228–30, 237.

68. Mueller 2002c. On Vietnam: Pike 1966, chap. 13.

69. *60 Minutes:* Bob Simon interviewing Michael Moore, February 16, 2003. Fragile: Gergen 2002. Existential: Krauthammer 2002–3, 9.

70. Ignatieff 1993; Hedges 2002, 163.

71. Disorders of the present time: Hobbes 1994, 496 (review and conclusion); actually, however, Hobbes had already previously worked out some of the notions in writings, such as *De Civi,* that were published before the Civil War. State of nature: Hobbes 1994, 76–78 (chap. 13). Not so solitary: Kraynak 1990, 148–49. In Hobbes's view, according to Robert Kraynak, people did once manage to lift themselves out of a barbaric, if somewhat innocent, state of nature into a form of ordered civilization. This progressive development proved fragile, however, because scholars, priests, and lawyers developed competing and incompatible religious doctrines based on authority rather than on objective science and then convinced their various co-religionists to engage in vicious and destructive doctrinal wars. In particular, notes Kraynak, in Hobbes's opinion the English Civil War emerged when "various intellectual authorities, driven by a desire for honor and glory, competed among themselves to corrupt and seduce the credulous people." For Hobbes, "the tragedy and folly of doctrinal politics" are that eventually "intellectual elites mobilize the masses against their rivals and foment rebellion" (Kraynak 1990, 86, 88). Hobbes held that the resulting brutish conditions of civil war are scarcely, if at all, distinguishable from those of the barbaric, precivilized state of nature (Kraynak 1990, 144).

72. This conclusion may be more Hobbesian than Hobbes, however. Russell Hardin points to a passage in which Hobbes notes that "law was brought into the world for nothing else but to limit the natural liberty of particular men, in such manner, as they might not hurt, but assist one another, and join together against a common enemy" (Hobbes 1994, 175, chap. 26). The suggestion is that the problem is with "particular men," not with the totality of humanity.

73. Arkan: Vasić 1996, 134; United Nations Commission of Experts 1994, paras. 92, 138. Lukić: Hedges 1996a; Vulliamy 1996a; Maass 1996, 12–14, 157; United Nations Commission of Experts 1994, paras. 246–50, 540–56; Sudetic 1998, 120–25; Hedges 2002, 113–14. Lukić is reported to be spending the post-war years in Serbia, a wealthy man (Vulliamy 1996a). He claims to be proud he killed so many Muslims in the war and that he has an almost uncontrollable urge to kill again. He has reportedly sought psychiatric care, become unhinged, sleeps with all the lights on, and drives around in a different car all the time (Sudetic 1998, 355–56, 358). Teslic: O'Connor 1996; see also Glenny 1993, 169–70; Bennett 1995, 249. Adolf: United Nations Commission of Experts 1994, para. 196. Srebrenica and Orić: Rohde 1997, xiv, 60, 107–9, 354, 355; Sudetic 1998, 223, 244. Orić was rumored to be profiting greatly on the black market and to be running a prostitution business (pimping, it's usually called), but he denied that, claiming to be "just a small businessman" who somehow managed to clear enough to be able to tear around the fuel-starved enclave in an Audi or a Mercedes or a Volkswagen and to find enough diesel oil to run his private electricity generator during the war and to open a floating restaurant after it was over (Rohde 1997, 63, 354–55, 381; Pomfret 1994).

74. Parker 1977, 78–79. Liberia: Reno 1998, 79. Guatemala: Valentino 2004, chap. 6. Colombia: Jenkins 2000–2001, 50. Chechnya: Lieven 1998, 4. Timor: Moore 2001, 13. Jamaica: *60 Minutes,* CBS, May 14, 2000. Somalia: Bowden 1999, 109, 368. Irish vote: Mitchell 1999, 188; this extraordinary result might be compared with the record in California, where the law has required hundreds of referendum votes on minor and often legalistic trivia, none of which over a half century has ever been approved by more than 65 percent (Mueller

1969, 1198). On the connection between crime and the Irish Republican Army and on the addictive quality of the war effort, see Grant 1998; George 1996.

75. Hall 1994, 210; Tambiah 1986, 120. See also Valentino 2004, chap. 2; Keeley 1996, 158; Fearon and Laitin 2003, 81, 88.

76. Apply rhetoric: Collier 2000, 92; Collier and Hoeffler 2001; Keen 2000, 35. Sankoh: Ourdan 1999; Singer 2003, 276n41.

77. Fearon and Laitin 2000, 869.

78. Keen 1998, 43. See also Howe 1996–97, 173; Genschel and Schlichte 1998, 114; Keen 2000, 27; Collier 2000, 104; Berdal and Malone 2000, 2; Andreas 2004.

79. Lebanon: Mackey 1989. Burma: Brown 1999. Colombia: Rabasa and Chalk 2001, xvi, 76; Jenkins 2000–2001, 55.

80. See also Collier, Hoeffler, and Söderbom 2001; Fearon and Laitin 2003, 77–78; Global Menace 2003.

81. Keen 2000, 26.

82. van Creveld 1991, 221; O'Connell 1995, 5, 225.

83. van Creveld 1991, 2, 205, 223.

7. ORDERING THE NEW WORLD

1. Truman 1966, 1201.

2. Thus, over a period of less than three years the world underwent something like the functional equivalent of World War III. As with World Wars I and II, a major empire was dismembered, important political boundaries in Europe were reorganized, and several nations were politically transformed. And as the ancient institution of monarchy met its effective demise in Europe in World War I and as the newer, but dangerous and seemingly virile, ideologies of Nazism and Fascism were destroyed by World War II, so a major political philosophy, Communism, over which a tremendous amount of ink and blood had been spilled, was discredited and apparently expunged in World War III.

3. Rummel 1994; Valentino 2004, 1.

4. However, most definitions of superpower status during the Cold War stressed the possession of stocks of nuclear weapons. If that criterion were continued to be embraced, Russia should still probably be considered a superpower.

5. Woodward 1991, 157–58 (altercations), 86 (campaign), 116 (unpleasant symbol), 129 (wimp), 164 (forces). Canal threat: Johns and Johnson 1994, 59–60.

6. Simpson 1991, 20, 107–8; see also Aburish 2000, 282.

7. Woodward 1991, 215–22.

8. Simpson 1991, 227. Wobbly: Smith 1992, 63. The Saudis were persuaded to allow the United States and other nations to station troops in their country to deter an Iraqi incursion, and they also agreed to increase their oil output to compensate for the shortfall in international supplies caused by the boycott of Iraq and occupied Kuwait.

9. Hufbauer, Schott, and Elliott 1990; Cortright and Lopez 2000, 43–44.

10. Coalition: Sciolino 1991, 233; Woodward 1991, 42. Lose face: Barnes 1991a, 11.

11. Emotionally absorbed: Woodward 1991, 255, 260; Barnes 1991b. Tested: Frost 1991. Yearn: Drew 1991, 83; Tucker and Hendrickson 1992, 91; Simpson 1991, 215–16; Aburish 2000, 296. No deals: Tucker and Hendrickson 1992, 91; also U.S. News and World Report 1992, 199–200; Smith 1992, 222; Drew 1991, 85; Fred Barnes observed at the time, in the first fifteen minutes of one television interview, that "Bush ruled out compromise nineteen separate times" (1991b, 8); on the possibility that Saddam was open to a face-saving deal, see Aburish 2000, 293, 301, also 303–4. Atrocities: Drew 1991; Woodward 1991; and especially Frost 1991; the Kuwait government in exile claimed that the Iraqis had killed 2,000 people in Kuwait during and after the invasion, while Middle East Watch put the number at between 500 and 700 (Cockburn 1991). Ass out: Barnes 1991b, 9; Drew 1991, 83; White House press secretary Marlin Fitzwater, however, insisted that this "wasn't macho talk" (Barnes 1991b, 9). Aspin: Schmitt 1991; Moore 1991a.

12. Suicidal: Freeman and Karsh 1993, 431; see also Viorst 1991a, 67–68; Sciolino 1991, 31;

Karsh and Rautsi 1991, 240–41; Freeman and Karsh 1991, 9n; Simpson 1991, 17, 228, 231, 274. Fatalism: Mueller 1994, 56–58. New world order: Frost 1991.

13. On these conclusions, see Mueller 1995b. Technologies: Krepinevich 1994, 40; for a more skeptical view, see Keaney and Cohen 1993, chap. 10. Simultaneity: Cooper 1994, 29. Lack of strategy: Freeman and Karsh 1993, 387. It has been suggested that the Iraqi commanders neglected the possibility of a flanking attack because they thought an army would get lost in the large desert areas in that locale. If so, this means they completely and casually discounted the value of the well-known global positioning system technology that was in wide use in the West by truckers and boaters. It has also been argued that Iraqi leaders were surprised because they reasonably assumed vehicles would get bogged down in the loose sand of the desert. Because most of the area of concern was within Iraq itself, it would have been possible, one would think, for the Iraqis at their leisure some time during the five months of war preparation to drive a few trucks and tanks over there (if they could avoid getting lost) to check out the terrain. As Stephen Biddle puts it laconically, "The Iraqis simply lacked the professional skills" (1997, 172). See also Press 2001.

14. Abandoned troops: Dunnigan and Bay 1992, 75; Sciolino 1991, 259; Cordesman 1993, 443. Tank battles: U.S. News and World Report 1991, 340, 355, 385. McCaffrey 1991, 113. Marine: Moore 1991b. Asked about tactics, one Iraqi artillery officer said simply, "There were no tactics. . . . We are not like the Americans; we are not logical. We do not plan; we do not train. . . . On a busy day we might train for one hour, but not hard. They just told us to shoot to the last bullet and the last man" (Liebl 1991). A measure of the inadequacy of the Iraqi military is furnished by the incredibly small number of U.S. forces it managed to kill. Of the 146 Americans who died in action, 35 were the victims of friendly fire, 11 of unexploded allied munitions, 18 of unexploded Iraqi munitions, and 28 of a freakish Scud missile strike on a barracks in Dhahran, Saudi Arabia (U.S. News and World Report 1992, ix). This leaves a maximum of 54 killed directly by the Iraqi defenders. As it happens, no Arab army has ever done well in conventional war against a reasonably skilled European-style army. At the battle of Tel-el-Kebir between England and Egypt in 1882, for example, some 10,000 Egyptians surrendered to a sergeant from the Shropshires who was armed with nothing but a stick (Newman 1928, 113). In the Gulf War, remnants of an entire Iraqi company surrendered to a female reporter from Virginia who was armed, one presumes, only with a pencil (Weil 1991).

15. Iraqi casualties: Heidenrich 1993; Mueller 1995b, 87–95. Effectiveness: Heidenrich 1993, 124.

16. See Freeman and Karsh 1993, 417; Gordon and Trainor 1995.

17. DiPrizio 2002, chap. 2.

18. Cortright and Lopez 2000, 48; United Nations 1999, paras. 43, 49.

19. Garfield 1997, 1999; Stahl 1996; O'Kane 1996; Simons 1996, chap. 3; UNICEF 1998; Ritter 1999, 147–50; Cockburn and Cockburn 1999, chap. 5; Mueller and Mueller 2000, 170–71; Cortright and Lopez 2000, 45–51; Baram 2000, 198–99, 204; Welch 2002; Pollack 2002, 125–40; Rieff 2003, 43; Mackey 2002, 365–67.

20. Material for rebuilding: Loeb 1998; Melby 1998, 121. Chlorine: Stahl 1996; Cockburn and Cockburn 1999, 131. Chlorine in World War I: Brown 1968, 4, 38. Insecticides: O'Kane 1998a. Delays: Crossette 1999.

21. Bush and Albright: Cockburn and Cockburn 1999, 43, 263, 98; see also Melby 1998, 118, 123. British: Aburish 2000, 342.

22. Weiner 1999a, 1999b; Lippman and Gellman 1999.

23. Aaron 1998; *Middle East International,* 13 November 1998; Cockburn and Cockburn 1999, 135; Gordon 2002; Cortright and Lopez 2000, 48–51; Rieff 2003, 43.

24. Memory of 1991: Cockburn and Cockburn 1999, chap. 1. Opposition: a cell of dissidents run by the Central Intelligence Agency was destroyed in September 1996 when it was betrayed by one of the Kurdish leaders as part of his power struggle with a rival in northern Iraq, an area that was being protected by the militaries of the sanctioning countries (Weiner 1998; Cockburn and Cockburn 1999, chap. 7).

25. Quoted in O'Kane 1996.

26. Lewis and Mayall 1996, 107–8. This phenomenon is hardly unique to Somalia; see Terry 2002, 35–41.

27. Lewis and Mayall 1996, 94, 111n (troop numbers). U.S. motivation: Western 2002; Maren 1997, 219; DiPrizio 2002, chap. 3.

28. Christopher: *MacNeil/Lehrer NewsHour*, PBS, March 2, 1995. Lower estimates: Hansch et al. 1994.

29. Lewis and Mayall 1996, 116–17; de Waal 1997, 186; Hirsch and Oakley 1995, 117–26; Bowden 1999, 71–76, 365.

30. Atkinson 1994; Bowden 1999; Hirsch and Oakley 1995, 127.

31. Hirsh and Oakley 1995, 124; Larson 1996; Strobel 1997, 166–83; Burk 1999, 66–67; Klarevas 1999.

32. See Herbst 1996–97.

33. *New York Times* columnist William Safire, in urging withdrawal, blandly observed of the venture that "the saving of hundreds of thousands of lives is no small thing" (1993). What, one might wonder, would he consider to be a truly *large* thing? The popularly accepted notion that the debacle in Somalia was caused by the UN (Dole 1995, 37) is not only wrong but grotesque; see Gordon and Friedman 1993.

34. See Dole 1995, 41. A poll conducted a few days after the October event found 60 percent agreeing that "nothing the U.S. could accomplish in Somalia is worth the death of even one more U.S. soldier" (Mueller 2002a, 162).

35. See Power 2002, chap. 10; Des Forges 1999 595–691; DiPrizio 2002, chap. 4.

36. Oberdorfer 2001, 314.

37. Oberdorfer 2001, 307; Harrison 2002, 213.

38. Prepared to go to war: Oberdorfer 2001, 308, 316; on this issue, see also Fallows 1994–95. Sanctions: Oberdorfer 2001, 318. Important figures: Oberdorfer 2001, 329. Full-scale war: Oberdorfer 2001, 324; see also Harrison 2002, 117–18.

39. Extortion: Eberstadt 1999; Oberdorfer 2001, 305, 336. Exceedingly pleased: Oberdorfer 2001, 327; see also Harrison 2002, 217. Carter's deal: Sigal 1998, chaps. 6–7; Harrison 2002, chap. 18. Expect collapse: Harrison 2002, chap. 1.

40. Famine toll: Oberdorfer 2001, 399; Natsios 2001, 215. U.S. efforts: Natsios 2001, 147–48.

41. Cortright and Lopez 2000, 95–97; DiPrizio 2002, chap. 3.

42. Clinton hyperbole: *Washington Post*, 16 September 1994, A31. American public: Strobel 1997, 184–89; Klarevas 1999. Pressure: DiPrizio 2002, 94–100.

43. Mitchell 1996. On the post-U.S. situation, see Fatton 2002.

44. Judah 1997, chap. 13; Andreas 2004. Of interest in this regard is that Serb forces never felt strong enough to take Sarajevo militarily, even though at the outset of the war it was defended mainly by police units, volunteers, and armed street gangs (Vasić 1996, 135–36; Rieff 1995, 131; Hedges 1997c; Burg and Shoup 1999, 138; Judah 1997, 211–12). Something similar happened in Srebrenica in 1992 (Rohde 1997, xiv–xv). They also had great difficulties in battles with a ragtag Croat army along the Bosnia–Croatia border (Judah 1997, 208–10). And although the Serbs eventually won the battle over the Croatian city of Vukovar, they did so at great cost and difficulty, even though they vastly outgunned the defenders, most of whom were untrained and hastily organized local militia (Cigar 1993, 325–26; Silber and Little 1997, 177; Mackley 1993; Kaldor 1999, 50).

45. Croatian build-up: Cviić 1996, 209; Vasić 1996, 134–35; Silber and Little 1997, 360; Silverstein 2000, 171–73; Tanner 1997, 284; Pavković 1997, 180; Binder 1998; Shearer 1998, 58–59; Singer 2003, 5, 125–27; Andreas 2004. Destroy criminal gangs: Vasić 1996, 136; Judah 1997, 217–18; Maass 1996, 33; Hedges 1997c; Burg and Shoup 1999, 138–39; Burns 1993a, 1993b; Merrill 1999, 285–86; Kaldor 1999, 46; Andreas 2004. Repudiate commanders: Burns 1993a. A third Sarajevo gang leader demonstrated the depth of his ethnic loyalty by deserting and joining the Croats. He later fled to Liège, Belgium, where he was assassinated on December 3, 1993, by two gunshots to the head administered by one of his own bodyguards (United Nations Commission of Experts 1994, para. 78; see also Burg and Shoup 1999, 139).

46. Bennett 1995, 228–29; Silber and Little 1997, 353; Tanner 1997, 288.

47. Tanner 1997, 294–97; see also Silber and Little 1997, 353–60; Vasić 1996, 135. In victory, however, the discipline of the Croat forces often broke down in arson, destruction, and looting: Heller 1996; Tanner 1997, 298. In many respects the war in Bosnia ended as it

had begun, as gangs of Serbs roamed the suburbs of Sarajevo to force Serbs to leave, only then to be replaced by Muslim thugs who beat and robbed those few Serbs who still remained: Wilkinson 1996a, 1996b.

48. Owen 1995, 331, Power 2002, 392, 439. NATO's formative military mission, of course, had simply been to deter a Soviet invasion. Because no invasion ever materialized, some jibed that NATO's initials stood for "No action, talk only." In an important sense, Bosnia was the first time in its history that NATO actually engaged in military action.

49. Holbrooke 1998, 73; see also Mueller 2000, 28, 36n82. Milošević's control: Owen 1995, 330. Milošević's affection for his Bosnian co-negotiators is indicated by his angry assertions to Holbrooke: "They are not my friends. They are not my colleagues. It is awful just to be in the same room with them for so long. They are shit" (1998, 105–6). Milošević on previous peace plans: Silber and Little 1997, chaps. 21, 27. Final agreement: Burg and Shoup 1999, 356.

50. NATO credibility: Judah 2000, 235–36; Clark 2001, 422; DiPrizio 2002, 145. Blair: News-Hour with Jim Lehrer, PBS, April 22, 1999.

51. Monitor withdrawal: Erlanger 1999e. Both ways: McManus 1999. No planning: Judah 2000, 252; Daalder and O'Hanlon 2000, chap. 4.

52. For assessments of the decision, see Judah 2000, 287–85; Hosmer 2001; Posen 2000; Stigler 2002–3; Daalder and O'Hanlon 2000, chap. 5; Lambeth 2000, 191–94; 2001, chap. 4.

53. Tiffen 2001, 75; Ryan 2000, 13–15.

54. Ryan 2000, 64–66, 131–35; Martinkus 2001, chap. 11. Last drop of blood: Fischer 2000, 1.

55. Economist, May 18, 2002, 12; Maren 2000. Student: Onishi 2000. Chege 2002; see also Jones 2001, 126; Reno 2003, 95–96. Something similar occurred in Ivory Coast in 2002 when the French intervened in a chaotic situation.

56. Anderson 2002, 173–74.

57. Woodward 2002, 253 (rent Afghans), 235 (suitcases). Additional information from a briefing by Enduring Freedom Special Forces veterans, Mershon Center, Ohio State University, November 19, 2002.

58. Biddle 2002, 13–15, 27–28.

59. Woodward 2002, 254 (50,000 troops), 253 (perception of victory), 298 (converted cascade), 329 ($70 million), 314 (officers and personnel). Warlords switch: Filkins 2001; Biddle 2002, 17–19. Casualties, strike missions: Birtle 2002. Chickens: O'Hanlon 2002, 52. See also Record 2002, 8–10.

60. Biddle 2002, 40. Casualties: Birtle 2002. Reliance on Afghans: O'Hanlon 2002, 56–57.

61. Tork Faradi on the NewsHour with Jim Lehrer, PBS, January 14, 2003.

62. On the abilities of the Iraq army, see also Ritter 1999, 199–201.

63. Mearsheimer and Walt 2003. The case for going to war is extensively put forward in Pollack 2002 and in Kaplan and Kristol 2003. For a debate on the issue, see Mueller and Lindsey 2003. For assessments questioning whether biological and particularly chemical arms should be considered weapons of "mass destruction," see Mueller and Mueller 1999, 45–48; Mueller and Mueller 2000,165–69; Easterbrook 2002.

64. Lind 2003; Roy 2003.

65. Reporter: Wilson 2003. Orders of an imbecile: Zucchino 2003.

66. Van Creveld 1991, 225; also 1999a, 36.

67. Minimum of fighting: Des Forges 1999, 692, Prunier 1995, 268. Simply ordered: Gourevitch 1998, 156–57. Several thousand refugees were saved in a Kigali stadium because the United Nations Mission in Rwanda (UNAMIR), which Prunier characterizes as "the powerless UN 'military' force," simply forbade the murder squads' entry (1995, 254, 377).

68. Wrong 2001, 259 (angry men), 263 (swiftest campaign). In the process, Zairian generals sold the invaders weapons, set fire to their storage warehouses to conceal the loss of supplies, and stole the best equipment for themselves. As one ambassador mused, "They were sabotaging their own campaign. But you have to regard these people as gangsters rather than politicians. And a gangster tries to make money until the very last moment" (Wrong 2001, 263). Liberia: Ellis 1999, 315; Howe 1996–97, 168. Georgia: Kaldor 1999, 93; hashishists: conversation with Georgi Derluguian. Afghanistan: Rashid 2000, chaps. 1–2.

69. Van Creveld 1991, 222.

8. THE PROSPECTS FOR POLICING WARS

1. There was an additional impediment in the case of the war in Bosnia. Outsiders tended vastly to overestimate the fighting tenacity of the defenders under the assumption that Serbs in particular were fanatically dedicated fighters. This notion derives from a World War II myth that maintains that the occupying Germans, confronted with a dedicated guerrilla opposition, were forced to divert a huge number of forces to maintain their control in Yugoslavia. But the Germans occupied the country in a matter of days and rarely found the Yugoslav occupation much of a diversion, although quite a few Yugoslavs managed to kill other Yugoslavs during and immediately after the war (Bennett 1995, 49–50). In Bosnia, suggests J. P. Mackley, no Yugoslav combat unit, regular or irregular, could successfully compete with the U.S. military "in anything but a drinking contest" (1993).

2. In addition to Korea, Vietnam, the Dominican Republic, Lebanon (1958), India (1962), Afghanistan, and Grenada, where troops from the United States, the Soviet Union, and/or China became directly involved, the Cold War can be said to have exacerbated violent conflict within Thailand, Burma, Guatemala, Nicaragua, El Salvador, Venezuela, Cuba, Greece, Peru, Uruguay, Argentina, Bolivia, Cambodia, Laos, Angola, India, Mozambique, Chile, Congo, Brazil, Ethiopia, Algeria, Iraq, various Yemens, Hungary, Zanzibar, South Africa, Guyana, French Indochina, Malaya, Iran, Indonesia, and the Philippines.

3. DiPrizio 2002, 7.

4. Tucker and Hendrickson 1992, 95; Mueller 1994, 146–51. See also Johnson 1994, chap. 9; Cortright and Lopez 2000, 44.

5. For comparisons of the reactions to this event and to that after Pearl Harbor, see Mueller 2003b. For the suggestion that the American response to Pearl Harbor was misguided and that a policy of containment and harassment would have eventually undermined Japan at far lower cost than the war launched in fury, see Mueller 1995a, 103–10.

6. Mueller and Mueller 1999, 52–53; 2000, 177–80; Mearsheimer and Walt 2003; Mueller and Lindsey 2003. Heavy weapons in Baghdad: O'Kane 1998b.

7. Schilling 1965, 389; Small 1980, 238–39; Russett 1972, 58–60. On threat exaggeration more generally, see Johnson 1994.

8. On this issue, see Mueller 1995a, 14–16.

9. Genschel and Schlichte 1998, 120.

10. Kaplan 1993b. See also Kaplan 1991 and 1993a, and, for his later doomsaying, now focused, with due agility, on Africa, Kaplan 1994. For a devastating critique of the argument, see Malcolm 1993 as well as Gagnon 1994–95, 133–34; Hardin 1995, chap. 6; Sadowski 1998; Hall 1996, 83. Kaplan paints an extreme picture in a poorly understood area like the Balkans by selective perception: in the words of Noel Malcolm, "as magpies make collections of shiny objects, so Mr. Kaplan goes through national histories, picking out the gory bits" (1993, 85). At the source of many of these perceptions is Rebecca West's two-volume *Black Lamb and Grey Falcon* of 1941. The work was written after the author had made three visits—the longest of which lasted less than two months—to Yugoslavia between 1936 and 1938, and it often propounds views that are essentially racist. For a superb assessment, see Hall 1996.

11. Huntington 1996, 259, 291, 294; also 1993b, s1993c. A bit earlier, Huntington had been a prominent member of what might be called the FLASH! JAPAN BUYS PEARL HARBOR! school. At that time he warned, apparently seriously, that "economics is the continuation of war by other means," and he admonished that the issue had become whether the United States could "meet the economic challenge from Japan as successfully as it did the political and military challenges from the Soviet Union." If not, the United States was destined to lose its "primacy in a crucial arena of power" (Huntington 1991a, 8, 10, 16). Danger signals arise, he argued, because Japan had become the largest provider of foreign aid and because it had endowed professorships at Harvard and MIT (1993a, 77, 80).

12. Somalia: Western 2002, 113, 119–21, 131–33. Gore and Clinton: Cohen 1998, 397–98; on Clinton's seduction by Kaplan's book, see Drew 1994, 157; on his belated, regretful, public recantation in 1999 of the Kaplan perspective, see Seelye 1999; for Kaplan's professed amazement that anybody should take his work that seriously, see Kaplan 1999. Kissinger 1999; Hall 1994, 68.

13. Kraynak 1990, 165, 176, 179 (radically insecure).
14. See Ellickson 1991; Keeley 1996, 178; Mueller 1999b, chap. 4.
15. Valentino 2004.
16. On the role of journalists as boosters for intervention in the war in Bosnia, see Bennett 1995, 195–96, 236.
17. Public opinion: Mueller 2002b, 212; see also Larson 1996, 2000. Spain: Hedges 1997a. Belgium: Des Forges 1999, 618–20; Gourevitch 1998, 114, 149–50; African Rights 1995, 1112. As Martin Bell puts it regarding Bosnia, "The unstated principle seemed to be that British and French and Dutch lives mattered more—much more—than Bosnian lives. That probably reflected majority opinion in the troop-contributing nations" (1995, 266).
18. Clinton polls: Larson 2000, 214. In fact, six months after the Bosnian venture began, support for it had still not risen, even though it was completely successful in that the Bosnians had stopped killing each other (even if they hadn't come to love each other) and, most importantly, no Americans had been killed (Mueller 2002b, 213). Bush 1991 polls: Mueller 1994, 29–34. Bush 2003 polls: see compilations at www.PollingReport.com.
19. Korea and Vietnam: Mueller 1973, 44, 48–49, 58, 100–101. Afghanistan: Mueller 2003b, 33. For a broader discussion of American casualty tolerance in military ventures, see Larson 1996; Mueller 2002b.
20. Rwanda: Gourevitch 1998, 150; Des Forges 1999, 22, 607–8; Feil 1998. Although appropriately stressing the logistic and other potential difficulties of such an intervention, particularly in light of the astonishing speed with which the genocide was carried out, Alan Kuperman still estimates that a force of 15,000 could have stopped the murdering if it could have gotten there in time and that a force of 5,000 could have averted the killing if it had already been in place when the genocide began (2001, 65, 97; see also Jones 2001, 126–27). Liberia: Ellis 1999, 4, 307.
21. Columnist: Hoagland 2003. Budget request: Tucker 2003.
22. Kettle 1999; Zelnick 1999; Page 1999; Balz and Neal 1999.
23. Almond 1960, 76. Bosnia: Sobel 1996, 162. Most important problem: Mueller 2002a, 149–53.
24. See Mueller 2002b, 183–87. A phenomenon similar to the one in Somalia had taken place when Ronald Reagan withdrew policing troops from Lebanon after a terrorist bomb had killed more than two hundred of them in 1983. The experience scarcely dampened his reelection success a year later. In a related episode, even though the Republicans tried to make political hay by bashing the United Nations after the 1993 fiasco in Somalia, public ratings of the institution remained steady (Mueller 2002a, 171n12). On the American reaction to the Vietnam debacle, see Mueller 1984.
25. Annan 1999. Legal ability: Gray 2002, 3–7; see also Rawls 1999, 81, 93n; O'Connell 2003, 450; Talentino 1998. There may be something of a precedent in the way the United States, for its own purposes, decertifies governments that it thinks engage in the drug trade or are insufficiently vigilant in their efforts against it: Herbst 1996–97, 142.
26. Numbers of missions: Gray 2000, chap. 6. Costs: Jett 2000, 12, 27–34.
27. Ryan 2000, 43 (refund of costs), 83 (bureaucratic model), 16 (baseline). Domestic defense: Maren 2000; see also Onishi 2000; Gray 2000, 198. On the UN nonpayment, see also Jett 2000, 12.
28. Gray 2000, 144.
29. See, for example, Urquhart 1993.
30. Ryan 2000, 91. For broad critiques of the process, see Maren 1997; de Waal 1997. On the UN's problems most generally, see Jett 2000; Singer 2003, 59–60.
31. Private security: Shearer 1998, 26. Policing and training missions: Shearer 1998, chap. 3; Silverstein 2000, chap. 4; Rubin 1999; Mallaby 2001; Singer 2003.
32. Answerable to client: Shearer 1998, 21. Sierra Leone costs: Shearer 1998, 51. UN problems: Maren 2000; Onishi 2000; Genschel and Schlichte 1998, 119. See also Singer 2003, chap. 14.
33. Shearer 1998, 43, 49; Singer 2003, 112.
34. For the argument that international law should evolve to fully legitimate such actions, see Slaughter 2003. On the issue more generally, see Gray 2000, 2002.

35. See Howard 2002; Mueller 2003.
36. Effects of blockade: Meilinger 1993, 112, 194. Sanctions in the 1990s: Cortright and Lopez 2000.
37. Judah 1997, 255–56; see also Kinzer 1993; Firestone 1993; Sudetic 1998, 128; Glenny 2003; Andreas 2004. Hedges 1998a; see also Judah 1997, 256–58; Harden 1999a; Glenny 2003. Arkan: United Nations Commission of Experts 1994, para. 131. Brain drain: Judah 1997, 276–78. Serb section of Bosnia: Hedges 1997b; see also Borger 1997c. Mostar: Hedges 1996b; Pomfret 1995. Arkan did not do nearly as well in politics, however: he formed a political party in 1993 and spent more than $3 million campaigning for elections that year, but despite such lavish spending and despite the apparent support of Milošević, his party failed to gain a single seat (United Nations Commission of Experts 1994, para. 136).
38. Downes 1998. See also Sharrock 1999; Mackey 2002, 273. Borger 1998; Rieff 2003.
39. Kirshner 1997. As he notes, sanctions against Panama failed to loosen Noriega's grip for much the same reasons that they failed to work in Iraq (50–56).
40. Jenkins 2000–2001, 51, 55; Bergquist, Peñarand, and Sánchez 2001, 267–73. In a related episode, American "decertification" of Nigeria for involvement in the international drug trade seriously undercut the financing of the ECOMOG troops, who were maintaining a shaky peace in Liberia (Howe 1996–97, 162). On the close relationship in Burma between the market for illegal drugs and the endless wars there, see Brown 1999.
41. Herbst 1996–97, 124n.
42. Congo: Wrong 2001, 53, 133, 118. Average wage: Greenhouse 1988. Angola: Brooke 1985.
43. Kaldor 1999, 113.

9. THE DECLINE OF WAR

1. See Mueller 1989, 240–44.
2. Ehrenreich 1997, 61. See also Forsberg 2001.
3. Garland 1990, 232.
4. Horowitz 2001, 560–65. Capital punishment: Garland 1990, 225–29. Homicide trends: Given 1977; Gurr 1981; Beattie 1984; Garland 1990, 230–31; Keeley 1996, 118; Tilly 2003, 60–61. Adult homicide: Rosenfeld 2000. Dueling faded mainly because it came to be taken as a ridiculous mode of behavior, not because it was superseded by some other method to resolve disputes (Mueller 1989, 10). Duels were only rarely fought over issues that the legal system could handle, either then or now. Typically they were inspired by conflicts over matters of honor and personal dignity; "dueling, like war, is the necessary consequence of offense," admonishes a dueling manual from 1847 (Stowe 1987, 15). Moreover, particularly in the United States, duelists were hardly alienated from the judicial system or disenfranchised from it. In fact, many were lawyers—some 90 percent of duelists in Tennessee, for example (Seitz 1929, 30).
5. See Mueller and Mueller 1999, 2000. This is all the more impressive because there seems to be remarkably little animosity toward the Iraqi people. Fully 60 percent of the American public has held the Iraqi people to be *innocent* of *any* blame for their leader's policies (Mueller 1994, 316). However, there was no notable public reaction in the United States when Madeleine Albright, then U.S. ambassador to the UN, was asked on her country's most popular television news magazine show whether she thought the deaths of perhaps half a million Iraqi children caused by the sanctions were "worth it" and replied, without taking issue with the death toll estimate, "I think this is a very hard choice, but the price—we think the price is worth it" (Stahl 1996). The statement became famous in the Arab world (Cockburn and Cockburn 1999, 263; Mackey 2002, 372). The phenomenon could also be seen during the Gulf War itself. Extensive pictures and publicity about civilian casualties resulting from an attack on a Baghdad bomb shelter had no impact in the United States on attitudes toward U.S. bombing policy in the war (Mueller 1994, 317). Moreover, the immunity the American public showed to the images of the "highway of death" and to reports at the end of the war that 100,000 Iraqis had died in the war (a figure, as noted in Heidenrich 1993 and in Mueller 1995b, that is almost certainly much too high, probably by a factor of more than 10) scarcely dampened the enthusiasm of the various "victory" and "welcome home" parades and celebrations.

6. See J. Gordon 1999 but also Baram 2000.

7. Interestingly, it would probably be illegal for U.S. Air Force officers to comply with an order to conduct an air campaign that would inflict the kind of damage, with such disproportionately little result, that has been caused in Iraq by sweeping trade sanctions. U.S. Air Force regulations specifically require that an attack be cancelled or suspended if it "may be expected to cause incidental loss of civilian life, injury to civilians, damage to civilian objects, or a combination thereof which would be excessive in relation to the concrete and direct military advantage anticipated" (U.S. Department of the Air Force 1976, 5–9). My thanks to Karl Mueller for researching this issue. On the phenomenon, see also Garland 1990, 242–43; Keeley 1996, 62. As Garland observes, even though sensibilities have changed so that corporal and capital punishment have been eliminated or greatly reduced, there remains considerable tolerance for long-term incarceration, which can produce acute mental and psychological suffering, physical deterioration, erosion of social and cognitive skills, social degradation and humiliation, and serious economic and emotional distress for a prisoner's family. But, "because these pains are mental and emotional rather than physical, because they are corrosive over an extended period rather than immediate, because they are removed from public view, and because they are legally disguised as simple 'loss of liberty', they do not greatly offend our sensibilities and they are permitted to form a part of public policy." More generally, most people seem to have a remarkable capacity for passively supporting, or remaining indifferent to, acts of violence or other methods for destroying life, particularly foreign life, even when the acts are committed in their name, something Benjamin Valentino calls "negative support." Sometimes, of course, people look away and do not want to know what is going on because they fear that if they did, they might be morally required to take actions that could be dangerous for their own well-being. But the indifference seems to be far from unusual—indeed, it is probably typical—even in instances in which there is no cost or physical sanction to opposition. Usually, only a small minority is repelled enough as a matter of principle to refuse to commit violence or to actively oppose it when the situation seems to require them to carry it out. See Browning 1998; Valentino 2004, 31–39.

8. Dahl 1971, 182–83, 188. See also Wendt 1999, chap. 3.

9. For example: Jervis 1988; Gaddis 1992, chap. 6; 1999; Johnson 1995; O'Connell 1998, 258; van Creveld 1999a, 30–33; 1999b, 337–44.

10. May 1999, 1–2. Elsewhere, and more specifically, Churchill advanced the "melancholy thought" that "nothing preserves Europe from an overwhelming military attack except the devastating resources of the United States in this awful weapon" (Churchill 1951, 356; see also Rosenberg 1999).

11. Waltz 1998; Rostow quoted in May 1999, 3.

12. For a much more extended development of this argument, see Mueller 1995a, chap. 5. See also Mueller 1985, 1988, 1999a.

13. In 1953, Averell Harriman, a former ambassador to the Soviet Union, observed that Stalin "was determined, if he could avoid it, never again to go through the horrors of another protracted world war." Quoted in *Newsweek*, March 16, 1953, 31. See also Howard 2000, 78.

14. It is also unlikely that the bomb had much to do with forging the Cold War alliance patterns. In fact, the postwar division of the world into two alliances centered on Washington and Moscow suggests that the participants were chiefly influenced by the experience of World War II because in general the alliances included a group of nations that contributed little to nuclear defense but possessed the capability unilaterally of getting the alliance into trouble. That is, the alliances, as Warner Schilling has observed, were "essentially pre-nuclear in their rationale" (Schilling 1961, 26; see also Schlesinger 1967, 6; Gaddis 1987, 230n).

15. See also Luard 1986, 396; 1988, 25–31; Ray 1989, 428–31; Holmes 1989, 238–48; Vasquez 1991. On military initiatives that nonnuclear countries have taken against nuclear ones, see Paul 1994.

16. Howard 1991, 176.

17. Howard 1991, 1. Actually, industrialization may have enhanced war's appeal by making possible the "splendid little war." As Luard observes, "Very short wars (two months or less)

have been virtually confined to the last century or so, since it is only in this period that mobility has been sufficient to allow the type of lightning military campaign required" (1986, 79).

18. Kaysen 1990, 49; see also Fukuyama 1992, 262.

19. Keeley 1996, 160; Milward 1977, 3. One partial caveat might be made to this argument. The moral notion about the sanctity of life (as opposed to the sanctity of the soul) seems to be a fairly new one, apparently arising in the course of the nineteenth century. If human life becomes more greatly treasured, the costs of war effectively rise as a consequence of such a change in perspective or values. However, in view of the remarkable lack of concern about foreign deaths noted earlier in this chapter, it is difficult to know how much emphasis to place on this development.

20. See, for example, Doyle 1986, Russett 1990, Singer and Wildavsky 1993, Russett and Oneal 2001.

21. On this process, See Mueller 1995a, 181–82; 1999b, chap. 8; Nadelmann 1990, 484.

22. For example, Layne 1994; Rosato 2003, 591–92; Elman 1997, chaps. 1–3; Pietrzyk 2002.

23. See Rosato 2003, 590–91.

24. On these issues and for the "preponderance" argument, see Rosato 2003, 599–600.

25. Fearon and Laitin 2003, 76.

26. See also Rosato 2003, 593–94, 596–97.

27. Mencken 1920, 203. On democracy and mystique, see Mueller 1999b, chaps. 6–8. On the rally round the flag effect, where people often tend, at least initially, to support leaders at points of international crisis, see Mueller 1973, 208–13. See also Schweller 2002, 184; Rosato 2003, 594–96.

28. Elman 1997, 484, 496.

29. Disputes reduce trade: Pollins 1989a, 1989b; Li and Sacko 2002. Yardeni 2000, 94. Russett and Oneal conduct a limited effort to test the proposition that militarized disputes disrupt trade (2001, 224–26). There is an effect, even though the analysis deals with militarized disputes (not war alone) and even though it only looks at the effect from one year to the next rather than over a longer term. On the process most generally, see Rosecrance 1986.

30. In fact some people at the time argued that economic interdependence made war more tolerable. For example, war glorifier Heinrich von Treitschke concluded that economics would keep war in Europe from becoming too unpleasantly costly. He explained his reasoning this way: "Civilized nations suffer far more than savages from the economic ravages of war, especially through the disturbance of the artificially existing credit system, which may have frightful consequences in a modern war. . . . Therefore wars must become rarer and shorter, owing to man's natural horror of bloodshed as well as to the size and quality of modern armies, for it is impossible to see how the burden of a great war could long be borne under the present conditions" (Treitschke 1916, 1:70; see also Howard 2000, 58). John Maynard Keynes was prominent among those who expected the 1914 war to be brief for such reasons, even after it started (see Mueller 1995a, 190). David Rowe (2002) argues that in many respects, rising economic interdependence in Europe set in motion processes that enhanced the likelihood of major war there. The economic growth it helped foster increased the difficulty and cost of staffing and maintaining armed forces by diverting potential recruits into the private sector. This in turn made an early war seem more necessary, urgent, and inevitable by undermining the assumptions and practices upon which the major countries had constructed their prewar peace.

31. Keeley 1996, 123, 126.

32. But they do: "The creation of a security community has made armed conflict between France and Germany . . . unthinkable" (Russett and Oneal 2001, 158). See also Ikenberry 2001, chap. 6.

33. Betts 1992, 23–24 (emphasis removed). See also Schweller 2001, 183.

34. Keegan 2001, 39. See also Andreas and Price 2001.

35. Tilly 2003.

36. Sadowski 1998, 174–76; Keegan 1998, 68. Eighty-five times: Ellingsen 2000, 243. See also Collier 2000, 97, 109–10; Hegre et al. 2001, 37, 40; Fearon and Laitin 2003, 83; Global Menace 2003.

37. Hegre et al. 2001; Oberschall 2001, 135–36; Russett and Oneal 2001, 70; Marshall and Gurr 2003, 19–20, 25; Fearon and Laitin 2003, 85, 88; Tilly 2003, chap. 2. See also Scanlon and Jenkins 2001.

38. Lawrence 1926, 196 (chap. 33). See also Fearon and Laitin 2003, 80.

39. See Valentino 2004, chap. 6.

40. Majority of the Timorese: Dunn 1995, 68. Indiscriminate brutality: Dunn 1995, 65, 68; Taylor 1991, chap. 5; 1995, 36; Gama 1995, 98; Schwartz 1994, 204. Ten thousand lives: Schwartz 1994, 205. Portuguese control: Dunn 1995, 72. A woman searching for information about her husband, an Australian journalist who been killed by the invaders, asked a sympathetic Indonesian officer why the Indonesian soldiers behaved so atrociously, and he replied, "We have our fair share of thugs in uniform" (Shackleton 1995, 117). The Indonesian military has also applied the same brutal and substantially counterproductive tactics in the potentially breakaway province of Aceh: see Murphy 2003; Malley 2003, 197–201. The Israeli invasion of Lebanon in 1982 seems, overall, to have followed a similar pattern, judging from Sandra Mackey's account. Outraged by a series of terrorist attacks and shellings perpetrated by Palestinian forces based in bordering Lebanon, the Israelis moved in with massive force. Many Arabs in southern Lebanon resented the Palestinian presence in their midst, and they welcomed the Israelis with flowers and smiles. But indiscriminate Israeli brutality and arrogance, in which numerous Arab villages were overrun and some 1,900 civilians were killed in the first stages in the advance, quickly turned, as Mackey puts it, "a confederate against the Palestinians into a formidable adversary of the State of Israel" (1989, 175, 204). The invasion did succeed in forcing most Palestinian fighters to flee the country, but within a year more than 5,000 had filtered back (Mackey 1989, 250). By the time Israeli forces were withdrawn in 2000, vastly more Israelis among the occupying forces had been killed by harassing Arab attacks than had been killed by terrorists before 1982. See also Jaber 1997, 14–21.

41. Algeria: Kalyvas 1999, 261. Sierra Leone: Keen 1998, 26–28. Liberia: Ellis 1999, 76–79, 113; Howe 1996–97, 149. Chechnya: Lieven 1998, 117–19, 130, 324–27; Oliker 2001; on the willingness of most Chechens to work out a reasonable compromise with Russia before the war: Lieven 1998, 45, 67–68, 82, 337–38. Guatemala: Valentino 2004, chap. 6. On army ineptitude in Sri Lanka, see Jenne 2003, 237.

42. Tambiah 1986, 21. See also Kloos 2001.

43. Kaufman 2001, 64. Also relevant is the experience in Lebanon. Its lengthy and exceedingly complicated civil war was triggered in 1975 by a pair of violent incidents between Christian and Muslim forces, but crucial to the escalation of violence and to the development of full-blown civil war was the government's utter inability to police the situation. There was "no government and no army to stand for Lebanon," notes Mackey. "The war was on and there was no one to stop it" (1989, 157–58). She points out that moderates soon found their only effective choice was "to throw in their lot with the radicals" from their own group (1989, 162). As it happened, however, there was yet another early opportunity to halt the conflict. Even though the chaotic civil war contained substantial elements of disciplined, not criminal, warfare, it was pacified fairly readily in 1976 by some 13,000 troops sent by Syria (Mackey 1989, 166). This peace proved temporary, however, because Syria was unable to control the situation overall by establishing a coherent government in which the various factions shared power and by bringing about the well-policed normalization that most people seem to have wanted (Mackey 1989, 166–68). In result, the situation soon degenerated again into warring militia fiefdoms, with the Syrians supporting one side or the other, and the occupying troops eventually becoming criminalized—or Mafiaized—in the process, smuggling untaxed goods to their own country and undermining its economy (Mackey 1989, 254).

44. Somalia: Bowden 1999, 71–76, 364–66. On this consideration, see also Judah 2000, 309; Fearon and Laitin 2003, 80.

45. On Bulgaria, see Ganev 1997; Barany 2002. On Bulgaria and also Lithuania, see Gordon and Troxel 1995. On Romania, see Brubaker 2002. On Romania and also Slovakia, see Linden 2000. On Kazakhstan, see Kaufman 2001, 78–80.

46. Macedonia poised: Kaplan 1991, 104. Ground zero: Kaplan 1993c, 15. Macedonian ac-

commodation: Kaufman 2001, 193–95; Lund 2000; Ackermann 2000. Slav gangs: Wood 2001. Under control: Gall 2001; Pearson 2002; see also Hislope 2002. On leadership failure in Georgia, see Kaufman 2001, 112.

47. Keen 1998, 21. Saint Augustine: Wright 2000, 124.

48. For similar patterns found using other data sets and other definitions of war, see Gantzel and Schwinghammer 2000, 112, 170; Gurr 2000; Marshall and Gurr 2003, 12–14; Fearon and Laitin 2003, 77–78; Tilly 2003, chap. 3; Global Menace 2003; Gleditsch et al. 2002.

49. On the connection between democratization and weak government, see also Collier 2000, 98, 108; Hegre et al. 2001; Jones 2001, 164–65; Marshall and Gurr 2003, 17–20; Fearon and Laitin 2003, 85. Snyder (2000) argues that democratizing states often cascade into war because the sudden and unnuanced opening up of the opportunity to speak and publish permits agile nationalist demagogues to incite their naive listeners to violence. The experience in the former Yugoslavia, detailed in chapter 6 above, suggests otherwise: it was not nationalist propaganda that causes the principal violence, but rather the mobilization of thugs. On the rise of democracy: Huntington 1991b; Mueller 1999b, chap. 8.

50. Berkeley 1997, 5; Reno 1998, chap. 2; Shearer 1998, 27–29; Keen 1998, 23; Ellis 1999, 306–7; Gray 2000, 163–64; Bates 2001, chap. 5; Wrong 2001, 200.

51. Rotberg 2002. On this trend, see also Marshall and Gurr 2003, 17–25.

52. In late 1993, economist Robert Barro applied an economic model and came to a grim, if decisive, conclusion about the prospects for democracy in South Africa: "Considering the country's level and distribution of income, the ethnic divisions, and the political and economic experiences of most of the countries of Sub-Sahara Africa, this event would perhaps be the greatest political accomplishment in human history. To put it another way, it's not going to happen." When that country unobligingly became a democracy a few months later, an unbent Barro predicted that "the political changes in South Africa in 1994 have probably already overshot the mark, and a substantial decline of political freedom is likely after this year."

53. O'Donnell and Schmitter 1986, 31 (emphasis in the original). Ridiculous antics: Kamm 1990. Perhaps the most spectacular case of a new, instant democracy created during this period is that of Paraguay, a country that had never known any kind of government except Jesuit theocracy or rigid military dictatorship. In 1989 Paraguay's guiding autocrat, entrenched since 1954, was overthrown by a man who had been one of his chief henchmen and who had become fabulously wealthy in the process. The new leader, however, was sensitive to the fact that democracy is what everyone is wearing nowadays—that "despots have gone out of style," as a reporter from the *Economist* put it (May 16, 1991, 48). Accordingly, he held fair elections and promised that if elected president, he would guide the country to full democracy in four years. Paraguayans, in the first free election in their grim history, took him at his word, and on schedule in 1993 another election was held and another man became president (Brooke 1993). See also Mueller 1999b, chap. 8; Solingen 1998. Early in the new century, there were signs that many countries in the Middle East—the least democratized area of the world—were beginning to liberalize in the fashion of Latin American and East Asia in the previous two decades. As the ruler of Qatar put it in 2003, "Any people [who] want to develop their countries, they have to practice democracy. That's what I believe. . . . if I look around the world, I could see the most progress [in] country who's practicing democracy" (*60 Minutes*, CBS, March 9, 2003).

54. Reno 2003, 74. Rotberg 2003, 22–23. See also Reno 2000, 59; Berkeley 2001, 226–42; Rotberg 2002.

55. See Yergin and Stanislaw 1998; Mueller 1999b, chap. 5.

56. Horowitz 2001, 561.

57. Keeley 1996, 152–56.

REFERENCES

Aaron, Craig. 1998. U.N. Official Resigns over Iraqi Sanction. *In These Times,* November 15, 4.

Aburish, Saïd K. 2000. *Saddam Hussein: The Politics of Revenge.* New York: Bloomsbury.

Ackermann, Alice. 2000. *Making Peace Prevail: Preventing Violent Conflict in Macedonia.* Syracuse, NY: Syracuse University Press.

Acton, Baron John Emerich Edward Dalberg. 1948. *Essays on Freedom and Power.* Glencoe, IL: Free Press.

African Rights. 1995. *Rwanda: Death, Despair and Defiance.* Rev. ed. London: African Rights.

Alexandroff, Alan, and Richard Rosecrance. 1977. Deterrence in 1939. *World Politics* 29 (3): 404–24.

Almond, Gabriel A. 1960. *The American People and Foreign Policy.* New York: Praeger.

Anderson, Jon Lee. 2002. *The Lion's Grave: Dispatches from Afghanistan.* New York: Grove.

Andreas, Peter. 2004. The Clandestine Political Economy of War and Peace in Bosnia. *International Studies Quarterly* 48 (1): 29–51.

Andreas, Peter, and Richard Price. 2001. From War Fighting to Crime Fighting: Transforming the American National Security State. *International Studies Review* 3 (3): 31–52.

Angell, Norman. 1951. *After All: An Autobiography.* New York: Farrar, Straus and Young.

Annan, Kofi. 1999. Two Concepts of Sovereignty. *Economist,* September 16.

Applebaum, Anne. 2003. *Gulag: A History.* New York: Doubleday.

Aristotle. 1958. *The Politics of Aristotle.* New York: Oxford University Press.

Atkins, James E. 1991. Hooray? The Gulf May Not Be Calm for Long. *New York Times,* March 3, sec. 4, 17.

Atkinson, Rick. 1994. The Raid That Went Awry. *Washington Post,* January 30 and 31.

Atkinson, Rick, and Gary Lee. 1990. Brutality in Soviet Army Has Ethnic Overtones. *Guardian Weekly,* December 9, 19.

Ayoob, Mohammed. 1998. Subaltern Realism: International Relations Theory Meets the Third World. In *International Relations Theory and the Third World,* ed. Stephanie Neuman, 31–54. New York: St. Martin's.

Ball, George W. 1982. *The Past Has Another Pattern.* New York: Norton.

Balz, Dan, and Terry M. Neal. 1999. Gore Benefits, but Will War Issue Stay Hot? *Washington Post,* June 6, A21.

Baram, Amatzia. 2000. The Effects of Iraqi Sanctions: Statistical Pitfalls and Responsibility. *Middle East Journal* 54 (2): 194–223.

Barany, Zoltan. 2002. Bulgaria's Royal Elections. *Journal of Democracy* 13 (2): 141–55.

Barclay, Thomas. 1911. Peace. In *Encyclopedia Britannica,* 11th ed., 21:4–16.

Barnes, Fred. 1991a. The Wimp Factor. *New Republic,* January 7 and 14, 10–11.

——. 1991b. The Hawk Factor. *New Republic,* January 28, 8–9.

Barro, Robert J. 1993. Pushing Democracy Is No Key to Prosperity. *Wall Street Journal,* December 14, A16.

——. 1994. Democracy: A Recipe for Growth? *Wall Street Journal,* December 1, A18.

Bartov, Omer. 1998. Ordinary Monsters. *New Republic,* April 29, 32–38.

Bates, Robert H. 2001. *Prosperity and Violence: The Political Economy of Development.* New York: Norton.

Baumeister, Roy F., and W. Keith Campbell. 1999. The Intrinsic Appeal of Evil: Sadism, Sensational Thrills, and Threatened Egotism. *Personality and Social Psychology Review* 3 (1): 210–21.

Bayart, Jean-François, Stephen Ellis, and Béatrice Hibou. 1999. *The Criminalization of the State in Africa.* Bloomington: Indiana University Press.

Beales, A. F. 1931. *The History of Peace: A Short Account of the Organized Movements for International Peace.* New York: Dial.

Beattie, J. M. 1984. Violence and Society in Early Modern England. In *Perspectives in Criminal Law,* ed. A. Doob and E. Greenspan. Aurora, Ontario: Canada Law Book.

Bell, Martin. 1995. *In Harm's Way.* London: Hamish Hamilton.

Bell, P. M. H. 1986. *The Origins of the Second World War in Europe.* London: Longmans.

Benard, Cheryl. 1993. Bosnia: Was It Inevitable? In *Lessons from Bosnia,* ed. Zalmay M. Khalilzad, 18–25. Santa Monica, CA: RAND Corporation.

Bennett, Christopher. 1995. *Yugoslavia's Bloody Collapse: Causes, Course and Consequences.* New York: New York University Press.

Berdal, Mats, and David M. Malone. 2000. Introduction. In *Greed and Grievance: Economic Agendas in Civil Wars,* ed. Mats Berdal and David M. Malone, 1–15. Boulder, CO: Lynne Rienner.

Bergquist, Charles, Ricardo Peñarand, and Gonzalo Sánchez G., eds. 2001. *Violence in Colombia: Waging War and Negotiating Peace.* Wilmington, DE: Scholarly Resources.

Berkeley, Bill. 2001. *The Graves Are Not Yet Full: Race, Tribe, and Power in the Heart of Africa.* New York: Basic Books.

Bernhardi, Friedrich von. 1914a. *Germany and the Next War.* New York: Longmans, Green.

——. 1914b. *Britain as Germany's Vassal.* New York: Doran.

Betts, Richard K. 1992. Systems for Peace or Causes of War? Collective Security, Arms Control, and the New Europe. *International Security* 17 (1): 5–43.

Bialer, Seweryn. 1986. *The Soviet Paradox: External Expansion, Internal Decline.* New York: Knopf.

Bialer, Uri. 1980. *Shadow of the Bomber: The Fear of Air Attack and British Politics, 1932–1939*. London: Royal Historical Society.

Biddle, Stephen. 1997. The Gulf War Debate *Redux:* Why Skill *and* Technology Are the Right Answer. *International Security* 22 (2): 163–74.

——. 2002. *Afghanistan and the Future of Warfare: Implications for Army and Defense Policy.* Carlisle Barracks, PA: Strategic Studies Institute, U.S. Army War College.

Binder, David. 1988. Soviet and Allies Shift on Doctrine: Guiding Terminology Changes—"Class Struggle" Is Out, "Struggle for Peace" In. *New York Times,* May 25, A13.

——. 1998. Gojko Susak, Defense Minister of Croatia, Is Dead at 53. *New York Times,* May 5, A25.

Birtle, Andrew J. 2002. *Afghan War Chronology.* Information paper, March 22. Washington, DC: U.S. Army Center of Military History.

Blainey, Geoffrey. 1973. *The Causes of Wars.* New York: Free Press.

Blass, Thomas, ed. 2000. *Obedience to Authority: Current Perspectives on the Milgram Paradigm.* Mahwah, NJ: Erlbaum.

Blight, James G., Joseph S. Nye Jr., and David A. Welch. 1987. The Cuban Missile Crisis Revisited. *Foreign Affairs* 66 (1): 170–88.

Block, Robert. 1993. Killers. *New York Review of Books,* November 18, 9–10.

Boardman, Andrew W. 1998. *The Medieval Soldier in the War of the Roses.* Phoenix Mill, UK: Sutton.

Borger, Julian. 1997a. Friends or Foes? *Guardian Weekly,* January 19, 23.

——. 1997b. The President's Secret Henchmen. *Guardian Weekly,* February 16, 8.

——. 1997c. Day of Reckoning for the Men of Death. *Guardian Weekly,* July 20, 7.

——. 1998. Iraq Élite Rides High Despite Sanctions. *Guardian Weekly,* March 8, 4.

Botterweck, G. Johannes, and Helmer Ringgren. 1986. *Theological Dictionary of the Old Testament.* Grand Rapids, MI: Eerdmans.

Bourke, Joanna. 1999. *An Intimate History of Killing: Face-to-Face Killing in Twentieth-Century Warfare.* New York: Basic Books.

Bowden, Mark. 1999. *Black Hawk Down: A Story of Modern War.* New York: Atlantic Monthly Press.

Bowen, John R. 1996. The Myth of Global Ethnic Conflict. *Journal of Democracy* 7 (4): 3–14.

Boyd, Charles G. 1995. Making Peace with the Guilty: The Truth about Bosnia. *Foreign Affairs* 74 (5): 22–38.

Boyle, Francis Anthony. 1985. *World Politics and International Law.* Durham, NC: Duke University Press.

Brent, Peter. 1976. *Genghis Khan.* New York: McGraw-Hill.

Breslauer, George W. 1987. Ideology and Learning in Soviet Third World Policy. *World Politics* 39 (3): 429–48.

Brett-James, Antony, ed. 1961. *Wellington at War, 1794–1815: A Selection of his Wartime Letters.* London: Macmillan.

Broder, John M. 1999. Clinton Underestimated Serbs, He Acknowledges. *New York Times,* June 26, A6.

Brodie, Bernard. 1959. *Strategy in the Missile Age.* Princeton, NJ: Princeton University Press.

——. 1973. *War and Politics.* New York: Macmillan.

——. 1976. The Continuing Relevance of *On War,* and A Guide to the Reading of *On War.* In *On War,* ed. Michael Howard and Peter Paret, 45–58, 641–711. Princeton, NJ: Princeton University Press.

Brooke, James. 1985. Angolan Coffee Trade in Shambles. *New York Times,* January 14, D4.

——. 1990. Colombian Guerrillas Forsake the Gun for Politics. *New York Times,* September 2, 14.

——. 1993. Governing Party's Candidate Wins Paraguay's Presidential Election. *New York Times,* May 11, A10.

Brooks, Stephen G., and William C. Wohlforth. 2000–2001. Power, Globalization, and the End of the Cold War. *International Security* 25 (3): 5–53.

——. 2002. From Old Thinking to New Thinking in Qualitative Research. *International Security* 26 (4): 93–111.

Brown, Catherine. 1999. Burma: The Political Economy of Violence. *Disasters* 23 (3): 234–56.

Brown, Frederic J. 1968. *Chemical Warfare: A Study in Restraints.* Princeton, NJ: Princeton University Press.

Brown, Stephen. 2002. Quiet Diplomacy and Recurring "Ethnic Clashes" in Kenya. Paper presented at the annual meeting of the American Political Science Association, August 29–September 1, Boston, MA.

Browning, Christopher R. 1998. *Ordinary Men: Reserve Police Battalion 101 and the Final Solution in Poland.* New York: HarperCollins.

Broyles, William, Jr. 1984. Why Men Love War. *Esquire,* November, 55–65.

Brubaker, Rogers. 2002. Ethnicity without Groups. *Archives Européennes de Sociologie* 43 (2): 163–89.

Brzezinski, Zbigniew. 1986. *Game Plan: A Geostrategic Framework for the Conduct of the U.S.–Soviet Contest.* Boston: Atlantic Monthly Press.

——. 1993. *Out of Control: Global Turmoil on the Eve of the Twenty-first Century.* New York: Scribner's.

Buford, Bill. 1991. *Among the Thugs.* New York: Norton.

Bullock, Alan. 1952. *Hitler: A Study in Tyranny.* London: Odhams.

——. 1993. *Hitler and Stalin: Parallel Lives.* New York: Vintage.

Bunce, Valerie. 1985. The Empire Strikes Back: The Evolution of the Eastern Bloc from a Soviet Asset to a Soviet Liability. *International Organization* 39 (1): 1–46.

Bundy, McGeorge. 1988. *Danger and Survival: Choices about the Bomb in the First Fifty Years.* New York: Random House.

Burg, Steven L., and Paul S. Shoup. 1999. *The War in Bosnia-Herzegovina: Ethnic Conflict and International Intervention.* Armonk, NY: Sharpe.

Burin, Frederic S. 1963. The Communist Doctrine of the Inevitability of War. *American Political Science Review* 57 (2): 334–54.

Burk, James. 1999. Public Support for Peacekeeping in Lebanon and Somalia: Assessing the Casualties Hypothesis. *Political Science Quarterly* 114 (1): 53–78.

Burns, John F. 1993a. Two Gang Leaders in Sarajevo Face Crackdown in Bosnia. *New York Times,* October 27, A6.

——. 1993b. Bosnian Forces Kill Reputed Gang Chief in Sarajevo Gunfight. *New York Times,* October 27, A6.

Bush, George H. W. 1990. *Public Papers of the Presidents of the United States: George Bush, 1989.* Washington, DC: U.S. Government Printing Office.

Butow, Robert J. C. 1961. *Tojo and the Coming of the War.* Stanford, CA: Stanford University Press.

Byman, Daniel L., and Kenneth M. Pollack. 2001. Let Us Now Praise Great Men: Bringing the Statesman Back In. *International Security* 25 (4): 107–46.

Caferro, William. 1998. *Mercenary Companies and the Decline of Siena.* Baltimore, MD: Johns Hopkins University Press.

Campbell, Bruce B., and Arthur D. Brenner, eds. 2000. *Death Squads in Global Perspective: Murder with Deniability.* New York: St. Martin's.

Campbell, John C. 1967. *Tito's Separate Road: America and Yugoslavia in World Politics.* New York: Harper and Row.

Chandler, David G., ed. 1988. *The Military Maxims of Napoleon.* Trans. George C. D'Aguilar. New York: Macmillan.

Chatfield, Charles. 1971. *For Peace and Justice.* Knoxville: University of Tennessee Press.

Checkel, Jeffrey T. 1997. *Ideas and International Political Change: Soviet/Russian Behavior and the End of the Cold War.* New Haven, CT: Yale University Press.

Chege, Michael. 2002. Sierra Leone: The State That Came Back from the Dead. *Washington Quarterly* 25 (3): 147–60.

Chickering, Roger. 1975. *Imperial Germany and a World Without War: The Peace Movement and German Society, 1892–1914.* Princeton, NJ: Princeton University Press.

——. 1988. War, Peace, and Social Mobilization in Imperial Germany: Patriotic Societies, the Peace Movement, and Socialist Labor. In *Peace Movements and Political Cultures,* ed. Charles Chatfield and Peter van den Dungen, 3–22. Knoxville: University of Tennessee Press.

Chirot, Daniel. 2000. What Was Communism All About? *East European Politics and Societies* 14 (3): 665–75.

Churchill, Winston S. 1932. *Amid These Storms: Thoughts and Adventures.* New York: Scribner's.

——. 1951. *In the Balance: Speeches, 1949 and 1950.* Boston: Houghton Mifflin.

Cigar, Norman. 1993. The Serbo-Croatian War, 1991: Political and Military Dimensions. *Journal of Strategic Studies* 16 (3): 197–338.

Clark, Wesley K. 2001. *Waging Modern War: Bosnia, Kosovo, and the Future of Combat.* New York: Public Affairs.

Clarke, I. F. 1966. *Voices Prophesying War, 1763–1984.* London: Oxford University Press.

Clausewitz, Carl Von. 1976. *On War.* Trans. Michael Howard and Peter Paret. Princeton, NJ: Princeton University Press.

Cockburn, Alexander. 1991. Beat the Devil. *Nation* 4: 114–15.

Cockburn, Andrew, and Patrick Cockburn. 1999. *Out of the Ashes: The Resurrection of Saddam Hussein.* New York: HarperCollins.

Cohen, Roger. 1998. *Hearts Grown Brutal: Sagas of Sarajevo.* New York: Random House.

Collier, Paul. 2000. Doing Well out of War: An Economic Perspective. In *Greed and Grievance: Economic Agendas in Civil Wars,* ed. Mats Berdal and David M. Malone, 91–111. Boulder, CO: Lynne Rienner.

Collier, Paul, and Anke Hoeffler. 2001. *Greed and Grievance in Civil War.* Washington, DC: World Bank.

Collier, Paul, Anke Hoeffler, and Måns Söderbom. 2001. On the Duration of Civil War. Paper presented at the conference Civil Wars and Post-Conflict Transition, May 18–20, Center for Global Peace and Conflict Studies, University of California, Irvine.

Colton, Timothy J. 1986. *The Dilemma of Reform in the Soviet Union.* Rev. ed. New York: Council on Foreign Relations.

Conquest, Robert. 1986. *The Harvest of Sorrow: Soviet Collectivization and the Terror-Famine.* New York: Oxford University Press.

Contamine, Philippe. 1984. *War in the Middle Ages.* Oxford: Basil Blackwell.

Cooper, Jeffrey R. 1994. *Another View of the Revolution in Military Affairs.* Carlisle Barracks, PA: Strategic Studies Institute, U.S. Army War College.

Cooper, Matthew. 1978. *The German Army, 1933–1945.* New York: Stein and Day.

Cooper, Sandi E. 1991. *Patriotic Pacifism: Waging War on War in Europe, 1815–1914.* New York: Oxford University Press.

Cordesman, Anthony H. 1993. *After the Storm: The Changing Military Balance in the Middle East.* Boulder, CO: Westview.

Cortright, David, and George A. Lopez. 2000. *The Sanctions Decade: Assessing UN Strategies in the 1990s.* Boulder, CO: Lynne Rienner.

Craig, Gordon A. 1956. *The Politics of the Prussian Army, 1640–1945.* New York: Oxford University Press.

———. 1989. Making Way for Hitler. *New York Review of Books,* October 12, 11–16.

Cramb, J. A. 1915. *The Origins and Destiny of Imperial Britain.* London: Murray.

Crawford, Neta C. 2002. *Argument and Change in World Politics: Ethics, Decolonization, and Humanitarian Intervention.* Cambridge: Cambridge University Press.

Crossette, Barbara. 1999. Iraq Is Said to Shun Vital Food and Medicine It Could Import under U.N. Sanctions. *New York Times,* January 13, A6.

Cubides C., Fernando. 2001. From Private to Public Violence: The Paramilitaries. In *Violence in Colombia: Waging War and Negotiating Peace,* ed. Charles Bergquist, Ricardo Peñarand and Gonzalo Sánchez G., 127–49. Wilmington, DE: Scholarly Resources.

Cviić, Christopher. 1996. Croatia. In *Yugoslavia and After: A Study in Fragmentation, Despair, and Rebirth,* ed. David A. Dyker and Ivan Vejvoda, 196–212. London: Longman.

Daalder, Ivo H., and Michael E. O'Hanlon. 2000. *Winning Ugly: NATO's War to Save Kosovo.* Washington, DC: Brookings.

Dahl, Robert A. 1971. *Polyarchy.* New Haven, CT: Yale University Press.

Davies, Godfrey. 1954. *Wellington and His Army.* Oxford, UK: Basil Blackwell.

de Waal, Alex. 1997. *Famine Crimes: Politics and the Disaster Relief Industry in Africa.* Bloomington: Indiana University Press.

Desch, Michael C. 1993–94. Why Ordinary Men Commit Extraordinary Crimes: The German Military, the War on the Eastern Front, and the Final Solution. *Security Studies* 3 (2): 359–68.

Des Forges, Alison. 1999. *"Leave None to Tell the Story": Genocide in Rwanda.* New York: Human Rights Watch.

Dessert, Daniel. 1995. The Financier. In *Baroque Personae*, ed. Rosario Villari, 57–81. Chicago: University of Chicago Press,

Dinmore, Guy. 1999. Milosevic's Last Stand. *Financial Times,* March 22, 12.

DiPrizio, Robert C. 2002. *Armed Humanitarians: U.S. Interventions from Northern Iraq to Kosovo.* Baltimore, MD: Johns Hopkins University Press.

Documents on German Foreign Policy, 1918–45. 1954. Series D. Vol. 8. Washington, D.C.: U.S. Government Printing Office.

Doder, Dusko, and Louise Branson. 1999. *Milosevic: Portrait of a Tyrant.* New York: Free Press.

Dole, Bob. 1995. Shaping America's Global Future. *Foreign Policy,* Spring, 29–43.

Dorsey, James M. 1999. From Serb Paramilitaries, Tales of Killing and Cash. *Wall Street Journal,* September 1, A18.

Dower, John W. 1986. *War without Mercy: Race and Power in the Pacific War.* New York: Pantheon.

Downes, Richard. 1998. Saddam's Men Use Sanctions to Secure Their Grip. *Independent* (London), December 12, 17.

Doyle, Michael W. 1986. Liberalism and World Politics. *American Political Science Review* 80 (4): 1151–69.

Drew, Elizabeth. 1991. Letter from Washington. *New Yorker,* February 4, 82–90.

——. 1994. *On the Edge: The Clinton Presidency.* New York: Simon and Schuster.

Dumas, Samuel, and K. O. Vedel-Petersen. 1923. *Losses of Life Caused by War.* London: Oxford University Press.

Dunn, James. 1995. The Timor Affair in International Perspective. In *East Timor at the Crossroads: The Forging of a Nation,* ed. Peter Carey and G. Carter Bentley, 59–72. Honolulu: University of Hawai'i Press.

Dunnigan, James F., and Austin Bay. 1992. *From Shield to Storm: High-Tech Weapons, Military Strategy, and Coalition Warfare in the Persian Gulf.* New York: Morrow.

Dupuy, R. Ernest, and George Fielding Eliot. 1937. *If War Comes.* New York: Macmillan.

Dyer, Gwynne. 1985. *War.* New York: Crown.

Easterbrook, Gregg. 2002. Term Limits: The Meaninglessness of "WMD." *New Republic,* October 7, 22–25.

Eberstadt, Nicholas. 1999. The Most Dangerous Country. *National Interest,* Fall, 45–54.

Edgerton, Robert B. 1992. *Sick Societies: Challenging the Myth of Primitive Harmony.* New York: Free Press.

Edmonds, James E., and R. Maxwell-Hyslop, eds. 1947. *Military Operations: France and Belgium, 1918.* Vol. 5. London: HMSO.

Ehrenreich, Barbara. 1997. *Blood Rites: Origins and History of the Passions of War.* New York: Metropolitan.

Ellickson, Robert C. 1991. *Order without Law: How Neighbors Settle Disputes.* Cambridge, MA: Harvard University Press.

Ellingsen, Tanja. 2000. Colorful Community or Ethnic Witches' Brew? *Journal of Conflict Resolution* 44 (2): 228–49.

Ellis, Stephen. 1999. *The Mask of Anarchy: The Destruction of Liberia and the Religious Dimension of an African Civil War.* New York: New York University Press.

Elman, Miriam Fendius, ed. 1997. *Paths to Peace: Is Democracy the Answer?* Cambridge, MA: MIT Press.

Emerson, Ralph Waldo. 1904. War. In *Miscellanies*, 148–76, vol. 11 of *The Complete Works of Ralph Waldo Emerson*. Boston and New York: Houghton Mifflin.

English, Robert D. 2001. *Russia and the Idea of the West: Gorbachev, Intellectuals, and the End of the Cold War*. New York: Columbia University Press.

———. 2002. Power, Ideas, and New Evidence on the Cold War's End. *International Security* 26 (4): 70–92.

Enthoven, Alain C., and K. Wayne Smith. 1971. *How Much Is Enough? Shaping the Defense Program, 1961–1969*. New York: Harper Colophon.

Erlanger, Steven. 1999a. In a Kosovo Town, the Serbs Feel Persecuted Too. *New York Times*, January 26, A4.

———. 1999b. Serb Conscripts Drift into Hiding. *New York Times*, April 5, A1.

———. 1999c. *New York Times*, May 12, A13.

———. 1999d. In Ruined Village, a Mother Lives with Her Son's Blood. *New York Times*, June 15, A1.

———. 1999e. Refuge for Kosovars in Serbian Monastery, after the Burning and Looting. *New York Times*, June 16, A15.

———. 1999f. For Serb Draftee in Kosovo, All His Patrols Were "Awful." *New York Times*, July 28, A1.

Esposito, Vincent J. 1979. World War I. In *Encyclopedia Americana*, 29:216–363. Danbury, CT: Americana.

Fallows, James. 1994–95. The Panic Gap: Reactions to North Korea's Bomb. *National Interest*, Winter, 40–45.

Farrar, L. L., Jr. 1973. *The Short-War Illusion: German Policy, Strategy and Domestic Affairs, August–December 1914*. Santa Barbara, CA: ABC-Clio.

Fatton, Robert, Jr. 2002. *Haiti's Predatory Republic: The Unending Transition to Democracy*. Boulder, CO: Lynne Rienner.

Fearon, James D., and David D. Laitin. 1996. Explaining Interethnic Cooperation. *American Political Science Review* 90 (4): 715–36.

———. 2000. Violence and the Social Construction of Ethnic Identity. *International Organization* 54 (4): 845–77.

———. 2003. Ethnicity, Insurgency, and Civil War. *American Political Science Review* 97 (1): 75–90.

Feil, Scott R. 1998. *Preventing Genocide: How the Early Use of Force Might Have Succeeded in Rwanda*. New York: Carnegie Corporation of New York.

Fest, Joachim C. 1974. *Hitler*. Trans. Richard Winston and Clara Winston. New York: Harcourt Brace Jovanovich.

Filkins, Dexter. 2001. Rebel Forces Say They Have Taken a Second Afghan City. *New York Times*, November 12, A1.

Finn, Peter. 1999. Albanians Squeeze Out Kosovo's Serbs. *Guardian Weekly*, January 17, 20.

Firestone, David. 1993. Serb Lawmaker Is Called Vicious Killer. *St. Louis Post-Dispatch*, January 3, 1A.

Fischer, Fritz. 1967. *Germany's Aims in the First World War*. New York: Norton.

———. 1975. *War of Illusions: German Policies from 1911 to 1914*. New York: Norton.

Fischer, Tim. 2000. *Seven Days in East Timor: Ballot and Bullets.* St. Leonards, Australia: Allen and Unwin.

Fitzgerald, Frances. 1972. *Fire in the Lake: The Vietnamese and Americans in Vietnam.* New York: Vintage.

Forero, Juan. 2000. A Child's Vision of War: Boy Guerrilla in Colombia. *New York Times,* December 20, A22.

Forsberg, Randall Caroline. 2001. Socially-Sanctioned and Non-Sanctioned Violence: On the Role of Moral Beliefs in Causing and Preventing War and Other Forms of Large-Group Violence. In *Gewalt und Konflikt in Einer Globalizierten Welt: Festschrift für Ulrich Albrecht,* ed. Ruth Stanley. Wiesbaden: Westdeutscher Verlag.

Freedman, Lawrence, and Efraim Karsh. 1993. *The Gulf Conflict, 1990–1991: Diplomacy and War in the New World Order.* Princeton, NJ: Princeton University Press.

Freud, Sigmund. 1930. *Civilization and Its Discontents.* London: Hogarth.

——. 1957. *The Standard Edition of the Complete Psychological Works of Sigmund Freud,* ed. James Strachey. London: Hogarth.

Friedrichs, Christopher R. 1979. *Urban Society in an Age of War.* Princeton, NJ: Princeton University Press.

Frost, David, interviewer. 1991. *Talking with David Frost: An Interview with President and Mrs. Bush.* PBS, January 2 (taped December 28, 1990).

Fukuyama, Francis. 1992. *The End of History and the Last Man.* New York: Free Press.

Fulbright, J. William. 1966. *The Vietnam Hearings.* New York: Vintage.

Fussell, Paul. 1975. *The Great War and Modern Memory.* New York: Oxford University Press.

——. 1989. *Wartime: Understanding and Behavior in the Second World War.* New York: Oxford University Press.

Gaddis, John Lewis. 1974. Was the Truman Doctrine a Real Turning Point? *Foreign Affairs* 52 (2): 386–401.

——. 1982. *Strategies of Containment.* New York: Oxford University Press.

——. 1987. *The Long Peace: Inquiries into the History of the Cold War.* New York: Oxford University Press.

——. 1992. *The United States and the Cold War: Implications, Reconsiderations, Provocations.* New York: Oxford University Press.

——. 1999. Conclusion. In *Cold War Statesmen Confront the Bomb: Nuclear Diplomacy since 1945,* ed. John Lewis Gaddis, Philip H. Gordon, Ernest R. May, and Jonathan Rosenberg, 260–71. Oxford: Oxford University Press.

Gagnon, V. P., Jr. 1994–95. Ethnic Nationalism and International Conflict: The Case of Serbia. *International Security* 19 (3): 130–66.

Gall, Carlotta. 1999a. With Flash in Sky, Kosovars Fear Ground Fighting. *New York Times,* March 25, A1.

——. 1999b. Ethnic Albanians Now Fear Wrath of Serbs. *New York Times,* March 26, A1.

——. 2001. Rebel Head in Macedonia Gives Order to Disband. *New York Times,* September 28, A5.

Gama, Paulino. 1995. The War in the Hills, 1975–85: A Fretilin Commander Remembers. In *East Timor at the Crossroads: The Forging of a Nation,* ed. Peter Carey and G. Carter Bentley, 97–105. Honolulu: University of Hawai'i Press.

Gamba, Virginia, and Richard Cornwell. 2000. Arms, Elites, and Resources in the Angolan Civil War. In *Greed and Grievance: Economic Agendas in Civil Wars*, ed. Mats Berdal and David M. Malone, 157–72. Boulder, CO: Lynne Rienner.

Ganev, Venelin I. 1997. Bulgaria's Symphony of Hope. *Journal of Democracy* 8 (4): 125–39.

Gantzel, Klaus Jürgen, and Torsten Schwinghammer. 2000. *Warfare since the Second World War.* New Brunswick, NJ: Transaction.

Garfield, Richard. 1997. The Impact of Economic Embargoes on the Health of Women and Children. *JAMWA* 52 (4): 181–85.

———. 1999. *Morbidity and Mortality among Iraqi Children from 1990 to 1998.* South Bend, IN: Kroc Institute for International Peace Studies, University of Notre Dame.

Garland, David. 1990. *Punishment and Modern Society: A Study in Social Theory.* Chicago: University of Chicago Press.

Garthoff, Raymond L. 1987. *Reflections on the Cuban Missile Crisis.* Washington, DC: Brookings.

———. 1994. *The Great Transition: American–Soviet Relations and the End of the Cold War.* Washington, DC: Brookings.

Gat, Azar. 2001. Isolationism, Appeasement, Containment, and Limited War: Western Strategic Policy from the Modern to the "Postmodern" Era. In *War in a Changing World*, ed. Zeev Maoz and Azar Gat, 77–91. Ann Arbor: University of Michigan Press.

Genschel, Philipp, and Klaus Schlichte. 1998. Civil War as a Chronic Condition. *Law and State* 58: 107–23.

George, Alexander, and Juliette L. George. 1956. *Woodrow Wilson and Colonel House: A Personality Study.* New York: John Day.

George, Terry. 1996. Lost without War in Northern Ireland. *New York Times,* July 17, A23.

Gergen, David. 2002. A Fragile Time for Globalism. *U.S. News and World Report,* February 11, 41.

Gilchrist, H. L. 1928. *A Comparative Study of World War Casualties from Gas and Other Weapons.* Edgewood Arsenal, MD: Chemical Warfare School.

Given, J. B. 1977. *Society and Homicide in Thirteenth-Century England.* Stanford, CA: Stanford University Press.

Gleditsch, Kristian Skrede. 2004. A Revised List of Wars within and between Independent States. *International Interactions* 30 (3).

Gleditsch, Nils Petter, Peter Wallenstein, Mikael Eriksson, Margareta Stollenberg, and Håvard Strand. 2002. Armed Conflict, 1946–2001: A New Dataset. *Journal of Peace Research* 39 (3): 615–37.

Glenny, Misha. 1993. *The Fall of Yugoslavia: The Third Balkan War.* New York: Penguin.

———. 2003. The Death of Djindjic. *New York Review of Books,* July 17, 32–34.

The Global Menace of Local Strife. 2003. *Economist,* May 22.

Glynn, Patrick. 1987. The Sarajevo Fallacy: The History and Intellectual Origins of Arms Control Theology. *National Interest,* Fall, 3–32.

Goldberg, Jeffrey. 1995. A War without Purpose in a Country without Identity. *New York Times Magazine,* January 22, 36–39.

Goldhagen, Daniel Jonah. 1998. *Hitler's Willing Executioners: Ordinary Germans and the Holocaust.* New York: Knopf.

Gooch, G. P. 1911. *History of Our Time, 1885–1911.* London: Williams and Norgate.

Gooch, John. 1981. *The Prospect of War: Studies in British Defense Policy, 1847–1942.* London: Frank Cass.

Gordon, Ellen J., and Luan Troxel. 1995. Minority Mobilization without War. Paper presented at the conference on Post-Communism and Ethnic Mobilization, April 21–22, Cornell University.

Gordon, Joy. 1999. A Peaceful, Silent, Deadly Remedy: The Ethics of Economic Sanctions. *Ethics and International Affairs* 13: 123–42.

——. 2002. Cool War: Economic Sanctions as a Weapons of Mass Destruction. *Harper's,* November, 43–49.

Gordon, Michael R. 1999. Civilians Are Slain in Military Attack on a Kosovo Road. *New York Times,* April 15, A1.

Gordon, Michael R., and Thomas L. Friedman. 1993. Disastrous U.S. Raid in Somalia Nearly Succeeded, Review Finds: Valorous Delay May Have Far-Reaching Impact. *New York Times,* October 25, A1.

Gordon, Michael R., and Bernard E. Trainor. 1995. *The Generals' War: The Inside Story of the Conflict in the Gulf.* Boston: Little, Brown.

Gould-Davies, Nigel. 1999. Rethinking the Role of Ideology in International Politics during the Cold War. *Journal of Cold War Studies* 1 (1): 90–109.

Gourevitch, Philip. 1998. *We Wish to Inform You That Tomorrow We Will Be Killed with Our Families: Stories from Rwanda.* New York: Farrar, Straus and Giroux.

Grant, Linda. 1998. Where Hard Men Face Hard Choices. *Guardian Weekly,* April 26, 32.

Gray, Christine. 2000. *International Law and the Use of Force.* Oxford: Oxford University Press.

——. 2002. From Unity to Polarization: International Law and the Use of Force against Iraq. *European Journal of International Law* 13 (1): 1–19.

Gray, J. Glenn. 1959. *The Warriors: Reflections on Men in Battle.* New York: Harper and Row.

Greenhouse, Steven. 1988. Zaire, the Manager's Nightmare: So Much Potential, So Poorly Harnessed. *New York Times,* May 23, A3. See also the correction, May 26, 1988, A3.

Griffith, Samuel B. 1961. Introduction. In *Mao Tse-tung on Guerrilla Warfare,* 3–34. New York: Praeger.

Grinker, Roy R., and John P. Spiegel. 1945. *Men under Stress.* Philadelphia: Blakiston.

Grossman, Dave. 1995. *On Killing: The Psychological Cost of Learning to Kill in War and Society.* Boston: Little, Brown.

Guilmartin, John F., Jr. 1997. Light Troops in Classical Armies: An Overview of Roles, Functions, and Factors Affecting Combat Effectiveness. In *The Military and Conflict between Cultures: Soldiers at the Interface,* ed. James C. Bradford, 17–48. College Station: Texas A&M University Press.

Gurr, Ted Robert. 1981. Historical Trends in Violent Crime: A Critical Review of the Evidence. *Crime and Justice* 3: 295–353.

——. 2000. Ethnic Warfare on the Wane. *Foreign Affairs* 79 (3): 52–64.

Haffner, Sebastian. 1979. *The Meaning of Hitler.* Trans. Ewald Osers. Cambridge, MA: Harvard University Press.

Halberstam, David. 1965. *The Making of a Quagmire.* New York: Random House.

Hale, J. R. 1985. *War and Society in Renaissance Europe, 1450–1620.* New York: St. Martin's.

Hall, Brian. 1994. *The Impossible Country: A Journey through the Last Days of Yugoslavia.* New York: Penguin.

——. 1996. Rebecca West's War. *New Yorker,* April 15, 74–83.

Halperin, Sandra. 1998. The Spread of Ethnic Conflict in Europe: Some Comparative-Historical Reflections. In *The International Spread of Ethnic Conflict,* ed. David A. Lake and Donald Rothchild, 151–84. Princeton, NJ: Princeton University Press.

Hamburg, David A. 1993. *Preventing Contemporary Intergroup Violence.* New York: Carnegie Corporation of New York.

Haney, Craig, Curtis Banks, and Philip Zimbardo. 1973. Interpersonal Dynamics in a Simulated Prison. *International Journal of Criminology and Penology* 1: 69–97.

Hansch, Steven, Scott Lillibridge, Grace Egeland, Charles Teller, and Michael Toole. 1994. *Lives Lost, Lives Saved: Excess Mortality and the Impact of Health Interventions in the Somalia Emergency.* Washington, DC: Refugee Policy Group.

Harden, Blaine. 1999a. Honor Compels Opposition to Rally around Belgrade. *New York Times,* March 25, A14.

——. 1999b. Reservists a Crucial Factor in Effort against Milosevic. *New York Times,* July 9, A1.

Hardin, Russell. 1995. *One for All: The Logic of Group Conflict.* Princeton, NJ: Princeton University Press.

Harrison, Selig S. 2002. *Korean Endgame: A Strategy for Reunification and U.S. Disengagement.* Princeton, NJ: Princeton University Press.

Harvard Nuclear Study Group. 1983. *Living with Nuclear Weapons.* New York: Bantam.

Hauser, William L. 1980. The Will to Fight. In *Combat Effectiveness: Cohesion, Stress, and the Voluntary Military,* ed. Sam C. Sarkesian, 186–211. Beverly Hills, CA: Sage.

Hedges, Chris. 1995. War Turns Sarajevo away from Europe. *New York Times,* July 28, A4.

——. 1996a. From One Serbian Militia Chief, a Trail of Plunder and Slaughter. *New York Times,* March 25, A1.

——. 1996b. A War-Bred Underworld Threatens Bosnia Peace. *New York Times,* May 1, A8.

——. 1997a. On Bosnia's Ethnic Fault Lines, It's Still Tense, but World Is Silent. *New York Times,* February 28, A1.

——. 1997b. Bosnian Serbs Sink in Poverty as Their Leaders Amass Wealth. *New York Times,* July 7, A3.

——. 1997c. Postscript to Sarajevo's Anguish: Muslim Killings of Serbs Detailed. *New York Times,* November 12, A1.

——. 1998a. Dejected Belgrade Embraces Hedonism, but Still, Life Is No Cabaret. *New York Times,* January 19, A1.

——. 1998b. Gun Battles in Serbia Raise Fear of "Another Bosnia." *New York Times,* March 6, A3.

——. 1998c. Kosovo Rebels' New Tactic: Attack Serb Civilians. *New York Times,* June 24, A1.

——. 1999. Kosovo's Next Masters? *Foreign Affairs* 78 (3): 24–42.

——. 2002. *War Is a Force That Gives Us Meaning.* New York: Public Affairs.

Hegre, Håvard, Tanja Ellingsen, Scott Gates, and Nils Petter Gleditsch. 2001. Toward a Democratic Civil Peace? Democracy, Political Change, and Civil War, 1816–1992. *American Political Science Review* 95 (1): 33–48.

Heidenrich, John G. 1993. The Gulf War: How Many Iraqis Died? *Foreign Policy,* Spring, 108–25.

Heller, Yves. 1996. How Croatia Reclaimed Its Accursed Land. *Guardian Weekly,* March 31, 14.

Henderson, Errol A., and J. David Singer. 2002. "New Wars" and Rumors of "New Wars." *International Interactions* 28: 165–90.

Herbst, Jeffry. 1996–97. Responding to State Failure in Africa. *International Security* 21 (1): 120–44.

Herman, Sondra R. 1969. *Eleven against War: Studies in American International Thought, 1898–1921.* Stanford, CA: Hoover Institution Press.

Hildebrand, Klaus. 1973. *The Foreign Policy of the Third Reich.* Trans. Anthony Fothergill. Berkeley: University of California Press.

Hinsley, F. H. 1963. *Power and the Pursuit of Peace: Theory and Practice in the History of Relations between States.* London: Cambridge University Press.

——. 1987. Peace and War in Modern Times. In *The Quest for Peace,* ed. Raimo Väyrynen, 63–79. Beverly Hills, CA: Sage.

Hirsch, John L., and Robert B. Oakley. 1995. *Somalia and Operation Restore Hope: Reflections on Peacemaking and Peacekeeping.* Washington, DC: United States Institute of Peace.

Hislope, Robert. 2002. Organized Crime in a Disorganized State: How Corruption Contributed to Macedonia's Mini-War. *Problems of Post-Communism,* May–June, 33–41.

Historicus [George Allen Morgan]. 1949. Stalin on Revolution. *Foreign Affairs* 27 (2): 175–214.

Hitler, Adolf. 1942. *The Speeches of Adolf Hitler, April 1922–August 1939.* London: Oxford University Press.

——. 1943. *Mein Kampf.* Trans. Ralph Mannheim. New York: Houghton Mifflin.

Ho Ping-ti. 1959. *Studies on the Population of China, 1368–1953.* Cambridge, MA: Harvard University Press.

Hoagland, Jim. 2003. Fusing Force with Diplomacy. *Washington Post,* June 19, A27.

Hobbes, Thomas. 1994. *Leviathan.* Ed. Edwin Curley. Indianapolis, IN: Hackett.

Hobsbawm, Eric J. 1987. *The Age of Empire, 1875–1914.* New York: Vintage.

Holbrooke, Richard. 1998. *To End a War.* New York: Random House.

Holmes, Richard. 1985. *Acts of War: The Behavior of Men in Battle.* New York: Free Press.

Holmes, Robert L. 1989. *On War and Morality.* Princeton, NJ: Princeton University Press.

Holsti, Kalevi J. 1991. *Peace and War: Armed Conflicts and International Order, 1648–1989.* Cambridge: Cambridge University Press.

Horowitz, Donald L. 2001. *The Deadly Ethnic Riot.* Berkeley: University of California Press.

Hosmer, Stephen T. 2001. *The Conflict over Kosovo: Why Milosevic Decided to Settle When He Did.* Santa Monica, CA: RAND.

Hosmer, Stephen T., and Thomas W. Wolfe. 1983. *Soviet Policy and Practice toward Third World Countries.* Lexington, MA: Lexington.

Hough, Jerry F. 1986. *The Struggle for the Third World: Soviet Debates and American Options.* Washington, DC: Brookings.

Howard, Michael. 1978. *War and the Liberal Conscience.* New Brunswick, NJ: Rutgers University Press.

——. 1984. *The Causes of Wars and Other Essays.* 2nd ed. Cambridge, MA: Harvard University Press.

——. 1989. A Death Knell for War? *New York Times Book Review,* April 30, 14.

——. 1991. *The Lessons of History.* New Haven, CT: Yale University Press.

——. 2000. *The Invention of Peace: Reflections on War and International Order.* London: Profile Books.

——. 2001. The Great War: Mystery or Error? *National Interest,* Summer, 78–84.

——. 2002. What's in a Name? How to Fight Terrorism. *Foreign Affairs* 81 (1): 8–13.

Howe, Herbert. 1996–97. Lessons of Liberia: ECOMOG and Regional Peacekeeping. *International Security* 21 (1): 145–76.

Hudson, G. F., Richard Lowenthal, and Roderick MacFarquhar, eds. 1961. *The Sino-Soviet Dispute.* New York: Praeger.

Hufbauer, Gary C., Jeffrey J. Schott, and Kimberly Ann Elliott. 1990. *Economic Sanctions Reconsidered: History and Current Policy.* 2nd ed. Washington, DC: Institute for International Economics.

Huntington, Samuel P. 1991a. America's Changing Strategic Interests. *Survival,* January–February, 3–17.

——. 1991b. *The Third Wave: Democratization in the Late Twentieth Century.* Norman: University of Oklahoma Press.

——. 1993a. Why International Primacy Matters. *International Security* 17 (4): 68–83.

——. 1993b. The Clash of Civilizations? *Foreign Affairs* 72 (3): 22–49.

——. 1993c. If Not Civilizations, What? Paradigms of the Post–Cold War World. *Foreign Affairs* 72 (5): 186–94.

——. 1996. *The Clash of Civilizations and the Remaking of the World Order.* New York: Touchstone.

Husarska, Anna. 1995. Rocky-Road Warrior. *New Republic,* December 4, 16–17.

Hyland, William G. 1990. *The Cold War Is Over.* New York: Times Books.

Ignatieff, Michael. 1993. The Balkan Tragedy. *New York Review of Books,* May 13, 3–5.

——. 1997. *The Warrior's Honor: Ethnic War and the Modern Conscience.* New York: Henry Holt.

Ikenberry, G. John. 2001. *After Victory: Institutions, Strategic Restraint, and the Rebuilding of Order after Major Wars.* Princeton, NJ: Princeton University Press.

Ingrao, Charles. 1999. It Will Take More Than Bombs to Bring Stability. *Los Angeles Times,* April 12, B11.

Jaber, Hala. 1997. *Hezbollah: Born with a Vengeance.* New York: Columbia University Press.

Jackson, Robert H. 1993. The Weight of Ideas in Decolonization: Normative Change in International Relations. In *Ideas and Foreign Policy: Beliefs, Institutions, and Political Change*, ed. Judith Goldstein and Robert O. Keohane, 111–38. Ithaca, NY: Cornell University Press.

James, William. 1911. *Memories and Studies*. New York: Longmans, Green.

Jefferson, Thomas. 1939. *Democracy*. Ed. Saul K. Padover. New York: Appleton-Century.

Jenkins, Brian Michael. 1970. *Why the North Vietnamese Keep Fighting*. Santa Monica, CA: Rand Corporation.

——. 2000–2001. Colombia: Crossing a Dangerous Threshold. *National Interest*, Winter, 47–55.

Jenne, Erin K. 2003. Sri Lanka: A Fragmented State. In *State Failure and State Weakness in a Time of Terror*, ed. Robert Rotberg, 219–44. Washington, DC: Brookings.

Jervis, Robert. 1988. The Political Effects of Nuclear Weapons. *International Security* 13 (2): 28–38.

——. 1989. *Implications of the Nuclear Revolution*. Ithaca, NY: Cornell University Press.

——. 2002. Theories of War in an Era of Leading-Power Peace. *American Political Science Review* 96 (1): 1–14.

Jett, Dennis C. 2000. *Why Peacekeeping Fails*. New York: St. Martin's.

Johns, Christina Jacqueline, and P. Ward Johnson. 1994. *State Crime, the Media, and the Invasion of Panama*. Westport, CT: Praeger.

Johnson, Paul. 1995. Another Fifty Years of Peace? *Wall Street Journal*, May 9.

Johnson, Robert H. 1994. *Improbable Dangers: U.S. Conceptions of Threat in the Cold War and After*. New York: St. Martin's.

Joll, James. 1984. *The Origins of the First World War*. New York: Longman.

Jones, Bruce D. 2001. *Peacemaking in Rwanda: The Dynamics of Failure*. Boulder, CO: Lynne Rienner.

Jones, E. L. 1987. *The European Miracle: Environments, Economies, and Geopolitics in the History of Europe and Asia*. 2nd ed. Cambridge: Cambridge University Press.

Josephus. 1982. *The Jewish War*. Ed. Gaalya Cornfeld. Grand Rapids, MI: Zondervan.

Judah, Tim. 1997. *The Serbs: History, Myth and the Destruction of Yugoslavia*. New Haven, CT: Yale University Press.

——. 1999. KLA Is Still a Force to Be Reckoned With. *Wall Street Journal*, April 7, A22.

——. 2000. *Kosovo: War and Revenge*. New Haven, CT: Yale University Press.

Kaeuper, Richard W. 1988. *War, Justice, and Public Order: England and France in the Later Middle Ages*. New York: Oxford University Press.

Kagan, Donald. 1987. World War I, World War II, World War III. *Commentary*, March, 21–40.

——. 1995. *On the Origins of War and the Preservation of Peace*. New York: Doubleday.

Kaldor, Mary. 1999. *New and Old Wars: Organized Violence in a Global Era*. Cambridge, UK: Polity Press.

Kalyvas, Stathis N. 1999. Wanton and Senseless? The Logic of Massacres in Algeria. *Rationality and Society* 11 (3): 243–85.

——. 2001. "New" and "Old" Civil Wars: A Valid Distinction? *World Politics* 54 (1): 99–118.

———. 2002. The Ontology of "Political Violence": Action and Identity in Civil Wars. *Perspectives on Politics* 1 (3): 475–94.

Kamm, Thomas. 1990. Democracy in Argentina Buoyed as Armed Revolt Is Ended Fast. *Wall Street Journal,* December 5, A13.

Kant, Immanuel. 1952. *The Critique of Judgement.* London: Oxford University Press.

Kaplan, Lawrence F., and William Kristol. 2003. *The War over Iraq: Saddam's Tyranny and America's Mission.* San Francisco: Encounter Books.

Kaplan, Robert D. 1991. History's Cauldron. *Atlantic,* June, 93–104.

———. 1993a. *Balkan Ghosts: A Journey through History.* New York: St. Martin's.

———. 1993b. A Reader's Guide to the Balkans. *New York Times Book Review,* April 18, 1, 30–32.

———. 1993c. Ground Zero: Macedonia: The Real Battleground. *New Republic,* August 2, 15–16.

———. 1994. The Coming Anarchy. *Atlantic,* February, 44–76.

———. 1999. Reading Too Much into a Book. *New York Times,* June 13, 4–17.

Karnow, Stanley. 1991. *Vietnam: A History.* Rev. ed. New York: Penguin.

Karsh, Efraim, and Inari Rautsi. 1991. *Saddam Hussein: A Political Biography.* New York: Free Press.

Katz, Fred E. 1993. *Ordinary People and Extraordinary Evil: A Report on the Beguilings of Evil.* Albany: State University of New York Press.

Katz, Jack. 1988. *Seductions of Crime: Moral and Sensual Attractions in Doing Evil.* New York: Basic Books.

Kaufman, Stuart J. 2001. *Modern Hatreds: The Symbolic Politics of Ethnic War.* Ithaca, NY: Cornell University Press.

Kaufmann, Chaim. 1996. Possible and Impossible Solutions to Ethnic Civil Wars. *International Security* 20 (4): 136–75.

Kaysen, Carl. 1990. Is War Obsolete? *International Security* 14 (4): 42–64.

Keaney, Thomas A., and Eliot A. Cohen. 1993. *Gulf War Air Power Survey Summary Report.* Washington, DC: Department of the Air Force.

Keegan, John. 1976. *The Face of Battle.* London: Penguin.

———. 1987. The Evolution of Battle and the Prospects of Peace. In *Arms at Rest: Peacemaking and Peacekeeping in American History,* ed. John R. Cinor and Robert L. Beisner, 189–201. New York: Greenwood.

———. 1989. Only One Man Wanted to Ignite World War II. *Los Angeles Times,* August 27, sec. V, 1.

———. 1993. *A History of Warfare.* New York: Knopf.

———. 1998. *War and Our World.* London: Hutchinson.

———. 2001. The Threat from Europe. *Spectator,* March 24, 38–39.

Keeley, Lawrence H. 1996. *War before Civilization: The Myth of the Peaceful Savage.* New York: Oxford University Press.

Keen, David. 1998. *The Economic Functions of Violence in Civil Wars.* Adelphi Paper No. 320. London: International Institute for Strategic Studies.

———. 2000. Incentives and Disincentives for Violence. In *Greed and Grievance: Economic Agendas in Civil Wars,* ed. Mats Berdal and David M. Malone, 19–41. Boulder, CO: Lynne Rienner.

Kellen, Konrad. 1972. 1971 and Beyond: The View from Hanoi. In *Indochina in Conflict,* ed. J. J. Zasloff and Ellen E. Goodman, 99–112. Lexington, MA: Heath.

Keller, Bill. 1988. New Soviet Ideologist Rejects Idea of World Struggle against West. *New York Times,* October 6, A1.

——. 1994. In Mozambique and Other Lands, Children Fight the Wars. *New York Times,* November 9, A14.

Kellett, Anthony. 1982. *Combat Motivation.* Boston: Kluwer-Nijhoff.

Kelman, Herbert C., and V. Lee Hamilton. 1989. *Crimes of Obedience: Toward a Social Psychology of Authority and Responsibility.* New Haven, CT: Yale University Press.

Kempe, Frederick. 1986. Gorbachev Task: Revamping Economy in the Face of Declining Soviet Exports. *Wall Street Journal,* February 25, 34.

Kennan, George F. [X]. 1947. The Sources of Soviet Conduct. *Foreign Affairs* 25 (4): 566–82.

Kennedy, Paul. 1987. *The Rise and Fall of the Great Powers.* New York: Random House.

Kennedy, Robert F. 1971. *Thirteen Days: A Memoir of the Cuban Missile Crisis.* New York: Norton.

Kershaw, Ian. 1985. *The Nazi Dictatorship: Problems and Perspectives of Interpretation.* London: Edward Arnold.

——. 1987. *The "Hitler Myth": Image and Reality in the Third Reich.* New York: Oxford University Press.

——. 2000. *Hitler, 1936–45: Nemesis.* New York: Norton.

Kettle, Martin. 1999. Kosovo Holds the Key to Gore's Prospects. *Guardian Weekly,* June 6, 6.

Khrushchev, Nikita. 1970. *Khrushchev Remembers.* Ed. Edward Crankshaw and Strobe Talbott. Boston: Little, Brown.

Kifner, John. 1999a. Refugees Tell of Methodical Emptying of Pristina. *New York Times,* April 2, A1.

——. 1999b. How Serb Forces Purged One Million Albanians. *New York Times,* May 29, A1.

King, Charles. 2001. Potemkin Democracy: Four Myths about Post-Soviet Georgia. *National Interest,* Summer, 93–104.

Kinnard, Douglas. 1977. *The War Managers.* Hanover, NH: University Press of New England.

Kinzer, Stephen. 1993. The Nightmare's Roots: The Dream World Called Serbia. *New York Times,* May 16, sec. 4, 1.

——. 1995a. Bosnian Muslim Troops Evade U.N. Force to Raid Serb Village. *New York Times,* June 27, A3.

——. 1995b. Yugoslavia Deports Refugee Serbs to Fight for Rebels in Bosnia and Croatia. *New York Times,* July 6, A6.

Kirshner, Jonathan. 1997. The Microfoundations of Economic Sanctions. *Security Studies* 6 (3): 32–64.

Kissinger, Henry A. 1977. *American Foreign Policy.* 3rd ed. New York: Norton.

——. 1979. *White House Years.* Boston: Little, Brown.

——. 1999. No U.S. Ground Forces for Kosovo. *Washington Post,* February 22, A15.

Klarevas, Louis J. 1999. American Public Opinion on Peace Operations: The Cases of Somalia, Rwanda, and Haiti. Ph.D. diss., American University.

Kloos, Peter. 2001. A Turning Point? From Civil Struggle to Civil War in Sri Lanka. In *Anthropology of Violence and Conflict,* ed. Bettina E. Schmidt and Ingo W. Schröder, 176–96. London: Routledge.

Knox, MacGregor. 1982. *Mussolini Unleashed, 1939–1941: Politics and Strategy in Fascist Italy's Last War.* New York: Cambridge University Press.

———. 1984. Conquest, Foreign and Domestic, in Fascist Italy and Nazi Germany. *Journal of Modern History* 56: 1–57.

Kramer, Mark. 1987. Soviet Arms Transfers to the Third World. *Problems of Communism* 35 (5): 52–68.

———. 1999. Ideology and the Cold War. *Review of International Studies* 25 (4): 539–76.

Kraus, Sidney. 1979. *The Great Debates: Carter vs. Ford, 1976.* Bloomington: Indiana University Press.

Krauthammer, Charles. 2002–3. The Unipolar Moment Revisited. *National Interest,* Winter, 5–17.

Kraynak, Robert P. 1990. *History and Modernity in the Thought of Thomas Hobbes.* Ithaca, NY: Cornell University Press.

Krepinevich, Andrew. 1994. Cavalry to Computer. *National Interest,* Fall, 30–42.

Kuperman, Alan J. 1998. In the Balkans, Time to Intervene?, October 5, A18.

———. 2001. *The Limits of Humanitarian Intervention: Genocide in Rwanda.* Washington, DC: Brookings.

Lambeth, Benjamin S. 2000. *The Transformation of American Air Power.* Ithaca, NY: Cornell University Press.

———. 2001. *NATO's Air War for Kosovo: A Strategic and Operational Assessment.* Santa Monica, CA: RAND.

Langer, William. 1951. *The Diplomacy of Imperialism, 1890–1902.* New York: Knopf.

Larson, Eric V. 1996. *Casualties and Consensus: The Historical Role of Casualties in Domestic Support for U.S. Military Operations.* Santa Monica, CA: RAND.

———. 2000. Putting Theory to Work: Diagnosing Public Opinion on the U.S. Intervention in Bosnia. In *Being Useful: Policy Relevance and International Relations,* ed. Miroslav Nincic and Joseph Lepgold, 174–236. Ann Arbor: University of Michigan Press.

Lawrence, T. E. 1926. *Seven Pillars of Wisdom.* New York: Dell.

Layne, Christopher. 1994. Kant or Cant? The Myth of the Democratic Peace. *International Security* 19 (2): 5–49.

———. 2000. Collateral Damage in Yugoslavia. In *NATO's Empty Victory: A Postmortem on the Balkan War,* ed. Ted Galen Carpenter, 51–58. Washington, DC: Cato Institute.

Lebow, Richard Ned. 1981. *Between Peace and War: The Nature of International Crisis.* Baltimore: Johns Hopkins University Press.

Lebow, Richard Ned, and Janice Gross Stein. 1994. *We All Lost the Cold War.* Princeton, NJ: Princeton University Press.

Leffler, Melvyn P. 1994. *The Specter of Communism.* New York: Hill and Wang.

Leites, Nathan. 1953. *A Study of Bolshevism.* Glencoe, IL: Free Press.

———. 1969. *The Viet Cong Style of Politics.* RM-5487-1-ISA/ARPA. Santa Monica, CA: RAND.

Lemarchand, René. 1998. U.S. Policy in the Great Lakes: A Critical Perspective. *Issue: A Journal of Opinion* 36 (1): 41–46.

Lerner, Max, ed. 1943. *The Mind and Faith of Justice Holmes.* Boston: Little, Brown.

Levy, Jack S. 1983. *War in the Modern Great Power System, 1495–1975.* Lexington: University Press of Kentucky.

Levy, Jack S., Thomas C. Walker, and Martin S. Edwards. 2001. Continuity and Change in the Evolution of Warfare. In *War in a Changing World*, ed. Zeev Maoz and Azar Gat, 15–48. Ann Arbor: University of Michigan Press.

Lewis, Ioan, and James Mayall. 1996. Somalia. In *The New Interventionism, 1991–1994: United Nations Experience in Cambodia, former Yugoslavia, Somalia*, ed. James Mayall, 94–124. Cambridge: Cambridge University Press.

Lewy, Gunther. 1978. *American in Vietnam*. New York: Oxford University Press.

Li, Quan, and David Sacko. 2002. The (Ir)Relevance of Militarized Interstate Disputes for International Trade. *International Studies Quarterly* 46 (1): 11–34.

Liebl, Vern. 1991. The View from the Other Side of the Jebel (Hill). *Command Magazine*, November–December, 33.

Lieven, Anatol. 1998. *Chechnya: Tombstone of Russian Power*. New Haven, CT: Yale University Press.

Lind, Michael. 2003. The Weird Men behind George W. Bush's War. *New Statesman*, April 7, 10–13.

Linden, Robert H. 2000. Putting on Their Sunday Best: Romania, Hungary, and the Puzzle of Peace. *International Studies Quarterly* 44 (1): 121–45.

Linderman, Gerald F. 1987. *Embattled Courage: The Experience of Combat in the Civil War*. New York: Free Press.

Link, Arthur S. 1957. *Wilson, the Diplomatist: A Look at His Major Foreign Policies*. Baltimore, MD: Johns Hopkins University Press.

Lippman, Thomas W., and Barton Gellman. 1999. U.N. "Helped U.S. to Spy on Saddam." *Guardian Weekly*, January 17, 17.

Lloyd George, David. 1933. *War Memoirs*. Vol. 1. London: Ivor Nicholson and Watson.

——. 1938. *The Truth about the Peace Treaties*. Vol. 1. London: Victor Gollancz.

Loeb, Vernon. 1998. Oil-for-Food Program Continues as Key Facet of U.S. Policy on Iraq. *Washington Post*, November 14, A16.

Luard, Evan. 1986. *War in International Society*. New Haven, CT: Yale University Press.

——. 1988. *The Blunted Sword: The Erosion of Military Power in Modern World Politics*. London: I. B. Tauris.

Lukacs, John. 1997. *The Hitler of History*. New York: Knopf.

Lukas, J. Anthony. 1987. Class Reunion: Kennedy's Men Relive the Cuban Missile Crisis. *New York Times Magazine*, August 30, 22ff.

Lund, Michael S. 2000. Preventive Diplomacy for Macedonia, 1992–1999: From Containment to Nation Building. In *Opportunities Missed, Opportunities Seized: Preventive Diplomacy in the Post–Cold War World*, ed. Bruce W. Jentleson, 173–208. Lanham, MD: Rowman and Littlefield.

Lundestad, Geir. 1999. *East, West, North, South: Major Developments in International Politics since 1945*. Trans. Gail Adams Kvam. 4th ed. New York: Oxford University Press.

——. 2000. "Imperial Overstretch," Mikhail Gorbachev, and the End of the Cold War. *Cold War History* 1 (1): 1–20.

Luvaas, Jay, ed. 1999. *Frederick the Great on the Art of War*. New York: Da Capo.

Lynn, John A. 2003. *Battle: A History of Combat and Culture*. Boulder, CO: Westview.

Maass, Peter. 1992. In Bosnia, "Disloyal Serbs" Share Plight of Opposition. *Washington Post*, August 24, A1.

——. 1996. *Love Thy Neighbor: A Story of War.* New York: Vintage.

Macdonald, Douglas J. 1995/96. Communist Bloc Expansionism in the Early Cold War: Challenging Realism, Refuting Revisionism. *International Security* 20 (3): 152–88.

Mack, Andrew. 2002. Civil War: Academic Research and the Policy Community. *Journal of Peace Research* 39 (5): 515–25.

Mackey, Sandra. 1989. *Lebanon: Death of a Nation.* New York: Congdon and Weed.

——. 2002. *The Reckoning: Iraq and the Legacy of Saddam Hussein.* New York: Norton.

Mackley, J. P. 1993. The Balkan Quagmire Myth: Taking on the Serbs Would Be More Grenada Than Vietnam. *Washington Post,* March 7, C3.

Maddison, Angus. 1983. A Comparison of Levels of GDP per Capita in Developed and Developing Countries, 1700–1980. *Journal of Economic History* 43 (1): 27–41.

Malcolm, Noel. 1993. Seeing Ghosts. *National Interest,* Summer, 83–88.

——. 1995. Bosnia and the West: A Study in Failure. *National Interest,* Spring, 3–14.

Malinowski, Tom. 2003. Broken Promises To Liberia. *Washington Post,* September 24, A29.

Mallaby, Sebastian. 2001. Paid to Make Peace: Mercenaries Are No Altruists, but They Can Do Good. *Washington Post,* June 4, A19.

Malley, Michael. 2003. Indonesia: The Erosion of State Capacity. In *State Failure and State Weakness in a Time of Terror,* ed. Robert Rotberg, 183–218. Washington, DC: Brookings.

Manchester, William. 1988. *The Last Lion, Winston Spencer Churchill: Alone, 1932–1940.* Boston: Little, Brown.

Mandelbaum, Michael. 1998–99. Is Major War Obsolete? *Survival* 40 (4): 20–38.

——. 2002. *The Ideas That Conquered the World: Peace, Democracy, and Free Markets in the Twenty-first Century.* New York: Public Affairs.

Maren, Michael. 1997. *The Road to Hell: The Ravaging Effects of Foreign Aid and International Charity.* New York: Free Press.

——. 2000. Outmanned, Outgunned in Sierra Leone. *New York Times,* May 9, A31.

Marshall, Monty G., and Ted Robert Gurr. 2003. *Peace and Conflict, 2003: A Global Survey of Armed Conflicts, Self-Determination Movements, and Democracy.* College Park, MD: Center for International Development and Conflict Management, University of Maryland.

Martinkus, John. 2001. *A Dirty Little War.* Sydney, Australia: Random House.

May, Ernest R. 1999. Introduction. In *Cold War Statesmen Confront the Bomb: Nuclear Diplomacy since 1945,* ed. John Lewis Gaddis, Philip H. Gordon, Ernest R. May, and Jonathan Rosenberg, 1–11. Oxford: Oxford University Press.

Mayer, Arno. 1959. *Political Origins of the New Diplomacy, 1917–1918.* New Haven, CT: Yale University Press.

McCaffrey, Barry R. 1991. Testimony. In *Operation Desert Shield/Desert Storm. Hearings before the Committee on Armed Services, United States Senate,* 103–75. 102nd Cong., 1st sess., May 9. Washington, DC: U.S. Government Printing Office.

McEvedy, Colin, and Richard Jones. 1978. *Atlas of World Population History.* New York: Penguin.

McMahon, Robert J. 1999. *The Limits of Empire: The United States in Southeast Asia since World War II.* New York: Columbia University Press.

McManus, Doyle. 1999. Debate Turns to Finger-Pointing on Kosovo Policy. *Los Angeles Times,* April 11, A1.

McNaugher, Thomas L. 1990. Ballistic Missiles and Chemical Weapons: The Legacy of the Iran–Iraq War. *International Security* 15 (2): 5–34.

McPherson, James M. 1997. *For Cause and Comrades: Why Men Fought in the Civil War.* New York: Oxford University Press.

Mearsheimer, John J. 1983. *Conventional Deterrence.* Ithaca, NY: Cornell University Press.

——. 1988. *Liddell Hart and the Weight of History.* Ithaca, NY: Cornell University Press.

Mearsheimer, John J., and Stephen M. Walt. 2003. Iraq: An Unnecessary War. *Foreign Policy,* January–February, 50–59.

Meilinger, Philip S. 1993. Winged Defense: Airwar, the Law, and Morality. *Armed Forces and Society* 20 (1).

Melby, Eric D. K. 1998. Iraq. In *Economic Sanctions and American Diplomacy,* ed. Richard N. Haass. New York: Council on Foreign Relations Press.

Mencken, H. L. 1920. *Prejudices: Second Series.* New York: Knopf.

Merrill, Christopher. 1999. *Only Nails Remain: Scenes from the Balkan Wars.* Lantham, MD: Rowman and Littlefield.

Milgram, Stanley. 1975. *Obedience to Authority: An Experimental View.* New York: Harper and Row.

Miller, Arthur G. 1986. *The Obedience Experiments: A Case Study of Controversy in Social Science.* New York: Praeger.

Miller, J. D. B. 1986. *Norman Angell and the Futility of War.* New York: St. Martin's.

Miller, T. Christian. 2001. Forgotten Land Where Only Rebels Dare to Roam. *Los Angeles Times,* July 8, A5.

——. 2002a. Paramilitary Rule Pleases the Locals. *Los Angeles Times,* August 18, A6.

——. 2002b. Colombia's Drug War Attracts Dubious Ally. *Los Angeles Times,* August 19, A1.

Millett, Allan R., and William B. Moreland. 1976. What Happened? The Problem of Causation in International Affairs. In *Historical Dimensions of National Security Problems,* ed. Klaus Knorr, 5–37. Lawrence: University Press of Kansas.

Milne, Alan Alexander. 1935. *Peace with Honour.* New York: Dutton.

Milward, Alan S. 1977. *War, Economy and Society, 1939–1945.* Berkeley: University of California Press.

Mitchell, Alison. 1996. Clinton Honors Troops That Served in Haiti. *New York Times,* March 19, A14.

Mitchell, George J. 1999. *Making Peace.* New York: Knopf.

Moore, Molly. 1991a. Aspin: War Would Start with Air Strikes, Escalate to Ground Battles. *Washington Post,* January 9, A15.

——. 1991b. Porous Minefields, Dispirited Troops and a Dog Named Pow. *Washington Post,* March 17, A1.

Moore, Samuel. 2001. The Indonesian Military's Last Years in East Timor: An Analysis of Its Secret Documents. *Indonesia* 72 (October): 9–44.

Morgenthau, Hans J. 1948. *Politics among Nations: The Struggle for Power and Peace.* New York: Knopf.

Moynihan, Daniel Patrick. 1990. *On the Law of Nations.* Cambridge, MA: Harvard University Press.

——. 1993. *Pandaemonium: Ethnicity in International Politics.* New York: Oxford University Press.

Mueller, John. 1969. Voting on the Propositions: Patterns and Historical Trends in California. *American Political Science Review* 63 (4): 1197–212.

——. 1973. *War, Presidents and Public Opinion.* New York: Wiley.

——. 1980. The Search for the "Breaking Point" in Vietnam: The Statistics of a Deadly Quarrel. *International Studies Quarterly* 24 (4): 497–519.*

——. 1984. Reflections on the Vietnam Protest Movement and on the Curious Calm at the War's End. In *Vietnam as History,* ed. Peter Braestrup, 151–57. Lanham, MD: University Press of America.*

——. 1985. The Bomb's Pretense as Peacemaker. *Wall Street Journal,* June 4, 32.

——. 1986. Containment and the Decline of the Soviet Empire: Some Tentative Reflections on the End of the World as We Know It. Paper presented at the Annual Convention of the International Studies Association, March 25–29, Anaheim, CA.*

——. 1988. The Essential Irrelevance of Nuclear Weapons: Stability in the Postwar World. *International Security* 13 (2): 55–79.

——. 1989. *Retreat from Doomsday: The Obsolescence of Major War.* New York: Basic Books.*

——. 1994. *Policy and Opinion in the Gulf War.* Chicago: University of Chicago Press.

——. 1995a. *Quiet Cataclysm: Reflections on the Recent Transformation of World Politics.* New York: HarperCollins.*

——. 1995b. The Perfect Enemy: Assessing the Gulf War. *Security Studies* 5 (1): 77–117.

——. 1999a. Epilogue: Duelling Counterfactuals. In *Cold War Statesmen Confront the Bomb: Nuclear Diplomacy since 1945,* ed. John Lewis Gaddis, Philip H. Gordon, Ernest R. May, and Jonathan Rosenberg, 272–83. Oxford: Oxford University Press.*

——. 1999b. *Capitalism, Democracy, and Ralph's Pretty Good Grocery.* Princeton, NJ: Princeton University Press.

——. 2000a. The Banality of "Ethnic War." *International Security* 25 (1): 42–70.

——. 2000b. The Banality of "Ethnic War": Yugoslavia and Rwanda. Paper presented at the Annual Meeting of the American Political Science Association, September 2, Washington, DC.*

——. 2002a. American Foreign Policy and Public Opinion in a New Era: Eleven Propositions. In *Understanding Public Opinion,* ed. Barbara Norrander and Clyde Wilcox, 149–72. Washington, DC: CQ Press.

——. 2002b. Public Support for Military Ventures Abroad. In *The Real Lessons of the Vietnam War: Reflections Twenty-five Years after the Fall of Saigon,* ed. John Norton Moore and Robert F. Turner, 171–219. Durham, NC: Carolina Academic Press.

——. 2002c. Harbinger or Aberration? A 9/11 Provocation. *National Interest,* Fall, 45–50.

——. 2003. Police Work or War? *Public Perspective,* March–April, 31–34.

——. Forthcoming. What Was the Cold War About? Evidence from Its Ending. *Political Science Quarterly.*

*Available at http://psweb.sbs.ohio-state.edu/faculty/jmueller/links.

Mueller, John, and Brink Lindsey. 2003. Should We Invade Iraq? *Reason*, January, 40–48.

Mueller, John, and Karl Mueller. 1999. Sanctions of Mass Destruction. *Foreign Affairs* 78 (3): 43–53.

——. 2000. The Methodology of Mass Destruction: Assessing Threats in the New World Order. In *Preventing the Use of Weapons of Mass Destruction*, ed. Eric Herring, 163–87. London: Frank Cass. Also published in 2000 in *Journal of Strategic Studies* 23 (1).

Mueller, Karl. 2000. The Demise of Yugoslavia and the Destruction of Bosnia: Strategic Causes, Effects, and Responses. In *Deliberate Force: A Case Study in Effective Air Campaigning*, ed. Robert C. Owen, 1–36. Maxwell Air Force Base, AL: Air University Press.

Murphy, Dan. 2003. Quagmire. *New Republic*, November 3.

Mussolini, Benito. 1935. The Political and Social Doctrine of Fascism. *International Conciliation*, January, 5–17.

Nadelmann, Ethan A. 1990. Global Prohibition Regimes: The Evolution of Norms in International Society. *International Organization* 44 (4): 479–526.

Natsios, Andrew S. 2001. *The Great North Korean Famine*. Washington, DC: United States Institute of Peace Press.

Newman, E. W. Polson. 1928. *Great Britain in Egypt*. London: Cassell.

Nougayrède, Natalie. 1999. Serb Propaganda Stifles Debate on Kosovo. *Guardian Weekly*, March 7.

Oberdorfer, Don. 1992. *The Turn: From the Cold War to a New Era*. New York: Touchstone.

——. 2001. *The Two Koreas: A Contemporary History*. Rev. ed. New York: Basic.

Oberschall, Anthony. 2001. From Ethnic Cooperation to Violence and War in Yugoslavia. In *Ethnopolitical Warfare: Causes, Consequences, and Possible Solutions*, ed. Daniel Chirot and Martin E. P. Seligman, 119–50. Washington, DC: American Psychological Association.

O'Connell, Mary Ellen. 2003. Re-Leashing the Dogs of War. *American Journal of International Law* 97 (2): 446–56.

O'Connell, Robert L. 1995. *Ride of the Second Horseman: The Birth and Death of War*. New York: Oxford University Press.

——. 1998. War: Institution Without Portfolio. In *The Columbia History of the 20th Century*, ed. Richard W. Bulliet, 248–61. New York: Columbia University Press.

O'Connor, Mike. 1996. Moderate Bosnian Serbs Plot in Secrecy for Unity. *New York Times*, July 31, A3.

——. 1998a. 12,000 Flee Serb Attack on a Town in Kosovo. *New York Times*, July 22, A6.

——. 1998b. Battle for Kosovo Town Grew in the Telling. *New York Times*, July 23, A8.

——. 1998c. Rebel Terror Forcing Minority Serbs out of Kosovo. *New York Times*, August 31, A3.

O'Donnell, Guillermo, and Philippe C. Schmitter. 1986. *Transitions from Authoritarian Rule: Tentative Conclusions about Uncertain Democracies*. Baltimore, MD: Johns Hopkins University Press.

O'Hanlon, Michael E. 2002. A Flawed Masterpiece. *Foreign Affairs* 81 (3): 47–63.

O'Kane, Maggie. 1996. The Wake of War. *Guardian* (London), May 18, T34.

——. 1998a. Sick and Dying in Their Hospital Beds, the Pitiful Victims of Sanctions and Saddam. *Guardian* (London), February 19, 1.

——. 1998b. Saddam Wields Terror—and Feigns Respect. *Guardian* (London), November 25.

Oliker, Olga. 2002. *Russia's Chechen Wars, 1994–2000: Lessons from Urban Combat.* Santa Monica, CA: RAND.

Onishi, Norimitsu. 2000. British Plans to Leave Sierra Leone Prompt Worry. *New York Times,* June 7, A14.

Ourdan, Rémy. 1999. Uneasy Peace Follows a Brutal Past. *Guardian Weekly,* December 16–22, 26.

Overy, Richard. 1982. Hitler's War and the German Economy: A Reinterpretation. *Economic History Review* 35 (2): 272–91.

——. 1989. Taming the Monster. *New Republic,* July 17 and 24, 37–39.

Owen, C. R. 1984. *Erich Maria Remarque: A Critical Bio-Biography.* Amsterdam: Rodopi.

Owen, David. 1995. *Balkan Odyssey.* New York: Harcourt Brace.

Page, Susan. 1999. Kosovo Can Help or Haunt Gore. *USA Today,* April 14, 4A.

Parker, Geoffrey. 1977. *The Dutch Revolt.* London: Allen Lane.

——. 1994. Early Modern Europe. In *The Laws of War: Constraints on Warfare in the Western World,* ed. Michael Howard, George J. Andreopoulous, and Mark R. Shuman. New Haven, CT: Yale University Press.

——. 1995. The Soldier. In *Baroque Personae,* ed. Rosario Villari, 32–56. Chicago: University of Chicago Press.

——. 1996. *The Military Revolution: Military Innovation and the Rise of the West, 1500–1800.* 2nd ed. Cambridge: Cambridge University Press.

——, ed. 1997. *The Thirty Years' War.* 2nd ed. New York: Routledge.

Parker, Geoffrey, and Angela Parker. 1977. *European Soldiers, 1550–1650.* London: Cambridge University Press.

Patterson, David S. 1976. *Toward a Warless World: The Travail of the American Peace Movement, 1887–1914.* Bloomington: Indiana University Press.

Paul, T. V. 1994. *Asymmetric Conflicts: War Initiation by Weaker Powers.* New York: Cambridge University Press.

Pavković, Aleksandar. 1997. *The Fragmentation of Yugoslavia.* New York: St. Martin's.

Pearson, Brenda. 2002. *Putting Peace into Practice: Can Macedonia's New Government Meet the Challenge?* Washington, DC: United States Institute of Peace Special Report.

Pentagon Papers. 1971. Senator Gravel ed. Boston: Beacon.

Perlez, Jane. 1998. Many Serbs Would Just Rather Not Fight to Keep Kosovo. *New York Times,* March 12, A6.

——. 1999. Unpalatable U.S. Options: NATO Air Strikes on the Serbs May Prove to Be a Bad Idea Whose Time Has Come. *New York Times,* March 23, A1.

Petersen, Roger D. 2002. *Understanding Ethnic Violence: Fear, Hatred, and Resentment in Twentieth-Century Eastern Europe.* New York: Cambridge University Press.

Pietrzyk, Mark E. 2002. *International Order and Individual Liberty: Effects of War and Peace on the Development of Governments.* Lanham, MD: University Press of America.

Pike, Douglas. 1966. *Viet Cong.* Cambridge, MA: MIT Press.

Pipes, Richard. 1984. *Survival Is Not Enough.* New York: Simon and Schuster.

Pollack, Jonathan D. 1984. China and the Global Strategic Balance. In *China's Foreign Relations in the 1980s,* ed. Harry Harding, 146–76. New Haven, CT: Yale University Press.

Pollack, Kenneth M. 2002. *The Threatening Storm: The Case for Invading Iraq.* New York: Random House.

Pollins, Brian. 1989a. Conflict, Cooperation, and Commerce: The Effect of International Political Interactions on Bilateral Trade Flows. *American Journal of Political Science* 33 (3): 737–61.

——. 1989b. Does Trade Still Follow the Flag? *American Political Science Review* 83 (2).

Pomfret, John. 1994. Weapons, Cash and Chaos Lend Clout to Srebrenica's Tough Guy. *Washington Post,* February 16, A14.

——. 1995. Gang Violence Imperiling Bosnia's Fragile Muslim–Croat Coalition. *Washington Post,* May 14, A21.

Posen, Barry R. 1984. *The Sources of Military Doctrine.* Ithaca, NY: Cornell University Press.

——. 2000. The War for Kosovo: Serbia's Political-Military Strategy. *International Security* 24 (4).

Power, Samantha. 2002. *"A Problem from Hell": America and the Age of Genocide.* New York: Basic Books.

Press, Daryl G. 2001. The Myth of Air Power in the Persian Gulf War and the Future of Warfare. *International Security* 26 (2): 5–44.

Prunier, Gérard. 1995. *The Rwanda Crisis: History of a Genocide.* New York: Columbia University Press.

Queller, Donald E. 1977. *The Fourth Crusade: The Conquest of Constantinople, 1201–1204.* Philadelphia: University of Pennsylvania Press.

Quindlen, Anna. 1991. The Microwave War. *New York Times,* March 3, sec. 4, 17.

Rabasa, Angel, and Peter Chalk. 2001. *Colombian Labyrinth: The Synergy of Drugs and Insurgency and Its Implications for Regional Stability.* Santa Monica, CA: RAND.

Rappard, William E. 1940. *The Quest for Peace since the World War.* Cambridge, MA: Harvard University Press.

Rashid, Ahmed. 2000. *Taliban: Militant Islam, Oil, and Fundamentalism in Central Asia.* New Haven, CT: Yale University Press.

Ravlo, Hilde, Nils Petter Gleditsch, and Han Dorussen. 2001. Colonial War and Democratic Peace. Oslo, Norway: International Peace Research Institute.

Rawls, John. 1999. *The Law of Peoples.* Cambridge, MA: Harvard University Press.

Ray, James Lee. 1989. The Abolition of Slavery and the End of International War. *International Organization* 43 (3): 405–39.

Read, Anthony, and David Fisher. 1988. *The Deadly Embrace: Hitler, Stalin and the Nazi–Soviet Pact, 1939–1941.* London: Michael Joseph.

Record, Jeffrey. 2002. Collapsed Countries, Casualty Dread, and the New American Way of War. *Parameters,* Summer, 4–23.

Rees, David. 1964. *Korea: The Limited War.* New York: St. Martin's.

Reeves, Richard. 1993. *President Kennedy: Profile of Power.* New York: Simon and Schuster.

Reno, William. 1998. *Warlord Politics and African States.* Boulder, CO: Lynne Rienner.

——. 2000. Shadow States and the Political Economy of Civil Wars. In *Greed and Grievance: Economic Agendas in Civil Wars*, ed. Mats Berdal and David M. Malone, 43–68. Boulder, CO: Lynne Rienner.

——. 2003. Sierra Leone: Warfare in a Post-State Society. In *State Failure and State Weakness in a Time of Terror*, ed. Robert Rotberg, 71–100. Washington, DC: Brookings.

Rich, Norman. 1973. *Hitler's War Aims: Ideology, the Nazi State, and the Course of Expansion*. New York: Norton.

Rieff, David. 1995. *Slaughterhouse*. New York: Simon and Schuster.

——. 2003. Were Sanctions Right? *New York Times Magazine*, July 27, 41–46.

Ritter, Scott. 1999. *Endgame: Solving the Iraq Problem—Once and for All*. New York: Simon and Schuster.

Robbins, Keith. 1976. *The Abolition of War: The "Peace Movement" in Britain, 1914–1919*. Cardiff: University of Wales Press.

Roberts, Geoffrey. 1999. *The Soviet Union in World Politics: Co-existence, Revolution and Cold War, 1945–1991*. London and New York: Routledge.

Rohde, David. 1997. *Endgame: The Betrayal and Fall of Srebrenica, Europe's Worst Massacre since World War II*. New York: Farrar, Straus and Giroux.

——. 1999. Where Neighbors Attacked Neighbors, Justice Is Far from Easy. *New York Times*, June 23, A10.

Rohter, Larry. 1996. A Chastened Latin Left Puts Its Hope in Ballots. *New York Times*, July 29, A6.

Ron, James. 2000a. Territoriality and Plausible Deniability: Serbian Paramilitaries in the Bosnian War. In *Death Squads in Global Perspective: Murder with Deniability*, ed. Bruce B. Campbell and Arthur D. Brenner, 287–312. New York: St. Martin's.

——. 2000b. Boundaries and Violence: Repertoires of State Action along the Bosnia–Yugoslavia Divide. *Theory and Society* 29 (5): 609–49.

Rosato, Sebastian. 2003. The Flawed Logic of Democratic Peace Theory. *American Political Science Review* 97 (4): 585–602.

Rosecrance, Richard. 1986. *The Rise of the Trading State: Conquest and Commerce in the Modern World*. New York: Basic Books.

Rosenberg, Jonathan. 1999. Before the Bomb and After: Winston Churchill and the Use of Force. In *Cold War Statesmen Confront the Bomb: Nuclear Diplomacy since 1945*, ed. John Lewis Gaddis, Philip H. Gordon, Ernest R. May, and Jonathan Rosenberg, 171–93. Oxford: Oxford University Press.

Rosenberg, Nathan, and L. E. Birdzell. 1986. *How the West Grew Rich: The Economic Transformation of the Industrial World*. New York: Basic Books.

Rosenfeld, Richard. 2000. Patterns in Adult Homicide. In *The Crime Drop in America*, ed. Alfred Blumstein and Joel Wallman. New York: Cambridge University Press.

Rotberg, Robert. 2002. New Breed of African Leader. *Christian Science Monitor*, January 9, 9.

——. 2003. Failed States, Collapsed States, Weak States: Causes and Indicators. In *State Failure and State Weakness in a Time of Terror*, ed. Robert Rotberg, 1–25. Washington, DC: Brookings.

Rowe, David M. 2002. The Tragedy of Liberalism: Globalization and the Origins of the First World War. Manuscript. Department of Political Science, Kenyon Colleg, Gambier, OH.

Roy, Oliver. 2003. Europe Won't Be Fooled Again. *New York Times*, May 13, A31.

Rubin, Elizabeth. 1999. Saving Sierra Leone, At a Price. *New York Times*, February 3, A27.

Rummel, Rudolph. 1994. *Death by Government*. New Brunswick, NJ: Transaction.

Ruskin, John. 1866. War. In *The Crown of Wild Olives: Three Lectures on Work, Traffic, and War*, 83–127. New York: Wiley.

Russett, Bruce. 1972. *No Clear and Present Danger: A Skeptical View of the United States' Entry into World War II*. New York: Harper and Row.

———. 1990. *Controlling the Sword: The Democratic Governance of National Security*. Cambridge, MA: Harvard University Press.

Russett, Bruce M., and John R. Oneal. 2001. *Triangulating Peace: Democracy, Interdependence, and International Organizations*. New York: Norton.

Ryan, Alan. 2000. *Primary Responsibilities and Primary Risks: Australian Defence Force Participation in the International Force East Timor*. Study Paper No. 304. Duntroon, Australia: Land Warfare Studies Centre.

Ryder, H.I.D. 1899. The Ethics of War. *Nineteenth Century* 45: 716–28.

Sacher, Howard M. 1976. *A History of Israel: From the Rise of Zionism to Our Time*. New York: Knopf.

Sadowski, Yahya. 1998. *The Myth of Global Chaos*. Washington, DC: Brookings.

Safire, William. 1993. Depart with Honor. *New York Times*, October 7, A29.

Sánchez G., Gonzalo. 2001. Problems of Violence, Prospects for Peace. In *Violence in Colombia: Waging War and Negotiating Peace*, ed. Charles Bergquist, Ricardo Peñarand, and Gonzalo Sánchez G., 1–38. Wilmington, DE: Scholarly Resources.

Scanlon, Stephen J., and J. Craig Jenkins. 2001. Military Power and Food Security: A Cross-National Analysis of Less-Developed Countries, 1970–1990. *International Studies Quarterly* 45 (1): 159–87.

Schandler, Herbert Y. 1977. *The Unmaking of a President: Lyndon Johnson and Vietnam*. Princeton, NJ: Princeton University Press.

Schilling, Warner R. 1961. The H-Bomb Decision. *Political Science Quarterly* 76 (1): 24–46.

———. 1965. Surprise Attack, Death, and War. *Journal of Conflict Resolution* 9 (3): 285–90.

Schlesinger, Arthur M., Jr. 1978. *Robert Kennedy and His Times*. Boston: Houghton Mifflin.

Schlesinger, James. 1967. *On Relating Non-Technical Elements to Systems Studies*. P-3545. Santa Monica, CA: RAND.

Schmitt, Eric. 1991. U.S. Battle Plan: Massive Air Strikes. *New York Times*, January 10, A17.

Schroeder, Paul W. 2001. The Life and Death of the Long Peace, 1763–1914. Paper presented at the conference Waning of Major War, April 6–8, Joan B. Kroc Institute for International Peace Studies, University of Notre Dame, South Bend, IN.

Schwartz, Adam. 1994. *A Nation in Waiting: Indonesia in the 1990s*. Boulder, CO: Westview.

Schweller, Randall L. 2001. The Problem of International Order Revisited: A Review Essay. *International Security* 26 (1): 161–86.

———. 2002. Correspondence. *International Security* 27 (1): 181–85.

Sciolino, Elaine. 1991. *The Outlaw State: Saddam Hussein's Quest for Power and the Gulf Crisis.* New York: Wiley.

Seelye, Katharine Q. 1999. Clinton Blames Milosevic, Not Fate, for Bloodshed. *New York Times,* May 14, A12.

Seitz, Don C. 1929. *Famous American Duels.* New York: Crowell.

Shackleton, Shirley. 1995. Planting a Tree in Balibo: A Journey to East Timor. In *East Timor at the Crossroads: The Forging of a Nation,* ed. Peter Carey and G. Carter Bentley, 109–19. Honolulu: University of Hawai'i Press.

Sharrock, David. 1999. Iraq Is Falling Apart, We Are Doomed. *Guardian* (London), April 24, 14.

Shearer, David. 1998. *Private Armies and Military Intervention.* Adelphi Paper No. 316. London: International Institute for Strategic Studies.

Sheehan, Neil. 1964. Much Is at Stake in Southeast Asian Struggle. *New York Times,* August 16, E4.

Sherif, Muzafer, O. J. Harvey, B. Jack White, William R. Hood, and Carolyn W. Serif. 1961. *Intergroup Conflict and Cooperation: The Robbers Cave Experiment.* Norman, OK: University Book Exchange.

Shevchenko, Arkady N. 1985. *Breaking with Moscow.* New York: Knopf.

Shils, Edward A., and Morris Janowitz. 1948. Cohesion and Disintegration in the Wehrmacht in World War II. *Public Opinion Quarterly* 12 (2): 280–315.

Shirer, William L. 1941. *Berlin Diary: The Journal of a Foreign Correspondent, 1934–1941.* New York: Knopf.

Shulman, Marshall D. 1963. *Stalin's Foreign Policy Reappraised.* New York: Atheneum.

Sigal, Leon V. 1998. *Disarming Strangers: Nuclear Diplomacy with North Korea.* Princeton, NJ: Princeton University Press.

Sikavica, Stipe. 1995. The Collapse of Tito's Army. In *Yugoslavia's Ethnic Nightmare,* ed. Jasminka Udovicki and James Ridgeway, 123–45. New York: Lawrence Hill.

Silber, Laura, and Allan Little. 1997. *Yugoslavia: Death of a Nation.* New York: Penguin.

Silverstein, Ken. 2000. *Private Warriors.* New York: Verso.

Simmons, Robert R. 1975. *The Strained Alliance: Peking, Pyongyang, Moscow, and the Politics of the Korean Civil War.* New York: Free Press.

Simons, Geoff. 1996. *The Scouring of Iraq: Sanctions, Law, and Natural Justice.* New York: St. Martin's.

Simpson, John. 1991. *From the House of War: John Simpson in the Gulf.* London: Arrow Books.

Singer, Max, and Aaron Wildavsky. 1993. *The Real World Order: Zones of Peace, Zones of Conflict.* Chatham, NJ: Chatham House.

Singer, P. W. 2003. *Corporate Warriors: The Rise of the Privatized Military Industry.* Ithaca, NY: Cornell University Press.

Sivard, Ruth Leger. 1987. *World Military and Social Expenditures, 1987–88.* Washington, DC: World Priorities.

Slaughter, Anne-Marie. 2003. Good Reasons for Going around the U.N. *New York Times,* March 18, A33.

Small, Melvin. 1980. *Was War Necessary? National Security and U.S. Entry into War.* Beverly Hills, CA: Sage.

Small, Melvin, and J. David Singer. 1982. *Resort to Arms: International Civil Wars, 1816–1980.* Beverly Hills, CA: Sage.

Smith, Dinitia. 1996. Challenging a View of the Holocaust. *New York Times,* April 1, C11.

Smith, Jean Edward. 1992. *George Bush's War.* New York: Holt.

Smith, M. Brewster. 1949. Combat Motivations among Ground Troops. In *The American Soldier: Combat and Its Aftermath,* ed. Samuel A. Stouffer, 105–91. Princeton, NJ: Princeton University Press.

Smith, Woodruff D. 1986. *The Ideological Origins of Nazi Imperialism.* New York: Oxford University Press.

Snyder, Jack. 1984. *The Ideology of the Offensive.* Ithaca, NY: Cornell University Press.

———. 1987–88. The Gorbachev Revolution: A Waning of Soviet Expansionism? *International Security* 12 (3): 93–131.

———. 2000. *From Voting to Violence: Democratization and Nationalist Conflict.* New York: Norton.

Sobel, Richard. 1996. U.S. and Foreign Attitudes toward Intervention in the Former Yugoslavia, 145–81. In *The World and Yugoslavia's Wars,* ed. Richard H. Ullman. New York: Council on Foreign Relations Press.

Solingen, Etel. 1998. *Regional Orders at Century's Dawn: Global and Domestic Influences on Grand Strategy.* Princeton, NJ: Princeton University Press.

Sorensen, Theodore C. 1965. *Kennedy.* New York: Harper and Row.

Spencer, Herbert. 1909. *The Principles of Sociology.* Vol. 2. New York: Appleton.

Spolar, Christine. 1995. Lesser Serbs in Greater Serbia: Refugees of Croatia Fighting Find Little Welcome from Fellow Serbs. *Washington Post,* May 25, A36.

Squires, James Duane. 1935. *British Propaganda at Home and in the United States from 1914 to 1917.* Cambridge, MA: Harvard University Press.

Stahl, Leslie. 1996. Punishing Saddam; Sanctions against Iraq Not Hurting Leaders of the Country, but the Children Are Suffering and Dying. *60 Minutes.* CBS, May 12.

Stalin, Joseph V. 1973. *The Essential Stalin,* ed. Bruce Franklin. London: Croom Helm.

Stanley, Alessandra. 1999. Kosovo Killings Bind Both Sides in Terror's Web. *New York Times,* April 5, A1.

Staub, Ervin. 1989. *The Roots of Evil: The Origins of Genocide and Other Group Violence.* New York: Cambridge University Press.

Steele, Jonathan. 1998. Kosovo Fighters Set No-Go Areas. *Guardian Weekly,* May 17, 4.

Steinert, Marlis G. 1977. *Hitler's War and the Germans: Public Mood and Attitude during the Second World War.* Athens: Ohio University Press.

Stigler, Andrew L. 2002–3. A Clear Victory for Air Power: NATO's Empty Threat to Invade Kosovo. *International Security* 27 (3): 124–57.

Štitkovac, Ejub. 1995. Croatia: The First War. In *Yugoslavia's Ethnic Nightmare,* ed. Jasminka Udovicki and James Ridgeway, 147–64. New York: Lawrence Hill.

Stoakes, Geoffrey. 1986. *Hitler and the Quest for World Domination.* Leamington Spa, UK: Berg.

Stockton, Richard. 1932. *Inevitable War.* New York: Perth.

Stoessinger, John G. 1982. *Why Nations Go to War.* 3rd ed. New York: St. Martin's.

Stouffer, Samuel A., Arthur A. Lumsdaine, and Marion Harper Lumsdaine. 1949. *Attitudes before Combat and Behavior in Combat.* In *The American Soldier: Combat and Its Aftermath,* ed. Samuel A. Stouffer, 3–58. Princeton, NJ: Princeton University Press.

Stowe, Steven M. 1987. *Intimacy and Power in the Old South: Ritual in the Lives of the Planters.* Baltimore, MD: Johns Hopkins University Press.

Strobel, Warren P. 1997. *Late-Breaking Foreign Policy: The News Media's Influence on Peace Operations.* Washington, DC: United States Institute of Peace Press.

Stromberg, Roland N. 1982. *Redemption by War: The Intellectuals and 1914.* Lawrence: Regents Press of Kansas.

Sudetic, Chuck. 1992. A "Wild East" Revival in Serbian-Held Croatia. *New York Times,* September 21, A6.

——. 1998. *Blood and Vengeance: One Family's Story of the War in Bosnia.* New York: Norton.

Suri, Jeremi. 2002. Explaining the End of the Cold War: A New Historical Consensus? *Journal of Cold War Studies* 4 (4): 60–92.

Tajfel, Henri, ed. 1982. *Social Identity and Intergroup Relations.* Cambridge: Cambridge University Press.

Talbott, Strobe. 1981. The Strategic Dimension of the Sino-American Relationship. In *The China Factor,* ed. Richard H. Solomon, 81–113. Englewood Cliffs, NY: Prentice-Hall.

Talentino, Andrea. 1998. Intervention in the International System. Ph.D. diss., UCLA.

Tambiah, Stanley J. 1986. *Sri Lanka: Ethnic Fratricide and the Dismantling of Democracy.* Chicago: University of Chicago Press.

Tanner, Marcus. 1997. *Croatia: A Nation Forged in War.* New Haven, CT: Yale University Press.

Taracouzio, T. A. 1940. *War and Peace in Soviet Diplomacy.* New York: Macmillan.

Taubman, William. 1982. *Stalin's American Policy.* New York: Norton.

Taylor, A.J.P. 1961. *The Origins of the Second World War.* 2nd ed. New York: Fawcett.

Taylor, John G. 1991. *Indonesia's Forgotten War: The Hidden History of East Timor.* London: Zed.

——. 1995. The Emergence of a Nationalist Movement in East Timor. In *East Timor at the Crossroads: The Forging of a Nation,* ed. Peter Carey and G. Carter Bentley, 21–41. Honolulu: University of Hawai'i Press.

Taylor, Maxwell. 1972. *Swords and Plowshares.* New York: Norton.

Taylor, Telford. 1979. *Munich: The Price of Peace.* New York: Doubleday.

Terry, Fiona. 2002. *Condemned to Repeat? The Paradox of Humanitarian Aid.* Ithaca, NY: Cornell University Press.

Thayer, Thomas C. 1977. We Could Not Win the War of Attrition We Tried to Fight. In *The Lessons of Vietnam,* ed. W. Scott Thompson and Donaldson D. Frizzell, 85–92. New York: Crane and Russak.

Thomas, Robert. 1999. *Serbia under Milosevic: Politics in the 1990s.* London: Hurst.

Thomson, Janice E. 1994. *Mercenaries, Pirates, and Sovereigns: State-Building and Extraterritorial Violence in Early Modern Europe.* Princeton, NJ: Princeton University Press.

Tiffen, Rodney. 2001. *Diplomatic Deceits: Government, Media, and East Timor.* Sydney, Australia: University of New South Wales Press.

Tilly, Charles. 1985. War Making and State Making as Organized Crime. In *Bringing the State Back In,* ed. Peter B. Evans, Dietrich Rueschemeyer, and Theda Skocpol, 169–91. Cambridge: Cambridge University Press.

——. 1990. *Coercion, Capital, and European States, A.D. 990–1990.* Cambridge, MA: Basil Blackwood.

——. 2003. *The Politics of Collective Violence.* New York: Cambridge University Press.

Tolstoy, Leo. 1966. *War and Peace.* New York: Norton.

Toynbee, Arnold J. 1950. *War and Civilization.* New York: Oxford University Press.

——. 1969. *Experiences.* New York: Oxford University Press.

Trachtenberg, Marc. 1985. Nuclear Weapons and the Cuban Missile Crisis. *International Security* 10 (1): 156–63.

Treitschke, Heinrich von. 1916. *Politics.* New York: Macmillan.

Trevor-Roper, Hugh R. 1953. The Mind of Adolf Hitler. In *Hitler's Secret Conversations, 1941–1944,* vii–xxx. New York: Farrar, Straus and Young.

Truman, Harry S. 1966. *Public Papers of the Presidents of the United States: Harry S. Truman, 1952–1953.* Washington, DC: U.S. Government Printing Office.

Tucker, Cynthia. 2003. If Afghanistan Stays Forgotten, It Won't Forget. *Atlanta Journal-Constitution,* April 27, 10E.

Tucker, Robert W., and David C. Hendrickson. 1992. *The Imperial Temptation: The New World Order and America's Purpose.* New York: Council on Foreign Relations Press.

Turner, Henry Ashby, Jr. 1996. Hitler's Impact on History. In *From the Berlin Museum to the Berlin Wall: Essays on the Cultural and Political History of Modern Germany,* ed. David Wetzel, 109–26. Westport, CT: Praeger.

Udovicki, Jasminka, and Stojan Cerovic. 1995. The People's Mass Murderer. *Village Voice,* November 7, 27.

UNICEF. 1998. Situation Analysis of Children and Women in Iraq. April 30. New York: United Nations.

United Nations. 1999. *Report of the Second Panel Established Pursuant to the Note by the President of the Security Council of 30 January 1999 (S/1999/100), concerning the Current Humanitarian Situation in Iraq.* New York: United Nations, 30 March.

United Nations Commission of Experts. 1994. *Final Report of the United Nations Commission of Experts Established Pursuant to Security Council Resolution 780 (1992), Annex III.A Special Forces,* ed. M. Cherif Bassiouni. New York: United Nations, 28 December.

Urquhart, Brian. 1993. For a UN Volunteer Military Force. *New York Review of Books,* June 10, 3–4.

U.S. Department of the Air Force. 1976. *International Law — The Conduct of Armed Combat and Air Operations.* AFP 110-31. November 19.

U.S. News and World Report. 1992. *Triumph without Victory: The Unreported History of the Persian Gulf War.* New York: Times Books/Random House.

Uvin, Peter. 1998. *Aiding Violence: The Development Enterprise in Rwanda.* West Hartford, CT: Kumarian Press.

Vagts, Alfred. 1959. *A History of Militarism.* New York: Norton.

Vale, Malcolm. 1981. *War and Chivalry*. Athens: University of Georgia Press.

Valentino, Benjamin. 2003. *Final Solutions*. Ithaca, NY: Cornell University Press.

van Creveld, Martin. 1991. *The Transformation of War*. New York: Free Press.

——. 1999a. The Future of War. In *Security in a Post–Cold War World*, ed. Robert G. Patman, 22–36. New York: St. Martin's.

——. 1999b. *The Rise and Decline of the State*. Cambridge: Cambridge University Press.

Van Evera, Stephen. 1984. The Cult of the Offensive and the Origins of the First World War. *International Security* 9 (1): 58–107.

Vasić, Miloš. 1996. The Yugoslav Army and the Post-Yugoslav Armies. In *Yugoslavia and After: A Study in Fragmentation, Despair, and Rebirth*, ed. David A. Dyker and Ivan Vejvoda, 116–37. London: Longman.

Vasquez, John A. 1991. The Deterrence Myth: Nuclear Weapons and the Prevention of Nuclear War. In *The Long Postwar Peace: Contending Explanations and Projections*, ed. Charles W. Kegley Jr., 205–23. New York: HarperCollins.

——. 1993. *The War Puzzle*. Cambridge: Cambridge University Press.

——. 1998. *The Power of Power Politics: From Classical Realism to Neotraditionalism*. Cambridge: Cambridge University Press.

Vassiltchikov, Marie. 1987. *Berlin Diaries, 1940–1945*. New York: Knopf.

Viorst, Milton. 1991. Report from Baghdad. *New Yorker*, June 24, 55–73.

Voslensky, Michael. 1984. *Nomenklatura: The New Soviet Ruling Class*. Garden City, NY: Doubleday.

Vulliamy, Ed. 1994. *Seasons in Hell: Understanding Bosnia's War*. New York: Simon and Schuster.

——. 1996a. Bloody Train of Butchery at the Bridge. *Guardian*, March 11, 9.

——. 1996b. Croats Who Supped with the Devil. *Guardian*, March 18, 8.

Waite, Robert G. L. 1952. *Vanguard of Nazism: The Free Corps in Postwar Germany, 1918–1923*. Cambridge, MA: Harvard University Press.

Waltz, Kenneth N. 1998. Presidential Address. Annual Meeting of the American Political Science Association, September, Washington, DC.

Wank, Solomon. 1988. The Austrian Peace Movement and the Habsburg Ruling Elite, 1906–1914. In *Peace Movements and Political Cultures*, ed. Charles Chatfield and Peter van den Dungen, 40–63. Knoxville: University of Tennessee Press.

Watson, Peter. 1978. *War on the Mind: The Military Uses and Abuses of Psychology*. London: Hutchinson.

Watt, Donald Cameron. 1975. *Too Serious a Business: European Armed Forces and the Approach to the Second World War*. Berkeley, CA: University of California Press.

——. 1989. *How War Came: The Immediate Origins of the Second World War*. New York: Pantheon.

Wedgwood, C. V. 1938. *The Thirty Years War*. London: Jonathan Cape.

Weidhorn, Manfred. 1974. *Sword and Pen: A Survey of the Writings of Sir Winston Churchill*. Albuquerque: University of New Mexico Press.

Weigley, Russell F. 1976. Military and Civilian Leadership. In *Historical Dimensions of National Security Problems*, ed. Klaus Knorr, 38–77. Lawrence: University Press of Kansas.

——. 1991. *The Age of Battles: The Quest for Decisive Warfare from Breitenfeld to Waterloo*. Bloomington: Indiana University Press.

Weil, Martin. 1991. Iraqis Surrender to Reporter: Loudoun County Woman Encounters Remnants of a Company. *Washington Post,* February 27, A32.

Weinberg, Gerhard L. 1970. *The Foreign Policy of Hitler's Germany: Diplomatic Revolution in Europe, 1933–36.* Chicago: University of Chicago Press.

——. 1980. *The Foreign Policy of Hitler's Germany: Starting World War II, 1937–1939.* Chicago: University of Chicago Press.

——. 1994. *A World at Arms.* New York: Cambridge University Press.

Weiner, Tim. 1998. Opponents Find That Ousting Hussein Is Easier Said Than Done. *New York Times,* November 16, A10.

——. 1999a. U.S. Spied on Iraq under U.N. Cover, Officials Now Say. *New York Times,* January 7, A1.

——. 1999b. U.S. Used U.N. Team to Place Spy Device in Iraq, Aides Say. *New York Times,* January 8, A1.

Welch, David A., and James G. Blight. 1987–88. The Eleventh Hour of the Cuban Missile Crisis: An Introduction to the ExComm Transcripts. *International Security* 12 (3): 5–29.

Welch, Matt. 2002. The Politics of Dead Children. *Reason,* March 2, 53–58.

Wells, H. G. 1914. *The War That Will End War.* New York: Duffield.

Wendt, Alexander. 1999. *Social Theory of International Relations.* New York: Cambridge University Press.

Werth, Alexander. 1964. *Russia at War, 1941–1945.* New York: Dutton.

West, Rebecca. 1941. *Black Lamb and Grey Falcon: A Journey through Yugoslavia.* New York: Viking.

Western, Jon. 2002. Sources of Humanitarian Intervention: Beliefs, Information, and Advocacy in the U.S. Decisions on Somalia and Bosnia. *International Security* 26 (4): 112–42.

Westmoreland, William. 1976. *A Soldier Reports.* Garden City, NY: Doubleday.

Whitney, Craig R., and Eric Schmitt. 1999. NATO Had Signs Its Strategy Would Fail Kosovars. *New York Times,* April 1, A1.

Wilde, Oscar. 1946. The Critic as Artist. In *The Portable Oscar Wilde,* ed. Richard Aldinton, 51–137. New York: Viking.

Wilkinson, Tracy. 1996a. Defiant Serbs Hand over Sarajevo Suburb. *Los Angeles Times,* March 12, A4.

——. 1996b. Bosnia Muslims Return with a Vengeance. *Los Angeles Times,* March 14, A10.

Williams, Daniel. 1999. Russian Conscripts Fear Enemy in Own Ranks. *Guardian Weekly,* January 24, 19.

Wilson, Edmund. 1962. *Patriotic Gore.* New York: Oxford University Press.

Wilson, George C. 2003. Why Didn't Saddam Defend His Country? *National Journal,* April 19, 1222.

Winter, J. M. 1989. *The Experience of World War I.* New York: Oxford University Press.

Wolf, Charles, Jr., K. C. Yeh, Edmund Brunner Jr., Aaron Gurwitz, and Marilee Lawrence. 1983. *The Costs of Soviet Empire.* Santa Monica, CA: Rand Corporation.

Wood, Nicholas. 2001. Killer Gangs Plot Revenge in Macedonia. *Observer* (London), May 6.

Woodward, Bob. 1991. *The Commanders.* New York: Simon and Schuster.

———. 2002. *Bush at War.* New York: Simon and Schuster.

Woodward, Susan L. 1995. *Balkan Tragedy: Chaos and Dissolution after the Cold War.* Washington, DC: Brookings.

Wright, Nicholas. 2000. *Knights and Peasants: The Hundred Years War in the French Countryside.* Woodbridge, UK: Boydell.

Wrong, Michela. 2001. *In the Footsteps of Mr. Kurtz: Living on the Brink of Disaster in Mobutu's Congo.* New York: HarperCollins.

Yardeni, Edward. 2000. The Economic Consequences of the Peace. In *Peace, Prosperity, and Politics,* ed. John Mueller, 91–110. New York: Westview.

Yergin, Daniel, and Joseph Stanislaw. 1998. *The Commanding Heights: The Battle between Government and the Marketplace That Is Remaking the Modern World.* New York: Simon and Schuster.

Zacher, Mark. 2001. The Territorial Integrity Norm: International Boundaries and the Use of Force. *International Organization* 55 (2): 215–50.

Zelikow, Philip, and Condoleezza Rice. 1995. *Germany Unified and Europe Transformed: A Study in Statecraft.* Cambridge, MA: Harvard University Press.

Zelnick, Bob. 1999. Kosovo Crisis Carries Grave Risks for Gore. *USA Today,* April 8, 13A.

Zimbardo, Philip G., Craig Haney, Curtis Banks, and David Jaffe. 1973. The Mind Is a Formidable Jailer: A Pirandellian Prison. *New York Times Magazine,* April 8, 38ff.

Zimmermann, Warren. 1996. *Origins of a Catastrophe: Yugoslavia and Its Destroyers.* New York: Times Books.

Zucchino, David. 2003. Iraq's Swift Defeat Blamed on Leaders. *Los Angeles Times,* August 11, A1.

Index

Note: Page numbers with an *f* indicate figures; those with an *n* indicate footnotes; those with a *t* indicate tables.

Aaron, Craig, 202
Abkhasia, 139
Abortion, 162–63, 167
Aburish, Saïd, 201, 202
Ackermann, Alice, 211
Adams, Henry, 37
Afghanistan, 41, 83, 144, 178
  Pakistan and, 108, 135
  Soviet Union and, 78, 80, 139
  United States and, 82, 120t, 134–36, 148, 149, 154
Agincourt, 25
Aidid, Mohammed, 113, 127
Albania, 52, 66, 95–97, 132–34, 173, 175
Albright, Madeleine, 125, 207
Alcohol, 10, 18, 25, 89–94, 97–99, 103
  See also Drugs
Alexandroff, Alan, 192
Algeria, 75, 107, 109, 130, 144, 173
Almond, Gabriel, 150
al Qaeda, 110–11, 135–36, 143, 156
Anderson, Jon Lee, 204
Andreas, Peter, 196, 197, 201, 203, 207, 209
Angell, Norman, 34–35, 49
Angola, 77, 82, 107, 154, 159
Annan, Kofi, 151
Anti-Semitism, 12, 15, 55, 184
  See also Racism
Applebaum, Anne, 193
Argentina, 83, 85, 169, 178
Aristotle, 187
Arkan's Tigers, 90, 112
  See also Ražnjatović, Željko

Armenians, 174, 185
Aspin, Les, 122
Asquith, H. H., 46–48
Astaire, Fred, 192
Atkins, James E., 124n
Atkinson, Rick, 184, 203
Augustine, Saint, 29, 175
Aum Shinrikyo, 110
Australia, 134, 137, 143, 144, 153, 188
Austria, 31n, 46, 58, 59, 62
Authority, obedience to, 11–12, 18, 21, 59, 116, 184
Ayoob, Mohammed, 199
Azerbaijan, 174

Baldwin, Stanley, 44
Ball, George, 74
Balz, Dan, 206
Baram, Amatzia, 202, 208
Barany, Zoltan, 210
Barclay, Thomas, 187
Barnes, Fred, 201
Barro, Robert, 211
Bartov, Omer, 185
Basque country, 110
Bates, Robert, 211
Baumeister, Roy, 183
Bayart, Jean-François, 200
Beales, A. F., 187
Beattie, J. M., 207
Beck, Josef, 62
Beck, Ludwig, 192
Belgium, 46, 48, 59, 61, 147, 158, 168, 203

John Mueller is the Woody Hayes Chair of National Security Studies, Mershon Center, and professor of political science at Ohio State University, where he teaches courses in international relations. He has published scores of articles, and his books include *War, Presidents, and Public Opinion, Astaire Dancing: The Musical Films, Retreat from Doomsday: The Obsolescence of Major War, Policy and Opinion in the Gulf War, Quiet Cataclysm: Reflections on the Recent Transformation of World Politics,* and *Capitalism, Democracy, and Ralph's Pretty Good Grocery.* Mueller is a member of the American Academy of Arts and Sciences, has been a John Simon Guggenheim Fellow and a Guest Fellow at the Norwegian Nobel Institute, and has received grants from the National Science Foundation and the National Endowment for the Humanities. He has also received several teaching prizes.